Terrorism and Counterterrorism

Terrorism and Counterterrorism

Theory, History, and Contemporary Challenges

Matthew Lippman

University of Illinois at Chicago

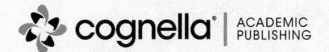

Bassim Hamadeh, CEO and Publisher
Mary Jane Peluso, Senior Specialist Acquisitions Editor
Alisa Munoz, Project Editor
Laureen Gleason, Production Editor
Emely Villavicencio, Senior Graphic Designer
Sara Schennum, Licensing Associate
Bumpy Design, Interior Designer
Natalie Piccotti, Director of Marketing
Kassie Graves, Vice President of Editorial
Jamie Giganti, Director of Academic Publishing

Cover: Copyright © 2017 iStockphoto LP/Gremlin.

Printed in the United States of America.

ISBN: 978-1-5165-2370-2 (pbk) / 978-1-5165-2371-9 (br)

Brief Contents

Preface xi
Acknowledgments xiii

CHAPTER 1
Defining Terrorism 1

CHAPTER 2
Theories of Terrorism 27

CHAPTER 3
Terrorist Tactics and Strategies 59

CHAPTER 4
The Foundations of Modern Terrorism 97

CHAPTER 5
Ethnonationalist and Revolutionary
Terrorism 119

CHAPTER 6
Religious Terrorism 137

CHAPTER 7
State Terrorism 167

CHAPTER 8
Terrorism in the United States 191

CHAPTER 9
The Media and Terrorism 227

CHAPTER 10
The Legal and Historical Basis of
Homeland Security 247

CHAPTER 11
Counterterrorism 271

CHAPTER 12
Donald Trump and Contemporary
Terrorism 307

Appendix 323
References 339
Index 351

Detailed Contents

Preface xi
Acknowledgments xiii

CHAPTER 1 Defining Terrorism 1

Test Your Knowledge 1
Introduction 1
Why Terrorism Matters 3
Defining Terrorism 5
Do We Need a Definition of Terrorism? 6
Problems With Defining Terrorism 6
Initial Thoughts on Defining Terrorism 7
Some Definitons of Terrorism 9

Terrorism, War, and Guerilla Warfare 12
Typologies of Terrorism 15
The New Terrorism 17
The Logic of Terrorism 21
Chapter Summary 24
Chapter Review Questions 25
Terminology 25

CHAPTER 2 Theories of Terrorism 27

Test Your Knowledge 27
Introduction 27
Psychological Theories 28
Radicalization 29
The Process of Radicalization 30
Lone-Wolf Terrorists 34
Structural Theory 38
Criminological Theories 40
Differential Association 40
General Strain Theory of Terrorism 41

Social Disorganization Theory 43
Social Activities Theory 43
Situational Approach 44
Marxism 45
Victimology 48
Women and Terorism 51
Chapter Summary 56
Chapter Review Questions 57
Terminology 58

CHAPTER 3 Terrorist Tactics and Strategies 59

Test Your Knowledge 59
Introduction 59
Terrorist Weapons and Targets 63
Types of Terrorist Groups and Violence 68
Terrorist Financing 70
Weapons of Mass Destruction 72
Chemical Weapons 74
Biological Agents 75

Nuclear Terrorism 77
Radiological Bomb 79
Suicide Bombing 82
Sri Lanka and Palestine 87
Cyberterrorism 90
Chapter Summary 95
Chapter Review Questions 95
Terminology 95

CHAPTER 4 The Foundations of Modern Terrorism 97

Test Your Knowledge 97
Introduction 97
Early Religious Terrorism 98
Religious Conflict In Europe 99
The French Revolution 100
Anarchism 102
Russian Revolutionary Violence 104

Ireland Ethnonationalist Violence 107
The Israeli-Palestinian Conflict 109
Palestinian Response 111
Chapter Summary 117
Chapter Review Questions 118
Terminology 118

CHAPTER 5 Ethnonationalist and Revolutionary Terrorism 119

Test Your Knowledge 119
Ethnonationalist Separatist Terrorism 119
Northern Ireland 120
The Basque Region of Spain 121
The Tamil Region of Sri Lanka 122
Chechnya 123
Turkey 124
People's Republic of China 124
Algeria 124
Ethnonationalist Communal Terrorism 125

Revolutionary Terrorism 127
Uruguay 129
Colombia 129
Peru 130
Revolutionary Terrorism in Europe 132
Predatory Terrorism 133
Chapter Summary 135
Chapter Review Questions 136
Terminology 136

CHAPTER 6 Religious Terrorism 137

Test Your Knowledge 137
Introduction 137
Religion and the New Terrorism 139
The Caliphate 141
Salafism 141
Apocalyptic Narratives 144
Al Qaeda 147

The Islamic State of Iraq 155
Islamic State of Iraq and the Levant 157
Shia Terrorism 162
Chapter Summary 166
Chapter Review Questions 166
Terminology 166

CHAPTER 7 State Terrorism 167

Test Your Knowledge 167
Introduction 167
Defining State Terrorism 171
Types of State Terrorism 174
Domestic State Terrorism 174
Domestic State-Sponsored Terrorism 179
State Sponsors of External Terrorism 179
External State Terrorism 181

External State-Sponsored Terrorism:
    Coup D'état 182
External State-Sponsored Terrorism:
    Terrorist Groups 185
Chapter Summary 188
Chapter Review Questions 189
Terminology 189

CHAPTER 8 Terrorism in the United States 191

Test Your Knowledge 191
Introduction 192

Right-Wing Terrorism 194
Ku Klux Klan 195

Neo-Nazi Extremists 198
Minutemen and Posse Comitatus 198
Christian Identity, Aryan Identity,
   and The Order 199
Militia Groups 201
Moralist Movements 202
Lone Wolves 203
Left-Wing Terrorism 203
Labor Violence 203
Anarchism 204
Modern Left-Wing Terrorism 205
Youth Violence: The Weather
   Underground 207
African American Liberation
   Movements 208
The Black Panther Party 208
Black Liberation Army 209
The Republic of New Afrika (New Afrikan
   Freedom Fighters) 209
Nationalist Violence: Puerto Rican
   Independence 210

Left-Wing Revolutionary Violence:
   Symbionese Liberation Army 212
Left-Wing Revolutionary Violence: The
   United Freedom Front 213
Left-Wing Revolutionary Violence: May 19
   Communist Organization 213
Single-Issue Terrorism 215
Radical Environmental and Animal-
   Liberation Groups 215
Lone Wolves: Biological Terrorism 216
International Terrorism in the United
   States 217
Jihad in America 218
September 11, 2001 Attacks 219
Post-9/11 International Jihadist Attacks 220
Post-9/11 Domestic Jihadist Attacks 220
Chapter Summary 223
Chapter Review Questions 225
Terminology 225

CHAPTER 9 The Media and Terrorism 227

Test Your Knowledge 227
Introduction 227
Mass-Mediated Terrorism 231
The Focus of Media Coverage
   of Terrorism 234
The Extent of Media Coverage
   of Terrorism 234

Media Contagion 235
Media Coverage of Counterterrorism 237
The New Media and Terrorism 239
Media Censorship 242
Chapter Summary 245
Chapter Review Questions 246
Terminology 246

CHAPTER 10 The Legal and Historical Basis of Homeland Security 247

Test Your Knowledge 247
Introduction 247
Department of Homeland Security 250
Critical Infrastructure 252
Federal Law Enforcement 252
Domestic and Foreign Intelligence 253
Federal Counterterrorism Laws 254
Identifing State Sponsors and
   Foreign Terrorist Organizations 256
Checks and Balances 256
International Counterterrorism
   Agreements 258

Historical Foundation of Homeland
   Security 264
Alien and Sedition Acts 264
The Civil War 265
The Palmer Raids 266
The Post-Depression Red Scare 266
The Cold War and The Red Scare 267
World War II Internment 268
Vietnam Protests 268
Homeland Security and Civil Liberties 269
Chapter Summary 269
Chapter Review Questions 269
Terminology 270

CHAPTER 11 Counterterrorism 271

Test Your Knowledge 271
Introduction 271
Drone Warfare 275
Guantánamo 281
Enhanced Interrogation 284
Military Commissions 287
Surveillance 290

Racial Profiling 293
Immigration 295
Social Media 300
Chapter Summary 305
Chapter Review Questions 305
Terminology 306

CHAPTER 12 Donald Trump and Contemporary Terrorism 307

Introduction 307
Nuclear Weapons 308
International Counterterrorism 310
Domestic Terrorism 315

National Security 317
Immigration 318
Future Challenges 321

Appendix 323
References 339
Index 351

Preface

Following the 9/11 attacks on the Pentagon and World Trade Center, I was asked by the College of Liberal Arts and Sciences at the University of Illinois at Chicago to teach a course on terrorism. This was a return to my educational roots. As a student I was fortunate to work for and study with some of the important pioneers in the study of terrorism. The years since 9/11 have witnessed a rapid increase in terrorism-related courses, programs, research centers, journals, and books. This text is an effort to consolidate some of these intellectual insights and developments in an accessible, relatively brief, and interdisciplinary introduction to the topic of terrorism. The focus of the book is on the theory and history on terrorism along with coverage of concrete contemporary developments and public policy issues. The book can be used as a primary or supplemental text.

CHAPTER ORGANIZATION

Each chapter is introduced by a *test your knowledge* feature which quizzes students on the extent to which they are familiar with the material in the chapter. This feature also stimulates interest in the chapter and helps students to organize the material. The chapter *introduction* in most instances presents a contemporary example of the topic discussed in the chapter. Each chapter also includes a *personality and events* feature which discuss important figures and events that relate to the content of the chapter. The *you decide* feature presents problems that challenge students to reach their own solution. The chapters conclude with a *chapter summary* and with *chapter summary questions* for discussion and *terminology*.

ORGANIZATION OF THE TEXT

The book follows a standard organizational scheme. A discussion of theory is followed by historical chapters and the last part of the book primarily is concerned with the media and public policy. The text is outlined below:

Definitions of terrorism. Chapter 1 surveys various approaches to defining terrorism and the strengths and weaknesses of these definitions.

Theories of terrorism. Chapter 2 provides an overview of psychological, criminological, and structural definitions of terrorism and discusses lone wolves and the involvement of women in terrorism.

Terrorist tactics and strategies. Chapter 3 provides an overview of the financing of terrorism, the weapons employed by terrorists, and their tactics and strategies, including cyberterrorism.

The history of terrorism. Chapter 4 outlines the foundations of modern terrorism, including religious terrorism, the French and Russian revolutions, anarchism, and an introduction to Irish terrorism and to the Israel–Palestine conflict.

Types of terrorism. Chapter 5 discusses ethnonationalist and revolutionary terrorism, Chapter 6 covers religious terrorism, and Chapter 7 outlines types of state terrorism.

Terrorism in the United States. Chapter 8 discusses right- and left-wing terrorism in the United States and international terrorism in America.

The media and terrorism. Chapter 9 discusses the relationship between the media and terrorism and the issues that arise in media coverage of terrorism.

Homeland security. Chapter 10 provides a brief introduction to the institutions involved in homeland security.

Counterterrorism. Chapter 11 is an introduction to contemporary public policy issues in counterterrorism, including Guantánamo, military commissions, domestic trials of terrorists, enhanced interrogation, racial profiling, and surveillance. Chapter 12 provides a sketch of developments since the election of President Donald Trump.

Acknowledgments

My thanks to the truly excellent reviewers whose comments and suggestions greatly improved the manuscript:

- Robert Cardigan, Boston University
- Chris Cook, University of Pittsburgh at Johnstown
- Christopher Cyr, Eastern Kentucky University
- Joseph Engler, City College of San Francisco
- Leslie Payne, Rand Corporation
- Jerome Randall, University of Central Florida
- Matthew Wahlert, Miami University

Special thanks to associate editor Leah Sheets, project editor Tom Pike, production editor Laureen Gleason, and acquisitions editor Mary Jane Peluso. My now retired editor and publisher at Sage Publications, Jerry Westby, has been with me from the beginning and is primarily responsible for developing and guiding the writing of the manuscript. As always, this book is dedicated to Natasha Barnes.

Defining Terrorism

INTRODUCTION

This introductory chapter explores the definition of **terrorism** and surveys **typologies of terrorism**. The definition of terrorism is far from straightforward and is hotly debated. We may label an act as terrorism in our daily conversation which does not fit the definition used by criminal justice and national security professionals or by academics. A vastly different definition is used by individuals and groups devoted to attacking the United States and its allies who view America as a "state sponsor of terrorism" (Schmid, 2011).

In November 2009 army psychiatrist and major Nidal Hasan opened fire and killed 13 people and wounded 30 at Fort Hood, Texas, the deadliest shooting ever to take place at an American military base. As he fired Hasan shouted "Allahu

Akbar" (commonly translated as *God is great*). He subsequently was convicted of multiple counts of murder and attempted murder by a military court-martial and sentenced to death.

The Department of Defense initially categorized the shooting as workforce violence and as the criminal act of a single individual although a Senate report classified the shooting as "the worst terroristic attack on U.S. soil since

FIGURE 1.1 & 1.2 Firefighters at the World Trade Center

Source: https://commons.wikimedia.org/wiki/File%3AFire_fighters_amid_smoking_rubble_after_September_11th_terrorist_attack_(29392249476).jpg.

Source: https://commons.wikimedia.org/wiki/File%3AFire_fighter_in_front_of_burning_building_and_rubble_following_September_11th_terrorist_attack_(29138236340).jpg.

September 11, 2001" (Swaine, 2013). Army investigators explained that they could not find links between Hasan and terrorist groups.

Hasan joined the military following his graduation from a Virginia high school and served as an enlisted soldier for 8 years while earning his college degree at Virginia Tech. After graduating in 1997 he was accepted into an elite medical program and received his medical training at a military-sponsored health facility. He was known by others as deeply religious, quiet, and unassuming. Several of his colleagues had complained to authorities that he expressed anti-American views and expressed misgivings about Muslims serving in the U.S. military in the Middle East. At one point while conducting research, Hasan was in regular email contact with Anwar al-Awlaki in Yemen, an inspirational Muslim cleric who advocated attacks on the United States.

Following the Fort Hood killings, investigators found that Hasan had been viewing jihadist websites and had made Internet posts comparing suicide bombers to soldiers who die for a noble cause. They also found that his business card identified him as an SOA (soldier or servant of God).

On the other hand, Hasan was extremely agitated over his reassignment to Afghanistan and was angry that authorities refused to prosecute his military patients who admitted to war crimes; he simply may have experienced an emotional breakdown. There was no evidence linking Hasan to radical groups in his family's native Palestine.

President Barack Obama, in discussing the events at Fort Hood, referred to the shootings as an example of extremist violence rather than using the terminology of *terrorism*. In April 2015 the Pentagon, in response to congressional legislation requesting a reexamination of the Fort Hood shooting, awarded Purple Hearts to the victims of the shootings, making them eligible for combat-related benefits.

In April 2014 Specialist Ivan A. Lopez, age 34, killed three individuals at Fort Hood and injured 16 before committing suicide. At the time he was being treated for depression and anxiety and was being evaluated for post-traumatic stress disorder.

Why was there a question whether Major Hasan as a terrorist? How does he compare to Specialist Lopez? The remainder of the chapter explores the definition of terrorism. First, let us consider why the study of terrorism has taken on importance in recent years.

WHY TERRORISM MATTERS

There are some worthwhile reasons for being concerned about and studying **terrorism.**

Violence. There is a significant human cost from terrorism. This includes the severely injured victims of the Boston Marathon bombing, the dead and injured from the 9/11 attacks, and the psychologically traumatized individuals who have experienced terrorist attacks. This cost is amplified manifold across the globe.

Daily life. Terrorism has significantly transformed the way people live their life. Think about the changes in foreign and domestic travel and even the experience when attending a concert or sporting event.

Resources. A vast amount of money, time, and human resources have been spent creating structures to combat terrorism and in maintaining national security. It is estimated that since 2001, somewhere between $1.4 and $4 trillion has been spent by the United States on the War on Terror. More than 1,200 government organizations and 1,900 private companies presently work on counterterrorism, homeland security, and national security at 10,000 locations across the United States (Masco, 2014).

Civil liberties. Terrorism has resulted in an expansion of government databases, surveillance, and expanded government powers of search and seizure.

Personal security. There is a general sense of psychological insecurity and fear.

Knowledge. The study of terrorism provides an introduction to the history, nature, and causes of violence and how to combat violence.

In 2015 there were 11,774 terrorist attacks worldwide. This was a slight decrease from 2014, in which there were 13,463 terrorist attacks worldwide—an increase from 9,707 terrorist attacks in 2013. A total of 28,328 individuals died during terrorist attacks in 2015, including 6,924 perpetrators. In 2015 there was a monthly average of 981 attacks, causing 2,361 deaths and 2,943 injuries. Each terrorist attack in 2015 resulted in an average of 2.5 deaths and 3.3 injuries (Bureau of Counterterrorism, 2015). The total number of terrorist attacks in 2016 decreased by 9 percent and the total number of deaths resulting from terrorist attacks decreased by 13 percent as compared to 2015. These attacks occurred in 104 countries, although they were heavily concentrated in Iraq, Afghanistan, India, Pakistan, and the Philippines. Other countries with a significant number of terrorist attacks included Nigeria, Somalia, Syria, Turkey, and Yemen (Bureau of Counterterrorism, 2016).

John Mueller challenges the conventional view that terrorism is an immediate and urgent threat. He contends, among other points, that the damage and threat of terrorism is exaggerated. The probability that an individual American will be killed in a terrorist attack is "microscopic" and that the United States is able to "readily absorb" the damage from an attack. The probability that a resident of the globe will die as a result of international terrorism is 1 in 80,000—roughly the chance that an individual will die from the impact of an asteroid or comet. Mueller advocates a less "exaggerated" and more reasoned approach to addressing terrorism (Mueller, 2006).

Lisa Stampnitzky asks in a related analysis whether terrorism is merely a name for a long-standing phenomenon. She points out that between 1961 and 1972 there were 85 planes hijacked en route from the United States to Cuba. These hijackings were viewed as air piracy or as a routine crime. In the mid-1970s these same acts, together with other criminal acts, were categorized as terrorism. Terrorism from this perspective is a relatively isolated event and is used by governments to create a climate of social fear and anxiety to justify governmental intrusion into our daily lives (Stampnitzky, 2013).

DEFINING TERRORISM

The definition of terrorism is a subject of constant and intense debate, and a dizzying number of definitions have been proposed by scholars and government agencies. The various branches of the American government do not even agree among themselves on a definition of terrorism. More than 100 definitions of terrorism have been proposed by scholars, government agencies, various countries, and commentators (Schmid & Jongman, 2005). There are a number of respected commentators who conclude that terrorism is too difficult to define and that an accurate definition is not possible. The best approach, according to these commentators, is to admit that "I cannot define terrorism, but I know terrorism when I see it" (Richardson, 2006).

This disagreement over the definition of terrorism may seem like the type of seemingly complicated question of primary interest to terrorist researchers and academics, and which is irrelevant to practitioners. The question, however, has real-world implications. Without a definition, the best we can do is to rely on our impressions, prejudices, and fears rather than evidence to label individuals and groups as terrorists. This may divert resources into areas that do not enhance national security. Does the United States enhance security by banning immigration from various countries or by requiring all Muslims to register with federal authorities or would a more selective strategy prove more successful?

How should we define terrorism or a terrorist? Think about the environmental group Greenpeace which intercepts whaling ships and harasses vessels that pose a threat to the environment. Greenpeace certainly engages in coercion to achieve political goals. Is Greenpeace a terrorist organization? What about groups dedicated to the protection of animals which in some instances have been accused of "freeing" laboratory animals or destroying laboratories that experiment on animals? Think about how freely we use the designation cyberterrorism. Is this a proper designation?

Keep in mind that an act may threaten the peace and stability of society and merit severe punishment although it is not terrorism. An example is a school shooting.

DO WE NEED A DEFINITION OF TERRORISM?

The designation of *terrorist organization* or *terrorist* carries a number of legal implications. In the United States, working on behalf of a designated terrorist organization, promoting the organization, or being involved in the organization in any capacity may result in criminal prosecution for material support of a terrorist organization. An organization designated as a terrorist organization in the United States may be dissolved and have its finances seized. These organizations in some instances may be subject to legal action for damages brought by the victims and families of victims of the violent activity sponsored by the group. Individuals who are reasonably believed to be engaged in terrorist activities may be placed under surveillance and have their phone and Internet communications monitored. Suspected terrorists will be prevented from entering the United States and may be subject to deportation from the country. They also may on rare occasions be detained on a material witness warrant until they testify before a grand jury or at trial. Even being suspected of terrorist activity can result in being placed on a no-fly list, which prevents an individual from travelling on a domestic or international airline. Individuals in countries with fewer legal protections that are considered terrorists may find their passports revoked, and in some instances may find themselves subject to preventive detention and lengthy prison terms for membership in a designated terrorist organization. Suspected terrorists in some areas of the world may be shot on sight rather than arrested, and when captured may be subject to harsh prison conditions. Consider that methods of interrogation are accepted against suspected terrorists that would be unacceptable if used against other types of criminals. In other words, we need to define who is a terrorist to counterterrorism.

PROBLEMS WITH DEFINING TERRORISM

Terrorism is a word that is used in our daily vocabulary without a great deal of precision or clear meaning. There are various interrelated obstacles to an objective definition of terrorism (Jackson, Jarvis, Gunning, & Breen-Smyth, 2011).

Perspective. The use of the term often depends on individuals' situations. Governments label critics and insurgents as terrorists and these groups, in turn, may label the response of governments as terrorism. An individual's perspective may dictate what is viewed as "illegitimate violence" and who is viewed as an "innocent individual."

Power. In most societies, governments exercise immense power to influence public perceptions, fund research, and to enforce the law, and they are able to shape public perceptions of which individuals and groups are considered terrorists and what types of acts are considered to be terrorism.

Diversity. Terrorism is a diverse phenomenon. A definition of terrorism that treats the violent acts of individuals in the United States, the People's Republic of China, Russia, or Rwanda as part of a common category provides limited insight or understanding.

Motive. The same act—such as assassination of a political leader—may be an act of terrorism, undertaken as an act of personal revenge, or based on some other motive. How do we determine, other than perhaps in retrospect, that the act was intended as terrorism?

History. The term *terrorism* has shifted throughout history and has had no consistent meaning. In the 19th and early 20th centuries, terrorists in many cases were viewed as romantic rebels who, in many countries—including the United States—were considered soldiers in the cause of democratic values, who should not be extradited to stand trial in their states of nationality. In the 1970s the United States refused to return several members of the Irish Republican Army to Great Britain on the grounds that they were political offenders fighting for a revolutionary cause.

As you read definitions of terrorism, consider the statement of the radical scholar Noam Chomsky that "we have to qualify the definition of 'terrorism' given in official sources; the term applies only to terrorism against us, not the terrorism we carry out against them" (Duyvesteyn, 2017).

INITIAL THOUGHTS ON DEFINING TERRORISM

If asked to develop a definition of terrorism most people would include some basic components.

Act. Unlawful acts of violence.

Motivation. Politically inspired violence or threat of violence.

Intent. Designed to achieve political change through violence.

Target. Attacking civilian targets or members of the government or government structures.

Tactic. Carried out by individuals who are members of a group that do not wear identifiable uniforms and act on behalf of a nation-state.

Of course, terrorism may be motivated by nonpolitical factors including religion, race, or ethnic rivalries, or may be motivated by opposition to a public policy such as abortion or LGBT rights. Some people might add that the purpose or consequence of a terrorist attack is to bring about change through intimidation or through the creation of fear. We may find definitions that specify the type of weapons employed by terrorist or list the types of harm to persons or property resulting from terrorist violence. Others might note that terrorism may include nonviolent acts of coercion such as a massive cyberattack. We also might find that some people include violent attacks by states—such as bombing attacks on civilians—as terrorism. There may be objections that attacks on the military or police are not terrorism and that terrorism is limited to attacks on civilians. Recent events remind us that there are lone-wolf terrorists who are not formally affiliated with any group. Another consideration is that violence undertaken in pursuit of a morally just cause may not be considered by some individuals to constitute terrorism. Finally, definitions might distinguish between domestic and international acts of terrorism, and between attacks undertaken by individuals who are citizens and noncitizens of a state.

A survey of definitions of terrorism found that the definitions variously mentioned the following factors: violence or force (83.5% of the definitions), political motivation (65%), creating fear or terror (51%), intentional and systematic (32%), particular strategies and tactics (30.5%), without regard for normal constraints (30%), coercion (28%), and over one third (37.5%) mentioned injury to victims that were not themselves the primary target of the attack. Infrequently mentioned in the definition were repetitive or serial violence (7%), covert nature (9%), and criminal character (6%) (Schmid & Jongman, 2005). Weinberg and his colleagues analyzed definitions of terrorism in academic journals and found that the focus was on politically directed violence and that very few definitions focused on the psychological impact of terrorism (Weinberg, Pedahzur, & Hirsch-Hoefler, 2012). Lisa Stampnitzky reports that 77% of political science journal articles on terrorism do not include a definition of terrorism, and the remainder offer a definition that is unrelated to previous definitions (Stampnitzky 2013). In other words, H. H. A. Cooper understandably concludes that there is "a problem in the problem of definition" of terrorism (Cooper, 2001).

Despite these complexities, terrorism experts and practitioners have proposed some thought-provoking definitions of terrorism some of which are discussed in the next section. As you read these definitions, pay attention to what is included and what is omitted from the various definitions. Do you agree with the statement of famed terrorist researcher Walter Laqueur (1999) that a "comprehensive definition of terrorism" (p. 5) does not exist and likely will not be formulated in the years to come?

SOME DEFINITONS OF TERRORISM

Israeli national security strategist Boaz Ganor writes that terrorism is the "intentional use of, or threat to use, violence against civilians or against civilian targets, in order to attain political aims" (Ganor, 2005). Note that the focus of this definition is on the identity of the victims. Ganor writes that his definition is based on three central elements. First, the essence of terrorism is the use of or the threat of violence. An activity that does not involve violence is not terrorism. Second, the aim of terrorism is political: changing the regime or modifying a policy. An act that is not directed to achieve a political aim is a criminal act and a criminal act is not terrorism. Ganor notes that the term *political* is sufficiently expansive to include a religious, ideological, or other motivation. Third, the targets of terrorism are civilians. The inadvertent injury to civilians is not terrorism. Ganor argues that the reason or motive for attacking civilians (for example, intimidation or to spread fear) is irrelevant and is insistent that national liberation groups fighting against foreign occupiers are not immune from being labeled as terrorists because of the alleged morality of their cause. He makes the important point that under his definition, states can be involved in terrorism by directing, sponsoring, or carrying out attacks (Ganor, 2005).

Harvard scholar Louise Richardson adopts a very similar definition. In discussing the characteristics of terrorism, Richardson notes that the act and victim typically have "symbolic significance." Terrorists are "outmanned" and "outgunned" by the opposition and select targets to enhance their perceived power and capacity. The victims of terrorism are usually a means to influence the government and are not themselves the focus of terrorist grievance or demands. Most importantly, Richardson diverges from Ganor and argues that terrorism is carried out by substate groups—not carried out by states. She recognizes that states target civilians, although such acts are punishable as war crimes or as violations of human rights, and are not terrorism (Richardson, 2006, pp. 4–5).

Important terrorism scholars Bruce Hoffman and Walter Laqueur further elaborate on the definition of terrorism by charactering terrorism as the use of "illegitimate force to achieve political ends by targeting innocent people" (Guiora, 2011, p. 4). The definition focuses on the criminal nature of terrorist violence, which targets innocent people, to achieve political objectives. Note that this approach does not limit the victims to civilians; it might include the police or members of the military. Professor Amos Guiora, a former commander in the Israel Defense

Force notes there is a problem in deciding when violence is "legitimate" or "illegitimate" and in agreeing who is an "innocent" (Guiora, 2011, p. 4).

Hoffman also has offered his own definition, which shifts the focus to the psychological impact of terrorism. He writes that terrorism is "deliberate creation and exploitation of fear through violence or the threat of violence in the pursuit of change" (Hoffman, 2006, p. 41).

Guiora also proposes a definition of terrorism. He first explains that the essence of terrorism is "acts of violence," suggesting that terrorism is a process that involves periodic attacks that exact a psychological toll on a population—rather than a single dramatic attack. These acts are undertaken to advance a "political, social, religious or economic" cause aimed at "innocent civilians defined as legitimate targets with the intent to cause physical harm" (Guiora, 2011, p. 4). Note that Guiora recognizes that terrorists define "innocent" victims as permissible targets for attack, although attacking civilians is both an act of terrorism and a crime under international law. He concludes by adding that terrorism in addition to causing physical harm may involve "psychological warfare against a population aimed at intimidating it from conducting its daily life in a normal fashion" (Guiora, 2011, p. 4) The focus of Guiora's definition is on the infliction of physical and psychological harm on innocent individuals who are defined as targets by terrorists. Note that he does not include attacks on the police or military as terrorism (Guiora, 2011).

A United Nations (UN) definition focuses on the types of acts that are terrorism and states that terrorism involves the infliction of death or serious bodily injury, serious damage to property, and damage to property that results in major economic loss when the purpose is to intimidate a population or compel a government or international organization to "do or to abstain from doing any act" (United Nations, 2002).

At this point you likely have reached your own definition of terrorism. There are some common elements that are included in most of these definitions.

Violence. Terrorism involves criminal violence or the threat of criminal violence.

Actor. Terrorism may be committed by subnational groups or by states.

Intent. Terrorism involves the intent to advance a political, social, religious, or economic cause.

Target. Terrorism is directed at innocent individuals defined as legitimate targets.

Harm. Terrorism involves physical harm or the creation of physical harm or psychological fear or intimidation.

Motive. Terrorism is unjustifiable whatever the motive or cause.

U.S. government departments and agencies have developed various definitions of terrorism.

The FBI defines international terrorism as violent acts that:

> appear to be intended to intimidate or coerce a civilian population; influence the policy of a government by intimidation or coercion; or affect the conduct of a government by mass destruction, assassination or kidnapping and occur primarily outside the territorial jurisdiction of the United States or transcend national boundaries in terms of the means by which they are accomplished, the persons they appear intended to intimidate or coerce, or the locals in which their perpetrators operate or seek asylum. (FBI, 2006)

The FBI also defines **domestic terrorism** as:

> activities that involve acts dangerous to human life that are a violation of the criminal laws of the United States or of any state; appear to be intended to intimidate or coerce a civilian population; to influence the policy of government by mass destruction, assassination, or kidnapping and occur primarily within the territorial jurisdiction of the United States. (FBI, 2006)

The U.S. Department of Defense defines terrorism as:

> the unlawful use of, or threatened use of, force or violence, often motivated by religious, political, or other ideological beliefs, to instill fear and coerce governments or societies in pursuit of goals that are usually political. (U.S. Department of Defense, 2010)

The Department of State defines terrorism as:

> premeditated, politically motivated violence perpetrated against non-combatant targets by subnational groups or clandestine agents. (Bureau of Counterterrorism, 2015)

The Department of Homeland Security states that terrorism is:

> any activity that is dangerous to human life or potentially destructive of critical infrastructure or key resources; and ... must also appear to be intended (1) to intimidate or coerce a civilian population; (ii) to influence the policy of a government by intimidation or coercion; or (iii) to affect the conduct of a government by mass destruction, assassination, or kidnapping. (Jackson et al., 2011, p. 102)

Federal law in the United States Code, 18 U.S.C. Section 3077, defines terrorism as unlawful violence that is intended to:

> intimidate or coerce a civilian population ... influence the policy of a government by intimidation or coercion; or ... affects the conduct of a government by assassination or kidnapping. (U.S. Code, n.d.)

1.1 You Decide

In July 1944 a group of German military officers led by Colonel Claus von Stauffenberg, who had lost an eye and hand in combat in North Africa, attempted to assassinate Adolf Hitler. The plan was to assassinate Hitler, deploy the reserve army to remove the high command, and seek a negotiated peace with the Allied Powers. Stauffenberg carried a bomb loaded with plastic explosives connected to an acid fuse into a military conference with Hitler. He placed the briefcase under the table adjacent to Hitler and left the room under the excuse that he needed to make a phone call. The bomb detonated a moment later reducing the room to rubble. Four individuals died although Hitler escaped with minor injuries. When Stauffenberg left the room, the briefcase was moved resulting in the blast being deflected from Hitler. Stauffenberg and the other conspirators were apprehended and together with hundreds of dissidents were later executed. Hitler later would boast that he was immortal and following the attack rarely was in public view. On April 30, 1945, Hitler committed suicide. A successful assassination would have spared some of the six million Jews and other individuals exterminated in death camps and may have resulted in the survival of tens of thousands of Allied military forces and German soldiers and civilians who died in the last months of the war.

Was the attempted assassination of Hitler an act of terrorism? []

TERRORISM, WAR, AND GUERILLA WARFARE

Terrorism, **war**, and **guerilla warfare** (*guerilla* translates to "little war") share the common characteristic that all involve armed combat that results in the loss of human life. These military operations, however, are distinct and different in important ways. Bruce Hoffman suggests that contrasting guerilla warfare with terrorism helps to clarify the nature of terrorism in the absence of a clear definition (Hoffman, 2006).

War may be defined as a "contention between two or more States through their armed forces, for the purpose of overpowering each other and imposing such conditions of peace as the victor pleases" (Detter, 2000, p. 7). Two less traditional although increasingly prevalent forms of war are noninternational armed conflicts to establish an autonomous regional government, or internal civil wars in which a government is in combat with an opposition force fighting to overthrow the central government or to attain regional autonomy. An example is the Bosnian War in the 1990s in which the Bosnian government engaged in a prolonged conflict with the Serbian population. War in the 20th century, beginning with the Hague Convention of 1898, became heavily regulated by international agreements—the most important of which are the four Geneva Conventions and Protocols. A violation of these treaties in theory may result in a monetary penalty on a state and criminal prosecution or court-martial of violators.

Virtually every country in the world is a signatory to the Geneva Conventions and have incorporated these conventions as part of their domestic military law. The Geneva Conventions regulate nearly every area of armed conflict including the conduct of hostilities, treatment of civilians and the wounded, sick, and prisoners of war, and the protection of cultural property and the environment. Violation of these restrictions can lead to criminal prosecution and to a state's liability to pay compensation to the victimized state.

Two provisions are most important for our discussion. The law of war specifies that civilians and civilian structures and material essential for human survival should not be made the intentional target of attack. A second important provision provides that to be treated as a prisoner of war, rather than as an irregular combatant, is that a combatant must carry arms openly, wear an identifiable and fixed uniform or insignia, operate under the authority of an organized command, and obey the law of war. This is important because a country must treat prisoners of war in a humanitarian fashion, and the protections for irregular combatants are far less extensive.

In a controversial decision, the international community in the Geneva Protocol loosened the requirements for recognition of prisoner-of-war status of combatants who are fighting internal wars of national liberation from a foreign power or repressive and racist regimes, and for internal opposition movements that control territory. Keep in mind, however, that civilians and the sick and wounded may never be made the intentional target of an attack other than when they are unavoidably part of an attack on a valuable military site.

Guerilla warfare often is labelled as terrorism although the two forms of irregular conflict are somewhat different. The term *guerilla war* was developed to describe Spanish resistance to Napoleon in 1808 and is derived from the Spanish term for war. Guerilla war typically is used to describe combat relying on irregular forces who rely on hit-and-run tactics to fight a more powerful organized government or foreign force.

Bruce Hoffman notes that both guerillas and terrorists—as a matter of strategy—may not wear formal uniforms or carry arms openly and may not be distinguishable from civilians. Guerillas, however—unlike terrorists—operate in military units, attack enemy military forces, and seize and hold territory, although this may be limited to the nighttime. They engage in propaganda and information campaigns to attract support and to criticize the government. In some cases guerillas abide by the rules of war in terms of the protection of civilians and wearing an identifiable insignia. Terrorists, in contrast to guerillas, do not operate in the open in armed units under responsible command, do not respect the law of war, in most cases do not seek to capture and hold territory, attack civilians rather than focus their attacks on the police and military forces, and rarely—if ever—wear an identifiable insignia.

A group may engage in guerilla warfare as well as terrorism. Examples of groups combining these forms of warfare are the Revolutionary Armed Forces of Colombia (FARC) and Liberation Tigers of Tamil Eelam (LTTE), also known as the Tamil Tigers. Brue Hoffman writes that roughly one third of the groups on the U.S. State Department list of designated foreign terrorist organizations could be considered guerillas. ISIS and **al Qaeda**, while fighting in Syria against the Assad regime, were examples of groups who engaged in both guerilla warfare and in terrorism. Another example of a group that combines terrorism and guerilla warfare are the Taliban in Afghanistan (Hoffman, 2006).

There are numerous historical examples of successful guerilla campaigns including the Chinese communists' defeat of the Chinese nationalists in 1949 and the Vietnamese defeat of the French colonial forces in 1954.

Hoffman also contrasts terrorism with conventional crime. Both terrorists and criminals may engage in acts such as kidnapping, bank robberies, and armed attacks. The difference is that the common criminal typically is motivated by self-interest, rather than by an intent to bring about political change. Criminals may terrorize victims through the infliction of violence, although, unlike terrorism, this typically is intended to punish victims or to force them to cooperate, rather than to intimidate society. According to Hoffman, terrorists also are distinct from the psychologically challenged individuals who may target a political leader as a result of a mental delusion rather than because of a political motive. John Hinckley, for example, attempted to kill President Ronald Reagan in an effort to impress his fantasy-lover actress Jodie Foster rather than because of a political motive.

Of course, individuals may have various motives that account for their behavior. Hoffman may go too far in arguing that terrorists—in contrast to criminals—are altruists who believe that they are serving a just cause, rather than the criminal who is motivated by a desire to achieve personal profit or revenge. There undoubtedly are terrorists who view their activities as a lucrative business involving drugs (narcoterrorists) or gun trafficking.

The next section of the chapter outlines typologies of terrorism.

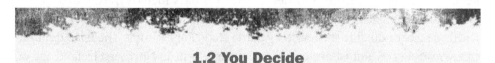

1.2 You Decide

In 2012 Edgar Morales, a member of a New York City street gang, was charged and convicted of terrorism stemming from a fight with members of a rival gang in which a young child was killed. A New York court reversed the decision, noting that violence between rival street gangs, however serious, was very different from the September 11, 2001, attacks on the World Trade Center and the Pentagon. These attacks were undertaken to intimidate or coerce the civilian population and to affect the policy of the United States in the Middle East. Bringing a prosecution against a member of a street gang for acts directed at another gang would mean that prosecutors "could invoke the specter of 'terrorism' every time a Blood [street gang member] assaults a Crip [street gang member]. ... The concept of terrorism has a unique meaning ... and risk[s] being trivialized if the terminology is applied ... in situations that do not match our collective understanding of ... a terrorist act" (*People v. Morales*, 2012).

Are street gangs terrorist organizations?

TYPOLOGIES OF TERRORISM

The term terrorism encompasses a wide variety of groups with different strategies, goals, and ideologies. A number of analysts have developed **typologies of terrorism**, which group these organizations according to shared characteristics. These typologies are somewhat misleading because terrorist organizations often cannot be easily categorized, and no two groups are precisely alike. Nonetheless typologies are useful for organizing terrorist organizations according to broad categories that provide a starting point for studying the characteristics of individual terrorist groups and for exploring the differences and similarities between terrorist groups.

Dr. Frederick Hacker developed an early categorization scheme based on the personality of terrorists. He broadly grouped terrorists as "crazies" with an addiction to violence, "crusaders" who possessed a religious zealotry, and "criminals" who used to terrorist activity to traffic drugs and weapons and to make money (Hacker, 1976).

Subsequent efforts at classification shifted the focus from the personality of terrorists to other bases for distinguishing terrorists. One prevalent scheme differentiates groups according to whether their primary focus is the use of domestic (national) or international violence. The question is whether the focus of attacks is within a state or outside the territory of the state. For example, the Irish Republican Army focused almost exclusively on violence within Northern Ireland and on occasion within Britain. Al Qaeda focuses their efforts across the globe. Another binary scheme is the difference between state and nonstate terrorism. State terrorism is distinguished by the government resources available to carry out attacks and by the need to simultaneously maintain a measure of popular support while conducting a domestic and/or international war against terror. States engaging in terrorism also may draw both support and criticism from other countries. Yet another binary division is between individual or lone-wolf terrorism carried out by individuals such as the Oklahoma bomber Timothy McVeigh and terrorism carried out in small groups. This differentiation is based on the differing capabilities of individuals and groups. There is a growing attention to drawing a difference between female and male terrorists.

Another common typology is based on the methods employed by terrorists. Weapons of mass destruction (WMD) terrorism is contrasted with "conventional" terrorism. The most frequently cited example of WMD terrorism is the sarin attack by Aum Shinrikyo in the Tokyo subway in 1995 (Lifton, 1999). Cyberterrorism is another form of terrorism which encompasses attacks on networks and information systems. Suicide bombing and suicide terrorism is another categorization scheme based on the methodology used by terrorists (Pape, 2005).

Categorizing terrorists and terrorist organizations based on ideology is the most prevalent and helpful scheme of categorization and is based on the underlying belief system of terrorist organizations. Keep in mind that this ideology may not be shared by each member of the terrorist organization. These ideological categories include the following:

Left-wing terrorism. These groups are dedicated to a restructuring of society and the economy and to the eradication of class differences. They tend to draw membership from peasants who want land redistribution and the poor and working class who want a redistribution of wealth and government ownership of industry. These groups include FARC in Colombia, Naxalites in India, and the now-disbanded Red Brigades in Italy and Baader-Meinhof in Germany.

Right-wing terrorism. Groups that support an authoritarian form of government with a commitment to racial or national purity and opposition to racial diversity and immigration. They generally articulate an extreme nationalism and oppose international obligations that limit the independence of the nation. Examples are various neo-Nazi groups in Europe and the Aryan Brotherhood in the United States.

Nationalist terrorism. These groups aspire to create a state based on religion or national identity. Examples are Hamas in Palestine, which is devoted to the creation of Palestinian state with an Islamic identity; Chechens who desire a state separate from Russia; and Kurds who want to create a unified country separate from Turkey. Other groups include the Tamil Tigers in Sri Lanka and the ETA in the Basque Country in Spain.

Religious terrorism. These terrorists are motivated by theological texts that they interpret as obligating the creation of a state based on a pure form of religion. Individuals demonstrate their religious devotion by their willingness to engage in armed struggle and self-sacrifice, as well as the cleansing of nonbelievers. Religious groups in most instances are led by charismatic leaders who provide religious inspiration. Examples include al Qaeda, ISIS, and the Lord's Resistance Army in Uganda.

Ecoterrorism. This category only recently has been recognized as a distinct form of terrorism. These terrorists are motivated by a desire to protect the natural environment and engage in vandalism against what they view as environmentally destructive activities and projects. A related form of terrorism involves individuals who act using extreme methods to protect animals against human abuse and exploitation.

These categories have been divided into additional "mixed" subcategories such as right-wing religious terrorists (Masters, 2008). There are various other schemes such as ancient and modern terrorism, single-issue terrorism, and high-casualty terrorism. One additional scheme worth mentioning is the difference between "new" and "old" terrorism although this remains an area of particular controversy.

The New Terrorism

A number of analysts argue that a new type of terrorism developed in the early 1990s which is distinguished from the "old terrorism" (Hoffman, 2006; Lesser, Hoffman, Arquilla, Ronfeldt, & Zanini, 1999). The **new terrorism** is characterized by the following:

Transnational. Targets are selected across the globe rather than being directed at a single country.

Leaderless resistance. Terrorists are organized in a series of independent cells with no chain of command or formal members. These cells are inspired by a common ideology and in some instances may be connected through cell leaders. This "leaderless resistance" prevents the detection or infiltration of one cell from leading to the detection of other terrorist cells.

Personnel. Terrorists tend to be drawn from amateurs ("clean skins") rather than professional fighters. The "new terrorist" is motivated by religion and is more fanatical and violent than in the past.

Technology. Terrorists communicate through encrypted messages and conduct sophisticated social media propaganda and recruitment campaigns.

Weaponry. The availability of powerful weaponry, powerful toxic chemicals, and even nuclear material provides terrorists with a formidable military capacity, and allows a single individual to pose a significant threat to inflict indiscriminate violence.

The "new terrorism" is dismissed by many experts as "old wine in bottles." For example, the notion that there is a "new terrorism" overlooks that 19th-century anarchists and the left-wing groups of the 1970s relied on autonomous cells. Amateurs historically were prevalent in terrorist groups and religion-based terrorism has long been an aspect of recorded history.

Personalites and Events

A discussion of contemporary terrorism inevitably involves a reference to *Osama bin Laden*. This is an uncomfortable topic because he is a figure with a massive amount of innocent blood on his hands.

Mohammed bin Laden, Osama's biological father, emigrated to Saudi Arabia from Yemen and started a construction company which profited from the country's oil-driven economy. He obtained contracts for high-profile projects and advised foreign construction companies doing business in Saudi Arabia. Mohammed bin Laden amassed significant wealth and developed an extravagant lifestyle, including a total of 22 wives, numerous concubines, and 54 children. Osama ("the Lion") was born in 1958 and was the product of a marriage between Mohammed and Alia Ghanem from Syria. Mohammed soon grew tired of Alia, divorced her, and arranged a marriage between Alia and an executive of his construction firm.

Osama was sent to an elite private school and at age fourteen experienced a religious transformation and embarked on a severe lifestyle of prayer and grew intolerant of Western influences, which he believed were corrupting Saudi society. Osama married while in high school and together with Najwa Gahnem, a Syrian cousin, and with three other wives subsequently gave birth to 11 children. He enrolled in King Abdul Aziz University in Jeddah in 1976 and studied economics although his interest in religion continued to grow. Bin Laden consciously patterned himself on the Prophet Muhammad, fasting on the days the Prophet fasted, wearing clothes reminiscent of the Prophet, and following a similar diet. Osama became a devoted student of a mystical Palestinian scholar, Abdullah Azzam, who was teaching Islamic theology in Jeddah.

Abdullah was an ardent supporter of the Afghan resistance to the Soviet Union's 1979 Soviet incursion and recruited young Saudis to join their struggle. Bin Laden established a hostel in Peshawar, Pakistan, for Arab fighters on their way to join the struggle in Afghanistan and devoted himself to raising money to fund the struggle from oil-rich Saudis. Bin Laden also served as a conduit for money from the Saudi regime.

Osama formed al Qaeda (meaning *the foundation*) in 1988, in the aftermath of the Russian defeat in Afghanistan, as an organization dedicated to the continuation of jihad (meaning *struggle*). Arab fighters now streamed into Afghanistan for a struggle against the Communist government of Afghanistan, which found itself weakened by the Russian retreat. Bin Laden provided salaries and health care for al Qaeda fighters who swore oaths of loyalty to the now-respected Emir bin Laden.

Bin Laden returned to Saudi Arabia in 1989 with a commitment to the defense of Islam across the globe. In the same year, he urged the Saudi royal family to allow him to raise an army to defend Saudi Arabia against Iraq, which under the leadership of strongman Saddam Hussein, had invaded neighboring Kuwait rather than allow the "infidel" United States to establish a base in the country.

Disappointed at the decision to allow the American military to enter Saudi Arabia, Bin Laden along with a handful of members of al Qaeda moved to Sudan in 1992 where Islamic scholar Hasan al-Turabi emerged a major figure following a military coup. Al-Turabi envisioned the creation of an international Muslim community centered in Sudan. Bin Laden provided the Sudanese with money and construction equipment to build a 300-kilometer highway as a gift to the nation.

(continues on next page)

(continued from previous page)

Bin Laden gradually established strong links with Islamic fighters from Egypt and other countries. He was viewed by various Muslim regimes as responsible for unrest in their countries and Saudi Arabia, and under pressure to take action, they revoked Bin Laden's citizenship. There now was little left to lose and in 1995 Bin Laden openly attacked the Saudi royal family for their extravagant lifestyle, irresponsible expenditures that were impoverishing the country, and for allowing American "infidels" to enter the country. In May 1996 Bin Laden was expelled from Sudan and traveled back to Afghanistan which now was under the control of the Taliban, a fundamentalist Islamic regime.

The United States viewed Bin Laden as a financial supporter of terrorism rather than a terrorist operative. Intelligence sources, however, warned that Bin Laden was building a military capacity in Afghanistan, and that he had established training camps, was recruiting fighters from across the globe, and had initiated efforts to obtain chemical and nuclear weapons. In 1996 Bin Laden issued the "Declaration of War Against the Americans Occupying the Land of the Two Holy Places," calling for jihad against American troops stationed in Saudi Arabia. The declaration was followed in February 1998 with a call for Muslims to kill Americans wherever they may be found.

The few glimpses of Bin Laden showed him in a cave. He likely was aware that the Prophet had encountered the angel Gabriel in a cave in Mecca, where the Prophet was embraced as a messenger of God. The underground cave for Bin Laden was a public message that he had retreated from the corruption of modern society and had removed himself from the influence of Western civilization.

In August 1998 al Qaeda orchestrated a simultaneous bomb attack on U.S. embassies in Kenya and in Tanzania, killing 12 Americans and more than 200 Kenyans and Tanzanians and injuring more than 4,000 people. In December 1999 Ahmed Ressam was detained by a U.S. custom officer while crossing from Canada into the United States and was discovered to be planning an attack on Los Angeles International Airport on New Year's Eve.

An August 1998 series of American cruise missile attacks failed to kill Bin Laden. The failure of Operation Infinite Reach to kill Bin Laden elevated his profile as a symbol of terrorist resistance to the United States and to the West.

On at least four occasions in 1998 and 1999, U.S. cruise missile strikes against Bin Laden were called off by the Clinton administration for various reasons, including the fear of collateral damage against innocents and because of what was viewed as unreliable intelligence.

On October 12, 2000, attackers in a skiff loaded with explosives rammed into the Navy destroyer the U.S.S. *Cole* in Aden, Yemen, killing 17 American sailors and nearly sinking the ship. In January 2000 an al Qaeda terrorist attack on the navy vessel the *Sullivan* failed when a skiff loaded with explosives sank before reaching the vessel.

Bin Laden's last and most tragic attack occurred on September 11, 2001, when al Qaeda operatives hijacked planes that hit the World Trade Center and the Pentagon. A plot to pilot a third plane into the White House was prevented by brave passengers whose resistance resulted in the plan crashing in Pennsylvania before it was able to reach its intended destination.

On May 2, 2011, Navy Seal Team Six descended by helicopter on Bin Laden's compound in Abbottabad, Pakistan, and killed him. His body was removed and buried at sea.

Historians will debate whether contemporary Islamic extremist terror would have developed to the same extent and pace without Osama bin Laden. ⬜

THE LOGIC OF TERRORISM

Terrorist groups have various goals. The general consensus is that the overwhelming number of groups fail to experience even a modest degree of success. A number of groups have been successful in achieving independence from a colonial power. A good example is the Kenyan anticolonial struggle against Great Britain. Other groups such as the Basque separatists (ETA) in Spain or Kurds in Turkey have been less successful in achieving regional autonomy from a central power. Basque agitation, however, likely has been partially responsible for granting Basque provinces significant regional autonomy. The social revolutionaries in early 20th-century Russia, although unsuccessful in overthrowing the Czarist regime, laid a foundation for the Russian Revolution led by the Bolsheviks in 1917. The 'Palestine Liberation Organization (PLO) engaged in a series of terrorist attacks between 1968 and 1972 which highlighted the Palestinian cause, established the PLO as the primary representative of the Palestinian people, and in recent years has led to limited self-rule on the West Bank and in Gaza, as well as to international endorsement by a number of nations and international organizations of a Palestinian state. Other groups may have limited policy goals like the release of what they consider to be political prisoners. Terrorist groups by demonstrating success hope to increase their recruitment and ability to raise money (Merari, 1993).

In the 1880s anarchist Johannes Most wrote a famous essay, *The Philosophy of the Bomb*, in which he sketched a blueprint for terrorist violence. Most's essay perceptively laid out the classic logic of terrorist violence which aspires to the overthrow of the established political order (Townshend, 2011).

Overthrow the established order. Terrorists have various goals, ranging from the creation of a separate state to the replacement of the existing government or the imposition of a religiously ordained order or policy reform.

Attention. The first strategic goal of any terrorist organization is to capture public attention to their cause and to communicate their grievances. This requires that as many people as possible witness or learn about a terrorist event. The media is the terrorists' best friend in ensuring an audience for their violence.

Psychological disorientation. A primary tactic to achieve terrorist goals is the creation of a climate of fear and intimidation through violence against individuals and the destruction of symbolically important property. The logic is that people will pressure the government to give the terrorists what they want rather than continue to live in fear and fright. There is a fine balance: Injuring and killing too many individuals may accelerate anger and desire for revenge and retribution against terrorists.

Social disruption and delegitimization. A related tactic is to disrupt the normal routine and way of life. Individuals will turn their anger towards the government for failing to protect them and will demand a change.

Social divisions. Terrorists hope to widen existing divisions in society by creating a climate that enhances social divisions and distrust between groups. The contemporary attacks by Islamic terrorists in Europe are designed in part to create a backlash towards Muslims and to drive the Muslim community into supporting the terrorist cause.

Overreaction. Terrorists hope to cause the government to react by curbing rights and liberties and cause dissatisfaction with the government for curtailing individual freedoms and for singling out innocent individuals for investigation and detention. These types of repressive policies may create sympathy for terrorists.

Propaganda. Terrorists want to dominate the media and to communicate the reasonableness of their cause and to highlight the corruption and ineptitude of the government to their intended audience. Terrorist violence reinforces the terrorists' objectives by, for example, targeting the troops of an occupying power. The ability to carry out terrorist violence projects power and, in turn, attracts the alienated and powerless youth.

Terrorists function in a social environment in which they are hoping to reinforce their message to their supporters and to appeal to individuals who potentially may be attracted to their cause.

The Morality of Terrorism

A perennial question is the moral justifiability of terrorism. Can the injury or death of individuals in pursuit of a social, political, or religious cause ever be moral? Most individuals labeled as terrorists, with the occasional exception, reject the notion that they are terrorists. In fact, they tend to accuse the individuals who affix this label to them as the true terrorists.

Individuals and groups offer a series of justifications for their actions (Jackson et al., 2011; Richardson, 2006).

Legal Alternatives. Efforts to achieve change through legal avenues such as elections, mass demonstrations, lobbying, and public pressure have proven unsuccessful and are clearly a waste of time and effort. These efforts have led to a repressive response in many instances. Even in democracies, the concentration of wealth and power makes meaningful change through legal avenues next to impossible. By foreclosing legal and nonviolent avenues for change, regimes force individuals to engage in violence as a last resort.

Violence. The government monopolizes force and cannot be confronted on equal terms. Terrorism or asymmetrical warfare is the only strategy available to the weak.

Effectiveness. The resort to violence brings attention and helps to attract other individuals to the cause.

Collective Guilt. There are no innocent individuals in the view of a terrorist. Even civilians bear moral responsibility. Osama bin Laden famously declared that the American people pay taxes that fund the armies that occupy Arab lands, which helps fund repressive Arab regimes. Acts that are labeled as Islamic terrorism are nothing more than acts of self-defense by Muslims against the violence inflicted against them by the United States.

Moral Equivalence. The claim is that the enemy regime engages in acts of violence and repression and that their condemnation of acts of terrorism is hypocritical. Terrorists believe that their cause is more righteous than that of the government and—unlike government forces—are willing to sacrifice themselves in the service of a moral cause. Osama bin Laden made constant references to America's dropping of the atomic bomb on Hiroshima and Nagasaki, which killed and maimed tens of thousands without differentiating between men, women, and children; he alleged that America was engaged in criminal attacks against civilians in Afghanistan and Iraqi. A subtle argument is that the violence imposed by governments often is not apparent because it is institutionalized violence. This is the violence that results from the inequality of education, opportunity, and income.

(continues on next page)

(continued from previous page)

Legitimacy. Resistance is legitimized by invoking religious justifications, historical mistreatment, and declarations by revered historical leaders.

In summary, terrorists view their violence as a means of accomplishing social or political change; they are no more violent than the government. Terrorists believe that they occupy the moral high ground and have been forced into violence in the service of an honorable and just cause. There are no other alternatives available to remove an authoritarian dictator or repressive regime and there are no "innocents" in this struggle (Honderich, 2002). Others respond that there is no justification for sacrificing the innocent lives of men, women, and children to advance a political cause. Even if violence is undertaken, it can be pursued in a fashion that respects the limits of the law of war and limits attacks to enemy combatants. Terrorism, in other words, is aggravated criminality (Meisels, 2014). What is your view?

A continuing debate revolves around the question whether terrorism has proven successful in the past. Proponents of terrorist violence point to Algeria, the establishment of Israel, and the end of apartheid in South Africa as examples of successful campaigns. On the other hand, these are dismissed as isolated examples whose success resulted from a broad combination of tactics (Richardson, 2006). ☐

CHAPTER SUMMARY

There are good reasons to study terrorism because of its impact on governmental policy and on the daily lives of individuals. Terrorism is part of our daily vocabulary, but there are various challenges in defining the term *terrorism*. There is no uniform definition of terrorism, although any definition should incorporate references to violence, actors, intent, targets, harm, and motive. Another approach to understanding the elements of terrorism is to distinguish terrorism from guerilla warfare—which, unlike terrorism, generally involves adherence to the laws of war and, for example, avoids intentional attacks on civilians. There are various typologies of terrorism; the most prevalent approach is to divide terrorist groups by the nature of their political or religious ideology. A heavily debated question is whether there is a "new terrorism."

The logic of terrorism involves the creation of social fear and intimidation in an effort to demonstrate the weakness of government and to provoke an overreaction which will erode support for the regime and persuade the population to accept the demands of terrorists. Terrorists generally view themselves as moral and acting in the cause of social justice. Others question the justification for attacking a civilian population.

CHAPTER REVIEW QUESTIONS

1. Discuss why terrorism matters or does not matter.
2. What are some the factors to be considered in defining terrorism?
3. List some various approaches to defining terrorism.
4. Distinguish between terrorism and guerilla warfare. Do you believe there is a meaningful difference?
5. What are some types of terrorism?
6. Discuss the logic of terrorism.
7. In your view, is terrorism ever morally justified?

TERMINOLOGY

al Qaeda
guerilla warfare
new terrorism

Osama bin Laden
terrorism

typologies of terrorism
war

Theories of Terrorism

INTRODUCTION

Ahmed Omar Saeed Sheikh (popularly known as Omar Sheikh) has been called an "unlikely terrorist." Born and raised in London in a comfortable home, his Pakistani businessman father was able to send Omar to the elite private Forest School where he was a member of the cricket team and an ardent chess player. His tutors considered him among the best and most polite students. Omar's performance on his English A-level exams (which determine entry into college) enabled him to gain entry to the prestigious London School of Economics to study applied mathematics, statistical theory, economics, and social psychology (Richardson, 2006).

Omar apparently had some sense of concern for others. As a young man he rescued a man who fell onto the subway tracks, at the risk of his own life. At age 18, he received a commendation from the London Underground for his rescue of the passenger. In an excerpt from a diary he kept while in India, he reveals that he responded compassionately to homeless people on the streets and once shared his one-room apartment with an old, one-legged beggar.

As a student in London, Sheikh was deeply affected by the atrocities suffered by Bosnian Muslims during the Bosnian War of the 1990s, fought between Bosnian Muslims and Bosnian Serbs. He came to believe that Muslims were being discriminated against and mistreated in various parts of the world and left to attend an al Qaeda training camp in Afghanistan. Sheikh subsequently was involved in a kidnapping plot to free imprisoned Muslim prisoners in India and was imprisoned himself. In prison his fellow prisoners, along with prison administrators, praised his compassion and concern for others. Sheikh was released from prison in 1999 and moved to Pakistan where he married and had a child.

In July 2003 Sheikh was convicted of the kidnapping and beheading of American journalist Daniel Pearl in Pakistan. After his conviction, Sheikh boasted about his involvement in the bombing of the Kashmir Parliament in October 2001, attacks on the Indian Parliament, and the attack on the American Cultural Center in Calcutta, India.

How to explain the involvement of Omar Sheikh in terrorism? Louise Richardson writes that the difficulty with explaining terrorism is based on the fact that terrorists are a diverse group, and that most people exposed to the same influences do not commit acts of terrorism. There are at least two broad theoretical approaches to explaining terrorism outlined in this chapter. The first focuses on individual psychology and the second on the social, economic, and political environment of an individual. Keep in that that there likely is no single approach that provides an adequate explanation.

PSYCHOLOGICAL THEORIES

In the early years of psychological analysis of terrorists, there was a strong sentiment that these individuals were abnormal and mentally challenged. In an early study of skyjackers, David Hubbard described skyjackers as seriously disturbed and characterized by a dysfunctional personality (Hubbard, 1971). Psychiatric examinations of terrorists have largely discredited this view, and therapists today view terrorists as having the same distribution of psychological traits as the general population. The consensus view is that it is unwise to assume that a particular psychological profile will cause an individual to engage in terrorism (Horgan, 2014).

Dismissing the notion that terrorists are psychologically unbalanced, Jerold Post notes that terrorist organizations are selective in the individuals they recruit and do not want individuals in their organization who will not follow orders and remain loyal (Post, 2007).

There are certain ways of looking at the world or perspectives that studies identify as characteristic of most terrorists. Louise Richardson writes that terrorists divide the world into "good" and "evil." They blame the enemy for all that is "bad" in the world. A second trait is an identification with the suffering of others. In justifying their behavior, terrorists invoke the injustice of harm being inflicted on the impoverished or on individuals driven from their homeland. Terrorists see themselves as acting in defense of others. While a student at the London School of Economics, Sheikh as noted above wrote that he was affected by films of Bosnian Muslims being murdered by Serbs and became involved in raising money for Muslim victims. He also took the step of contacting al Qaeda militants in Afghanistan. Osama bin Laden viewed the 9/11 attacks as revenge for the violence inflicted by the United States on Muslims and as an act of defense of Muslims throughout the world. The call to violence is reinforced when individuals witness what they view as an injustice on a daily basis, such as British troops patrolling Catholic areas of Northern Ireland or Jewish settlements on the West Bank, in what Palestinians consider their land. A crucial factor in the terrorist worldview is the "culture surround"—whether there is a social environment and a tradition of resistance to the enemy that reinforces the terrorist worldview (Richardson, 2006).

The predominant approach today is focus on the psychological processes involved in producing terrorists. In other words, terrorists are "made" rather than born. In his book on the psychology of terrorism, John Horgan argues that rather than looking for the social, political, and economic causes of terrorism, attention should be devoted to the psychological pathways to terrorism (Horgan, 2014). The psychological process of becoming a terrorist is termed *radicalization*.

RADICALIZATION

Radicalization is defined by Webber and Kruglanski (2017) as "the process whereby an individual adopts radical means as the method of choice for goal attainment." A *radical means* is a method that is out of the ordinary. Individuals who are unhappy with a foreign military base on their territory could adopt a nonviolent approach to the problem by working through conventional political channels, or they could adopt a radical approach by forming a terrorist organization and bombing the military base (Webber & Kruglanski, 2017). In plain English, radicalization is the process through which an individual evolves to the point that they are willing to support or join a terrorist organization and, in some cases, take the next step and engage in terrorism.

Radicalization is related to another concept, **alienation** (or anomie). This is described as a psychological condition in which an individual abandons the beliefs and values that are held by most people in society. A terrorist's willingness to commit violence against innocent individuals violates the basic respect for human life and for other individuals that is shared by most individuals in society. This theory is applied most frequently to explain lone-wolf terrorism (see below).

In sum, when we look at a terrorist we are looking at an individual who is the product of the process of radicalization.

THE PROCESS OF RADICALIZATION

Marc Sageman is a leading terrorism analyst and medical doctor who conceptualizes the process of radicalization as involving several steps, which he illustrates through individuals' embrace of Islamic terrorism. Sageman argues that the most important explanation for Islamic radicalization is an individual's network of friends and family, and that the process of radicalization is a group phenomenon. Once involved in this network, individuals gradually develop a political awareness which culminates in involvement in terrorist activity (Sageman, 2004).

Social affiliation. The first step is social affiliation with the jihad (struggle) through friendship, kinship, and discipleship.

Progressive intensification. An increasing commitment to belief and faith and moral outrage over the perceived unjust treatment of Muslims, leading to an embrace of the jihad ideology.

Recruitment. A formal connection to jihad or the terrorist struggle.

In this process, a group forms based on friendship, family relations, or membership in a mosque, church, or social organization (social affiliation). Over a period that can last as long as several years, individuals' ideology or religious belief system becomes stronger, and members of the group reinforce one another's religious or ideological commitment (progressive intensification). The group is increasingly isolated from outside influences, and when the opportunity arises, it makes the transition to terrorism and connects to a terrorist organization (recruitment). The group context is crucial to Sageman's analysis.

In Sageman's view, the global jihadist movement is a product of the self-organization of small clusters of individuals united by strong bonds of friendship, family, and worship. This process typically involves Muslim students who have left their homelands to study in the West, or the male children of immigrant parents in Europe or the United States who find themselves unemployed, poorly educated, and with a criminal history. Sageman's approach also applies to online radicalization, in which individuals are embraced by recruiters on the Internet who make them feel like they are part of a religious or political community.

The radicalized young men view themselves as warriors who are willing to sacrifice themselves to protect Islam against the evil of the West. This mission provides a sense of meaning to their lives and a sense of community with their fellow terrorists.

Sageman illustrates this process of "group" radicalization through the radicalization of the Hamburg, Germany, cell that carried out the 9/11 attack on the United States. Mohamed Atta arrived in Hamburg from Egypt in 1996 and met Mounir Motassadeq and Abdelgham Mzoudi, who had arrived 3 years earlier and were enrolled at the technical university there. The three eventually moved in together and attended a study group at the local mosque taught by Mohammad Belfas in which they learned about Salafism, an extremely conservative form of Islam. Three other foreign Muslim students soon joined the study group and became regular visitors to the apartment: Ramzi bin al-Shibh (originally from Yemen), Ziad Amir Jarrah (originally from Lebanon), and Said Bahaji. Bahaji, a German Moroccan whose father owned a discotheque and whose mother was a Prussian Protestant who quickly adopted the Salafi ideology—going so far as to lecture his Christian aunt on the proper behavior for a woman. The group eventually added two additional members, Marwan al-Shihi from the United Arab Emirates and Zakarya Essabar from Morocco.

In 1998 Atta, bin al-Shibh, and Bahaji moved into an apartment together, which they called "House of the Supporters of the Prophet"—the name of a guest house in Peshawar, Pakistan, for al Qaeda recruits. The group spent time watching battlefield videos, singing songs about martyrdom, praying, and discussing the need to protect Islam against the abuse of Western powers. They entertained Belfas and veterans of the Afghan struggle against the Soviets who recruited them to join al Qaeda in Afghanistan. Once they arrived in Afghanistan, they were recruited to carry out the 9/11 attacks, which had been in the planning stages for many years. They spoke English, possessed technical skills, and had no criminal records. Motassadeq and Mzoudi were the only two members of the group who were not directly involved in the 9/11 terrorist attacks, remaining in Hamburg where they were subsequently prosecuted and imprisoned.

Ehud Springzak views terrorism as a process of delegitimization in which individuals—as part of a group—move from conventional politics to violence. His complex theory can be boiled down to a three-stage process. First, in the "crisis of confidence" stage, individuals strongly reject a political policy or political decision maker or decision makers. In the "conflict of legitimacy" stage, individuals become disillusioned with the entire political process and political system and develop an alternative vision. In the "crisis of legitimacy" phase, the entire society is viewed as corrupt and individuals within the society are dehumanized. In this last phase, individuals are transformed into "brutal and indiscriminate killers" and are in a state of "transformational delegitimization" (Springzak, 2012).

An alternative approach to radicalization views personal experience as the key to entry into the world of terrorism—rather than group influence. Webber and Kruglanski describe this process as the "3N" approach: needs, narratives, and networks. The first step is a "trigger" that changes the way an individual perceives the world. Terrorists refer to an ethical or moral awakening that drives them to join the struggle (needs). A 2015 study in Pakistan found that 90% of militants in the Swat Valley claimed to have been drawn to terrorism by U.S. drone strikes that injured or killed individuals whom they viewed as innocent. Relatively few of the individuals who were interviewed personally experienced drone strikes, although they identified with the victims. They explained their involvement in terrorism as a way to defend their community. Other researchers find that terrorists often progress from nonviolent and peaceful involvement in issues like the eradication of poverty, and that their lack of success leads them to terrorism (Horgan, 2014).

This new perception of the world provides a sense of identity and connects individuals to a larger ethnic, national, or religious community with a history of resistance. They look to earlier terrorists as heroes and as role models (narrative).

Individuals now gradually descend a "staircase" of terrorism. They embrace the terrorist ideology, enter a training camp, and play a supportive role in the organization—and the process terminates in an act of terrorism (network).

A similar framework is proposed by Johnny Ryan who describes a four-step process of radicalization: persecution, precedent, piety, and perseverance. Individuals feel that they are treated unjustly (persecution) and in response, they find support for the use of violence within a group's history of resistance (precedent). Terrorist activity is viewed as a religious or moral mission to correct an injustice (piety), and this struggle is embraced as a lifetime commitment (perseverance) (Ryan, 2007).

Theories of radicalization that focus on individuals (rather than on the influence of groups) are more useful for explaining the radicalization of individuals who are not part of a network.

A number of studies find that imprisonment is a source of radicalization. The radicalization of inmates frequently results from the proselytizing of fundamentalist religious clerics, attracting individuals who lack detailed knowledge about religious doctrine and are easily seduced by a radical message. Other individuals find a sense of belonging or personal safety in a religious community in prison. In the United States, prison radicalization tends to most frequently involve White supremacists, racial nationalism, and Islamic fundamentalism; radicalization in Europe tends to be focused on Islam. Keep in mind that there are researchers who find very little evidence of prison radicalization (White, 2017).

In his study of prison radicalization, Mark S. Hamm recognizes that only a small percentage of inmates emerge from prison as terrorists, and that there is no clear causal link between exposure to fundamentalist religion and prison radicalization. He also notes that prisons do not manufacture radicals—although he documents a modest but growing link between prison radicalization and terrorism. A crucial step is recruitment by a charismatic figure while in prison and the existence of a social group in prison that replicates the structure of a gang. After being released, individuals gravitate to an environment—such as a mosque or a trip abroad—that exposes them to individuals who reinforce radical ideas and promote terrorist violence. In cases of the radicalization of detainees at the Guantánamo prison camp, the process involved a regeneration of an individual's religious beliefs—rather than a religious conversion. Hamm concludes with the observation that whether an inmate will be attracted to terrorism is dependent on whether an individual is ready to embrace terrorism. A good example is Abu Bakr al-Baghdadi, the leader of the Islamic State in Syria (ISIS), who emerged from imprisonment by American forces following the war in Iraq to direct a group which at one time was the most formidable terrorist group in the Middle East and in Europe (Hamm, 2013).

Several psychological processes are important to understanding how terrorists cope emotionally with engaging in acts of terrorism. A crucial factor is for an individual to dehumanize the victims and to view them as objects rather than as human beings. A second psychological process is to view the victims as deserving of their fate. A third process is for terrorists to deny responsibility for their actions and to view themselves as acting in accordance with divine demands, or to view themselves as part of a struggle of good versus evil in which they are merely following the orders of their leader (Horgan, 2014).

These theories of radicalization do not fully explain why some individuals are radicalized and resort to violence in spite of the fact that the vast majority of individuals exposed to similar influences do not make this transition.

There are several additional anger-based theories of terrorism that, although relatively straightforward, are viewed as inadequate to explain the range of factors that lead individuals to resort to terrorism as opposed to other forms of criminal or antisocial behavior.

The *physiological* approach argues that terrorists have unique chemical characteristics that, when stimulated, cause an individual to engage in acts of terrorism. There are also three psychological theories. The *frustration-aggression* theory states that when individuals are unable to achieve their ambitions and goals, they blame society and engage in violence and terrorism. The *negative-identity approach* argues that terrorism results from an inability to meet societal standards, which leads individuals to engage in self-destructive terrorist violence. The *narcissistic-rage* approach views terrorists as self-centered individuals with a high and often unrealistic sense of self-worth. They are incapable of self-examination or taking responsibility for their actions. They tend to blame and to lash out at other individuals when they encounter adversity, and they lack the capacity for genuine concern for other individuals. These individuals are driven to lash out in violence by what they view as a lack of appreciation of their value and worth. There also are theorists who adopt a *sexual-social* approach and attribute terrorism to sexual frustration (Hudson, 1999).

Siblings and Terrorism

There is a striking prevalence of siblings being involved in terrorism. In March 2017 Khalid and Ibrahim al-Bakraoui acted as suicide bombers in an attack on an airport in Brussels, Belgium. The brothers appear to have been connected to a cell that committed an earlier attack in Paris that killed 130 people and involved brothers Saleh and Ibrahim Abdesalam. Three sets of Saudi brothers were among the 19 hijackers in the 9/11 attacks. Siblings are ideal recruits. They tend to radicalize and reinforce one another's views and willingness to conduct the attack. Family members who live together are able to communicate with one another without the risk of detection or infiltration. They also are protective of their siblings and are unlikely to implicate a sibling or family member if apprehended and interrogated. Other terrorist brothers include Cherif and Said Kouachi, who killed 12 people in an attack on the Paris office of the French satirical magazine *Charlie Hebdo*, and Dzhokhar and Tamerlan Tsarnaev, who carried out the Boston Marathon bombing. In 2004 Amanta Nagayeva detonated a bomb while on a flight from Moscow. A week later, her sister Roza ignited a bomb outside a Moscow subway station, killing 10 individuals. An estimated 30% of terrorists have family members who are also terrorists. Another example is the husband and wife who committed the San Bernardino attacks that killed 14 people. []

LONE-WOLF TERRORISTS

There are a surprising number of **lone-wolf terrorists**, individuals acting by themselves who are not formally affiliated with a terrorist organization who commit acts of terrorism. An example is the killing of 49 individuals at the Pulse nightclub by Omar Mateen in Orlando, Florida. This was the most lethal attack by a single shooter and the most lethal crime ever carried out against LGBT individuals in American history. In a call to 911 during the shooting, Mateen identified himself as an "Islamic soldier" and as a "Soldier of God" and pledged allegiance to the

Islamic State of Iraq and al-Sham (ISIS). Mateen proclaimed that the shooting was provoked by a U.S. airstrike that had occurred 6 weeks earlier, killing Abu Wahib, an Islamic State commander. Mateen had not flown under the radar of surveillance; he had been investigated in 2013 and 2014 by the FBI as a result of reports from his coworkers that he had expressed strong sympathy for jihadist groups.

One study of lone-wolf terrorism in 15 countries found that between 1968 and 2010, lone-wolf attacks accounted for almost 2% of all terrorist attacks in these countries. The statistics indicate that this type of attack increased in frequency in the last few years of the study (Simon 2016,).

In recent years, ISIS has urged sympathizers in Europe and in the United States to take violent action in their homeland. Lone-wolf terrorism in the United States is committed by individuals who adhere to virtually every religious and political belief. Anders Breivik, a white nationalist, ignited a car bomb near government buildings in Oslo, Norway, and then went to a summer camp on the nearby island of Utoya, where he killed 77 young people.

It is for good reason that in 2013 President Barack Obama, in a statement echoed by various foreign leaders, announced that his biggest concern was lone-wolf terrorism. Lone-wolf terrorists are thought to pose a greater threat than terrorists affiliated with an organization because they are not constrained by a desire to attract popular support and act in unpredictable and extremely violent ways; and because of their isolation, they often are nearly impossible to detect prior to their attack. The Internet has given lone wolves instructions on how to construct bombs and WMDs and has provided a community of like-minded and supportive activists. Consider the fear spread by lone-wolf terrorist Bruce Ivins who is alleged to have been responsible for mailing letters containing anthrax in the United States. In two waves of attacks, 5 people died, 17 others were infected, and 10,000 more people who were thought to have been exposed to anthrax spores were given treatment.

Jeffrey D. Simon lists five types of lone-wolf terrorists (Simon, 2016).

Secular. These lone wolves act on behalf of a political or ethnonationalist cause. An example is Timothy McVeigh, who bombed the Alfred P. Murrah Federal Building in Oklahoma City in 1995, resulting in the death of 168 individuals. McVeigh, a right-wing gun rights activist, was retaliating for what he believed was the murder of eight members of the Branch Davidian cult by the federal government during a siege on the group's compound.

Religious. Religious lone wolves act based on a religious motivation which may lead them to attack individuals and institutions viewed as contrary to the tenets of their religion. In 2009 James von Brunn killed a security guard at the U.S. Holocaust Museum before being killed himself. He identified with the racist Christian

Identity movement and believed that the Jews were intent on destroying all the gentile nations in the world.

Single issue. These individuals are motivated by a specific issue. In 1996 Eric Rudolph ignited a bomb during a concert at the Atlanta Olympics in protest of abortion. He subsequently carried out the bombing of abortion clinics in Atlanta and in Birmingham, Alabama, and at a gay nightclub before being apprehended after a lengthy manhunt.

Financial gain. These individuals commit acts of terrorism based on a desire for money. In 1995 John Gilbert Graham placed several sticks of dynamite and a timer in his mother's airline luggage. The explosion killed 43 people, along with Graham's mother. His plan was to collect on an insurance policy on his mother's life that he had purchased before she boarded the plane.

Idiosyncratic. Terrorists who act in the name of principle whose criminal acts are in fact based on a mental challenge or psychiatric disorder. Ted Kaczynski, the "Unabomber," was responsible for sending 16 package bombs, resulting in the deaths of three people and the injury of 23; most of victims were academic scientists. Kaczynski lived an isolated existence and was motivated by his opposition to science and technology. He was diagnosed as a paranoid schizophrenic.

Simon writes that most lone wolves exhibited long-term adjustment problems and prior to their attacks demonstrated extreme changes in their behavior.

As noted above, there is no template for American lone wolves although Mark S. Hamm and Ramón Spaaij find that most are single, unemployed White males who have a criminal record. They tend to be older, less educated than other terrorists, and suffer from some mental challenge or psychiatric disorder. Lone wolves are alienated from society and do not tend to be formal members of a terrorist group or to identify with a specific group. They have a sense of resentment over being deprived of socioeconomic rewards and direct their resentment at the government, women, immigrants, and minorities (Hamm & Spaaij, 2017).

Hamm and Spaaij developed a theory of lone-wolf terrorism based on a comprehensive database and interviews with imprisoned lone wolves. They theorize that lone wolves progress through various stages and do not impulsively embrace terrorism. They begin with a sense of personal or political grievance, become engaged with online sympathizers (or in some instances with an extremist group), are influenced by an enabler who has a strong personality, begin to broadcast their intent, and a triggering event leads them to commit an act of terrorist violence. An important aspect is that lone wolves often are mobilized by the terrorist acts of other lone wolves and engage in "copycat" attacks. Most, if given the opportunity, "go out in a blaze of glory."

Consider Boston Marathon bomber Dzhokhar Tsarnaev whose aspirations to attend a top-tier university were hampered by financial obstacles; as a result, he lost interest in his university studies and became absorbed in the drug culture. His older brother Tamerlan, who likely had connections to Chechen terrorists, exposed him to fundamentalist ideology. Tamerlan kept his political views to himself but shared with his college roommates that he felt there were ideas in the Koran worth sacrificing your life to uphold. Six days before the Boston bombing he posted a video on social media tagged with the line "Syria is calling. Will answer."

Keep in mind that analysts divide lone-wolf attacks into three types based on the extent of the lone wolf's identity with and connection to a terrorist group:

terrorist-coordinated lone-wolf attack: A terrorist group provides support for lone-wolf terrorism.

terrorist-directed lone-wolf attack: A terrorist group supervises a lone-wolf terrorist.

terrorist-inspired lone-wolf attack: A terrorist group encourages a lone-wolf terrorist.

Sociological and criminological theories of terrorism, which are discussed in the next sections of the chapter, focus on the role of economic, social, and political factors to explain terrorism.

Personalities and Events

Fjotolf Hansen, born Anders Behring Breivik in February 1979, is a Norwegian terrorist who killed eight people by detonating a fertilizer bomb in a van in Oslo outside the prime minister's residence, and then shot and killed 69 young participants—including a victim as young as 14—in a Workers' Youth League summer camp on the island of Utoya. A total of 319 people were injured in these attacks. A year later he was convicted of mass murder, causing a fatal explosion, and terrorism and was sentenced to 21 years in prison.

Breivik, prior to the attacks, distributed several texts entitled *2083: A European Declaration of Independence* outlining his right-wing ideology including his denunciation of Islam and feminism. After his arrest Breivik proclaimed this purpose was to prevent a Muslim takeover of Norway and of Europe and to punish the Labour Party for "letting down" Norway and the Norwegian people for allowing Muslim immigration.

(continues on next page)

(continued from previous page)

Breivik was found to be sane and guilty, and he was sentenced to 21 years in prison. He is required to serve 10 years in detention with the possibility of one or more extensions for as long as he is considered a danger to society. Breivik continued to insist that he does not accept the legitimacy of the court and stated that for that reason he would not appeal his sentence.

As a young man, Breivik was attracted to extreme conservative philosophies and as he was exposed to fascist and Nazi ideology moved to the extreme fringes of society. These different sources of hate influenced his manifesto, an often confused mixture of ideas he cut and pasted from the Internet intermingled with some of his own thoughts. Breivik's essential belief is that Europe is being invaded by Muslims, and governments are doing nothing to stop this catastrophe. He warned that a failure to act against Muslims will result in Europe being absorbed into the Islamic caliphate (Selerstad, 2016). Breivik is emblematic of a right-wing philosophy which views multiculturalism and immigration as leading to the dominance by Muslims and other minorities and to "cultural genocide" and to the creation of what he termed "Euroarabia."

Breivik, despite his inability to successfully pursue a career or find his place in society, viewed himself as the savior of Europe and as an individual destined for greatness. His personality when combined with an anti-Islamic ideology created a dangerous and lethal combination.

Breivik began buying weapons and ammunition and rented a farm so that he could accumulate hundreds of kilograms of fertilizer and other ingredients for a bomb. Isolated on the farm in the dense forests near the Swedish border he planned his attack on so-called political traitors and their children. Breivik aspired to spark a religious war in Europe that would end with the Christians finally defeating the Muslims. At that point, he anticipated all Muslims would be able to choose from deportation, converting to Christianity and changing their names, or death. Mosques would be demolished or used for other purposes, all Muslim artwork would be destroyed, and the use of Arabic, Farsi, Urdu, and Somali would be banned (Selerstad, 2016).

What does Breivik tell us about the process of radicalization?

STRUCTURAL THEORY

Sociological **structural theory** views terrorism as the product of the political, economic, and social structure of society. Terrorism is the response of a racial, ethnic, economic, or racial group's sense of deprivation. The resort to terrorism is an intentional decision taken to remedy the situation and violence typically is viewed as the only realistic avenue for change. Consider the case of apartheid in South Africa between 1948 and 1991. South Africa was ruled by a White government dominated by Dutch Afrikaners who governed a predominantly African and minority population. The government introduced a policy of apartheid or "separate development." Black South Africans were deprived of the right to vote and of virtually all civil rights and liberties. They were assigned to live in one of four separate, segregated "homeland" areas, obligated to carry pass books containing their personal information, and required to have a pass allowing them to travel and to work in White areas. Africans were subjected to mass arrests, preventive detention, and imprisonment; demonstrations were greeted with lethal violence. The African National Congress (ANC) headed by imprisoned leader Nelson Mandela resisted apartheid through demonstrations and labor strikes, and they also resorted to sabotage and bombings. In 1993 the ANC retaliated against an attack by the South African police by igniting a bomb at the central office of the South African air force, which killed 19 and wounded 200. The efforts of the ANC eventually led to a power-sharing agreement, and Mandela was elected to the presidency (Miller, 2013).

Martha Crenshaw (2012) notes that among the direct causes of terrorism are concrete grievances among an identifiable subgroup of the population. This subgroup may be a national group in a region of a country, such as the French in Quebec, Canada, or the Tamils in Sri Lanka, or they may be an economically disadvantaged group like Catholics in Northern Ireland. A second factor, according to Crenshaw, is a lack of opportunity for political participation. A third factor is a precipitating event which symbolizes the plight of the downtrodden and highlights the lack of availability of alternative methods for achieving social change. In South Africa the shooting and killing of 69 African workers on strike in the Sharpeville massacre of 1960 mobilized opposition to the government and demonstrated that the apartheid regime would resist granting civil rights to Africans. Sixteen years later the resistance against apartheid accelerated, following the killing of 575 young Africans during an uprising in the Soweto township. On January 30, 1972, British paratroopers fired on Catholic demonstrators in Londonderry, Northern Ireland, killing 13 individuals. The incident inspired the vast majority of Catholics to support the Irish Republican Army (IRA) in its campaign to establish an independent Northern Irish state.

There are two concepts to consider in applying structural theory. We commonly think about violence being sparked by discrimination, lack of socioeconomic opportunities, and poverty. In his classic volume *Why Men Rebel*, Ted Gurr (1970) developed the notion of **relative deprivation**, which is the gap between expectations and aspirations and the reality of the situation. This gap between the *is* and the *ought* creates frustration that provides a desire for violence. Relative deprivation explains why we find highly educated individuals—who are frustrated by their lack of opportunity—being involved in terrorist violence. Gurr notes that the Mau Mau revolt against the British in Kenya in the 1950s was an organized response to the frustrations of Westernized and educated young Kenyans who experienced a sudden lack of opportunity after a generation of improvement. On the other hand, **absolute deprivation**, occurs when reality coincides with expectations and leads to an acceptance of an individuals' life situation, discouraging a violent response (Gurr, 1970).

Structural theory assumes that terrorism is an intentional choice by individuals in response to their situation. It draws on **rational choice theory** by viewing terrorism as a reasoned and deliberate goal-oriented decision to pursue a goal through the use of violence. This violence is a reasoned response to their situation.

Criminological theories are used to explain individual criminal behavior. In recent years, these theories have been relied on to explain why individuals engage in terrorism.

CRIMINOLOGICAL THEORIES

There are at least four sociological theories that are used by criminologists to explain deviant behavior that have also been used to explain terrorism. These theories explain terrorism based on individuals' social environment rather than on individuals' personal characteristics (Grabosky & Stohl, 2010). Martha Crenshaw famously noted that an individual's interaction with other individuals in a group may prove much more important than an individual's psychology (Crenshaw, 2012).

Differential Association

Edwin Sutherland is credited with developing **differential association** theory in the late 1930s. Rather than explaining criminal behavior based on an individual's personal characteristics, he focused on the impact that other people have in shaping human behavior. In other words, differential association views our behavior as a product of the social context in which we live.

Differential association theory explains deviant behavior by the commonsense notion that we learn behavior, values, attitudes, and points of view from the individuals with whom we associate. We are shaped by and learn from the primary group with which we interact. Primary groups range from parents to friends to gangs. Individuals often are exposed to more than one group. Differential association theorizes that a group's impact on behavior is dependent on the intensity, frequency, and duration of an individual's relationship with the group. Deviant behavior results when messages that promote a violation of the law outweigh the messages that that are received that promote obedience to the law. Several researchers rely on **social learning theory**, an approach which is similar to differential association theory (Sutherland, 1939).

Individuals who are relatively isolated from larger society are most susceptible to being influenced by the group with which they associate. Terrorist groups tend be composed of relatively young individuals with limited life experience and access to outside influences. In 1999, Buford Furrow emerged from an isolated Aryan Nations encampment in Idaho where he was taught that a race war was imminent and that he could ignite a race war by committing a violent atrocity. He attempted to provoke a race war by driving to a Los Angeles Jewish Community Center and firing 70 rounds from an Uzi, wounding five individuals—including three children.

Social learning theory extended differential association theory by stressing the process through which attitudes and behavior are communicated to individuals. This includes an individual's entire network of friends, family, and influences. *Imitation* is the process of copying the behavior of other individuals, *definitions* label certain behaviors as good or bad, and *differential reinforcement* involves rewarding or punishing certain behavior (Atkins & Winfree, 2017).

Terrorist analysts stress the role of al Qaeda training camps in transmitting a sense of solidarity and in teaching skills in bomb making and in weapons training. Taylor Armstrong and Jonathan Matusitz relied on social learning theory to explain how the Lebanese Shi'a group Hezbollah transmitted a radical Islamic ideology, skills and techniques of violence to new members recruited into the organization (Armstrong & Matusitz, 2013). Other researchers partially attribute the willingness of individuals to become suicide bombers to the strong community encouragement and support for this type of terrorism—which in some countries was as high as nearly 70% of the population (Pape, 2005).

Critics assert that differential association theory fails to account for individual autonomy and the capacity of individual to make up their own mind about how to behave. Consider the young person who rebels against his or her religious background and engages in immoral or criminal behavior. Differential association theory does not fully explain lone-wolf terrorists, although online jihadist communities may be considered the modern equivalent of a social group. The focus on combating online messages promoting jihadism is based on the notion that messages promoting obeying the law from influential figures can outweigh and defeat messages promoting jihad.

General Strain Theory of Terrorism

General strain theory (GST) is a criminological theory that has primarily been used to explain interpersonal violence, property crimes, and drug use. In an important and much-cited article, Robert Agnew applied general strain theory to explain terrorism in what he termed **general strain theory of terrorism (GSTT)** (Agnew, 2010). Criminogenic strains are conditions that create pressure or incentive for an individual to respond with criminal behavior. These include factors such as rejection or abuse by a parent, negative school experiences, or chronic unemployment which leads to anger, frustration, and depression. Anger creates pressure for revenge and reduces concern about the consequences and legal ramifications of individual action.

Agnew notes that terrorism involves more extreme violence than ordinary crime although he views GSTT as explaining why some individuals and certain groups engage in terrorism. GSTT is the most frequently cited criminological theory relied on to explain terrorism and is based on a number of propositions.

Collective strains. Terrorism results from collective strains experienced by members of a group—typically a racial, ethnic, religious, economic, political, or some other identifiable group. Although an individual may not personally experience the strain, it is perceived as being experienced by a group with whom the individual identifies.

Magnitude. Strains are high in magnitude—that is, they are long lasting and widespread, causing physical or mental harm such as systematic violent attacks, sexual assault, starvation, confiscation of property, or dispossession of land.

Unjust. Collective strains promote terrorism when the cause of the strain is viewed as unfair and imposed in an undemocratic fashion.

Social distance. Strains are most likely to lead to terrorism when the individuals responsible for the strain are of a different race, ethnicity, nationality, or class and are viewed as more powerful. Civilians often are targeted by terrorists because they are viewed as supportive of the policies causing the strain or are viewed as benefiting from the situation.

Anger. Conditions of strain are likely to lead to anger. Anger is a powerful emotion that promotes a desire for violent revenge. Individuals experiencing high-magnitude strains come to believe that they have little to lose by engaging in terrorism. Terrorism also is promoted by a sense that the violence is justified by the violence inflicted on the terrorists' community.

Alternatives. Terrorism is most likely to be caused when there are limited alternatives because of a lack of education, resources, or democratic opportunities.

Group identification. The experience of a strain strengthens group identification among individuals who are undergoing a common experience. Members of the group share the opinion that terrorism is a justified response. Terrorism is encouraged by membership in a group with a history and tradition of violent resistance.

In other words, poverty and unemployment are most likely to lead to violence when viewed as unjust and are severe, prolonged, believed to be caused by a distant, powerful group, and perceived as being supported by a civilian population. A sense of anger fuels a desire for revenge among members of a group experiencing a common sense of unjust deprivation of their rights who lack alternatives to terrorism.

Daphna Canetti-Nisim and her coauthors find that strain theory also explains support for harsh governmental policies toward racial and ethnic groups perceived as being affiliated with terrorist movements. Canetti-Nisim and her colleagues find that one of the consequences of being exposed to the threat of terrorism is an increased identification with an individual's own group and the development of hostile attitudes and intolerance toward groups perceived as posing a threat. This, in turn, translates into support for repressive governmental policies (Canetti-Nisim, Halperin, Sharvit, & Hobfoll, 2009).

GSTT is a complex theory which is difficult to test in the "real world." The theory also does not specify which strains or collective strains are most likely to lead to terrorism, and it fails to account for the traits that will lead some individuals to engage in violence when others in a similar position do not engage in violence. There also is a question why privileged individuals who do not suffer a strain themselves engage in violence.

Social Disorganization Theory

Social disorganization theory. Criminal conduct is a product of a social environment. These areas tend to be transient, impoverished areas lacking a police presence. Gary LaFree and Bianca Bersani find that a significant number of terrorist attacks in the United States occur in densely populated urban areas with a large population turnover and language diversity. In Europe urban areas that suffer from high unemployment and inadequate services and schools tend to be the center of terrorist activity (LaFree & Bersani, 2014).

Social Activities Theory

Lawrence Cohen and Marcus Felson (1979) pioneered the **social activities theory** of criminal behavior and criminal victimization. There are three primary elements of social activities theory which may at any given time coincide to facilitate terrorism.

Suitable target. A vulnerable and relatively defenseless target.

Offender. A motivated and determined offender.

Security. A lack of a capable and effective guardian force.

Social activities theory explains why buses and subway trains are frequently singled out for terrorist attacks; these are vulnerable targets that cannot be easily defended. The nature of targets differs depending on the ideology of the attacker; an international terrorist may focus on an airport whereas a White supremacist may target an African American church.

Situational Approach

The **situational approach** to explaining terrorism focuses on the conditions that are required to exist for terrorists to carry out a successful attack. The assumption is that terrorists want to act as efficiently and effectively as possible. As summarized below, terrorists require attractive targets, appropriate weapons, and the proper tools to plan and to carry out an attack.

In *Outsmarting the Terrorists* Ron Clark and Graeme Newman (2006) describe the targets that attract terrorists with the acronym *EVIL DONE*. These factors are not present in every instance; although they are taken into consideration by terrorists when deciding whether to attack.

Exposed. Isolated and vulnerable victims.

Vital. Electricity grids, transportation systems, and communications that are important to the functioning of society.

Iconic. Targets with high symbolic value, such as the World Trade Center.

Legitimate. Targets viewed as consistent with the terrorist message, such as attacks on Shia Muslims or Coptic Christians by Sunni Muslim terrorists in parts of the Middle East.

Destructible. A target that with the right weapon can be severely damaged or destroyed.

Occupied. A target which will result in the loss of human life.

Near. A target that is easily reached from the terrorists' base of operation.

Easy. A target that is not well defended.

The most important factor is proximity to the target, because the logistics of organizing the attack are relatively uncomplicated and terrorists will be familiar with the area of the target.

The next step is the selection of the type of weapon required to accomplish the terrorists' goal. An assassination, for example, requires a precise and easily hidden weapon. Clark and Newman (2006) write that terrorists' choice of weaponry will be determined by the acronym *MURDEROUS*.

Multipurpose. A single rifle or explosive may be all that is required depending on the target.

Undetectable. Weapons that are not easily detected and may be smuggled into a building in order to facilitate attacks.

Removable. Weapons must be easily transported.

Destructive. In most instances the greater the lethality of the weapon, the better.

Enjoyable. Terrorists favor weapons with which they are familiar.

Reliable. Terrorists favor weapons that are easily employed.

Obtainable. Weapons are used that are easily obtained.

Uncomplicated. A weapon must be easily used without complications.

Safe. Weapons should be relatively easy and safe to use and easily produced without complications.

Terrorists also will require tools—including means of communication, transportation, cash or credit cards, identification, maps, surveillance cameras, and Internet access. The final consideration is whether there are factors that will facilitate the attack. These include whether the terrorists' culture endorses acts of heroic violence, and the depth of the terrorists' motivation to attack.

In situations in which terrorists are frustrated by counterterrorist measures, they will shift their attack to other targets. For example, following the increase in security of airplanes and embassies, terrorists shifted the focus of their attacks to concerts and streets crowded with individual shoppers. A significant number of terrorist groups disintegrate because they lack the capacity to respond to counterterrorist measures.

Marxism

Radical Marxist criminological theory is an influential theoretical perspective which draws on the classical economic theory that Karl Marx developed during the 1870s. Marx believed that wealth and property were concentrated in an economic elite. The elite owned the means of production and exploited and extracted profit from the working class through long and harsh working conditions, low wages, and limited social benefits. Members of the working class were inculcated with a "false consciousness" from the educational system and media, which led them to falsely believe myths, such as that class does not matter and that anyone can attain economic success. Marx believed that the contradictions of the capitalist system—a wealthy and powerful elite with an interest in exploiting an increasingly impoverished working class—made conflict inevitable and predicted a revolt by the proletariat (that is, the working class). The outcome of this revolt would be a government by and for the working class with the abolition of private property.

The influence of **Marxist theory** can be seen in the ideology of various late 20th-century Latin American nations. The Revolutionary Armed Forces of Colombia (FARC) was a Marxist guerilla force formed in 1964 as the armed wing of the Colombian Communist Party. FARC has signed an armistice with the Colombian government, and at one point the group boasted as many as 10,000 combatants and thousands of armed supporters. FARC preached a redistribution of wealth, the seizure of the assets of multinational corporations, and the end to American influence in Colombia. FARC's noble aspirations were in significant contradiction to the group's heavy involvement in the narcotics trade, which funded the organization. European terrorist groups such as the Red Army Faction in the late 1960s in West Germany adopted the rhetoric of Marxism to justify their utopian aspirations to transform society. The Red Army Brigade in Japan was another Marxist group committed to worldwide revolution that engaged in airline hijackings, kidnappings, and attacks on embassies and on American military bases. Their most infamous attack was a 1972 assault on what is now named Ben Gurion International Airport in Israel which resulted in the death of 26 and wounding of 80. One Red Army attacker was shot and killed, another committed suicide, and a third survived.

The question of whether economic deprivation is linked to terrorism is open to debate. Louise Richardson notes that if poverty alone caused terrorism, we would see terrorists streaming out of refugee camps in Africa and in the Middle East. At the same time, she notes the comfortable and privileged background of many al Qaeda terrorists, including the 9/11 attackers. Richardson concludes that if there is a relationship between poverty and terrorism, it is based on relative rather than absolute deprivation (Richardson, 2006). Marc Sageman finds that most Islamic terrorists are from upper class or solidly middle-class homes. However, he agrees with Richardson that these individuals are motivated by identifying with impoverished individuals—rather than by their own impoverishment (Sageman, 2008).

There are a number of sophisticated quantitative studies that fail to find a relationship between poverty and terrorism. Terrorist nationals of the 10 poorest countries in the world were responsible for just 2% of terrorist attacks between

2002 and 2010, and only Ethiopia (among the poorest countries) experienced significant terrorist violence within its borders. The countries that experienced the greatest number of terrorist incidents vary in their economic development and are not noticeably unequal with regard to the gap between rich and poor. Poorer regions within countries also do not experience more terrorism than wealthier regions. In addition, there is no significant relationship between economic growth and terrorism. However, and most importantly, research finds that the economic deprivation of a minority group discriminated against within a country is a breeding ground for terrorism (Piazza, 2014).

2.1 You Decide

In 2002, during a firefight with American forces in Afghanistan in which several armed forces were killed, Omar Khadr (age 15) allegedly threw a grenade at two unsuspecting American soldiers, wounding and blinding sergeant Layne Morris and killing sergeant Christopher Speer. Khadr was wounded in the firefight and was interrogated by American forces at Bagram Air Base before being transferred at age 16 to Guantánamo. Khadr pled guilty to war crimes in 2010 in return for an 8-year sentence, and in 2012 he was repatriated to Canada—his country of birth—and subsequently was released on bail in 2015. Khadr was the first person who committed a war crime as a juvenile who was criminally prosecuted since World War II. Critics claimed that as a juvenile that he should have been treated in accordance with the protections to be accorded a juvenile rather than as an adult offender. At Guantánamo, Khadr alleged that he was subjected to solitary confinement and shackling and to intense interrogation. Although some officials at Guantánamo believed that Khadr was capable of rehabilitation and did not harbor radical views, other individuals who interrogated Khadr disagreed and pointed to the fact that he was a proven killer and that his family was linked to terrorism. His father worked for Islamic charities in Pakistan and Afghanistan, was linked to Osama bin Laden, and died during a firefight with Pakistani forces in 2003, in which one of Omar's brothers was paralyzed and a second brother was detained for 5 years on suspicion of trafficking in firearms for al Qaeda. Khadr to this day continues to insist on his innocence and states that he only confessed based on a promise that he would be transferred to Canada. An initial report filed by military investigators raised the possibility that the grenade may have been thrown by an enemy combatant who died during the firefight rather than by Khadr. Should Khadr have been detained at Guantánamo and prosecuted as an adult for war crimes? Should he have been repatriated to Canada?

(continues on next page)

(continued from previous page)

After being repatriated to Canada, Khadr was released on bail 3 years later, in 2015. The Canadian Supreme Court subsequently held that Canada had been complicit in Khadr's mistreatment, and the Canadian government subsequently paid him roughly $8 million in compensation. In the United States, a Utah jury awarded more than $130 million to the widow of Christopher Spear and to a soldier wounded in the attack.

There are an estimated 30,000 child soldiers involved in conflicts across the globe; thousands are involved with terrorist groups and are directly responsible for war crimes.

How should the legal system respond to juvenile terrorists? []

VICTIMOLOGY

Victimology is a new and controversial area of terrorism research that analyses the victims of terrorism. Victims are understandably viewed as having suffered random and inexplicable violence. William S. Parkin, however, finds that individuals with certain characteristics or patterns of behavior are more likely to be victimized by terrorist attacks. In Israel students are more likely to be on public transport and thus to be victims of a suicide attack, and Israeli individuals whose lifestyle puts them in a public space are more likely to be a victim of terrorism. The probability of being a victim of terrorism of course also differs by country and by region of the world (Parkin, 2017).

Personalities and Events

For most of the world, Osama bin Laden was the face of the Islamic terrorist movement. In reality Egyptian Ayman al-Zawahiri, directly below Bin Laden in the organization's hierarchy, was the primary force in planning assaults on American troops in Somalia in 1983 (the Battle of Mogadishu, also known as the "Black Hawk down" attack), the embassy bombings in east Africa in 1998, and the attacks on the S.S. *Cole* and on the World Trade Center and Pentagon on September 11, 2001.

Al-Zawahiri, born in 1949, was a surgeon and a member of the Egyptian terrorist organization al-Jihad which was devoted to the overthrow of the Egyptian government and to the installation of an Islamic theocratic government (a *theocracy* is a government based on religious doctrine).

The al-Zawahiri family was one of the most prominent families in Egypt; it included dozens of doctors along with chemists, pharmacists, an ambassador, a judge, a member of parliament, and Grand Imam of al-Azjar, a 1,000-year-old university in Cairo. The other side of Ayman al-Zawahiri's family, the Azzam, was one of the most prominent political families in the country (Wright, 2016).

FIGURE 2.1 Osama Bin Laden and Ayman Al-Zawahiri

Copyright © Hamid Mir (CC BY-SA 3.0) at https://commons.wikimedia.org/wiki/File%3AHamid_Mir_interviewing_Osama_bin_Laden_and_Ayman_al-Zawahiri_2001.jpg.

Despite the prominence of the al-Zawahiri family they lived extremely modestly and had little or no contact with the British and European colonial residents who dominated the local social life and clubs. Ayman attended a state secondary school rather than the prominent local English preparatory school.

Ayman al-Zawahiri's thinking was shaped by the Egyptian Sayyid Qutb who, after returning from a year in the United States, was appalled by what he viewed as the decadence of America and turned away from secularism, rationality, tolerance, and individualism, advocating a strict form of Islam (termed the Salafist tradition) that does not recognize the legitimacy of any Islamic religious developments after the death of the Prophet. Al-Zawahiri and those in his circle of dissidents blamed Egypt's defeat in the 1967 war with Israel on the country's embrace of a secular (nonreligious) lifestyle. Al-Zawahiri advocated a return to religion and the creation of an Islamic state which would unify the Middle East with Egypt as the capital state (a caliphate).

(continues on next page)

(continued from previous page)

Al-Zawahiri graduated from medical school in 1974 and after 3 years as a surgeon in the army, he spent several months as a doctor in Pakistan treating Afghans wounded in the fight to expel the Soviet Union. Al-Zawahiri returned to Egypt fired by the spirit of resistance to the infidels in Afghanistan. He viewed the fight in Afghan as a prelude to a larger global struggle against the United States and Europe. The overthrow of the Shah and his royal family in Iran by a broad coalition led by Ayatollah Ruhollah Khomeini and the installation of theocratic Shia Muslim regime made the possibility of establishing an Islamic government in Egypt a realistic aspiration.

In 1979 President Anwar Sadat of Egypt signed a peace treaty, prohibited the covering of women's faces (the article of clothing that does this is the *niqab*), banned religious student associations on university campuses, and declared that religion had no role in politics in Egypt and should be confined to mosques. Egyptian underground terrorist cells responded by assassinating Sadat on October 6, 1981. Al-Zawahiri was arrested as he was on his way to the airport to board a flight to Pakistan.

Although he claimed to be unaware of the assassination plot, al-Zawahiri was tried for various crimes, including possession of a firearm. During his trial al-Zawahiri, along with 400 other Islamists, was detained in a zoo-like cage. In a video of the trial that was viewed across the Middle East, al-Zawahiri defiantly shouted, "We are Muslims"; he was intent on establishing an Islamic state and an Islamic society. Following his conviction, he was detained for 3 years and beaten and tortured on a daily basis. Al-Zawahiri emerged from this period as angry and violent and eager for revenge.

Al-Zawahiri and a small band of followers left for Saudi Arabia where he encountered Osama bin Laden, whom he followed to Peshawar, Afghanistan; and after the Soviets were driven out of Afghanistan, al-Zawahiri joined Bin Laden in Sudan. The two of them were natural allies; both were from distinguished families, and they were educated and devoutly religious. Both advocated Islamic resistance to the West and the establishment of a Caliphate uniting Sunni Muslims.

Al-Zawahiri and members of the Egyptian terrorist group al-Jihad used Sudan as a base of operations to initiate attacks on Egypt, which retaliated by arresting more than 100 Islamists, six of whom were sentenced to death. Sudan expelled al-Zawahiri, along with Bin Laden, in reaction to pressure from other Muslim regimes; they both relocated to Afghanistan. In February 1998 al-Zawahiri formally combined his organization with Bin Laden, forming the International Islamic Front for Jihad on Jews and Crusaders. The founding document claimed that Muslims possessed a religious duty to kill Americans and their allies—whether civilian or military. The front included jihad groups from Muslim countries across the globe.

The United States responded later in 1998 by tracking members of al-Zawahiri's organization that were living abroad and returning them for trial, imprisonment, and—allegedly—torture in Egypt. In August al-Zawahiri, although out of the country, was sentenced to death by an Egyptian court. Al-Zawahiri proclaimed that a response was being prepared. The next day the American embassies in Kenya and in Tanzania were bombed, killing 223 individuals.

President Bill Clinton responded on August 2, 1998, by launching 79 Tomahawk cruise missiles against Bin Laden's training camp in Afghanistan and against a chemical factory in Sudan that allegedly was manufacturing poison gas. Both Bin Laden and al-Zawahiri survived the missile strikes. Al-Zawahiri responded by announcing that the war had only just begun and that America should expect an answer.

Can you apply the theoretical approaches discussed in this chapter to explaining al-Zawahiri's involvement in terrorism?

WOMEN AND TERORISM

Historically, women were primarily involved in terrorism behind the scenes, acting as couriers, engaging in intelligence gathering, operating "safe houses," and purchasing provisions. An exception was the Russian terrorists of the late 19th century—perhaps a quarter of whom were women, and many of whom occupied leadership positions. Sophia L. Perovskaya, 27, orchestrated the assassination of Czar Alexander II in 1881 and was the first female terrorist executed in Russian history. The consensus is that women began to assume an increasingly prominent role in terrorist organizations in the 1960s and 1970s, and that today terrorism is an equal-opportunity enterprise, with women comprising between 20% and 30% of terrorists. Fusako Shigenobu was commander of the Japanese Red Army and Gudrun Ensslin and Ulrike Meinhof were leaders in the German Red Army Faction in the 1970s. Cynthia Combs notes that 10 of the 14 most wanted West German terrorists in the 1980s were women. The so-called Black Widows were the widows of Chechen insurgents killed during the Chechens' struggle to gain independence from the Russian Federation. Between 2000 and 2002 Black Widow suicide bombers were reportedly responsible for hundreds of deaths of Russian troops—150 in 2003 alone. In Sri Lanka in the 1970s, a number of terrorist attacks (including suicide bombings) were carried out by the Freedom Birds (Combs, 2013).

FIGURE 2.2 Wall Poster of Leila Khalid

The available data finds that women are overwhelmingly affiliated with left-wing groups that advocate for utopian principles. Some commentators speculate that this is explained by the fact that women are attracted to terrorism in societies in which they are frustrated by the lack of opportunity in the existing political system and aspire to achieve fundamental change and to establish a new role for women in the future (Hudson, 1999).

Women are valued in various terrorist groups because of their ability to move around without drawing suspicion. In May 1999, while placing a garland around the neck of Indian prime minister Rajiv Gandhi, a female Tamil suicide bomber ignited a bomb, killing herself, Gandhi, and 17 others.

The explanations for female involvement in terrorism generally are characterized by unproven assumptions and stereotypes rather than fact, and commentators at times contradict one another. Consider the often-quoted claim of Walter Laqueur that women tend to be "more fanatical" and have a "greater capacity for suffering." Laqueur claims that women's motivations tend to be emotional, and for that reason, when they are captured they are able to defy efforts to interrogate them or to break their will and spirit (Laqueur, 1999, pp. 38–39).

On the other hand, women are described by other analysts as cool and composed under pressure; as loyal and trustworthy with an inner strength and ruthlessness; and as single minded and dedicated (Hudson, 1999).

Laqueur also speculates that many women may engage in terrorism to defy gender roles. Wafa Idris was the first Palestinian suicide bomber. Her bomb ignited (allegedly by accident), killing one Israeli and wounding 140 others. Young Palestinian women celebrated Idris as having shattered traditional gender roles. Mia Bloom suggests that women fighting as low-level terrorists are repeating the traditional role of women sacrificing themselves on behalf of others, questioning whether women will fundamentally change the patriarchal structure of their societies by acting as suicide bombers (Bloom, 2007).

Another persistent theme dismisses women by viewing them as being drawn to terrorism by a romantic attachment (Hudson, 1999). In an analysis of newspaper accounts of female terrorists, Brigitte L. Nacos notes that women were often portrayed in sexual terms and as being politically uneducated thrill seekers (Nacos, 2013). Others note that female terrorism is motivated by a desire to revenge the loss of family members and to gain retribution for their mistreatment by security forces (Bloom, 2007).

Most of these theories fail to capture women's genuine political commitment and dedicated involvement in terrorist organizations. Leila Khalid, raised in a refugee camp, was a terrorist commando in the Popular Front for the Liberation of Palestine. In August 1969, at the age of 23, Khalid hijacked a Trans World Airlines plane flying between Rome and Athens and directed the plane to land in Damascus, Syria, and released all 113 passengers unharmed. Because of her notoriety, she underwent plastic surgery to alter her appearance. Roughly a year later, Khalid, along with a colleague, unsuccessfully attempted to hijack an El Al plane as part of a planned operation to hijack five planes. Khalid's fellow terrorist was shot and killed, and Khalid was apprehended and incarcerated; she was later released by Great Britain in a brokered deal with Palestine. She survived an assassination attempt by Mossad (the Israeli intelligence service) in 1976 and shifted her focus to political activism on behalf of the Palestinian cause.

In the 1960s the Irish Republican Army (IRA) merged the male and female wings of the organization. As male terrorists were apprehended and imprisoned, the organization began to increasingly rely on female fighters. The Price sisters (called the Sisters of Death) were involved in a notorious bombing campaign in London in 1973. Ten years later, Anna Moore received a life sentence for her role in bombing a Northern Irish pub in which 17 individuals died. Ella O'Dwyer and Martina Anderson each received a life sentence for a plot to bomb 17 seaside resorts. A study of these young women and other IRA female terrorists found that they shared an intense hatred for the British occupiers of Northern Ireland and were committed terrorist fighters (Hudson 1999).

Before we leave the topic of female terrorists consider Jeffrey D. Simon's explanation for the absence of female lone-wolf terrorists. He argues that women feel more comfortable in the protection offered by a group, are risk averse, and have a lower incidence of personality disturbance. Roshonara Choudhry is an example of a female lone wolf. She was the daughter of poor Bangladeshi migrants in Great Britain and yet managed to gain admission to the prestigious King's College London. Choudhry dropped out of the university in her final year and apparently was radicalized over the Internet by radical Yemenese cleric Anwar al-Awalaki and attempted to assassinate Stephen Timms, a member of Parliament who was an ardent supporter of the Iraq War (Simon, 2016).

In sum, Caron Gentry and Laura Sjoberg note that women terrorists are portrayed as either mothers (vengeful rage), monsters (psychologically disturbed), or whores (seduced by a lover); they are not credited with making a rational political decision. They also make the interesting point that little attention is paid to the terrorism of domestic violence and spousal abuse inside the home (Gentry & Sjoberg, 2016).

Can you explain why female terrorists are not fully credited with acting out of a political motive?

2.2. You Decide

Terrorists in a country as large as the United States are difficult to detect, and waiting until terrorists have attacked to initiate an investigation places Americans at risk. In roughly 40% of terrorist prosecutions, federal authorities rely on the use of informants or undercover agents to locate potential terrorist plots. One study of terrorist prosecutions after 9/11 finds that of the 580 prosecutions involving terrorists across the ideological spectrum, 317 involved informants or undercover agents (Norris & Grol-Prokopczyk, 2015).

The use of informants or undercover agents allows the government to penetrate terrorist cells, arrest individuals, and disrupt plots before terrorist plans can be carried out. This is straightforward in those instances in which informants or undercover agents can detect an ongoing plot. The use of undercover investigative techniques is much more controversial when a suspect has not yet engaged in a criminal act and federal agents need to determine whether an individual poses a threat. The FBI and federal counterterrorism officials rely on a theory of radicalization that suggests that a significant percentage of individuals who have accepted a terrorist ideology eventually will progress to the point that they commit acts of terrorism. The strategy is to arrest these individuals before they commit a terrorist act.

The government may monitor a suspect—but if law enforcement enables criminal activity, a suspect may be acquitted of criminal activity on the grounds that their actions were a product of the government and that they were entrapped. This is a far-from-simple determination.

Entrapment requires the government to influence someone to commit a criminal act, thus directly causing the defendant to commit a crime. A defendant who is predisposed to commit the crime may not plead entrapment. *Predisposition* means that the defendant would have committed the crime without the government's influence. In determining whether a defendant who pleads entrapment was predisposed to commit a crime, courts consider whether the defendant proposed the criminal activity, whether the defendant had a history of involvement in this type of activity, the defendant's character and reputation, the nature of the inducement (for example, a large sum of money), and whether the defendant resisted a proposal to commit a crime.

There is no instance since 9/11 in which a defendant has successfully raised the entrapment defense in a terrorist prosecution. Jesse J. Norris and Hanna Grol-Prokopczyk find a number of cases in which they conclude a defendant would have committed a crime even if the government had not been involved. For example, Jason Abdo, a former soldier, confided to an informant that he possessed bomb-making equipment and shared what appeared to be concrete plans to attack American soldiers at Fort Hood, Texas. Norris and Grol-Prokopczyk, however, draw the controversial conclusion that the use of undercover agents and informants were only partially effective in apprehending individuals who—if not arrested—would have engaged in terrorism. They conclude that only 16 threats were at least "somewhat likely to have been thwarted by the government's counterterrorism prosecutions ... thirty-one defendants were involved in these cases." This amounts to 5% of the jihadi defendants in cases involving informants (Norris & Grol-Prokopczyk, 2015, pp. 663–664).

A Study by Human Rights Watch and Columbia Law School along with Norris and Grol-Prokopczyk find that in a number of cases, FBI informants were significantly involved in persuading individuals to engage in terrorism who otherwise would not have committed an act of terrorism. Adel Daoud was a 19-year-old student at a Chicago Islamic high school. Daoud is described a mentally challenged, socially isolated, and heavily involved with the Internet. FBI employees began corresponding with him shortly after he turned 18 and an FBI undercover employee met with Daoud and introduced the topic of jihad. Members of Daoud's mosque, along with his parents, told him that jihad required giving money to the poor and taking care of his parents, and that violence was contrary to Islam. The FBI employee assured Daoud that religious approval was not required for him to engage in terrorism and in September 2012 the employee drove Daoud to downtown Chicago in a Jeep loaded with fake explosives. Daoud then was instructed to drive the Jeep to the target location and proceeded to attempt to detonate the device and was arrested by the FBI.

(continues on next page)

(continued from previous page)

In the Newburgh Four case an informant offered James Cromitie, an unemployed White nationalist, as much as $250,000 to fire rocket-propelled grenades at Stewart Air Base and to place bombs at a synagogue in Riverdale, New York. Federal district court Judge Colleen McMahon concluded that Cromitie's initial enthusiasm indicated his predisposition to commit the terrorist acts. However, she noted that the government's eagerness to protect society led the government to target a "bigoted and suggestible [man] ... incapable of committing an act of terrorism on his own ... who was ... utterly inept. Only the government could have made a terrorist out of Mr. Cromitie" (Norris & Grol-Prokopczyk, 2015, p. 612).

In the Liberty City Seven case the suspects were offered $50,000 to bomb the Sears Tower in Chicago. In several other cases, informants provided violent videos and jihadist material to suspects and continued to encourage and in some instances berated them into participating in a terrorist plot. A particularly controversial aspect of entrapment is the use of informants who possess criminal records and are promised leniency or money in return for their cooperation.

Keep in mind that federal investigations using undercover agents and informants are based on what we know about the process of radicalization. Individuals who claim entrapment are arrested and prosecuted for at least agreeing to and in most instances attempting to commit an act of terrorism.

The FBI guidelines require that agents employ the least intrusive means possible in carrying out an investigation. The FBI explains that entrapment is required to detect terrorists who otherwise are able to remain anonymous through the use of encrypted communications. In other instances, the FBI has approached individuals who have indicated their terrorist sympathies on social media. Current statistics indicate that more than 65% of terrorist prosecutions currently rely on undercover operations.

As a federal official, how would you balance the need to investigate terrorism with the risk that individuals may be convicted who would not have otherwise committed an act of terrorism? ☐

CHAPTER SUMMARY

In reading this chapter, it is easy to see terrorists as individuals who are driven by personal or social influence, rather than by political principle to engage in violence. Keep in mind that each and every one of us is the product of various experiences and influences, and terrorists are no different in this respect than other individuals.

Some commentators note that the type of theoretical perspectives discussed in this chapter may lead us to avoid taking terrorists seriously.

Analysis of the path to terrorism has implications for counterterrorist strategies. A few obvious points emerge from the discussion in this chapter. There clearly is a need to remain attentive to individuals who appear to be socially alienated; to publicly respond to grievances that may result in individuals feeling that they are being treated unjustly; to counter radical messages with an alternative accounting of the facts; and to prevent groups from being isolated from society at large. There is also a need to maintain the capacity for a strong and forceful response to terrorism.

Terrorists, although often labelled as "crazy," are generally "normal" individuals. Terrorists are "made," not born, and they progress through a radicalization process. There are various approaches to radicalization and these primarily differ with regard to the most important factor in radicalization—that is, whether it is a social network or an individual's reaction to a "triggering" event. Lone-wolf terrorists are a separate group with diverse motivations for engaging in terrorism.

Structural theory finds the causes of terrorism in individuals' socioeconomic and political environment. There are various criminological theories that also focus on an individual's surrounding environment. Differential association explains terrorism based on an individual's personal relationships; general strain theory focuses on the gap between an individual's expectations and the satisfaction of these expectations; social activities theory looks at whether individuals' activities place them at risk; social disorganization theory focuses on an individual's environment; and Marxist theory finds the explanation for terrorism in the economic structure of society.

Victimology is a fairly new approach to terrorism that explains the identity of the targets of terrorism based on the victims' behavior.

There are a number of explanations for the involvement of women in terrorism, several of which seem to be based on stereotypes rather than firm evidence. There is no question that women have proven to be dedicated fighters who have performed crucial roles in a number of terrorist organizations.

A persistent debate is whether terrorists are recruited by centralized terrorist organizations, or whether contemporary terrorists are radicalized through small networks of friends or are inspired by their online activities, possessing loose (rather than formal) ties to specific terrorist organizations (Hamm, 2013).

CHAPTER REVIEW QUESTIONS

1. Discuss the various psychological steps in the radicalization of terrorists. What factors do you consider most important in this process?
2. List the various factors that motivate lone-wolf terrorists.

3. What is structural theory? How does structural theory differ from psychological theories?

4. Explain differential association theory, general strain theory, social disorganization theory, social activities theory, social disorganization theory, and Marxist theory. Which one of these theories do you believe makes the most sense?

5. Discuss the various explanations for women's involvement in terrorism. Which theory makes the most sense? Makes the least sense?

6. How does understanding the process of radicalization and the process by which individuals become terrorists assist in designing counterterrorist tactics and strategies?

7. Explain why terrorists' personality profiles are not considered to be indicative of whether an individual will engage in terrorist acts.

TERMINOLOGY

absolute deprivation

alienation

differential association

entrapment

general strain theory of
   terrorism (GSST)

lone-wolf terrorists

Marxist theory

radicalization

rational choice theory

relative deprivation

situational approach

social activities theory

social disorganization theory

social learning theory

structural theory

terrorist-coordinated lone-
   wolf attack

terrorist-directed lone-wolf
   attack

terrorist-inspired lone-wolf
   attack

theocracy

victimology

CHAPTER 3

Terrorist Tactics and Strategies

INTRODUCTION

On January 7, 2013 two brothers, Saïd and Chérif Kouachi, burst into the offices of the Paris satirical magazine *Charlie Hebdo* and opened fire with AK-47 Kalashnikov rapid-fire weapons, killing 13 and wounding several others. During the attack the two assailants allegedly shouted "God is great" and "the Prophet is avenged." They fled, and on exiting the building, the attackers killed a police officer as he lay wounded in the street. Then they carjacked an automobile. The brothers were tracked to a rural area and 2 days later were killed in an exchange of gunfire with the police.

FIGURE 3.1 The Kouachi Brothers

Source: https://commons.wikimedia.org/wiki/File%3ASa%C3%AFd_et_
Ch%C3%A9rif_Kouachi.jpg.

Charlie Hebdo was known for poking fun at the rich and powerful politicians and important religious figures. The magazine had been a target for Islamic terrorists in the past for its provocative coverage of issues like wearing of veils and Islamic law, and the headquarters had been firebombed 3 years earlier. One controversial cover pictured a weeping Prophet Muhammad under the caption "Muhammad overwhelmed by fundamentalists." In the cartoon, Muhammad is complaining that "it's hard being loved by jerks." Those who adhere to a strict conservative interpretation of Islam consider it blasphemous to produce images of the Prophet, and radicals vowed retribution. The magazine added fuel to the fire by running a controversial cartoon poking fun at the leader of Islamic State, Abu Bakr al-Baghdadi.

The Kouachi brothers had been orphaned at a young age. They drifted into a life of only-occasional employment and petty crime. Chérif had spent time in jail and was known to the police for his militant activities. The brothers had been recruited by the Islamic State and were in communication with a French Tunisian commander Boubaker Hakim in Syria—who was later killed by an American drone in a retaliatory strike.

The assault on *Charlie Hebdo* was apparently coordinated with an armed attack the next day on a French policewoman and a pedestrian, as well as with a hostage-taking incident at a Jewish supermarket. The hostage-taking incident resulted in the death of known Islamic militant Amedy Coulibaly as well as four hostages during a police siege on the market. These terrorist attacks may have inspired a beheading and attempt to bomb an American-owned industrial gas plant in France later in the summer, as well as the killing of three randomly targeted individuals by a machine gun–toting attacker.

In response to the *Charlie Hebdo* attack, hundreds of thousands of Parisians and people throughout the world demonstrated solidarity by rallying in the streets. Several million copies of the magazine *Charlie Hebdo* were sold, and journalists across the globe spoke out for the sanctity of freedom of the press—even when the media expressed controversial ideas. Dissident voices criticized the magazine for irresponsible and unnecessarily provocative coverage that disregarded religious sensibilities and offended Muslims.

Any thought that these were isolated attacks quickly disappeared when, in November 2015, ISIS terrorists carried out a coordinated series of attacks in France. The first occurred in a northern suburb in which three suicide bombers

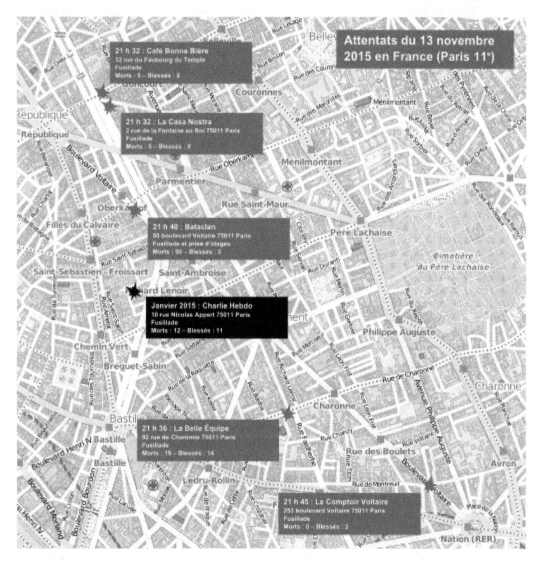

FIGURE 3.2 The 2015 Paris Attacks

initiated an attack outside a sports stadium during a World Cup football match. This was immediately followed by several mass shootings, as well as a targeting several crowded restaurants in the heart of a Paris entertainment district. Three gunmen then carried out a mass atrocity at the Bataclan theatre where a crowd of young people had gathered for a heavy metal concert. The attackers took 100 hostages; after the terrorists threatened to behead a hostage every 5 minutes, French counterterrorism squads laid siege to the theater, killing the assailants. The terrorists who conducted the November operations ultimately killed 130 individuals, 89 of whom were killed at Bataclan. There are reports that hostages at Bataclan were subject to unspeakable abuse. Five of the seven attackers were residents of France or Belgium; two reportedly were Syrian refugees who had entered Europe as part of the mass migration from the Syrian war zone.

On Bastille Day 2016, Mohamed Lahouaiej Bouhlel, a French resident from Tunisia with a criminal history of domestic assault, battery, and weapon possession—but no known extremist ties—drove a hijacked semitrailer into a crowd on the beach in Nice, France, killing 86 individuals. Evidence later revealed that Bouhlel was a radical sympathizer and had possible terrorist connections.

On the eve of the May 2017 French presidential election, French national Karim Cheurfi killed one police officer and wounded two in an apparent attempt to anger the French electorate into voting for an extremist candidate who would promote divisions in society. Cheurfi had a criminal history of car theft and shooting a police officer, and he had been released from prison the year before the May attack. He was known to the police—but had no history of militancy.

A year later, Khmzat Azimov, 20, stabbed and killed one pedestrian and wounded four others in a knife attack near the Paris Opera House. Azimov, born in Chechnya, was on the terrorism watchlist. Following the attack, a video was released in which Azimov called for attacks throughout Europe and the United States.

What lessons does the *Charlie Hebdo* attack (and other attacks in France) hold for understanding the nature of terrorist targets, attacks, and ideology? *Charlie Hebdo* was a senseless attack, the effects of which reverberated across the world. It was viewed as a violation of fundamental democratic values. An armed assault against prominent journalists and cartoonists in the middle of Paris was certain to draw attention and to spread anxiety and fear. There was little likelihood that the civilian victims in the *Charlie Hebdo* attack were prepared to resist a terrorist attack—particularly when the terrorists employed powerful assault weapons. Attacking *Charlie Hebdo* made sense to the assailants because the magazine was a symbol of Western arrogance and disregard for Islam, and targeting the magazine's headquarters was aligned with ISIS's message that it would strike against enemies of the Islamic faith. The attack sparked a debate over the role of freedom of expression, and it widened the division between Muslims and non-Muslims in France. There was logic, in the mind of the terrorists, to attacking the police who are an arm of the state and a symbol of law and order and public safety.

The Bataclan and Nice attacks contributed to the sense that terrorist attacks are unpredictable, difficult to anticipate and defend, and may target the most innocent of individuals. A focus on protecting monumental structures like the Eiffel Tower may leave other targets vulnerable. Although there may be a lull in terrorist attacks, terrorist violence emerges in a new form, in a new place, and using different tactics. Terrorism attacks—although often dismissed as inconsequential as compared to the number of those killed from drug overdoses or car accidents—are magnified in terms of their psychological impact.

These attacks may be indicative of a new pattern of terrorism, in which one attack inspires other attacks by individuals who are independent of one another. Terrorist groups like ISIS are inspiring "stay-at-home terrorism," in which individuals are urged to fight in their own country—rather than traveling to fight in Syria or in the Middle East.

There are more than 1,500 suspected Islamist radicals on France's list of suspected and potential terrorists, a total that has roughly doubled in the past 2 years. A more extensive list is estimated to include as many as 20,000 names. Twenty-four-hour surveillance on a suspect requires roughly 20 agents—which is far beyond existing French resources. The open European border means that it is relatively easy for terrorists to travel from nearby Belgium and other countries to France. An additional 1,600 French nationals left to fight in the Middle East, and at some point they may return to France. As a result of these attacks, the French are acutely aware that the enemy is within their society and difficult to detect.

Terrorist violence in France also has increased support for nationalist politicians who are opposed to immigration and to cultural diversity. This nationalist reaction also may take the form of violence against immigrants. In 2018, French police arrested members of a vigilante group called Operational Forces Action, which had planned to attack Muslims throughout France as well as mosques and stores owned by Muslims.

Other European countries face similar challenges. The British domestic intelligence agency M15 estimates that there are 3,000 individuals of interest in the United Kingdom, and at any given time M15 is conducting about 500 active investigations. Between 2013 and 2017 M15 claims to have foiled 18 active terrorist operations. Government officials note that attacks always are in the process of being planned or in the process of being carried out.

TERRORIST WEAPONS AND TARGETS

The hallmark of terrorism is the unpredictable nature of terrorist targets. Terrorists may attack an airline, train, subway, power plant, school, concert, or water or power supply (Masco, 2014). A number of commentators note that the tactics used by terrorists in the past are fairly limited and include hijackings, assassinations, kidnappings, armed assault, barricades, hostage taking, contamination of agriculture and water, the use of chemical and biological weapons, cyberterrorism, and suicide bombings (Simon, 2016). Three of the weapons of choice relied on by terrorists are outlined below (Combs, 2013).

Explosives. Bombs have the advantage of being easily deployed, and a rudimentary explosive can be constructed out of household products and only requires limited expertise. In 1988 a bomb that was smuggled onto Pan Am Flight 103 by Libyan agents was detonated, killing more than 200 people. In 1995 a car packed with fertilizer destroyed the Murrah federal building in Oklahoma City, killing 167 individuals. The so-called Unabomber Ted Kaczynski deployed crude mail bombs to kill three individuals and injure a further 23. Al Qaeda pioneered the tactic of detonating a bomb and igniting another explosive in the area to which the individuals targeted had fled. The improvised explosive device (IED) is a crude explosive device regularly used in Afghanistan, Iraq, and other insurgencies. It is concealed in a bag, container, or artillery shell and then enhanced by way of packing the bomb with steel ball bearings or pipes, and it may be ignited using a cell phone or timer.

In May 2017 in an ISIS-directed attack 22-year-old Salman Abedi detonated an IED on a public concourse during an Ariana Grande concert, killing 22 people—including children.

Assault weapons. The mass murderers in *Charlie Hebdo*, San Bernardino, California, and the Pulse night club in Orlando all were carried out with assault weapons. These rapid-fire weapons are equipped with ammunition clips and can fire many bullets very quickly. They are reliable, easily available, can be concealed with a folding stock, and are relatively light and easily transported. The AK-47 Kalashnikov is generally the weapon of choice for terrorists.

Portable rockets. There has been increased access to **precision-guided munitions** (PGMs). Most of these weapons are light and portable, and they can be fired by one or two individuals. Because their trajectory can be corrected in flight, they have been successfully used to bring down helicopters and aircraft. The most popular PGMs are the American Stinger, Soviet Strela, and British Blowpipe. These weapons are equipped with infrared devices that guide the missile to a heat source and have a range of well over a mile. In July 2014 Russian separatists in the Ukraine used a surface-to-air missile to bring down a Malaysian airliner, killing the crew and 283 passengers.

Knives. On June 3, 2017, three assailants drove a car into a crowd on London Bridge, crashed into a pub at the end of the bridge, and exited the car and began stabbing individuals with knives before being shot dead. They killed seven individuals and wounded 48. Palestinians stabbed over 84 Israelis and visitors to Israel in 2016; the most common weapon was a kitchen knife. These attacks are difficult to anticipate and to deter, and they spread insecurity and fear.

Terrorists engage in **asymmetrical warfare**. They cannot match the firepower or manpower available to the government and seek to accomplish their goals by targeting **soft targets**—targets that are accessible, lightly guarded, and which will result in maximum psychological impact. As targets are "hardened," terrorists shift their focus from **hard targets** to new soft targets. Targets are selected that have the maximum psychological impact. These targets include the following:

Assassinations. Political leaders are targeted who are in the public eye and lightly guarded and therefore present attractive targets. These assassinations demonstrate the capacity of terrorists to strike at the heart of the government. Israeli prime minister Yitzhak Rabin was assassinated by a right-wing Israeli student who believed that Rabin had made too many concessions to the Palestinians. Pakistani prime minister Benazir Bhutto was killed in 2007 by Islamic militants during her election campaign.

Susan Fahey (2017) defines *assassination* as including attacks intended to kill one or more specific individuals. She finds that the period between 2010 and 2014 accounts for 18% of this kind of attack since 1970. Roughly 30% of these attacks were directed against government officials, followed by private citizens, the police, and military officials. Assassinations were successful roughly 75% of the time, and firearms were usually the weapon of choice. Thirty countries account for 90% of attacks—with the United Kingdom, Colombia, Pakistan, Iraq, and India experiencing the greatest number of assassinations (Mandala, 2017).

Trains. Trains and subways are attractive targets because of the difficulty of protecting these targets. Trains have multiple stops, infrequent checks of baggage, a constant stream of passengers boarding and exiting, and accessible and unprotected tracks. An attack on a train can injure or kill a significant number of people. In 2004 an al Qaeda simultaneous bombing of 10 Madrid subway trains killed 191 people and injured hundreds. In August 2015 three American passengers subdued Moroccan-born 25-year-old Ayoub el Khazzani as he prepared to commit mass murder with an assault weapon on a train travelling between Amsterdam and Paris.

Maritime. In his study of naval terrorism, Bo Jiang recorded 183 maritime attacks on vessels between 1971 and 2013. Virtually all of the attacks relied on either firearms, shoulder-fired missiles, or explosives. Although 44 countries experienced maritime attacks, nearly 50% of attacks occurred in Colombia, Nigeria, Philippines, Somalia, and Sri Lanka. The Liberation Tigers of Tamil Eelam (LTTE) account for 81% of all maritime attacks in Sri Lanka and 50% in the South Asian region. The group committed more than twice as many attacks as any other terrorist group. LTTE attacks resulted in 113 killed and 26 wounded (Jiang, 2017).

Airliners and airports. One of the first major air hijackings took place in July 1968, when three Palestinian attackers affiliated with the Popular Front for the Liberation of Palestine (PFLP)—a group affiliated with the Palestine Liberation Organization (PLO)—hijacked an Israeli El Al airliner traveling from Rome to Tel Aviv. This was the 12th hijacking in 1968, although the other incidents were primarily undertaken by individuals who were fleeing the United States and were seeking asylum in Cuba. In contrast, the PFLP incident was intended to highlight the Palestinian cause by hijacking an Israeli plane. The Palestinians also had the strategic goal of holding the passengers hostage and exchanging them for Palestinian prisoners held in Israel (Hoffman, 2006).

The Bojinka plot, by Ramzi Yousef and Khalid Sheikh Mohammed, was planned for January 1995 and involved the assassination of Pope John II, along with the bombing of 11 airplanes in flight from the United States, with the potential of killing 4,000 passengers—as well as crashing a plane into CIA headquarters in Virginia. The attack was only uncovered when authorities responded to a fire in a terrorist-controlled bomb factory. Terrorists have continued to try to outmaneuver technology and in 2017, American and British authorities—fearful of bombs inserted into computers—banned laptops from the passenger cabins of overseas flights from various countries into the United States and other European countries.

Susan Fahey recorded 275 air hijackings between 1970 and 2011, which accounted for 0.22% of all terrorist incidents. One quarter of air hijackings took place in the Middle East and in North Africa, roughly 14% took place in western Europe, and an equal percentage occurred in South America. Firearms were the weapon of choice in these attacks and only 5% of hijackings resulted in the loss of five or more lives (Fahey, 2017).

As precautions have been taken against attacks on airliners, terrorists moved their attack zone outside of the screening checkpoints. In March 2016 three coordinated suicide bombings were launched in Belgium—two at the Brussels Airport and one at the Maalbeek metro station. Three attackers and 32 victims were killed, and more than 300 were injured in this Islamic State attack.

Crowds and public spaces. Crowded venues like nightclubs and concert arenas allow terrorists to kill large numbers of people with limited resources. Examples are the massacre at the Pulse nightclub in Orlando, the killings at the Bataclan theater in Paris in 2015, and the suicide attack in Manchester, England, in 2017.

A terrorist steered a stolen van into a holiday market in Berlin, killing 12 and wounding dozens of others in December 2016. As mentioned above, on Bastille Day 2017, an attacker drove a semitrailer into a beachgoing crowd in Nice, France, killing more than 80 individuals. In May 2017 a suicide bomber drove a water tanker packed with explosives to the outskirts of the embassy district in Kabul, Afghanistan, killing 80 individuals in a massive explosion.

In 2017 London experienced three motor vehicle attacks. In March, in an ISIS-inspired attack, Khalid Masood drove an SUV onto the sidewalk on the Westminster Bridge, killing two and injuring as many as 40 individuals. In June three terrorists drove a van onto the sidewalk of the London Bridge, running over pedestrians and fled the vehicle and stabbed people in bars and restaurants in Borough Market. They killed seven and injured dozens of others. Roughly 3 weeks later, Darren Osborne drove a rented van into a crowd of Muslims as they were exiting the Finsbury Park Mosque in London.

Hostage taking. The taking of hostages to place pressure on governments to meet demands or to pay ransom is illustrated by the Italian Red Brigades' abduction of former Italian prime minister Aldo Moro in March 1978. When the government refused their demands, Moro was killed and his body was left in an abandoned car. The Nigerian insurgent group Boko Haram notoriously kidnapped 262 schoolgirls in April 2014, and after several years of captivity released roughly 100 of the young women. Other hostages may have been killed, forced to marry insurgents, or have been radicalized. It is estimated that Boko Haram has kidnapped thousands of people and that as many as 20,000 individuals have been killed during the insurgency. The terrorists' ability to force the government to negotiate provides the group status and legitimacy, and it communicates to the public that the group is reasonable and open to a political solution. Governments find themselves under constant pressure to negotiate release of the hostages.

Sabotage. Terrorist plots have targeted nuclear power plants, electrical grids, the Wall Street financial district, and iconic landmarks. Iyman Faris, an Ohio truck driver, in 2003 pled guilty to an al Qaeda plot to blow up the Brooklyn Bridge and was sentenced to 20 years in prison.

Jonathan Matusitz writes that terrorist groups develop a **signature method** of violence that communicates that the group is strong and is to be feared. The IRA was known for "kneecapping"—shooting the back of an individual's knee joint, permanently impeding their ability to walk. This method was used against British agents. ISIS, in part, has developed a reputation for ruthless terror by circulating videos of the beheading of Western hostages and of captured enemy combatants. Signature methods are a method of communicating strength and resolve to both the domestic and the global audience (Matusitz, 2013).

TYPES OF TERRORIST GROUPS AND VIOLENCE

Bruce Hoffman writes that terrorist groups focus on targets that reflect their ideology and which they view as legitimate. These attacks call attention to the group's belief system and reinforce the loyalty of supporters. Left-wing Marxist groups focus on economic targets that reflect their belief that economic elites exploit the working class. Religious groups target nonbelievers. Right-wing groups focus their attacks on immigrants and minorities. Hoffman argues that even when an attack is seemingly brutal and bloody, the terrorists view the target as justified based on their worldview and view the attack as advancing their cause (Hoffman, 2006).

Hoffman uses an analogy of sharks to describe terrorist groups—sharks must keep moving forward and consuming the fish in the water in order to survive. Similarly, terrorist attacks often occur every few weeks. The worst imaginable fate for a group is to be ignored, and when events overshadow the terrorists' cause, they will resort to more innovative or spectacular attacks. Terrorist groups are in competition for attention, support, and finance. They are under pressure to commit ever more spectacular acts of violence to distinguish themselves from other groups. A gruesome attack may also result from the simple fact that violence is difficult to control once initiated (Hoffman, 2006).

Even an unsuccessful (although bold) attack attracts public attention and creates the perception that a group is powerful and potent. The IRA's nearly successful remote-bomb attack on British prime minister Margaret Thatcher in 1984 reinforced the perception that the IRA was capable of evading defenses and possessed technological sophistication. Individuals may question the ability of the government to protect them from the terrorist threat and may be persuaded to negotiate with the terrorists (Hoffman, 2006).

Terrorist groups share a belief in the future victory of their righteous cause, although this vision may take decades of dedication and sacrifice to be achieved. The reality is that a significant number of groups collapse within their first year, and at least half of those who survive this length of time do not survive beyond a decade. National groups that have a natural geographic home and a base of popular support and historical tradition are more likely to have the capacity to sustain themselves. National groups also have a clear and concrete goal; this contrasts with the goal of left-wing groups to create a classless society in which private property is abolished and the goal of right-wing groups to cleanse society of immigrants and minorities. Without a natural base of popular support, terrorist groups need to devote time and effort to building popular support and to providing an appealing intellectual justification for their efforts. The success of ISIS is based in part on the group's propaganda activities on the Internet.

Terrorist organizations that sustain themselves are "learning organizations" that adjust their inner workings to defeat counterterrorist tactics and pay attention to the experiences of other groups. The Baader-Meinhof gang in Germany, also known as the Red Army Faction (RAF), learned that security forces were lifting fingerprints off the bottom of toilet seats, inside refrigerators, and from other spaces and began to apply an ointment to their fingers so as to avoid leaving fingerprints (Hoffman, 2006).

Terrorist groups also must maintain the capacity to respond to the technological advancement of counterterrorism strategies. The first-generation Irish Republican Army (IRA) bombs were little more than nails or ball bearings wrapped around TNT, which required the lighting of a fuse. Other bombs used commercial detonators ignited by an alarm clock. These bombs proved unreliable, and between 1989 and 1996 roughly 120 IRA fighters lost their lives in bomb manufacture or attacks. The IRA pioneered the method of igniting bombs from a safe distance using radio controls for model aircraft purchased at hobby stores. The British responded by jamming the electronic transmission of signals. The IRA once again developed techniques to circumvent the jamming which, in turn, was defeated by British technology. The IRA adjusted by developing a system using radar guns, similar to those employed by the police to measure drivers' speed. Another technique of bomb ignition developed by the IRA involved the use of a photo flash that could be ignited half a mile away from the target. In both instances the signal was instantaneous, preventing the British from blocking the signal (Hoffman, 2006).

3.1. You Decide

The U.S. government traditionally has followed a policy of nonnegotiation with terrorists that hold hostages, along with a policy of refusing to pay a ransom in return for hostages. The families of hostages and third parties who negotiate with terrorists, in theory, were subject to criminal penalties. In practice, this policy has not been followed by every president. There has been an exception for negotiating the return of members of the military. In 2014 President Obama exchanged three Taliban fighters interned at Guantanamo for sergeant Bowe Bergdahl—a negotiation that generated controversy.

The refusal to negotiate with terrorists is based on the belief that this would indicate weakness, provide terrorists with undeserved legitimacy, and reward and encourage hostage taking. On the other hand, critics contend that it was cruel to abandon Americans—many of whom worked on behalf of the U.S. government in dangerous hotspots around the world.

(continues on next page)

(continued from previous page)

The Obama administration was subject to criticism by the families of four hostages killed by the Taliban in 2014, who argued that their loved ones had been abandoned by the United States. President Obama responded by lifting the prohibition on the families of hostages and third parties negotiating with terrorists. The directive maintained the ban on government payments and concessions to terrorists, although it indicated that the families and other individuals were free to negotiate.

President Obama stated that families and the government would work together as partners. The Department of State created a "family engagement" team to maintain contact with the families of individuals taken hostage, to keep them informed, and to assist them with any issues that may arise. European countries, unlike the United States, openly negotiate with terrorists and pay ransoms and, in most instances, obtain the safe return of their nationals who were held hostage.

Should countries whose nationals are taken hostage negotiate with terrorists? ▯

TERRORIST FINANCING

Terrorist organizations require money for weapons, supplies, travel, and communication. Groups differ on the methods they use to generate funds. Al Qaeda reportedly paid their fighters salaries, along with providing health care. Keep in mind that although an individual attack may require limited funds, the terrorist organization requires money to sustain itself. The attack on the U.S.S. *Cole* in October 2000 may have cost as little as $10,000; the Madrid train bombing in March 2004 likely cost roughly the same amount of money.

The intergovernmental Financial Action Task Force in Paris, composed of countries representing major global economies, documented the sources of terrorist financing in 2015. The task force currently has singled out North Korea, Iran, Iraq, Syria, Yemen, and Ethiopia as financing terrorism and has warned Pakistan to take more assertive action to prevent charities from funneling money to terrorists.

It is not surprising that a significant number of groups rely on criminal activity to fund their missions. The FARC in Colombia and the Taliban in Afghanistan have engaged in narcotics trafficking to support their operations. Hezbollah in Lebanon has relied on the hashish, opium, and heroin to fund itself and allied rebel groups. It is estimated that as much as one third of the Taliban's funding in Afghanistan is from the poppy trade. Another source of income is in smuggling and selling of cigarettes and tobacco. Additional income is derived from the sale of ancient artifacts that were seized from significant archeological sites. ISIS established a bureau of antiquities and has made tens of millions of dollars selling ancient artifacts.

Other illegal sources of income include credit card fraud, the sale of counterfeit goods (such as cigarettes falsely labeled as a major brand), the sale of illegally copied DVDs, obtaining fraudulent bank loans, and bank robberies. Shipping stolen vehicles abroad for sale also is a fairly prevalent source of funding.

The Islamic State and al Qaeda affiliates in Yemen and the Sahel have generated huge amounts of cash though taking hostages and demanding ransom payments. Somali pirate networks have made roughly $10 billion by commandeering ocean vessels and holding the ship and crew for ransom. ISIS, the Taliban, and other terrorist groups extract taxes and rents from individuals and businesses in the territories they control and impose fines for violations of their local laws.

Eight former company executives of the French company Lafarge SA have been indicted on charges of financing terrorism by paying money to Islamic terrorists during the conflict in Syria. In return for the more than $5 million paid to terrorist groups, the company was provided with safe passage for its employees to travel to the company's cement plant. Money also allegedly was paid to move supplies and employees through dangerous areas of Syria. A civil suit alleges that the company acted as an accomplice to the crimes against humanity committed by terrorist groups and placed the lives of its employees at risk (Alderman, 2018).

Terrorist organizations also have successfully raised funds from the diaspora—individuals living abroad who share their nationality or religion. The Irish Republican Army raised significant amounts of money from sympathizers in the United States. This type of funding is often accomplished through use of the Internet. Hoffman writes that the Palestinian group Hamas listed the amount of donations required to purchase a bullet, a kilogram of dynamite, and AK-47s for their fighters (Hoffman, 2006). A lucrative source of funding has been the establishment of charitable organizations which—unknown to donors—either direct funds to terrorist organizations or which devote money to providing medical care or financial support for the wives and children of terrorists.

It would be a mistake to view terrorist organizations as relying exclusively on criminal activity to raise money. Many groups are large conglomerates that run businesses, hold stock portfolios, have bank accounts throughout the world, and solicit contributions from wealthy donors in the Middle East. James Adams estimates that in the mid-1980s, the PLO presided over a $5 billion financial empire (Adams, 1986). Osama bin Laden was able to devote his personal wealth to the support of al Qaeda. Bin Laden also relied on private donors and the illicit trade of "conflict diamonds" (diamonds mined in areas of conflict), the trade of uranium and tanzanite, and on commercial activity (such as the sale of honey throughout the Middle East). The PLO owned dairy and poultry farms and duty-free stores in several African countries.

At the height of its influence and power, ISIS was earning as much as $350 million per year in oil sales.

Terrorist groups also finance themselves by carrying out attacks on behalf of other groups. The Japanese Red Army (JRA) carried out attacks on American embassies in Indonesia, Spain, and Italy on behalf of former Libyan leader Muammar Gaddafi in retaliation for an American air strike against Libya. The air strike was made in response to Libyan involvement in the bombing of a Berlin nightclub that killed an American soldier.

Finally, Iran and other countries engage in **state-sponsored terrorism**—providing financial support to terrorist organizations. Iran has provided support for the Houthi rebels in Yemen who fight against another armed faction supported by Saudi Arabia and the United States.

A problem that confronts terrorist organizations is how to move cash around the globe. Banking regulations make it difficult to deposit large amounts of cash into a bank and to transfer the funds. The use of "dummy corporations" (which only exist on paper) is important for **money laundering**, which involves claiming that money obtained through criminal activity was actually generated by a legitimate business. This money can then be transferred to other banks and used to establish bank accounts or to purchase houses, cars, and other goods and services. A number of international banks have been fined in recent years for knowingly allowing terrorism-related funds to be deposited and transferred across the globe.

Money also is transferred using couriers who personally deliver funds. Islamic groups often rely on the **hawala system**. This ancient system involves contacting a hawaladar, or an individual involved in arranging for the moving of money. The hawaladar takes a small percentage of the money for himself or herself and contacts a hawaladar in the city in which the money is to be picked up. The second hawaladar then pays the designated recipient. The advantage of this system is that money is not physically transferred across borders and there is no record of the transfer. The two hawaladars keep track of how much each of them has paid the other dealer's clients and periodically settle any debts. In contrast to the ancient hawala system, money is increasingly being transferred using alternative currencies and the dark web.

WEAPONS OF MASS DESTRUCTION

Weapons of mass destruction (**WMDs**) are weapons that are capable of inflicting severe, mass destruction. WMDs are commonly defined as chemical and biological weapons, and radiological and nuclear weapons (**CBRN**).

The traditional view was that terrorist groups employed violence to attract attention and supporters and to spread fear. The use of violence was thought to be discriminating and precise, focusing on targets whose destruction reinforced the terrorist groups' political aims. The IRA—with some tragic exceptions—targeted

The Organization of Terrorism: al Qaeda

The need of terrorist organizations for money can be appreciated by looking at the original organizational structure of al Qaeda. Al Qaeda once possessed one of the most sophisticated terrorist organizations, which has since been significantly degraded and today exists largely on paper. At the top of the structure sat the emir-general—this position was formerly held by Osama bin Laden. The next most powerful entity was the consultative committee, composed of individuals with a significant amount of experience in combat and administration. Individuals were recruited to the consultative committee based on family, friendship, and the desire to represent various countries. Immediately below this counsel were four operational committees: military; finance and business management; Islamic study; and publicity.

The military wing was responsible for recruiting, supervising military operations, obtaining weapons, and coordinating contacts with terrorist cells. Training at isolated camps proved important for building morale among the al Qaeda fighters and for transmitting military skills and theological knowledge. Individuals were invited to join al Qaeda based on their commitment to the jihadist cause and were required to swear allegiance to Bin Laden.

The O55 was al Qaeda's guerilla warfare branch, which at one time had close to 2,000 members. The brigade was based on regional units, although soldiers were recruited for special missions. Finances for al Qaeda were handled by a committee of accountants and bankers. The committee raised and distributed money to regional entities and invested in and ran businesses—ranging from agriculture to the selling of bicycles.

The strength of al Qaeda was partly based on the fact that below the top levels, the organization was based on autonomous cells in which only one or two individuals therein would know the identity of the cell's leader. As a result, finding one cell would not lead to the detection of other cells.

At the height of al Qaeda's global presence it was allegedly active in more than 70 countries. These groups were organized based on "families"— for example, the North African "family" (Algerians, Egyptians, Tunisians, Moroccans, Libyans) or the Southeast Asian "family" (Malaysians, Indonesians). Each "family" was headed by a regional leader. Occasionally, a fighter would be assigned to assist another regional "family" with an operation. Al Qaeda fighters were also sent to affiliated terrorist groups to help create affiliates across the globe.

The highest duty of an al Qaeda fighter was martyrdom or sacrifice for Allah. Rohan Gunaratna argues that before 9/11, al Qaeda was a utopian organization that sought to create a new order in society that conformed to Islamic principles; after 9/11, al Qaeda was transformed into an apocalyptic group that was devoted to mass destruction—without regard for whether an attack advances political goals (Gunaratna, 2002).

British occupying forces, Protestant police, and British politicians to communicate that their cause was directed against the British government rather than the British people. The thinking was that the use of WMDs would kill too many people or lead to an intense reaction against terrorists, and therefore would impede the terrorists' ability to attract public support for their cause and weaken their ability to present themselves as a legitimate force in negotiating with an opposition government. In other words, the belief was that terrorists operated on the "principle of minimum force" and that there was too little to gain and too much to lose by relying on CBRN. In this frequently cited comment, Brian Jenkins states that "terrorists want a lot of people watching and a lot of people listening and not a lot of people dead" (Hoffman, 2006, pp. 269–270).

Experts have considered terrorist groups as content to rely on weapons such as high-powered firearms and the occasional bomb, both of which have proven reliable in the past. Hoffman reports that the Rand database on terrorist incidents indicates that between 1968 and 1998, only around 60 attacks involved an attempt to rely on CBRN (Hoffman, 2006).

Richard Jackson and his colleagues note that a rogue state is unlikely to provide WMDs to a terrorist organization and thus risk retaliation. They also claim that the impact of a WMD attack is greatly exaggerated and point to the fact that various societies have been the target of devastating attacks without suffering mass disruption (Jackson et al., 2011).

A number of analysts challenge the conventional wisdom and argue that a "new generation of terrorists" has adopted a more lethal approach. They argue that there is less centralized restraint on terrorist cells, which determine their own tactics and weaponry. There is a proliferation of splinter terrorist organizations that lack well-defined goals and, in some instances, have adopted an apocalyptic philosophy of mass destruction; these groups would be eager to embrace CBRN.

CHEMICAL WEAPONS

Chemical agents include various poisons. There are several types of **chemical agents** that may be weaponized by terrorists: nerve agents, blood agents, choking agents, and blistering agents.

Nerve agents. Compounds like sarin, tabun, and soman enter the body through food, the air, or direct contact with the skin. These agents result in convulsions and affect the nervous system.

Blood and choking agents. Compounds like chlorine, phosgene, and cyanide enter the body though the air or skin contact. They lead to the accumulation of fluid in the lungs and cause vital bodily functions to shut down.

Blistering agents. A compound such as mustard gas enters the body though the skin or the air and causes burns, choking, and lung impairment.

A number of toxic chemical agents are employed for medical purposes (as well as for insecticides and cleaning agents) and are both relatively inexpensive and relatively easy to obtain and do not require sophisticated training. Chemical agents do have drawbacks. They are generally dangerous to handle, and a significant amount of agent is required to pose an effective threat. Chemical weapons require a delivery system that can effectively distribute the mixture. Explosive bombs risk incinerating the chemicals and once released, chemicals can be neutralized by rain, wind, and water. As a result, these weapons are most effective in a confined space. Some chemicals, like cyanide, are employed for assassinations of individuals rather than in mass attacks.

Nerve agents are the most lethal of the chemical agents and were used by Saddam Hussein against Iraqi Kurds in Halabja in 1988 and in his war against Iran in the 1980s. There have been various reports that terrorist groups possess chemical weapons. In August 1998 President Clinton ordered a missile attack on the al-Shifa pharmaceutical factory in Khartoum, Sudan, under what appears to have been the mistaken belief that the factory was manufacturing chemical weapons for use by al Qaeda. There were a series of reports that al Qaeda had established laboratories in Pakistan to manufacture chemical weapons, and captured documents indicate that Bin Laden had acquired chemical weapons. Apprehended al Qaeda operatives claimed to have seen the chemicals used in experiments on dogs. However, these reports were never corroborated (Richardson, 2006). A somewhat obscure American White nationalist terrorist group, the Covenant, the Sword and the Arm of the Lord, was found to possess significant supplies of potassium cyanide, which the group intended to use to poison water supplies (Martin, 2016).

Another use of a chemical weapon was a chlorine gas attack by the Tamil insurgents (LFTE) on a Sri Lankan military base in 1990.

In April 2017 (and again in 2018), the United States launched a missile attack on Syria in retaliation for Syria's use of chemical weapons to attack civilians.

In March 2018, a Russian initiated a nerve agent attack in Great Britain against a double agent and his daughter. A second attack resulted in the death of an ordinary British citizen. These were the first chemical weapons attacks in Europe since World War II.

BIOLOGICAL AGENTS

Biological agents are sometimes referred to as the poor man's nuclear bomb. These weapons are inexpensive to manufacture and are capable of inflicting significant harm to a large population. Botulinum, if enough were used, could wipe out a population in a 100-square-kilometer area (Combs 2013: 347–348).

There is evidence that al Qaeda had launched a biological warfare program to develop various toxins.

Jonathan White (2017) writes that there are four types of biological agents: natural toxins (these agents occur without human modification), viruses, bacteria, and plagues. He writes that the most threatening of these agents are smallpox, anthrax, plague, botulism, tularemia, hemorrhagic fever, and the Ebola virus.

The impact of biological agents is illustrated by tularemia an infectious organism developed by the United States as a weapon in the late 1950s. If sprayed in an aerosol cloud, within 3 or 5 days, those affected experience fever, chills, headaches, and inflammation and hemorrhaging—and even death. A number of countries have tried to weaponize smallpox. The disease is virulently infectious and would cause pain and disfigurement to about 30% of those affected. Viral hemorrhagic fevers (VHF) such as Ebola and Marburg can cause fever, fatigue, dizziness, and loss of strength. As the disease progresses, victims suffer internal bleeding, the collapse of internal organs and of the nervous system, seizures, and coma.

A weapons-grade anthrax strain can be produced in a laboratory. A cloud of anthrax spores ingested by a population would release deadly toxins into individuals' bodies and result in the death of 80% of those inhaling the spores within 1 or 2 days. Anthrax, however, is best delivered in a closed space to limit the impact of the weather.

Between 30 and 40 countries possess the capacity to manufacture biological weapons—most of whom are able to take advantage of their domestic pharmaceutical industry to produce these weapons.

The United States has suffered two well-documented biological attacks since 1980. In 1984 followers of Rajneesh, a public speaker and founder of a mystic cult, moved to a small town in Oregon and established a commune. Rajneesh's followers spread *Salmonella* at local salad bars in an effort to create mass sickness and immobilize local residents to prevent them from voting in a local election. More than 750 people were affected and 45 were hospitalized in the attack, which was planned as a precursor to the poisoning of the town's water supply and to the electoral takeover of the town by Rajneesh's followers.

Following 9/11, anthrax spores were mysteriously sent through the mail to two prominent news anchors and to a tabloid newspaper in Florida. In October 2011 a package of anthrax was delivered to the office of former Senate majority leader Thomas Daschle and to the office of senator Patrick Leahy, resulting in the closure of the Senate office building 2 two months. Instances of anthrax being sent through the mail also were recorded in Washington, D.C., and in four East Coast states; by December 2011, anthrax attacks had killed five people and infected 20 others. The Washington, D.C., post office that handled the letters sent to Capitol Hill was closed for roughly 2 years for decontamination. Thousands of false reports of anthrax sent through the mail surfaced, and as a precaution people across the country began to take an antibiotic to counter the anthrax infection. An extensive FBI investigation of hundreds of potential suspects eventually led to a focus on Dr. Bruce Ivins. Ivins had worked on the army's anthrax vaccination program and committed suicide before being formally charged. He allegedly wanted to create a panic to put pressure on the military to direct increased funding to the anthrax program.

Biological weapons are not only employed against people. Roughly 13 countries have developed biological agents that are intended to decimate a country's livestock and agriculture.

NUCLEAR TERRORISM

A week after the 9/11 attacks, the Bush administration was informed that al Qaeda possessed a 10-kiloton suitcase bomb they had stolen from the Russians. This was the so-called "problem from hell" feared by counterterrorism experts. The threat had an air of credibility because Bin Laden was known to have been attempting to purchase key ingredients for manufacturing a nuclear weapon since 1993. Vice President Cheney was ordered to a secure location where he lived for several weeks to ensure that the government would continue to function in the event of a crippling attack. Nuclear emergency support teams (NESTs) were deployed to New York to search for the bomb, which experts suspected was stored in a suitcase. In the end this bomb scare was a false alarm (Allison, 2004).

The incident nonetheless reminded decision makers of the potential devastation that would result from **nuclear terrorism**. A nuclear attack would decimate the city that was targeted. Harvard professor Graham Allison (2004) wrote that a nuclear bomb ignited in Times Square in New York City would kill half a million people within a half-mile radius. Hundreds of thousands of others would be killed from collapsing buildings, fire, and nuclear fallout within the next several hours. The electromagnetic pulse would shut down all communication and the medical system would be overwhelmed and paralyzed by the sheer number of victims. First responders would themselves be placed at risk and would be clearing debris and bodies and fighting fires for months.

Nine months following the false nuclear alarm, al Qaeda's press spokesperson, Suleiman Abu Gheith, claimed that al Qaeda possessed the right to kill 4 million Americans and to injure thousands more in retribution for the harm inflicted by the United States on the Islamic world. Radical Islamic clerics proclaimed that it was consistent with Islamic teachings to accomplish this task through the use of a nuclear weapon, and Osama bin Laden announced in 1998 that it was a religious duty for Muslims to obtain these weapons. In August 2001 al Qaeda contacted two Pakistani scientists responsible for that country's nuclear program. The scientists allegedly spent 3 days conferring with al Qaeda leaders and provided them with designs for a nuclear weapon. Pakistan responded by arresting the scientists and withdrawing their passports (Allison, 2004).

There were persistent rumors that al Qaeda possessed nuclear weapons. The fear of a nuclear attack was fueled by the January 2002 discovery of designs for a "superbomb" in an abandoned al Qaeda guest house in Afghanistan (Richardson, 2006). In 2003 an influential Saudi cleric issued a **fatwa** (religious pronouncement) that the possession and use of nuclear weapons was authorized by Islamic law, and members of a Saudi Arabian al Qaeda cell were arrested for attempting to purchase a nuclear device. There were several well-documented attempts by Japanese and Chechen terrorists to obtain nuclear weapons (Bunn, 2014).

There are two basic methods of constructing a nuclear bomb. The "gun design" involves forcing two pieces of highly enriched uranium (HEU) to collide at a high speed, causing a nuclear explosion. A plutonium "implosion-type" bomb requires compressing the material to cause a nuclear explosion. This style of bomb requires a greater degree of sophistication.

Various barriers create challenges for terrorists to manufacture a nuclear bomb. The first barrier is the difficulty of obtaining the required amount of fissile material—either uranimum-235 or plutonium-239. *Fissile material* is purified uranium or plutonium, both of which are capable of producing a self-sustaining chain reaction that causes a nuclear explosion. It is incredibly expensive and time consuming to produce weapons-grade material and although uranium-based fissile material is easier to produce, large amounts of uranium are required.

Uranium occurs in nature, and when first mined the ore contains a small percentage of uranium. In order to create a chain reaction, the uranium must be enriched. Uranium enriched to 20% is known as *HEU*. The United States uses HEU at 90% for its nuclear weapons. Plutonium must be manufactured in a complex process and also poses challenges (Capron & Mizrahi, 2016).

The next challenge is to construct the bomb. The estimate is that even with the required equipment and expertise, this may require as long as a decade. This length of time might be significantly reduced if terrorists are able to obtain weapons-grade material. In the first 3 years following the breakup of the Soviet Union, the German government reported more than 60 instances of attempted sale of nuclear material (Allison, 2004). In 2011 there was a documented effort by smugglers to sell a significant amount of HEU for $31 million to an interested buyer, which Bunn (2014) writes is only one of 20 documented cases of the theft and smuggling of the amount of plutonium or uranium required to build a bomb.

Terrorist groups have attempted to expedite the manufacture of a bomb by recruiting nuclear scientists. Of course, the possibility cannot be dismissed that terrorists may purchase a bomb from a rogue state like North Korea, that terrorists may raid a poorly protected nuclear facility in a country like Pakistan, or that terrorists may overthrow a regime and come to power along with jihadist members of the military. Another potential source of nuclear material is the HEU-operated research nuclear reactors around the world. In 2007 two teams of armed men successfully attacked and entered a South African nuclear power plant in an unsuccessful attempt to obtain nuclear material.

Terrorists can easily deliver a bomb in a suitcase or evade sensors at a seaport and smuggle the material into the United States. This allows them to manufacture a dirty bomb (see below). They are unlikely to have the capacity to mount a bomb on a delivery device such as a missile.

In 2008 a presidential commission found that "it was more likely than not" that a biological or nuclear attack would be initiated in the next 5 years. This alarmist conclusion is disputed by most analysts (Commission on the Prevention of WMD Proliferation and Terrorism, 2008). Bunn (2014) estimates an almost 30% chance of a nuclear attack in the next 10 years.

Keep in mind that although the possibility of a nuclear attack is likely still confined to the realm of science fiction, the world is awash in nuclear material that is not always well secured. In the United States alone, there are 10 sites housing nuclear material. More ominously, North Korea possesses nuclear material and along with Iran possesses the expertise to manufacture and to deliver a nuclear weapon. There also is the constant threat that a jihadist group could seize a nuclear weapon or nuclear material in Pakistan. It is always possible that a rogue nuclear state may enlist a terrorist organization to carry out a nuclear attack. On the other hand, the state would risk retaliation from the United States.

So-called realists believe that a nuclear attack would not be aligned with the goals of most terrorist groups, which for the most part do not include mass destruction, and that terrorist groups are more comfortable relying on weapons with which they are familiar (Martin, 2016).

The most realistic scenario involving nuclear material is the use of a so-called dirty bomb.

RADIOLOGICAL BOMB

Once they obtain radiological material, terrorists can merely wrap a small amount in a so-called **dirty bomb** (a radiological dispersal device), which can be ignited using a triggering device like TNT. Finely ground particles are spread by the explosion and infect a wide area. A dirty bomb requires less material than a nuclear bomb and is readily available in medical devices or in HEU-powered nuclear plants. The radiological materials that might be included in a dirty bomb include uranium, plutonium, cobalt-60, strontium, and cesium-137. Creating a dirty bomb also does not involve the complications associated with constructing nuclear devices. A radiological bomb can potentially contaminate an extensive area, which can result in radiological burns and poisoning for individuals within the radius of the attack, may cause cancer once inside the lung, and can create large-scale psychological panic. Another approach would be to attack a nuclear power plant with a bomb, plane, or armed assault. The meltdown of the core reactor would spread radiation and result in the contamination of the surrounding area.

The prestigious American Federation of Scientists estimated that if a bomb made with cobalt exploded in the heart of New York City, it would require the evacuation of the entire borough of Manhattan. One in every 100 persons would develop cancer. Before allowing citizens back into the area, there would have to be extensive decontamination of buildings and removal of vegetation and topsoil. It is possible that massive demolition of building and relocation of portions of the population would be required (Allison, 2004).

Following 9/11, there were a series of reports indicating that al Qaeda had obtained medical isotopes (these isotopes are used in body scans) or material from nuclear power plants that could be used to make a dirty bomb. In May 2002 former gang member José Padilla was arrested as he entered the United States. He allegedly planned to carry out an al Qaeda plot to ignite a dirty bomb. He was later charged and convicted of planning to use natural gas at two apartments to blow up the buildings (Richardson, 2006).

FIGURE 3.3 Criminal Wanted Poster for Members of Aum Shinrikyo

The Japanese sect **Aum Shinrikyo** (which translates to *Supreme Truth*) was founded in 1987 by Shoko Asahara, a half-blind owner of a chain of yoga studios and self-anointed prophet. Asahara predicted that the world would come to an end in a nuclear disaster in the late 1990s, precipitated by America and its allies. Only Asahara's followers would survive this catastrophe and his adherents were rumored to be required to drink his blood to demonstrate their belief in him and in his prophecy. Asahara preached that he was chosen to be leader of the survivors of the forthcoming catastrophe. This disaster, however, might be prevented if he was able to assume the role of "King of Japan."

The evolution and dynamics of Aum are recorded in exacting detail by psychologist Robert Lifton in his classic book, *Destroying the World to Save It* (1999).

Asahara, who proclaimed that he was the reincarnation of Jesus Christ and Buddha and had achieved "supreme truth" and was the "savior of the century," had previously been criminally convicted for selling unregulated medicine. Around the time of his conviction, he experienced a revelation while meditating that he had been chosen to lead a divine army to establish the "Kingdom of Shambhala."

Asahara continued to descend into paranoia and by the mid-1990s his list of enemies had expanded to include freemasons, Jews, bankers, and the Japanese government—which he held responsible for the Kobe earthquake in 1995.

Asahara then announced that a nuclear catastrophe could be averted if his adherents armed themselves with WMDs. Aum also contracted with Russian elite forces to train members of Aum in clandestine warfare tactics and to develop skills in martial arts, small arms, and advanced weaponry. Fearful that the authorities were about to seize the cult's cache of sarin nerve gas and weapons, Asahara ordered cult members to attack the population within cities. The cult's goal had previously been to seize power rather than to engage in mass murder of the Japanese population.

On March 20, 1995, adherents of Aum released sarin gas in subway cars during the morning rush hour, killing 12 people and injuring as many as 5,500. The 10 cult members in the assault team were divided into five teams, dressed in business suits and carrying umbrellas, and concealed bags of sarin gas in copies of the morning newspaper. As five trains left the station, they punctured the bags with their umbrellas, fled the trains, and immediately swallowed antidotes to prevent complications. The trains were scheduled to converge on Kasumigaseki central station, the heart of Japanese government, within 4 minutes of one another. Individuals in the trains began sweating, coughing, suffering from nosebleeds, and vomiting and had difficulty breathing. The trains continued on their routes and more individuals fell victim as they entered the trains. The failure of the Aum chemists to concoct a stronger odorless dose fortunately limited the human toll from the attack.

(continues on next page)

(continued from previous page)

A search of Aum's facilities resulted in the seizure of enough sarin to kill more than 4 million people. There also was a large cache of psychedelic drugs, which were used in conjunction with electric shock to discipline and to brainwash members of the sect.

Aum was in a position to carry out a WMD attack, which is not shared by most terrorist groups. The cult had almost 50,000 members in Japan and in six other countries, an estimated $1 billion in assets, and had hired scientific graduates of leading universities. The Aum scientists and engineers working at the group's 12-acre weapons laboratory experimented with producing chemical weapons like VX, taban, soman, and cyanide, along with biological weapons involving anthrax, botulism, and Q fever. They worked for 5 years to weaponize sarin. Aum also had attempted to obtain samples of Ebola virus in Africa. In June 1993 the group launched an experimental sarin gas attack on an apartment building in the city of Matsumoto, which injured three judges presiding over Asahara's trial for land fraud. Seven people were killed and more than 260 were injured. The group carried out a total of 12 sarin attacks, and only the subway and apartment attacks claimed a significant number of victims.

Prior to the subway attacks, Aum had sprayed sarin and botulism from vans in downtown Tokyo and had tried to distribute sarin packed in briefcases with vents powered by electric fans. On several occasions, Aum unsuccessfully attempted to spread anthrax spores throughout Tokyo. They also had plans to attack U.S. naval bases in Japan with botulism.

Even more terrifying were documents that established that Aum had purchased 500,000 acres of land in Australia to mine uranium and had purchased equipment to refine the material and to construct a nuclear bomb. The documents also indicated that the group had recruited Russian scientists and had been exploring purchasing a nuclear warhead.

In September 1995 Aum was disbanded by the Japanese government. A court subsequently sentenced Asahara to death. He and six other prominent Aum members were executed in July 2018. Based on Japan's experience with Aum, one might question whether the nuclear glass is half-full or half-empty. On the one hand, the group failed to manufacture a WMD arsenal. But on the other hand, a threshold had been crossed. Aum demonstrated that nonstate groups would be willing to employ WMDs, and that these weapons were theoretically within reach of a well-funded and sophisticated organization. ☐

SUICIDE BOMBING

Suicide bombing is a terrorist attack in which attacker intends to inflict damage to the target and take his or her own life in the process. This commonly involves the use of an explosive; although as illustrated by 9/11 it may involve other tactics, such as ramming an airplane or vehicle into a target or a terrorist carrying out an attack and then killing him- or herself. A suicide bombing may involve an explosive that is remotely ignited by an individual other than the attacker. It is distinguishable from a high-risk attack in which an attacker may or may not survive and from a no-escape attack in which the attacker is fairly certain to die. In both of these instances, the death of the attacker is neither required nor self-inflicted (Lewis, 2012).

There is a significant amount of literature on the subject of suicide bombing. Since 9/11, more than 17 separate suicide-bombing campaigns have been launched in more than 24 countries across the globe. These campaigns have resulted in more casualties than any other form of terrorism (Pape, 2005).

Suicide bombing is not limited to a specific religion, ideology, or country. On July 7, 2005, Mohammad Sidique Khan (aged 30) and Shehzad Tanweer (aged 22), along with two friends, boarded four different London subway trains and detonated bombs, killing themselves along with 56 others and injuring 700. Al Qaeda claimed responsibility for the attacks. Khan was born in Leeds to parents born in Pakistan. He was married with a 14-month-old child and worked as a teacher and mentor for elementary-school children with disabilities. Tanweer was a successful athlete who was studying sports science. His father was a prosperous businessperson and the family was economically comfortable (Richardson, 2006).

On May 23, 2017, Salman Abedi (aged 22) detonated a bomb in Manchester, England as a concert by American singer Ariana Grade was ending, causing a panic in which 22 young people were killed and more than 60 others were injured in attack celebrated by ISIS. Abedi's backpack was loaded with triacetone triperoxide (TATP)—the same explosive used in the attacks in London and Paris in 2005 and in Brussels in 2016. Abedi was an English citizen of Libyan descent who was born in Manchester. His family had fled Libya and later returned after the country's authoritarian leader Muammar Gaddafi was overthrown in 2011. Abedi had little knowledge of religion or global affairs and was described as easily misled; apparently, he had been trained for the attack while visiting Libya. Members of the Libyan community had reported Abedi's radical sympathies to British authorities who determined after the bombing that he had received training abroad.

The origin of suicide bombing is traced to the **Assassins**, members of a **Shia** Muslim sect known as the Ismailis. They were based in the mountains of what is now Iran between 1100 to 1300 CE. They viewed the ruling **Sunni** Muslim Turks as heretics and believed that they possessed a religious duty to kill the Turks. They targeted high-ranking political officials who were surrounded by armed bodyguards in most instances. The assassins were known for attacking their victims with daggers at close range. The assassins demonstrated little concern for their own safety and at times passively submitted to a retaliatory blow or to arrest and execution. Some commentators note that the assassins were not the clear forerunners of the modern-day suicide attacker because they did not take their own life as a means of committing an act of terror (Rapoport, 1990).

There were instances in the early 20th century of Russian terrorists igniting bombs knowing that they might die in the explosion. The Party of Socialist Revolutionaries (PSR) carried out most of the dynamite attacks in Russia between 1902 and 1906. The PSR had a group of bombers, the Terrorist Brigade, that carried out the bombings, risking their own deaths in the explosion. An often-cited example is Ivan Kalyayev who in February 1904 ran full tilt to within several feet of the carriage of Grand Duke Sergei Alexandrovich, governor-general of Moscow, before igniting the bomb that killed the grand duke. Kalyayev survived, although he wrote from prison expressing a willingness to die as a martyr to advance the revolutionary cause (Lewis, 2012).

The most infamous use of suicide bombers were the *Tokubetsu Kougekitai* ("special units") commonly referred to as *Kamikaze*. These pilots were ordered by the emperor of Japan to fly their aircraft into the target, and they generally accepted that their death was required to carry out these aerial attacks. As Japan faced defeat in World War II, the Japanese escalated these Kamikaze attacks. This resulted in the death of more than 3,000 pilots. The attacks were designed to limit the capacity of the U.S. Navy to operate in the Pacific and to intimidate U.S. forces. Although ultimately unsuccessful in stopping the American advance, the attacks damaged or sank nearly 400 U.S. vessels (Pape, 2005). These martyrdom attacks differ from contemporary suicide attacks because they involved combatants attacking other combatants during organized military combat.

There is disagreement as to when the first suicide bombing was carried out by modern terrorists. High-profile suicide bombing appears to have been introduced in the Middle East when a bomber drove an explosive-laden truck into the Iraqi embassy in Beirut, Lebanon, killing 61 people. The driver was from al-Dawa, a Shia group opposed to Saddam Hussein's Baathist regime.

The Israel Defense Forces (IDF) entered Lebanon in August 1982 to drive the Palestine Liberation Organization (PLO) out of the country. Hezbollah (an Iran-affiliated Lebanese organization of Shia Muslims) asserted its commitment to jihad against Israelis when 17-year-old Ahmad Qassir drove a Mercedes packed with 500 kilograms of explosives into the IDF headquarters in Tyre, killing 75 Israelis.

As Lebanon degenerated into a three-sided civil war between Sunni and Shia Muslims and Israel's Christian allies, the United States was increasingly viewed as aligned with Israel. Hezbollah's 1982 suicide attack was followed by an attack on the U.S. embassy in Beirut by a Shia terrorist organization using a pickup truck loaded with 400 pounds of explosives, killing 63 and injuring more than 100. The United States suffered yet another tragic blow 6 months later when a truck rammed into a Marine operations center and detonated the equivalent of 6 tons of TNT, killing 241 marines and federal agents. Twenty seconds later, a second vehicle rammed into the headquarters of French military forces, killing 58 elite paratroopers. One month later, yet another truck loaded with half a ton of explosives penetrated an Israeli military base, killing 60 individuals. In December 1983 the wave of suicide bombings came to an end with an attack on the U.S. embassy in Kuwait, killing six individuals and injuring as many as 90 others.

The use of suicide bombing spread to various countries across the globe. Why was suicide bombing such an attractive tactic? There are various reasons that have been suggested in what Robert Pape (2005) terms the "strategic logic of terrorism." The fundamental point is that suicide terrorism offers certain advantages that make it a rational policy.

The core purpose of suicide terrorism is the coercive use of violence to force a government to change its policy. Suicide terrorism, for the most part, involves a series of attacks and is not an isolated event. In general, suicide attacks are much more lethal than other types of assaults because an individual who is willing to die is better able to conceal a weapon, penetrate defenses, and position him- or herself near the target. Suicide attacks are a relatively inexpensive method of attack and are especially effective because individuals who are willing to die are clearly committed to their cause. Historically, this type of attack is particularly terrifying because security forces and the general population develop a state of anxiety about where the next attack is likely to occur. An additional advantage of suicide terrorism is that the attacker is dead and cannot be captured and interrogated.

Mia Bloom suggests that terrorist groups resort to suicide bombing to "outbid" one another. Groups compete for attention, funds, and notoriety; the use of suicide bombing is a method that groups can use to distinguish themselves from other organizations and to project strength (Bloom, 2007).

Robert Pape argues that suicide is used by a nationalist or religious group resisting occupation of their country by a democracy. A democracy is vulnerable to suicide attacks because public opinion will respond negatively to large-scale casualties and demand withdrawal from the country. Finally, suicide bombing is encouraged when there is a difference in religion between the "occupiers" and "occupied" individuals. However interesting and helpful, Pape's theory cannot easily explain many attacks. Is Saudi Arabia attacked because the regime is perceived as a puppet of the United States, viewed as a corrupt and repressive regime, or because of the regime's antagonism toward Iran and Shia Islam (Pape, 2005; Pape & Feldman, 2010)?

Jeffrey William Lewis argues that suicide bombing may be explained in terms of technological innovation. The combination of advancement in explosive devices, the development of suicide vests, the possibility of remote detonation through cell phones, and the capability of making videos of attacks have made suicide bombing an attractive tactic for terrorist groups. The availability of this inexpensive technology across the globe has helped to spread the use of suicide bombing. Terrorist groups cannot compete with the weaponry of nation-states and suicide bombing provides a means for them to attack effectively (Lewis, 2012).

Bloom views the use of suicide terrorism as the result of a number of factors. An important consideration is the acceptance of this tactic by the local population and whether this tactic will demonstrate strength and attract money, recruits, and local support. Suicide terrorism is more likely to be endorsed when used again noncivilians who are from a different ethnic, national, or religious group. There is also the consideration as to whether the terrorists are experiencing success with existing tactics and whether suicide terrorism will prove successful in overcoming existing counterterrorism measures. An overriding consideration is whether the terrorist group's ideology supports suicide bombing.

There are various descriptions of how an organization creates the conditions for individuals' willingness to sacrifice themselves in committing an act of terrorism. Ariel Merari (1993) integrates various explanations in his four-pronged approach.

Cultural factors. There must be a prevailing ethic that supports self-sacrifice. This may be a system of religious belief or a history that celebrates self-sacrifice.

Indoctrination. A process that prepares individuals to undertake suicidal terrorism.

Situational factors. The terrorist group possesses limited alternative modes of attacking which makes suicide attacks a logical and attractive alternative.

Personality factors. An individual must have psychological characteristics that make them receptive to suicide terrorism.

Pape and Feldman (2010) take a somewhat different approach. They argue that suicide bombing results from the gradual radicalization of a group of like-minded individuals, whose agreement to act is sparked by a specific triggering event. The London subway bombers spent time together sharing their anger and frustration, became increasingly isolated from outside influences, and were inspired to act after the bombing of subway trains in Madrid that led to a change in the Spanish government and to the withdrawal of Spanish troops from Afghanistan. The London bombers were secular Muslims, reasonably well educated and from economically advantaged families and, according to Pape and Feldman (2010), were motivated by opposition to Western occupation of Afghanistan rather than by religion.

Keep in mind that in recent years there has been a dramatic increase in suicide bombing by women. Bloom suggests that women are motivated by personal reasons to a greater extent than men, such as a desire to avenge personal mistreatment or the death of a loved one. She also notes—with some degree of unhappiness—that some women are attracted to suicide terrorism in a misguided attempt to challenge women's second-class status in a society (Bloom, 2007). In a shocking development, a family of six individuals all detonated themselves in separate attacks on three Christian churches in Indonesia, killing 43 persons. Puji Kuswati, with her two daughters, ages 9 and 12, were denied entry to a church. Kuswati then detonated a bomb (Cochrane, 2018).

Americans became familiar with suicide terrorism on 9/11 when 19 hijackers took control of U.S. airplanes, fully expecting to die as religious martyrs. Suicide bombings in Sri Lanka and in Palestine illustrate the use of suicide bombing as a method of terrorism.

SRI LANKA AND PALESTINE

The Liberation Tigers of Tamil Eelam (LTTE) was formed in the 1976 after the majority Sinhalese Buddhist population endorsed discrimination against the Tamil Hindu population in the 1972 constitution of the renamed state of Sri Lanka (formerly Ceylon). Velupillai Prabhakaran, unhappy with the lack of militancy of Tamil United Liberation Front (TULF), created the LTTE as an efficient fighting force dedicated to creating a Tamil homeland—Tamil Eelam. The LTTE was able to recruit young people from rural families that had suffered at the hand of the Sinhalese armed forces. In 1983 Prabhakaran, in an effort to distinguish the LTTE from other militant organizations, announced that every LTTE fighter would be required to wear a glass capsule around his or her neck containing potassium cyanide, which was to be swallowed in the event of capture (Bloom, 2007).

Prabhakaran was inspired by the 1983 Hezbollah suicide attack on U.S. Marine barracks, realizing that suicide bombings could elevate the domestic and inter-national profile of the LTTE. He is credited with creating a culture among the Tamil that supported suicide bombing. These attacks—rather than being described as suicide—were termed as a "gift of the self," a "self-gift," or as an "oath to the nation" that were freely given as a contribution to creation of a Tamil homeland.

Special Tamil suicide units, the "Black Tigers" and "Sea Tigers," were created, which promoted a belief among members of these units in their "determination and invincibility." These fighters were praised and celebrated for their willingness to make the supreme sacrifice of their lives. Suicide squadrons were strictly dis-ciplined and regimented in every aspect of their lives, including sexual relations and marriage.

Female suicide bombers were termed "Birds of Freedom" because of their valued ability to penetrate targets without suspicion and apprehension.

The LTTE promoted an image as a liberation group and avoided attacking civilians. Suicide attacks were used in rural areas against the Sri Lankan armed forces; in urban areas, attacks were aimed at critical infrastructure and against prominent Sinhalese figures and government leaders. The group intentionally avoided claiming credit for attacks in which civilians were injured or killed.

In 2009 the LTTE was defeated by Sri Lankan forces and Prabhakaran was killed in battle.

Max Abrams (2014) argues that suicide terrorism is ineffective in accomplishing a terrorist organization's goals. He disputes Robert Pape's contention that groups that use suicide bombing are successful in achieving their goals 50% of the time. Abrams also asserts that suicide bombing against civilians is ineffective and in fact is counterproductive. The terrorist organizations that have experienced success, according to Abrams, have limited their attacks to military targets. He explains that suicide terrorism against civilians is met with a strengthened resolve by leaders and the populace to resist concessions and negotiation. Abrams supports his conclusion by pointing to the responses to suicide terrorism in Egypt, Indonesia, Jordan, the Philippines, and Russia.

Targeting innocents undermines an organization's credibility and leads Abrams (2014) to conclude that suicide bombing decreases rather than increases a group's probability of success. Keep in mind that Pape argues that suicide bombing can achieve limited goals like American, French, and Israeli withdrawal from Lebanon; although it cannot coerce a state to abandon goals central to its security such as a loss of territory (Abrams, 2014).

Suicide attacks clearly do impact a government. The March 11, 2004, explosions on a commuter train in Madrid killed 191 people and caused the defeat of the Conservative Party and election of the Socialist Party. On the other hand, the small-scale terrorist attacks on the eve of the 2017 presidential election in France did not result in the electorate swinging in favor of the conservative candidate Marine Le Pen as the terrorists likely had hoped. The 9/11 attacks in the United States clearly has transformed the personal freedom enjoyed by Americans.

The Palestinian group Hamas was formed in 1987 and confronted the challenge of establishing itself as a credible alternative to the established Palestine Liberation Organization (PLO). The group was an outgrowth of the first Intifada (uprising) by young people against Israel. Hamas was led by a youthful, university-educated group that attracted popular support in the Gaza Strip based on politics and religion. Hamas called for a popular jihad to establish a Palestinian state that integrated the Gaza Strip and West Bank, along with the existing territory of the Israel.

In September 1993 Yasser Arafat—head of the PLO—and Israeli prime minister Yitzhak Rabin signed a treaty that marked a significant step towards peace. Hamas could not accept the end of the armed conflict, and in reaction to an attack by Israeli Baruch Goldstein on Muslim worshippers at a mosque in Hebron, carried out the first of a series of suicide operations on April 6, 1994. A young Palestinian rammed into a bus and detonated a bomb, killing eight Israelis and injuring 44. The following week, a second suicide attack on a bus killed five Israelis and injured 30. Six months later a 27-year-old Palestinian ignited a bomb on a bus, killing 20 people and injuring 48 persons.

The wave of bombings drew to a close in November 1996 after a total of 39 suicide attacks, which left 171 dead and 1,049 injured. The bombings were stopped after having proven unpopular with the Palestinian population, which harbored hopes for the peace process. A combination of Israeli retaliation and efforts by Arafat to prevent attacks also had taken a significant toll on Hamas (Lewis, 2012).

A second Intifada erupted in September 2000 when Israeli troops, reacting to crowd of rock-throwing Palestinians who were exiting Al-Aqsa Mosque in Jerusalem, shot and killed eight Palestinians. In 2001 a suicide-bombing campaign was launched by Hamas, which culminated in 30 attacks by the end of the year. This was followed by 50 more attacks by various Palestinian groups in 2002. Suicide attacks comprised 0.5% of all Palestinian attacks from 2000 to 2006—although they accounted for 50% of all casualties (Lewis, 2012).

Palestinian suicide bombers were selectively recruited to ensure that they were stable and reliable and would not panic. At times, they were recruited along with friends and typically came from communities that supported suicide bombing. The recruits were exposed to indoctrination throughout the training process. This was intended to reinforce their commitment. This preparation often occurred in small "suicide cells" which promoted a sense of group solidarity and accountability to the group. Prior to the suicide attack, Hamas recorded videos in which the prospective bomber expressed his or her intent to conduct an attack. The main purpose was to create a memorial to the attacker and to make him or her feel obligated to carry out the attack. Following the bomber's death, the family was customarily rewarded with monetary compensation, and they held a celebration with friends and neighbors to honor the bomber's heroism. The images of successful suicide bombers were displayed on murals and calendars which featured a "martyr of the month" (Richardson, 2006).

The process of socializing Islamic attackers into the acceptance of suicide bombing is reinforced by a religious ideology which promises a direct route to the "milk and honey" of Paradise along with 70 of their friends and relatives. Suicide bombers are considered *shaheed batal*, "martyr heroes," whose sacrifice is divinely rewarded and is distinguished from suicide, which is prohibited under

Islamic law. There is also the promise that male martyrs will enjoy the company of multiple virgins (Hoffman, 2006).

In 2018, the Israeli Knesset (parliament) voted to withhold a portion of the tax monies that Israel collects on behalf of the Palestinian Authority. The amount withheld is equivalent to the money that Israel alleges is paid as stipends to the families of suicide bombers and Palestinian prisoners in Israeli jails. The United States and Australia have suspended a portion of the monies they pay to the Palestinian Authority in protest over the stipends paid to Palestinian suicide bombers (Kershner, 2018).

Palestinian martyrs thus achieve revenge, renown, and rewards in Paradise, along with a sense that they have advanced the cause Palestinian independence. The next section provides an overview of the newly developing area of cyberterrorism.

CYBERTERRORISM

Peter Singer and Allan Friedman write that over 31,000 articles have been written on **cyberterrorism**. The FBI defines cyberterrorism as "premeditated, politically motivated attack against information, computer systems, computer programs, and data which results in violence against non-combatant targets by sub-national groups or clandestine agents" (Singer & Friedman, p. 96). This definition focuses on politically motived efforts to affect all aspects of civilian and nonmilitary governmental computer systems, carried out by terrorist groups or groups working on behalf of governments. The requirement that the attack results in "violence" presumably encompasses damage to computer systems that results in harm ranging from loss of data to the malfunctioning of banking systems—and in a worst-case scenario, the crash of an aircraft or release of radiation from a nuclear power plant into a civilian population (Singer & Friedman, 2014).

Several terrorism experts reject the term *cyberterrorism*, because terms like *sabotage* or *property theft* adequately describe the illicit conduct involved (Richardson, 2006). It also is a fact that few, if any, individuals have been killed because of cyberterrorism, and the anticipated consequences of such an attack are far worse than what has thus far occurred. Singer and Friedman (2014) mention two frequently cited instances of cyberterrorism: the attempt by a detainee at Guantánamo to take down the website of the prime minister of Israel, and a series of denial of service (DoS) attacks on five U.S. banking firms by the "Izz ad-Din al-Qassam Cyber Fighters." The authors note that these two examples are better described as a *nuisance* rather than as *terrorism*.

This is not to dismiss the potential consequences of cyberterrorism. In 2011 a team of hackers conducted a simulated attack on a local California computer system, penetrated the network, and potentially could have disrupted the area's infrastructure. The same type of attack could be launched against hydroelectric generators, nuclear power plants, transportation systems, and the electric power grid. An attack on the electric grid would affect almost every aspect of modern life. This may seem alarmist, but the United States, according to every American intelligence agency, already witnessed interference in the presidential election of 2016 by hackers aligned with Russian security services.

USA Today reports that the U.S. national power grid is attacked either physically or online approximately once every 4 days. Between 2011 and 2014, the U.S. Department of Energy received 362 reports from electric utilities of physical or cyberattacks that interrupted power services (Reilly, 2015). A 2012 video from As-Sahab, the media wing of al Qaeda, called for waves of cyberattacks on the U.S. electrical grid. There are numerous reports of al Qaeda conducting online research on a wide variety of crucial aspects of the American infrastructure.

Keep in mind that China, Iran, North Korea, and Russia have all penetrated American governmental and private computer systems—which potentially poses a serious threat to national security.

The Internet also provides a platform for terrorist recruitment and for the transmission of information. Gabriel Weimann documented that by 2006, terrorist websites increased from a few dozen in the 1990s to more than 4,000. Weimann explains that the Internet is an ideal platform for terrorists due to ease of access, the difficulty of limiting and censoring content, and the ability to shape content (Bergin, 2016). Terrorism experts refer to cyberspace as "terrorism university" because of the availability of resources and directions for carrying out terrorist attacks. An example is the *Mujahideen Poisons Handbook* which is a guide to preparing homemade poisons and lethal gases. The *Encyclopedia of Jihad* includes chapters like "How to Kill," "Explosive Devices," and "Assassination with Mines." Boston marathon bomber Dzhokhar Tsarnaev and his brother learned how to construct a pressure-cooker bomb from an al Qaeda online magazine article titled "Make a Bomb in the Kitchen of Your Mom" (Goodman, 2015).

As previously noted, terrorists have hacked Western bank accounts and financial sites to fund attacks. A prime example is the 2002 Bali bombing carried out by the al Qaeda affiliate Jamaah Islamiyah, which killed more than 200 residents and visitors to the idyllic island. Imam Samudra, the leader of the group, penned a manifesto which detailed techniques for hacking and urged his followers to take the "holy war" into cyberspace. A number of other attacks have been partially funded from hacking, including the 2004 Madrid bombing in which 190 people were killed and close to 2,000 were wounded (Goodman, 2015).

Internet hacking also was used to fund and to direct the infamous November 2008 attack on Mumbai, India, in which 10 gunmen killed 166 people. The incident demonstrated how the Internet can be used to coordinate an attack. Gunmen from the Pakistani al Qaeda affiliate Lashkar-e-Taiba (LeT) entered the room of 69-year-old K. R. Ramamoorthy at the luxurious Mahal Palace hotel. The terrorists phoned in Ramamoorthy's name to a command center where an internet search was conducted. The command center reported that their captive was chairperson of one of India's largest banks, ING Vysya, and that he fit the online photo. The terrorists were ordered to kill Ramamoorthy—but he miraculously survived. The command center monitored the radio and Twitter throughout the operation to alert the attackers of counterterrorism steps that were being taken by authorities. There were reports that attackers were checking their cell phones while simultaneously killing hostages (Goodman, 2015).

The Internet also is used by terrorist groups to communicate with adherents within countries and across the globe.

The most prevalent use of the Internet is as a "force multiplier" which is used to recruit individuals and to incite attacks. Anwar al-Awlaki, an American Yemenite cleric who was killed in an American drone strike in 2011, was called the "Bin Laden of the Internet." He was a powerful orator whose lectures continue to radicalize and attract Muslim youth. His online manifesto, "44 Ways to Support Jihad," has been referenced by numerous young recruits as having influenced their thinking. Al-Awlaki was in communication with Nidal Hasan, the Fort Dix shooter, as well as with Umar Farouk Adulmutalib, the so-called underwear bomber, who was arrested in December 2008 for attempting to ignite a bomb as his flight approached Detroit. Faisal Shahzan who was arrested in 2010 for a plot to bomb Times Square, and Roshonara Choudhry who stabbed British cabinet minister Steven Timms both stated that they were inspired by Al-Awlaki.

Terrorists use every conceivable form of social media to recruit to communicate with young people. Peter Bergin found that 40% of the 330 United States–based militants that he studied maintained an online social media profile and/or communicated through encrypted messages (Bergin, 2016). The Somali terrorist group Al-Shabaab experienced significant success in recruiting in Minneapolis, and a large number of European and North American young people have been recruited through the Internet to fight for the Islamic State in Syria.

The Internet performs critical functions for terrorist groups (Hoffman, 2006). They are summarized below.

Propaganda. The Internet is important for recruitment and funding.

Training and education. The Internet provides a mechanism for providing technological skills, ideological justifications for violence, and distributing propaganda.

Planning. The Internet is used to coordinate and to inspire attacks.

3.2 You Decide

FIGURE 3.4 Hunger Strike Mural

Copyright © Keith Ruffles (CC by 3.0) at https://commons.wikimedia.org/wiki/File%3AHunger_Striker_mural_-_panoramio.jpg.

In the early 1970s the United Kingdom implemented a policy of recognizing special category status for imprisoned Irish Republican Army (IRA) members and for arrested fighters loyal to Great Britain. Inmates were permitted to wear their own clothes, were able to associate with one another, and were provided special visiting privileges. This was important to the IRA because it implicitly recognized that the detainees were prisoners of war who had been captured while waging a war to liberate Northern Ireland from British control and to unite the six counties of Northern Ireland with the Republic of Ireland (O'Malley, 1990; McConville, 2003; McConville, 2014).

In 1976 the United Kingdom shifted policy and announced that IRA and Protestant loyalist detainees would be treated as "common criminals" and would be detained in newly constructed prison facilities in 8-by-12-foot cells in the newly named Maze prison. Prisoners convicted before March 1, 1976, would continue to be held in special category status in the adjoining Long Kesh prison.

In September 1980 there were a total of 1,400 prisoners at Maze and Long Kesh; 370 enjoyed special category status evenly divided between the IRA and British Protestant loyalists.

(continues on next page)

(continued from previous page)

The IRA detainees demanded the return of special category status. They refused to wear their prison uniforms and wrapped themselves in their blankets, refused to clean their chamber pots and food trays, and smeared feces on the walls of their cells. The "blanket men" were surrounded in their cells by rotting food, urine, feces, and maggots.

In March 1980 a group of IRA prisoners went on a hunger strike. Prison authorities responded by confining prisoners to their cells, deprived them of visits and "good time credits," and denied them access to the media and to reading and writing materials. When inmates smashed furniture, their cells were stripped bare—leaving only mattresses and blankets.

The most recognizable of the hunger strikers was Bobby Sands who refused food beginning on March 1, 1981, and died 66 days later. Roughly 2 weeks after Sands's funeral, Francis Hughes, Raymond McCreesch, and Patsy O'Hara passed away within a period of 17 days. Six weeks later Joe McDonnell became the fifth hunger striker to die. A total of 10 hunger strikers had died at the time that the strike was called off at the insistence of family members in October 1981.

The strike failed to achieve its primary goals, although it succeeded in inspiring support for the IRA. During the strike, Bobby Sands was elected to Parliament and 100,000 persons lined the streets for his funeral. The strike focused global attention on the Irish nationalist cause although following Sands' death, the hunger strikers increasingly attracted less attention.

There have been periodic hunger strikes at Guantánamo Bay housing alleged Muslim terrorist detainees. At the height of the protest in 2013, as many as 100 inmates were involved. The military has stopped reporting on hunger strikers. Unlike the British, American authorities under the Obama administration force-fed detainees by inserting tubes in various portions of the hunger strikers' anatomy. The policy of force feeding is considered contrary to medical ethics, which respects the right of individuals to refuse medical treatment. The navy decided against disciplinary action against a nurse who refused to force-feed striking detainees. The Trump administration reportedly adopted a policy of refusing to force-feed hunger strikers until they were in danger of death. In April 2017 Palestinians detained in Israel went on a hunger strike over prison conditions, including an end to administrative detention of individuals without trial.

As a prison administrator, would you negotiate with hunger-striking inmates? Should hunger strikers be force-fed? ▢

CHAPTER SUMMARY

Terrorist organizations traditionally have relied on various weapon systems to target "soft" targets that result in as much psychological impact as possible. There tends to be an alignment between a terrorist group's ideology and the target selected. Groups rely on various criminal and conventional methods for funding. The hawala is a traditional form of transmitting funds across borders without actually physically handling the funds.

WMDs present a particularly threatening form of terrorist violence but are not easily manufactured, obtained, or weaponized. WMDs include chemical, biological, and nuclear weapons and nuclear "dirty bombs." Suicide attacks are a particularly powerful mode of terrorist violence which has distinct strategic advantages. Although some analysts reject the notion of cyberterrorism, in recent years there is an increased awareness of the threat posed by cyberterrorism to America's infrastructure. The Internet also provides an effective "force multiplier" in recruiting terrorists and in inspiring attacks.

CHAPTER REVIEW QUESTIONS

1. Discuss why terrorists engage in asymmetrical warfare and the relevance of "hard" and "soft" targets in understanding terrorism.

2. Explain the connection between a terrorist group's ideology and decision where and who to attack. Do you agree with the notion that there is an alignment between a group's ideology and the selection of targets of terrorist violence?

3. List some ways terrorist groups obtain funding.

4. Distinguish between chemical and biological weapons and between nuclear and radiological bombs. What are the advantages and disadvantages of each of these types of WMD?

5. What are the challenges in a terrorist group producing a nuclear weapon? How might a terrorist group obtain a nuclear weapon?

6. Discuss the strategic logic of suicide bombing? What are some differing views on the conditions in which terrorist groups rely on suicide bombing?

7. Why do some commentators dispute the notion of cyberterrorism? Should the term *cyberterrorism* be used?

TERMINOLOGY

assassins	dirty bomb	signature methods
asymmetrical warfare	fatwa	soft targets
Aum Shinrikyo	hard targets	state-sponsored terrorism
biological agents	hawala system	Sunni
chemical agents	money laundering	WMDs
CBRN	nuclear terrorism	
cyberterrorism	Shia	

The Foundations of Modern Terrorism

TEST YOUR KNOWLEDGE

1. List the three religious terrorist groups that established the foundation of modern religious terrorism.
2. Describe the Gunpowder Plot.
3. Understand why Maximilien Robespierre is a significant figure in the history of terrorism.
4. Understand the importance of the Carbonari.
5. Understand the role of anarchists in the historical development of terrorism.
6. List the various groups involved in terrorist violence against the Russian monarchy in the 19th and 20th centuries.
7. Understand the reasons for 19th-century and early 20th-century violence by Irish dissidents aspiring to be independent from Great Britain.
8. List the causes and important events in the Israeli–Palestinian conflict.

INTRODUCTION

Terrorism is not limited to the modern age. The foundations of terrorism can be traced to three early religious sects, the Zealots, Assassins, and Thugs. Religious rivalries between Catholics and Protestants in Europe characterized the next phase of terrorism, exemplified by the religious conflict in England. In 18th-century France, political ideology—rather than religion—became the fundamental division between rivals for power during the French Revolution. The events surrounding the revolution established the beginning of what is termed *modern state-sponsored political terrorism*. Following the revolution organized terrorist groups emerged in Europe. These groups were committed to violent opposition to ruling monarchies, a development which culminated in violent revolution in Russia. The movement for Irish independence introduced the use of terrorism to achieve ethnonationalist territorial independence.

EARLY RELIGIOUS TERRORISM

The Israeli-Palestinian conflict has been at the center of terrorism in the 20th and 21st centuries and involves the various themes that historically have motivated terrorist violence. The **Zealots** (66–73 CE) or *Sicari* were a Jewish cult. Their name originated from the use of daggers similar to the Roman *sicae*. They adhered to the creed of "no master above God" to oppose the Romans in the area variously referred to today as Israel, Judea, and Palestine. The Zealots kidnapped public figures for ransom, committed public assassinations, and spread chaos and unrest. In 66 CE they inspired an open revolt against the Romans; the revolt was quickly subdued. The *Sicari* had already withdrawn to Masada, a mountain fortress, where 1,000 fighters committed suicide rather than surrender to the larger and more powerful Roman forces (Chaliand & Blin, 2016).

The **Assassins** were a Muslim sect in Persia and in Syria. They held a distinctive belief in the required line of succession to the Prophet Muhammad that varied from other groups. They first formed in the 11th century and managed to exist until the late 13th century, when they were subdued by the Mongols. The Assassins operated in secrecy, relied on the dagger, and welcomed death and martyrdom, perpetuating themselves through a series of alliances with dominant regional powers. They are credited with assassinating the Marquis de Montferrat, king of Jerusalem, and in so doing they intimidated the Christian crusaders, who paid tribute to the assassins in order to maintain peaceful relations (Chaliand & Blin, 2016).

The **Thugs** were a Hindu terrorist group that killed wealthy travelers as an act of tribute to Kali, the goddess of death. They believed that the universe could only be kept in equilibrium by engaging in these acts of religiously inspired violence, thus providing the blood required by Kali to create life. The Thugs were known for supporting themselves by infiltrating and attacking groups of travelers, strangling their victims, and dismembering the bodies. The killing was prolonged to amuse Kali. The Thugs were active for roughly 600 years between the 12th and 19th centuries. They indoctrinated their children into their beliefs and practices and only were extinguished by the British in the 1830s. Some scholars estimate that the Thugs killed as many as half a million individuals, making them the most lethal terrorist group in history (Rapoport, 2012; Laqueur 1999).

A number of points emerge from this sketch of three early religious terrorist groups. First, terrorism is a tactic of fear and intimidation that was exploited by small, weak sects confronting more powerful opponents. These groups relied on religion as their organizing principle to maintain group cohesion and to inspire attacks which otherwise might be viewed as immoral. In the next foundational phase of terrorism, religion continued to provide the justification for acts of terrorism.

RELIGIOUS CONFLICT IN EUROPE

The controversy surrounding the Protestant Reformation boiled over in the 16th century. The French Calvinist Huguenots comprised nearly 10% of the population in an overwhelmingly Catholic France. On St. Bartholomew's Day in 1572, Charles IX ordered the killing of prominent Huguenots in Paris, sparking the slaughter of thousands of Huguenots throughout the country (Law, 2016).

Across the channel in England, religious rivalry also raged. Mary I (1516–1558) ruled from July 1553 until her death in 1558. Her imprisonment and execution of Protestants led to her being referred to as "Bloody Mary." The return of the English throne to Protestantism with the ascendancy of Elizabeth I (who ruled from 1558 to 1603) following Mary's death was never fully accepted by the Catholic population. Protestant king James I (1556–1625) was the target of a daring assassination attempt known as the **Gunpowder Plot**. A number of Catholic insurgents smuggled 1,800 pounds of gunpowder into the basement below Westminster Palace. Guy Fawkes planned to ignite the explosives on the opening day of Parliament on November 5, 1605. An informant tipped off authorities to the plot which, if successful, would have killed James and the entire parliament and would have ravaged an area a mile in diameter. The plotters were hanged, drawn, and quartered in the yard of Westminster Palace (Law, 2016).

The English Civil War of 1642 led to a parliamentary army headed by Oliver Cromwell (1599–1658) defeating the forces of Charles I (1600–1649). Charles's assertion of the "divine right of Kings" and claim to unlimited powers, along with his seeming support for Catholicism, alienated a significant percentage of the population. Cromwell and his supporters abolished the monarchy, placed Charles on trial, and executed him as a "tyrant, traitor, and murderer, and public enemy" (Law, 2016, p. 96). Cromwell proved an unpopular leader and found himself involved in a bitter military campaign in Ireland and Scotland. He was succeeded by his son, whose failures in office led to the restoration of the monarchy in England.

The events in England and the English Civil War illustrate that religion remained a dramatic dividing line in society. The conflict in England also was one the first expressions of the belief that monarchs are not above the law and that government should rest on the will of the people rather than on royal succession. These very same principles were behind the French Revolution of 1789.

FIGURE 4.1 Democracy Figure Holding the Heads of Louis XVI and Marie Antoinette

Source: https://commons.wikimedia.org/wiki/File%3AThe_democracy_of_France.png.

THE FRENCH REVOLUTION

The term "terrorism" became part of the public vocabulary with the French Revolution (May 1789–November 1799).

In France under Louis XVI, a small group of his royal brethren along with members of the church hierarchy prospered while an overwhelming percentage of the population were condemned to remain landless peasants and factory workers, nearly all of whom lived on subsistence wages while paying high taxes and being called on to fight in France's European war campaigns. The middle class found themselves frustrated by their limited opportunities and lack of liberty and freedom.

In June 1789 a popular national assembly was declared and less than a month later, a Parisian mob seized the fortress of the Bastille. Peasants burned down mansions and destroyed government offices that housed records of their debts.

In 1792 the monarchy was abolished, and France was declared a republic in which power resided in the populous. Louis XVI was placed on trial; he was found guilty and executed.

An event that proved of significant importance occurred in July 1793 when Charlotte Corday stabbed Jean-Paul Marat to death. Marat was a journalist sympathetic to the Jacobins, a powerful radical faction in the Convention (France's parliament). The Jacobins responded by establishing a centralized revolutionary command under the leadership of **Maximilien Robespierre**. The Convention quickly issued a decree that terrorism was the new legal order of France and 12 days later passed a Law on Suspects that authorized the arrest of the revolutionaries. This broad law was the basis for the killing of 16,000 individuals in a 10-month period beginning in September 1793. In some instances, arrestees were turned over to local groups who summarily carried out executions—with little concern about conducting a trial (Law, 2016).

The Jacobins openly acknowledged that a totalitarian system based upon fear had been established in France. Terror was regarded by Robespierre as a swift and certain form of justice and as a mechanism to cleanse society of the enemies of the people. In June and July 1794, the killing proceeded at a fever pitch resulting in as many as 1,400 individuals being condemned to death. At this point, even Robespierre's supporters began to feel threatened and a group of legislators organized his arrest, trial, and execution (Chaliand & Blin, 2016).

In 1799 Napoleon Bonaparte came to power in France in a military coup. Napoleon deported and executed thousands of supporters of the monarchy and crowned himself as emperor. He then embarked on a 16-year campaign of European conquest, and eventually suffered a series of military setbacks as well as a crushing defeat in Russia at the hands of roving bands of guerillas. The guerilla warfare waged against Napoleon in Spain and in Russia, according to some historians, helped to establish terrorism as a "weapon of the weak" that could be effectively employed against a stronger force (White, 2017, p. 9). In 1815 Napoleon was exiled by the European powers to the small island of St. Helena. At the Congress of Vienna, the French monarchy was restored and legitimacy of monarchies across Europe was strengthened (Miller, 2013).

The French Revolution was famously denounced and dismissed by conservative English political thinker Edmund Burke as the work of "hell hounds called terrorists ... let loose on the people" (Law, 2016, p. 64).

The events of France, however, eroded the legitimacy of monarchies across Europe and unleashed nationalistic and democratic forces throughout Europe.

In the late 18th and early 19th centuries, the struggle was primarily based on a clash of political rather than religious ideologies. The primary dividing line was between individuals supporting (versus individuals opposing) the rule of royal monarchs.

A number of secret societies developed in Europe. They were devoted to democratic rule in which ultimate power was invested in the people. The most important was the **Carbonari**, established in 1807 in Naples, to combat Napoleon in southern Italy and later Ferdinand I who presided over the Kingdom of Naples. The influence of the Carbonari spread throughout Italy and to France, Germany, and Spain, and they were involved in uprisings against the French and Austrians in Italy.

Those initiated into the Carbonari underwent an elaborate ritual and received a crown of thorns to symbolize the desire to pierce the head of a tyrant; they also received a cross to symbolize the crucifixion of a tyrant. They were given a cord to signify the desire to lead the oppressors to the gallows. The Carbonari's weapon of choice was the dagger, although adherents were encouraged to employ poison against their adversaries. Historians view the Carbonari as perhaps the first highly organized international insurgent terrorist groups—although their political impact was limited (Miller, 2013).

An interesting group in the period between 1811 and 1826 was the **Luddites** comprised of English artisans who sabotaged textile looms and other newly developed industrial technology that threatened the jobs of skilled knitters and other workers. The group was named after Ned Ludd who—legend has it—destroyed two knitting machines in the 1770s. The British Parliament responded to the Luddites by adopting a law punishing economic sabotage and by executing seventeen Luddites in 1813 (Law, 2016).

The spread of the desire for democracy led to a series of political uprisings across Europe in 1848. The revolt included factory workers and landless peasants demanding economic reform. These movements were ultimately crushed, and monarchies were restored across the European continent.

In 1849 **Karl Heinzen** (1809–1880), a radicalized former German civil servant, published the influential essay, *Murder*, which is considered a foundation document of modern terrorism. Heinzen argued that although the taking of a human life is a very serious crime, murder has historically been relied upon by regimes to maintain power. Individuals devoted to liberty possessed no alternative other than to resort to assassination and to violence in self-defense. Heinzen argued that governments should not be permitted to possess a monopoly on violence. The weakness of democratic movements for change in terms of willing fighters, as well as resources, could be overcome by employing technological advances in weaponry—primarily the bomb (Miller, 2013).

Heinzen concluded by advising that murder was the engine of historical progress. He concluded that an individual who is not ready to sacrifice him or herself to put a million "barbarians in their coffins" does not possess a true commitment to democracy (Miller, 2013, p. 55).

The next stage in the development of terrorism was the epidemic of anarchist violence.

ANARCHISM

Anarchism is the rejection of all authority; in political terms, anarchism aspires to eradicate of all government authority. A more moderate wing believed in mutual sharing of power, the reorganization of society, and the ownership of businesses and industries by the worker collectives. Anarchists viewed the concept of private property as a form of theft, and this so-called criminal ownership allowed landlords and industrialists to exploit others by charging high rents and paying low wages. This, according to anarchism, resulted in the perpetuation of a wealthy class that used their money to control government officials.

Anarchist violence was promoted in 1866 by the discovery of dynamite by Swedish scientist Alfred Nobel. Dynamite was nearly 20 times more powerful than black powder, and although dynamite was developed for mining it was quickly employed as the weapon of choice by terrorists. Bombs packed with dynamite provided a weapon that transformed terrorists into a significant threat and enabled terrorists to inflict substantial damage. However, the bombs—although now significantly lighter nonetheless—remained bulky and difficult to place adjacent to a target.

Johann Most (1846–1906) is viewed as the foremost theoretician of anarchism. A former German member of parliament, Most founded the influential newspaper *Die Freiheit (Freedom)*, which he continued to publish after arriving in New York. He advocated what he termed "anarchist vengeance" and called for the rescue of humankind through "blood, iron, poison, and dynamite" (as cited in Law, 2016). Most argued that terrorist attacks would mobilize the people to revolt against government authority. The best strategy for terrorists to ignite a revolt was to assassinate well-known individuals, thus drawing attention to the anarchist cause, and to place posters at the site of the killings explaining the reason for the violence. Most provided recipes for manufacturing bombs, grenades, and other weapons.

The Russian anarchist Pyotr Kropokin (1842–1921) pioneered the notion of *propaganda by deed*, which was the guiding principle of terrorist groups. This was the belief that revolutionary violence could awaken the awareness and willingness of workers and peasants to act. On July 14, 1881, the International Workingmen's Association (IWA) met in London and various anarchist delegations announced that the time had come to engage in propaganda by deed and insurgent violence (Hubac-Occhipinti, 2016).

Italian anarchists engaged in both mass revolts and in assassinations. Particularly notable was the assassination of Umberto I in 1900 after two previous unsuccessful attempts. This was an act of revenge for Umberto's decoration of a general who had ordered his troops to open fire on a crowd during bread riots in 1898 (Hubac-Occhipinti, 2016).

Anarchists also attracted support from landless agriculture workers in Spain, a country which was divided by regional movements that advocated autonomy from the central government in Madrid. Beginning with an attempt to assassinate Alfonso XII in 1878, Spain experienced 20 years of anarchist violence. Terrorists began to target the general population for the first time. In November 1893 an anarchist threw two bombs into the crowd at the Liceu Opera House in Barcelona. Despite a mass crackdown on anarchists, an anarchist ignited a bomb during Barcelona's annual Corpus Christi religious procession, killing more than 40 people. In 1906 an anarchist tossed a bomb onto the carriage carrying Alfonso XIII of Spain and his bride Victoria Eugenie on their wedding day, killing 15 and injuring at least 50 people (Hubac-Occhipinti, 2016).

France experienced a wave of worker unrest and strikes. In 1886 an unsuccessful anarchist attack on the Paris Stock Exchange demonstrated the widening targets of terrorist violence. Between 1892 and 1894, 10 bombings were carried out against industrialists, political leaders, and judicial officials. In December 1893 the French government was directly challenged when a bomb was thrown from the gallery of the Chamber of Deputies. A year later bombs were hooked up to the doors of two hotel rooms, killing the officers who were called to investigate a reported suicide (Hubac-Occhipinti, 2016).

In February 1894 prominent French anarchist Émile Henry (1872–1894) ignited a bomb at the fashionable Café Terminus in Paris, killing one person and injuring more than 20 others. Henry explained that in persecuting anarchists, the government held all anarchists responsible for the work of a few; he was responding in kind by holding the mass of the wealthy, privileged economic class responsible for the crimes committed by the government and its corporate partners. At his trial Henry famously proclaimed that there are "no innocents" (Hubac-Occhipinti 2016, p. 130).

As the decade of the 1890s drew to a close, President Sadi Carnot of France was stabbed to death. In 1897 Premier Antonio Canovas of Spain was assassinated, and a year later Elizabeth, the empress of Austria, was murdered.

In 1898 the Great Powers in Europe met in Rome and 4 years later in St. Petersburg, Russia, to agree on a strategy to rid Europe of anarchist violence. They declared that anarchist publications were to be shut down, anarchists were to be swiftly apprehended and prosecuted, and the death penalty was to be imposed for the attempted assassinations of government officials and heads of state.

Anarchist violence seemingly had little rhyme or reason. The attacks were symbolic statements of protest against the prevailing political system and economic inequality. Anarchists tended to act on their own and did not share a specific goal. Famed criminologist **Cesare Lombroso** (1835–1909) explained the violence by pointing to the physical features of anarchists, including their large jaw, curved nose, and high cheek bones. At the time, these features were also associated with criminals, degenerates, and the insane. The anarchists' violent nature had been unleashed by the decline of religion and by the weakening of monarchies.

RUSSIAN REVOLUTIONARY VIOLENCE

The steady growth in politically motivated terrorist violence against government authorities reached its height in 19th-century and early 20th-century Russia. Russia was ripe for revolutionary violence. It was the least developed of the European states, and a small landholding elite dominated a vast impoverished peasant population. There was no provision for rights or liberties (Law, 2016).

Philip Pomper describes Russia as going through various stages of terrorist violence. The initial phase was **nihilism**. This was a movement of mostly privileged students in the 1860s who rebelled against social conventions. Determined to bring down the existing order, Dmitrii Karakozov attempted to assassinate Alexander II in April 1866 (Pomper, 2001).

In the period between 1867 and 1868, young student leader **Sergei Nechaev** emerged as the dominant and charismatic leader of a group of roughly 80 terrorists known as the Axe, who were dedicated to the assassination of Alexander

II. Nechaev fled abroad and wrote an influential road map for terrorists titled "Catechism of a Revolutionary." He wrote that the terrorist must be dedicated to the movement and must be ready to undergo torture and die. The immediate task was to spread fear among government leaders and to overthrow the regime. The question of what came next could wait until the regime had been eliminated. Nechaev was apprehended in Switzerland and died in prison in 1882 (Miller, 2013).

In 1876 student activists known as the **Populists** (*narodniki*) established the Land and Freedom movement. The primary focus was on the political organization of the peasantry in preparation for a mass revolutionary uprising. Members of Land and Freedom, however, were willing to engage in acts of violent retribution. In one infamous incident in 1878, Vera Zasulich shot and killed F. F. Trepov, the governor-general of St. Petersburg, in retribution for his ordering of the flogging of a young imprisoned party member who had refused to remove his hat during a prison inspection.

Russia's humiliation in the Russo-Turkish War of 1877–1878 weakened the government and ushered in what has been characterized as a turning point in Russian terrorism (Pomper, 2001). Various students, frustrated by the inability to mobilize the peasantry and by the effectiveness of government countermeasures, formed a new urban terrorist group, **People's Will** (*Narodnaia Volia*), which was active from 1878 to 1882. They believed that their violent attacks would inspire the peasantry to revolt in a mass uprising. A prominent figure in the People's Will was Nikolai Morozov, who called for small groups to carry out the assassination of government officials—which he predicted would inspire escalating violence and lead to overthrow of the regime. He proclaimed that every individual has the right to kill a tyrant and a nation cannot take this right away from its citizens. In 1880 the People's Will infiltrated the Winter Palace and ignited a bomb that killed 12 people and almost killed Alexander II. They finally succeeded in assassinating Alexander on March 1, 1881, which led the government crushing the movement (Miller, 2013).

The **Socialist Revolutionary (SR) Party** emerged in the early 20th century. The SR organized a revolutionary arm, the **Combat Organization (CO)**. The CO assassinated minister of the interior Dmitrii Sipiagin—as well as his successor von Plehve—in 1902. In 1905 a bomb killed the czar's uncle, Grand Duke Sergei, the governor-general of St. Petersburg. CO terrorism culminated in the killing of Prime Minister Peter Stolypin at the Kiev Municipal Theater (Miller, 2013).

In 1904 Russia entered a war with Japan. The hardships caused by the war increased discontent. A peace procession of thousands of workers in January 1905 gathered to present the czar with a petition listing grievances and asking for reforms. Soldiers fired on the demonstrators in what became known as "Bloody Sunday." Strikes and peasant uprisings spread throughout the country, forcing Nicholas II to issue various progressive reforms, most of which were never implemented.

The total number of state officials killed or seriously wounded reached nearly 4,500 by the end of 1907. An additional 2,180 individuals loosely affiliated with the government were killed and 2,530 were wounded. Government records list 20,000 acts of revolutionary violence, which included bank robberies in which millions of rubles were seized by terrorist groups. Sixteen thousand suspected terrorists were brought to trial. Nearly 3,700 were sentenced to death and the others were sentenced to hard labor in Siberia (Miller, 2013).

Terrorism and the costs of World War I weakened the Russian regime and laid the foundation for the 1917 revolution and the creation of a Soviet communist state. The monarchy was replaced by an unelected multiparty provisional government. The plan was to hold elections, form a parliament, draft a constitution, and to provide for an equitable distribution of land to the peasantry. The Bolshevik faction of the Social Democrats managed to seize power and established a government based on Marxist principles. In September 1918 the regime implemented a "Red Terror," an edict that proclaimed that in order to protect the Soviet Republic from internal enemies that a policy of terror was required. Experts estimate that the number of individuals killed by the Communist regime range from 500,000 to close to 2 million (Chaliand & Blin, 2016).

Personalities and Events

FIGURE 4.2 Karl Marx

Source: https://commons.wikimedia.org/wiki/File%3AKarl_Marx.jpg.

An account of 19th-century revolutionary thought and movements is not complete without reference to **Karl Marx** (1818–1883). Although Marx was not a central figure in the events in this period, his thinking was fundamental to the philosophy that guided the postrevolutionary regime in Russia and has influenced a long list of revolutionaries and terrorists across the globe who have claimed to embrace a Communist ideology. A journalist, political philosopher, and activist, Marx has left a rich legacy that has been the topic of tens of thousands of articles and book.

A brief discussion cannot do justice to Marx's complex philosophy. Along with his colleague Friedrich Engels (1820–1895), he argued that history is fraught with class struggle. Marx and Engels contended that under industrial capitalism, society was divided between two primary groups, the capitalists (*bourgeoisie*) who owned the means of production, and a vast proletariat working class who survived by selling their labor and who were paid less than the value that they created through their work. Economic dominance was reinforced by the capitalist-dominated superstructure of media, education, and religion that combined to create a "false consciousness" among the working class. This "false consciousness" led workers to believe that the existing system was fair and just and that individuals earned the success or failure that they deserved.

Marx believed that this exploitative system would only disappear when the working class rose in revolution and private property was replaced by communism in which the workers own the means of production, wealth is shared among the population, and economic classes disappear.

Marx and Engels expressed sympathy and support for the Russian terrorism as a response to the immorality of the country's ruling elite. However, Marx generally was no friend of terrorism—particularly seemingly purposeless anarchist attacks. Marx believed that society evolved through various stages which inevitably led to the revolutionary creation of a Communist society. He was skeptical about the revolutionary potential of peasants and advocated organizing the working class in preparation for revolutionary action. Marx was critical of terrorist actions that, however satisfying, often strengthened the patriotic loyalty of workers and the repressive power of the state and in his view did not advance the cause of revolution. Marx believed that political organizing—rather than violence—was the engine of change. He also was an internationalist and was critical of movements that were based on national pride rather than on opposition to economic exploitation and the plight of workers across the globe.

Because of his support for workers, Marx was nonetheless denounced as a terrorist. His basic notion that the state is stacked against the peasants and workers and that capitalists are impediments to social change—for better or worse—has inspired revolutionaries ranging from Vladimir Lenin in Russia, Mao Zedong in China, Ho Chi Minh in Vietnam, and Fidel Castro in Cuba. []

IRELAND ETHNONATIONALIST VIOLENCE

In the 16th and 17th centuries, the British began settling colonists on the most desirable land in northeastern Ireland, designated as the Plantation of Ulster. The influx of English migrants pushed the indigenous population from the

FIGURE 4.3 Lenin and Stalin, Pictured on an Albanian Stamp Commemorating the October Revolution

Source: https://commons.wikimedia.org/wiki/File%3ALenin-and-stalin.jpg.

land and reduced them to tenant farmers. Relations were further strained by the fact that these new settlers were Protestant while the indigenous population was predominantly Catholic. Yet another division was based on desire of the British settlers to remain part of England (Unionists or Loyalists) and the desire of the Irish to form an independent country (Republicans) (Law, 2016).

Each group sponsored and supported vigilante groups that persecuted members of the other religion. The primary indigenous Irish resistance group was the Fenian Brotherhood also known as the Irish Revolutionary Brotherhood (IRB). In the Phoenix Park murders of May 1882, the Fenians assassinated Thomas Burke—the third most powerful British official in Ireland—along with the nephew of the British prime minister. The British responded by forming the Special Irish Branch of the London Metropolitan Police to hunt down the Fenian terrorists.

The Fenians retaliated in the 1880s by carrying out what has become known as the dynamite war on targets within England such as Scotland Yard, the House of Commons, and railroad trains and stations.

In the 1916 **Easter Uprising** several thousand Republicans revolted and proclaimed Irish independence. The British suffered as many as 200 fatalities and only restored order after killing several thousand civilians, damaging property valued at over two million dollars, and executing 15 rebels.

The Irish Republicans continued the struggle against British control for 3 decades under the banner of the **Irish Republican Army (IRA)**, formed in 1918. Irish dissidents realized that their guerilla force was no match for the British in open combat and organized so-called flying squads or small mobile cells of fighters. The goal was to harass, demoralize, and weaken the British occupation force and the Protestant-dominated Royal Irish Constabulary (RIC) and drive the British out of Ireland. The decentralization of terrorist operations had the added benefit of making it difficult for the British to gather intelligence on terrorist operations. Flying squads carried out roughly 3,000 attacks on the police and army barracks (Carr, 2007).

Famed IRA strategist Michael Collins formed a group of assassins, the Twelve Apostles, which focused on attacking the RIC and its informants and spies. In 1920 the Apostles killed 450 members of the RIC, killing 14 on a single day in November 1920 (Law, 2016).

The British countered by forming a new military unit comprised of 12,000 army veterans referred to as the Black and Tans because of their mismatched uniforms. The Black and Tans, however, lacked training in counterinsurgency and frequently resorted to tactics of terror and to mass killings.

British casualties continued to climb; more than 1,000 police or military were killed or wounded by the IRA in the first half of 1921. By this time, the British had stationed nearly 150,000 troops in Ireland and began interning suspected IRA fighters in concentration camps.

The British eventually relented and recognized an independent Irish state within the British Commonwealth. However, the northern portion of Ireland, where the English Protestants had settled, was to remain part of the United Kingdom. This temporarily suspended IRA violence, which was reignited in Northern Ireland later in the 20th century.

THE ISRAELI-PALESTINIAN CONFLICT

The conflict between Israel and Palestine over the territory constituting modern Israel (or what the Palestinians term Palestine) has been at the center of terrorism in the 20th and 21st centuries. This struggle combines issues of religion, ethnonationalism, and state and international terrorism, and has involved issues such as airline hijacking, suicide bombings, and Islamic-inspired violence—which later would challenge the entire global community. This section outlines the enormously complicated issues in the Israeli–Palestinian conflict and by no means presents a comprehensive account.

In the 1870s a movement called **Zionism** developed in Europe. Zionists believed that the Jews, like other people, were entitled to live in a single unified homeland. An important event in fueling the Zionist movement was the Dreyfus affair in France. In 1894 captain Alfred Dreyfus, a young French officer, was convicted of espionage and imprisoned for life on Devil's Island, French Guiana. He was later exonerated. Jewish intellectual Theodor Herzel was outraged by the entire episode and penned a book titled *The Jewish State* in which he argued that the Jews would never be accepted in Europe and argued for the creation of a Jewish homeland in Palestine.

By the early 20th century, nearly 25,000 Jews had settled in Palestine and shared the land with the Palestinian Arab population. The so-called first wave of resettlement was followed by a second wave between 1904 and 1914, increasing the Jewish population to more than 350,000. As the Ottoman Empire was broken up as a result of Turkey's defeat in World War I, Great Britain and France divided vast areas of the Middle East between themselves. Britain assumed control over Palestine, which was experiencing increasing tension between the recently arriving Jews and the Arab population. Beginning in 1921, a series of riots took place. These riots were provoked by Arab fears of the growing Jewish presence, the purchase of Arab lands by Jews, and fears that the Jews were arming themselves in order to prepare to take control of Palestine.

The British seemingly were on both sides of the issue. In 1917 British prime minister Arthur James Balfour wrote that his government "view with favor the establishment in Palestine of a national home for the Jewish People" (Balfour Declaration, 1917). At the same time, the British has promised the Arabs that they would support an independent Arab state in Palestine in return for Arab assistance in fighting the Turkish Ottoman forces, which were aligned with the Germans during World War I.

British control was formally recognized by the world community in 1922 when the soon-to-be-defunct League of Nations recognized a British mandate (or administrative responsibility) over Palestine. The Jews, as well as the Arabs, resented British control; tensions between the two rival religious groups led to the formation of the Haganah, a Jewish defense force. The conflict boiled over in 1929 when an attack against Jewish worshippers resulted in the killing of more than 130 Jews. This led the Jews to form a new and more formidable defense force, the Irgun Zvai Leumi, known as the Irgun (Law, 2016).

The Irgun adopted an aggressive terrorist campaign of bombings. In July 1938 Irgun attacks on markets and on homes left 76 Arabs dead and more than 170 wounded. The strategy was to provoke the Arabs into a conflict with the Jews and then to mobilize the necessary military might to drive the Arabs out of Palestine. The British reacted in 1939 by restricting Jewish immigration to Palestine and announcing that it would end Jewish immigration entirely within 5 years. The Irgun responded by initiating terrorist attacks on the British.

The Irgun declared a ceasefire in September 1939 with the beginning of World War II. One faction of the Irgun, popularly known as the **Stern Gang**, continued the attacks on the British throughout the war.

The Irgun is said to have provided a model of urban terrorist violence which subsequently served as an example for terrorist movements across the globe. The goal was to weaken the British to the point that they could no longer effectively govern Palestine, resulting in the loss of popular support at home for Britain's continued presence in the Middle East. The British at this point would be left with no alternative other than to leave Palestine. Between 1945 and 1948, the Irgun unleashed an organized campaign of violence against the British in Palestine, destroying infrastructure, launching assaults on hated symbols of British power (such as office on immigration), and assassinating British officials and soldiers.

On July 22, 1946, the Irgun bombed the King David Hotel in Jerusalem, the headquarters of the British general staff, leaving 91 dead. The following year the Irgun used what is considered the world's first truck bomb to kill four British soldiers. The British and Jews found themselves locked into a cycle of violence (Law, 2016).

The UN adopted a plan on November 29, 1947, partitioning Palestine between the Jews and the Arabs with Jerusalem designated as an international city. The British subsequently left Palestine; in May 1948, the Jews declared the independent state of Israel. Egypt, Jordan, Syria, Iraq, and Lebanon immediately invaded the newly established state. The conflict led to an overwhelming Israeli victory and to a ceasefire rather than to a peace settlement. This was the first of various conflicts between Israel and its Arab neighbors. The two most significant were the 1967 Six-Day War—leading to Israel taking control over Jerusalem and the West Bank—and the so-called 1973 Yom Kippur War.

Over 700,000 Arab inhabitants of Palestine—half of the Arab population—flooded out of the territory during the 1948 war in what is called the **Nakba** or "Disaster." The Palestinians found themselves in UN-sponsored refugee camps, most of which were located in neighboring Jordan.

PALESTINIAN RESPONSE

Israel appeared to be invulnerable to a conventional military attack. In 1959 **Yasser Arafat**—along with students studying in Cairo, Egypt, and Beirut, Lebanon, and professionals working in the Gulf States—formed a guerilla force, Fatah, to battle with Israel. Fatah was a secular movement dedicated to the reclaiming of Palestinian lands and to the creation of a Palestinian state. The small-arms attacks waged by Fatah were viewed by the Israelis as more of an irritant than a threat. In 1964 Arafat merged Fatah into the **Palestine Liberation Organization (PLO)**, which became the leading Palestinian rights organization under his leadership.

From roughly 1967 to 1982, the Palestinian movement was divided between various groups which competed for control of the liberation movement. One of the most militant was Black September, a militant Palestinian terrorist group affiliated with Arafat, which retaliated for the expulsion of the PLO from Jordan by assassinating the Jordanian prime minister in 1971. Black September captured the attention of the world when commandos entered the Summer Olympic Village, killing a number of Israeli athletes and taking several more hostage. The Palestinian terrorists negotiated transportation to Libya for themselves and the surviving hostages. German forces attacked the Palestinians at the airport, resulting in the death of the terrorists as well as the remaining hostages. The Israelis later tracked down and killed members of Black September who had been released from German custody.

The year 1974 was a turning point for the PLO, whose terrorist attacks seemingly had placed the plight of the Palestinians on the global agenda. The group was recognized as the sole legitimate representative of the Palestinian people and the pistol-wielding Arafat was invited to address the UN General Assembly.

The terrorist violence nonetheless continued. In June 1976 two members of the Popular Front for the Liberation of Palestine hijacked an Air France flight en route from Israel to France. The terrorists landed the aircraft at Entebbe airport in Uganda. They demanded the release of 53 prisoners associated with various groups held in Israel, France, Kenya, Switzerland, and West Germany. This was an act of international terrorism directed outside the Middle East and demonstrated that terrorism posed an urgent threat to the global community.

Over the next 2 days, the terrorists released 148 non-Jews, leaving 94 Jews and 12 members of the Air France crew hostage. In a raid that would contribute to the impressive reputation of the Israeli counterterrorism forces, Israeli commandos rescued the hostages—only three of whom were killed in the raid. A single Israeli commando, the brother of future Israeli prime minister Benjamin Netanyahu, was killed in the raid (Boot, 2013).

In March 1979 the seemingly impossible occurred when President Jimmy Carter succeeded in orchestrating a peace treaty between President Anwar Sadat of Egypt and Prime Minister Menachem Begin of Israel. In October 1981 Islamic militants exacted revenge by assassinating Sadat at a military parade.

In an effort to stop attacks from southern Lebanon by the Palestinians, the Israelis sent their troops into Lebanon in 1982 in an effort to weaken—if not eliminate—the PLO and found themselves embroiled in a raging conflict between Christian, Islamic, and outside Syrian forces competing for power. Arafat found his forces fighting alongside Shia Muslim militias against Christian forces supported by Israel, the United States, and Syria. The fighting resulted in more than 10,000 dead and left Beirut, called the Paris of the Middle East, in ruins.

Arafat, realizing that his situation was precarious, evacuated more than 10,000 fighters to Tunisia. In an event that symbolizes the violence of the Israeli–Palestinian conflict, Israeli military commanders failed to prevent their Christian Phalangist allies from entering a Palestinian refugee camp in Lebanon and killing several thousand older men, women, and children.

The continuous terrorist attacks and counterterrorism responses over the next few decades are too extensive to be easily summarized. An example is October 7, 1985, when four members of the Popular Front for the Liberation of Palestine took control of the *Achille Lauro*, a cruise ship that was traveling from Israel to Egypt. The crew and passengers were taken hostage, and the terrorists later killed Leon Klinghoffer—an elderly wheelchair-bound passenger—and threw his body overboard. In 1985 the Palestinian organization Abu Nidal launched attacks on the Israeli airline El Al at airports in Rome and Vienna. Roughly 16 individuals died and nearly 100 were wounded in the Rome attack; nine were killed and 39 were wounded in the Vienna attack.

In 1987 Palestinian anger boiled over in the first **Intifada** (uprising) which involved demonstrations, strikes, and a series of armed attacks. It resulted in the death of more than 1,400 Palestinians and 185 Israelis. An estimated 18,000 Palestinians were arrested. The Palestinians primarily relied on stones, Molotov cocktails, and crude weapons; Israeli forces, equipped with modern weaponry, too often appeared to be the aggressors. The first Intifada ended with the 1993 Oslo Accords; in 1995 a second agreement was reached. This agreement established the Palestinian Authority (PA) as an independent Palestinian governing institution in return for recognition of Israel as a sovereign state. The Accords recognized the PA's power to establish governmental and judicial institutions, internal security and health, welfare, and educational services. Yasser Arafat was elected as first president of the PA. The agreement was opposed by conservative and ultra-religious groups within Israel that resisted any settlement with the Palestinians on the grounds of what they viewed as Israel's biblical claim to the West Bank. In 1995 Israeli prime minister Yitzhak Rabin, who had negotiated the Oslo Accords, was shot dead at a peace rally by a young religious student. Rabin was succeeded in office by Ariel Sharon, an outspoken opponent of Israeli negotiations with the Palestinians.

In 2000 at Camp David, Maryland, Israeli prime minister Ehud Barack offered to recognize a Palestinian state with control over East Jerusalem, most of the West Bank, and the Gaza Strip. Arafat, who was apparently concerned about opposition from militants within the PLO who favored the destruction of Israel, turned down the agreement.

The second Intifada was initiated in September 2000, following the visit of Sharon to the Muslim holy site of the Temple Mount, a site with religious import to both Muslims and Jews. In the ensuing months as many as 1,000 Israelis and thousands of Palestinians were killed. The death and destruction in the second Intifada far exceeded the violence in the first Intifada and was marked by suicide bombings and armed attacks. The violence gradually subsided over the course of the 5 years of the second Intifada. Nearly 700 Israelis were killed and more than 4,000 were wounded; roughly 1,300 Palestinians were killed and close to 10,000 were wounded. Israel responded by building a controversial wall separating Israel from Palestinian settlements on the West Bank. The Israelis also launched a military operation on the West Bank, which resulted in the death of 500 alleged militants and in the arrest of nearly 7,000 (Boot, 2013).

In July 2006 Israel invaded southern Lebanon to halt rocket attacks from Hezbollah, an Iran-sponsored group loosely aligned with **Hamas**. The 34-day siege resulted in more than 4,000 rockets being fired into Israel and the death of more than 1,000 Lebanese, and more than 150 Israeli soldiers, and nearly 50 Israeli civilians.

Following the Intifada in 1987, the Islamic Resistance Movement (Harakat al Muqawama al Islamiyya), or Hamas, was founded to support Palestinian youth involved in the protests. Hamas initially rejected violence, viewing a return to Islam as practiced by the founding figures of the religion as the first step towards liberation from Israel. Hamas was initially supported by Israel, which viewed the religious group as an alternative to the PLO. In the 1990s Hamas became swept up in the global Islamic movement and turned to violent jihad. They opposed peace negotiations and advocated the destruction of Israel. The group emerged as a rival to Arafat and to the more secular PLO. Hamas built a power base on the Gaza Strip by providing social welfare services like health, schools, and health clinics, and the group maintains a separate militant armed wing, Izz el Din al Qassam Brigades.

The PLO maintains control over the West Bank, although Hamas exercises a tight grip on Gaza. In August 2005 Sharon withdrew Israeli forces from the Gaza Strip, thinking that safeguarding Israel with security barriers and check-points would provide needed security and protect the lives of Israeli soldiers who were under constant harassment and attack by the residents of Gaza. The wall has become a point of controversy because it separates parts of Palestinian communities and because of the difficulty experienced by Palestinians in entering Israel for work.

The possibility of peace between Israel and the Palestinians seemed promising, but Hamas interrupted the momentum toward a settlement by launching rocket attacks on Israel in December 2008. In an effort to eradicate Hamas, Israel invaded Gaza and launched a violent campaign that resulted in the death of thousands of Palestinians and in the destruction of infrastructure. Israeli forces withdrew a month later. After withdrawing its troops, Israel continued to blockade construction equipment and certain other goods from coming into Gaza. The country became an object of severe international criticism when nine Turkish nationals died after Israel seized ships allegedly carrying relief supplies to Gaza (DeFronzo, 2015).

In October 2017 the two Palestinian entities reached a reconciliation agreement to form a united Palestinian front in negotiations with Israel.

Beginning in April and throughout the summer in 2018, thousands of Palestinians protested at the security fence separating Israel and the Gaza Strip. The Palestinians explained that they were asserting their right to return their former homes in Israel and were calling for an end the Israel blockade of the Gaza Strip. Crowds were dispersed by tear gas, and some protestors who attempted to scale the security fence were shot by Israeli troops, who claimed that demonstrators were throwing Molotov cocktails and attaching firebombs to kites in an effort to burn Israeli farmland (Halbfinger & Abuheweila, 2018; Halbfinger & Patel, 2018).

Personalities and Events

Since the country's inception, Israel has relied on a covert strategy of targeted assassination to eliminate the leadership of terrorist organizations. This policy is designed to weaken these organizations, deter other individuals from participating in terrorist organizations, and to protect Israel by killing those who pose an immediate threat. The logic behind this policy is that these assassinations enable Israel to avoid a larger military response and the resulting loss of human life. In recent years these attacks have extended beyond the Palestinian territories and have taken place across the globe. For example, the individuals who carried out the massacre of Israeli athletes at the Munich Olympics were hunted down and killed. The message is clear: "If you are an enemy of Israel we will hunt you down and kill you."

Targeted killings— termed *extrajudicial killings*—by Israel are limited to individuals against whom there is "accurate and reliable information" that the individuals carried out attacks or ordered attacks. Assassins are to avoid killing innocents, and attacks are never authorized if there is a risk of killing children. Killings only are to be carried out if there is visual confirmation of the target's identity. Mistakes, however, have been made—killing the wrong person or killing innocents.

In the case of high-profile targets, a dossier is compiled detailing the individual's terrorist activities. Intelligence operatives develop a profile of a target's movements and a plan is developed to kill the individual. The plan and killing is approved by a series of government officials, including a legal team, and by the Israeli prime minister. Individuals within the Israeli defense establishment have expressed apprehension that the program which was intended to be used selectively has become a frequently employed counterterrorism tactic. Combating suicide bombing, for example, required the targeting of potential bombers, their trainers, and bomb makers, along with individuals planning the attack.

A series of bold attacks by Israel between 2007 and 2017 targeted several Iranian scientists working on the development of nuclear weapons. These killings were intended to eliminate individuals that knew how to create a nuclear weapon and to deter scientists from working on the project (Bergman, 2018).

According to Ronen Bergman (2018), Israel has assassinated more people than any country in the world. In recent years, assassinations have become easier to conduct because of the advancement of technology allowing for aerial drone attacks. Since the second Intifada, Israel has carried out more than 800 targeted killing operations, most of which were conducted against Hamas in the Gaza Strip, against Palestinians in Europe and the Middle East, and against individuals in Syria and Iran.

(continues on next page)

(continued from previous page)

Salah Shehade, a Palestinian social worker from the Gaza Strip, was released from prison by Israel in 2000 as a gesture of good will. A brilliant strategist, he resumed his terrorist activities and, according to the Israelis, he had direct involvement in attacks that killed 474 individuals and wounded over 2,500 in a period of 1 year. On two occasions, authorization to kill Shehade was withdrawn because of the risk of killing a large number of civilians, including his wife and child. In July 2002 the decision was made to bomb Shehade's apartment—regardless of whether his wife was present or whether neighbors might be killed. The elusive Shehade was subsequently spotted in a three-story building in a densely populated neighborhood in Gaza City. On three occasions the mission was cancelled because of the number of civilians on the street or because of the risk of killing Shehade's wife and child. Aerial surveillance indicated that there were shacks surrounding the three-story apartment where Shehade was located, although there was no positive intelligence that they were inhabited. On July 22, 2002, an F-16 dropped a bomb on the apartment house. Shehade was killed, along with his wife, his daughter, his assistant, and 10 other civilians—including seven children. One hundred and fifty people were injured. Bergman writes that common sense was overwhelmed by the exciting prospect of killing Shehade. A number of pilots subsequently announced that they were trained to defend the country in times of war and that they would refuse to participate in attacks in the Palestinian territories. On the other hand, Israel asserts that there is no alternative other than to eliminate individuals who pose a continuing threat to the country despite the loss of innocent lives. ☐

4.1 YOU DECIDE

The assassination of Julius Caesar (100–44 BCE) by members of the Roman senate was a vivid example of a question that has been a persistent focus of commentators: whether tyrannicide or regicide (killing of royalty) is justifiable. In other words, when, if ever, can assassination of a political leader be justified? Roman philosopher and statesman Seneca wrote that "nothing pleases the Gods so much as the killing of a tyrant" (Laqueur, 1999, p. 10). The revered Greek philosopher Aristotle (384–322 BCE) wrote that there were three primary forms of government: monarchy, aristocracy, and democracy; the corrupt form of each system diverts society from the cause of justice. There is therefore a civic responsibility of individuals to rid society of tyranny.

The Roman politician and political commentator Cicero (106 BCE–43 CE) proclaimed that it is virtuous to kill a tyrant and that tyrants should be eliminated to prevent them from infecting the entire political system.

John of Salisbury (1120–1180), the bishop of Chartres in France, noted that tyrants rule by force. He argued that the killing of tyrants is necessary to allow society to be aligned with God.

European philosophers like Jean-Jacques Rousseau (1712–1778) argued that government is based on the popular will and that a ruler who deviates from this mandate should be assassinated.

As justifications for tyrannicide evolved, commentators argued that it was justified to kill individuals who implemented unpopular and destructive public policies or who misled the population.

The problem, of course, is how to distinguish a tyrant from a legitimate leader and whether tyrannicide can ever be justified in a democracy. Does a foreign country have the right to intervene to assassinate or to overthrow a foreign leader? Consider the number of authoritarian rulers in the world who are guilty of documented human rights violations. American law prohibits the American president from ordering the assassination of a foreign leader.

As a member of Congress, would you vote to waive this restriction in certain extraordinary cases? ▯

CHAPTER SUMMARY

The foundation of the various categories of modern terrorism can be traced to the historical developments discussed in this chapter. The Zealots, Assassins, and Thugs illustrate how religion can provide a terrorist group with justification for terrorist violence. Religious terrorism continued with the conflict between Protestants and Catholics in England. The French Revolution ushered in an age of politically motivated terrorism. The aftermath of the French Revolution provided an example of state-sponsored terrorism—the use of terrorist violence by a regime to maintain authority and power. Anarchists and various Russian revolutionary groups challenged state authority and engaged in terrorism against the established political order. The Irish, inspired by nationalism and a desire for independence from Great Britain, engaged in a successful terrorist campaign against the occupying English forces. The Israeli–Palestinian conflict involves terrorism and state terrorism motivated by ethnicity, territory, and religion, and it is characterized by both domestic and international terrorism. The conflict set the stage for the various forms of terrorism discussed in the next several chapters.

CHAPTER REVIEW QUESTIONS

1. Describe the origins and activities of the Zealots, Assassins, and Thugs.
2. Outline the conflict between Catholics and Protestants in England.
3. Discuss the French Revolution, particularly the aftermath and impact of the French Revolution.
4. Describe the terrorist violence in Russia that led to the Russian Revolution.
5. Outline the struggle for Irish independence from Great Britain.
6. How do the developments in this chapter create a foundation for later developments in the history of terrorism?
7. Sketch the history and causes of the Israeli–Palestinian conflict.
8. Do you believe it is worthwhile to take a historical approach to understanding terrorism?

TERMINOLOGY

anarchism
Arafat, Yasser
Assassins
Carbonari
Combat Organization (CO)
Easter Uprising
Gunpowder Plot
Hamas
Heinzen, Karl
Intifada

Irish Republican Army (IRA)
Lombroso, Cesare
Luddites
Marx, Karl
Most, Johann
Nakba
Nechaev, Sergei
nihilism
Palestine Liberation
     Organization (PLO)

People's Will
Populists
Socialist Revolutionary (SR)
     Party
Stern Gang
Thugs
Zealots
Zionism

CHAPTER 5

Ethnonationalist and Revolutionary Terrorism

ETHNONATIONALIST SEPARATIST TERRORISM

Ethnonationalist separatist terrorism is terrorism inspired by the desire of an ethnic group to separate from a country and create an autonomous region or an independent country. In contrast to this *separatist terrorism*, **anticolonial separatist terrorism** involves a movement to expel a colonial power from a country and to achieve independence.

Daniel Byman theorizes that ethnonationalist terrorist groups have the goal of forging an ethnic identity and mobilizing an ethnic population. This may involve promoting ethnic pride, fostering animosity towards other groups, and encouraging interethnic conflict (Byman, 1998).

These ethnonationalist movements possess the advantage of a definite and unifying goal and a natural loyalty among a portion of the general population. The groups tend to identify themselves as part of a historical tradition of struggle and tradition, and they are able to sustain themselves for multiple generations. In many instances, the national and ethnic groups comprise a significant percentage of the population within a part of a country and the indigenous population is receptive to appeals based on a sense of injustice in terms of education, employment, income, and cultural expression. Various ethnonationalist groups are also able to attract financial support from abroad.

A textbook example of this type of terrorism was the Front de Liberation du Quebec (FLQ; Quebec Liberation Front) which was committed to an autonomous French-speaking Quebec within Canada. The FLQ conducted more than 160 violent attacks between 1963 and 1970 and killed eight individuals. In 1969 the group bombed the Montreal Stock Exchange. This was followed by the October Crisis of 1970 in which James Cross (the British trade commissioner) was kidnapped, and Quebec labor minister Pierre Laporte was kidnapped and killed. Members of the FLQ were later arrested or fled to Cuba.

A successful example of separatist **anticolonial terrorism** was the National Organization of Cypriot Fighters (EOKA) on Cyprus which employed a campaign of violence to achieve independence for the Greek population of Cyprus from Great Britain in 1960. Yet another example was in Kosovo, where the Albanian majority—with the assistance of the United States and Europe—achieved independence from Serbia in 2008.

The first section of this chapter outlines separatist terrorism in Northern Ireland, Spain, Sri Lanka, Chechnya, Turkey, and the People's Republic of China. Anticolonial separatist violence is discussed next, with focus on the Algerian struggle against French occupation. Another type of ethnic-based terrorism is ethnonationalist communal terrorism, which is covered in the next section. The second part of the chapter discusses revolutionary terrorism and predatory terrorism.

Northern Ireland

The recognition of the 26 counties of Ireland as the Republic of Ireland left the remaining six counties in Northern Ireland as part of the United Kingdom. A faction of the Irish Republican Army (IRA) favored a peaceful political effort to unify Ireland. A militant wing of the IRA, the **Provisional IRA** (Provisionals), called for continued armed resistance. Their armed attacks alienated both Catholic Republicans (favoring independence) and Protestant Loyalists (favoring continued affiliation with Great Britain) and as a result by the early 1960s the Provisional IRA had become largely inactive.

The IRA was revived in 1969 with the organization of a mass civil rights movement in Northern Ireland protesting the lack of economic opportunity, housing, education, and civil rights for the Catholic population, which comprises roughly 45% of the country. The Northern Ireland government responded by banning demonstrations. Catholic groups reacted by organizing a protest march from Londonderry to Belfast during which they were gassed and beaten by the Royal Ulster Constabulary police force and a volunteer police force called the B Specials. As Northern Ireland spiraled into street violence the British army intervened to impose peace and stability.

The British did not play the role of a neutral arbiter and instead occupied Catholic neighborhoods. They often conducted searches and seizures, detentions, and abuse. In response, membership in the Provisionals significantly increased and the group launched an aggressive campaign of attacks on the police and military and bombings in Northern Ireland and in England.

The British realized that the military occupation of Northern Ireland was coming at a high price in terms of money, lives, and international public opinion. In 1990 they reached a ceasefire; in 1998 they negotiated a peace accord that included both Northern Irish Catholics and Protestants.

The Basque Region of Spain

The Basque region is centered in Spain and extends over the Pyrenees into France. The region was absorbed into Spain, but it was considered to be semiautonomous. Following the Spanish Civil War (1936–1939) and the victory of the fascist forces led by General Francisco Franco, the central government in Madrid banned the Basque language and culture.

The struggle to assert Basque identity intensified in 1959 with the formation **of Basque Nation and Identity (ETA)**. The ETA turned to terrorism in 1961 and attempted to derail a train transporting fascist civil war veterans to a memorial ceremony. Franco responded with the harsh suppression of the group, leading to a cycle of terrorism and counterterrorism. The

FIGURE 5.1 ETA Symbol

Source: https://commons. wikimedia.org/wiki/File%3AETA_ Symbol.svg.

escalating violence was in line with the ETA's belief that the Franco regime would inevitably overreact and target innocent people, inspiring a mass revolt.

Beginning in the 1970s, the ETA launched a campaign of the assassination of government officials, the police, and the military; kidnappings for ransom, and bank robberies. In 1973 the ETA assassinated Spanish prime minister Luis Carrero, Franco's heir apparent. The government responded by imposing martial law and authorizing the use of death squads—which freely functioned outside the legal system and kidnapped, tortured, and murdered suspected ETA members and supporters.

Franco's death in 1975 led to political reform and a new constitution in 1978. The Basque language and educational rights for Basques were recognized; and although a Basque police force was formed, the Basques were not granted autonomy to govern their own affairs. The ETA continued its struggle, but after realizing that as a result of its continued terrorism that the group had lost popular support, halted its military activities in 2011. Although the ETA claimed to only attack political targets in order to avoid killing innocents, roughly one third of the group's victims were civilians (Law, 2016). An effort in 2017 by the Basque region to assert autonomy from Spain through a referendum resulted in the arrest and imprisonment of various regional politicians.

The Tamil Region of Sri Lanka

Sri Lanka is an island roughly 20 miles from southeastern India. The population of Sri Lanka is 17 million, 74% of whom are Sinhalese (most Sinhalese are Buddhist), 18% Tamil (most Tamils are Hindu), with the remainder being of various nationalities and religions. The Tamils historically have populated the north and east of the island. Sri Lanka achieved independence from Great Britain in 1948, and the Tamils initially played a prominent role in the country. The Sinhalese resented what it viewed as the disproportionate influence and power of the Tamils, and in 1955 the group initiated a "Sinhalese-only" policy. The Tamil language and culture were restricted, quotas were imposed on Tamil admission to universities and to the civil service, and some Tamils were denied citizenship. An effort was made to repatriate various Tamils to India even though they were born in Sri Lanka (Law, 2016).

The **Liberation Tigers of Tamil Eelam (LTTE)**, popularly known as the Tamil Tigers, emerged as the vanguard of Tamil resistance. Their goal was to create the Tamil homeland of Eelam. They closely identified with their leader, Velupillai Prabhakaran, whose strategy included the use of suicide bombers, the organization of a naval military wing, and the combined deployment of both guerilla and terrorist fighters.

The Tigers attacked the military and the police and bombed civilian objects, including passenger planes, trains, commercial businesses, and Buddhist temples. The Tigers also engaged in kidnapping for ransom. A bomb in a market in the capital city of Columbo in 1987 killed 113 people and injured nearly 200. Nine years later a bomb destroyed the capital city's financial center, killing 86 people and injuring 1,400 others (Law, 2016).

The signature of the Tamil Tigers was the use of suicide bombers—particularly young female bombers. Between 1987 and 2000, the Black Tigers (males) and Birds of Freedom (women) carried out nearly 2,000 attacks. The Tigers' most infamous attack was the assassination of Indian premier Rajiv Gandhi in 1991 in retribution for his involvement in attempting to achieve a peaceful resolution of the conflict.

The LTTE also proved capable of launching conventional military attacks. In 1996, 4,000 Tamils attacked a Sinhalese military base, killing 1, 2000 Sinhalese soldiers (Whittaker, 2012).

The Tamil Tigers proved to be a fanatical terrorist group. In a strategy known as the "Unceasing Wave," they launched continuous and simultaneous attacks on government officials, the armed forces, public buildings, and infrastructure. Combatants were provided cyanide; in the event a combatant was captured, they would commit suicide by ingesting the cyanide.

The LTTE, much like the IRA, was able to depend on a large population living around the globe for financial support. They also were suspected of being involved in drug smuggling from Asia to Europe.

The LTTE neglected to pursue several opportunities to peacefully resolve the conflict, including a 1995 offer of autonomy. In 2009 the Sinhalese military overwhelmed the Tigers, killing Prabhakaran. The Sinhalese military moved the Tamil population into "no-fire zones" in order to isolate the Tamil terrorists from the rest of the population and flooded the area with military units. At the conclusion of the conflict, Sri Lankan terrorism and counterterrorism claimed as many as 58,000 lives (Whittaker, 2012).

Chechnya

As the Soviet Union splintered and various Eastern European and Baltic states declared independence, the Chechens proclaimed the new Chechen Republic of Ichkeria. Russia refused to recognize Chechen independence and in 1994 sent 40,000 troops into the region. Russia withdrew after nearly 80,000 Chechens and Russians had died. A second Russian invasion in 1999 led to the death of an additional 100,000 people, mostly Chechens, and to the reintegration of Chechnya into Russia.

The Russians have characterized the Chechens as part of the jihadist threat, although their primary motivation is the achievement of independence. The Chechens have engaged in a number of bloody and ruthless terrorist attacks on Russian soil. In October 2002, 50 Chechen terrorists seized 800 hostages during a performance at a Moscow theater and threatened to ignite bombs and to destroy the entire building. Russian special forces swept into the building with by "knockout gas," resulting in the death of all the terrorists. During the counterterrorist attack on the theater, a total of 129 hostages were killed. An August 2004 bombing of a subway killed 39 and wounded more than 100, which was followed by what is suspected to be the suicide bombing of two Russian airliners.

On September 1, 2004, Chechens entered an elementary school in Beslan, seizing 1,200 hostages. More than 330 individuals, most of whom were children, died during the Russian counteroffensive against the terrorists. The Chechens continue to engage in low-level terrorism; in 2010, 39 people were killed in a Moscow subway attack, and a year later, 36 people were killed in an attack on a Moscow airport.

Turkey

Turkey has confronted terrorist threats in the past from Iraqi jihadist militants and, more recently, ISIS. The primary threat to the Turkish government in the past 20 years, however, has been from the Kurds—an ethnic group within Turkey whose population is divided between southern Turkey, northern Iraq, and northern Iran. The primary opposition force is the Marxist **Kurdistan Workers' Party (PKK)**, established in 1977. The PKK has shifted its focus from political ideology and staging revolution, to nationalist appeal and a campaign of terror. Their ultimate goal is the establishment of a semiautonomous Kurdish state within Turkey that respects the Kurdish language and culture. The PKK primarily operates in mountainous areas, although the group has also engaged in suicide bombings, the assassination of diplomats, and armed resistance. Turkey has responded with vigorous counterinsurgency operations. An estimated 40,000 individuals have lost their lives in the conflict.

People's Republic of China

The **Uyghur** are a Turkic Muslim group that has lived in the Xinjiang province of the People's Republic of China (PRC) for more than 200 years. The PRC annexed the region in the 18th century and since that time has confronted periodic rebellions. China prizes the area's oil and gas reserves and in recent years, the Chinese have resettled ethnic Chinese in the area to reduce the percentage of Uyghur. In response, the Uyghur have initiated a low-level terrorist campaign, and some Uyghur have aligned themselves with Islamic terrorist groups.

Algeria

Randall Law (2016) refers to the struggle for Algerian independence as the bloodiest example of *anticolonial separatist terrorism* in the 20th century, along with Vietnam.

The French first began colonizing Algeria in 1830. They repressed the population in the interior and settled the coasts with French migrants. The north of the country was absorbed into France in 1881 and anyone born in the country was considered a French citizen. The Algerians, suffering from a lack of educational and economic opportunity, to the great surprise of the French, campaigned for independence from France.

Frustrated at French opposition to their independence, the Algerians formed the **National Liberation Front (NLF)**, which by November 1954 turned to a terrorist strategy to drive the French out of the country. At the time Algeria was populated by 1 million French and 8 million Algerians of Berber and Arab descent. The NLF initially launched a campaign of "blind terrorism"—random, indiscriminate assassinations and sabotage. NLF members slipped into French neighborhoods, killing entire families and slitting the throats of their victims.

A key strategic decision by the NLF was to focus terrorist attacks on the urban center of Algiers. The strategic rationale was that these attacks would receive media attention and would have a significant impact on the French population, a large number of whom lived in and around Algiers. Simply stated, the impact of 10 people being killed in a rural area does not equal the impact of the killing of a single individual in an urban area. The NLF initially killed 49 civilians in 4 days. This was followed in November 1954 by attacks on stores, restaurants, and airports.

The French Army adopted many of the tactics that it had used in fighting in Indochina, responding with mass arrests, dragnet searches, widespread interrogation, systematic torture, summary executions, reprisals against the population thought to be aligned with the NLF, and population displacement. These methods alienated the mass of the Algerian population, which aligned itself with the NLF. As many as 300,000 lives were lost in the conflict, most of whom were Algerians. In 1962 an exhausted France recognized Algerian independence (Law, 2016).

ETHNONATIONALIST COMMUNAL TERRORISM

Ethnic or nationalist tensions may erupt into terrorism and violence when groups claim ownership of the same land or live in close proximity to one another. In these instances of communal competition, violence primarily is directed against members of other ethnic communities—rather than the government. The differences between groups may be based on differences in ethnicity, nationality, race, or religion. There are countless examples of **ethnonationalist communal terrorism** including the conflict between the Hutu and Tutsi in Rwanda and Burundi, which has resulted in the deaths of more than 1 million people. In some instances, these conflicts result in one group seeking to carve out special cultural rights—or even a separate autonomous state. Two examples of a group seeking a separate state were the armed conflict between Serbs and the Bosnian government in the 1990s in what is now Bosnia and the effort by the Christian Igbos in Nigeria to create a separate state of Biafra. In other instances groups desire to align themselves with another country. An example is violence between Armenians and Azeri Turks in the region of Nagorno-Karabakh in which Armenians desire to transfer the region from Azerbaijan to Armenia.

Another area of tension is Punjab, India. There are 20 million people in the world who practice the Sikh religion. The religion is centered in the Punjab region and the most sacred site is the Golden Temple in Amritsar, Punjab. Sikh fundamentalists have campaigned for almost 50 years for an independent Sikh state of Khalistan within India.

In 1984 Sikh activists occupied the Golden Temple. The Indian army stormed the temple with tanks and artillery, killing hundreds of people. Half a million Indian troops occupied Punjab between 1984 and 1992, resulting in the death of roughly 250,000 individuals. In October 1984 Prime Minister Indira Gandhi was assassinated by her Sikh bodyguards in retribution for the attack on the Golden Temple.

Pakistan and India have engaged in long-standing conflict in Jammu and Kashmir, a region on the border of India and Pakistan which is divided by a line of control (LOC). The confrontation is between the roughly 70% of the population that are Muslim and aligned with Pakistan and the remainder of the population, which are Hindus, Sikhs, and Buddhists that are aligned with India. Pakistan has sponsored and supported armed militias which at times have relied on terrorism in a low-level war against the Indian army.

Perhaps the primary example of contemporary communal terrorism is in Darfur, Sudan. Various rebel groups organized armed resistance against the government to protest a lack of investment in the region. The central government in Khartoum employed nomadic Arab camel herders to launch an ethnic cleansing campaign against the largely African agriculturist population of Darfur. Villages and crops have been destroyed, women have been raped, and millions of people have been killed or displaced. Additionally, many humanitarian workers have been harassed. The Sudanese government alleges that Darfur poses a terrorist threat to global peace. The situation in Darfur has been recognized as a genocide by a number of international organizations.

Personalities and Events

Frantz Fanon was born in 1925 on French-Caribbean island Martinique. He served with French forces in World War II and following the war, he attended medical school in France. Between 1953 and 1956, Fanon worked as a psychiatrist in Algerian hospitals and treated victims of French abuse and torture, and he observed the impact of counterterrorism tactics on French forces and society.

In a series of writings, Fanon theorized that colonialism is perpetuated by persuading the subject population of their inferiority, primitiveness, and lack of personal value. The indigenous-educated colonial middle class, convinced of the bankruptcy of their own history, eagerly embraced colonial culture and provided a ruling elite loyal to the colonial power. The colonial elites were all too willing to maintain law and order and to allow the colonial power to seize local resources, in return for their appointment to important governmental positions and acceptance by the colonial power.

Fanon believed that there were three alternatives for colonized peoples. The first was to accept the existing situation in hopes that despite a history of exploitation, conditions would improve. The next was to emigrate abroad—noting that the colonized may confront racial discrimination and a second-class status. The third option was resistance.

In *The Wretched of the Earth*, Fanon made the controversial argument that psychological liberation and cleansing of the colonial population could be achieved through violent resistance. Striking out against a colonial power can restore a sense of power and self-worth, and it reveals the weakness of the colonial power. This sense of personal effectiveness and self-worth would lead to a rediscovery of the value of domestic art, writing, music, tradition, and culture.

An often overlooked aspect of Fanon's work was his observation that the torture and often brutal violence carried out by the French forces took an enormous psychological toll on the military. He argued that involvement in the torture and abuse of the colonial population resulted in a long-lasting psychological impact on the French.

Fanon passed away in 1961, but his writings had a major impact on anticolonial movements throughout the world. 〔〕

REVOLUTIONARY TERRORISM

Martha Crenshaw (1972) developed a theory of **revolutionary terrorism**, which she defines as a nonstate insurgency undertaken with the goal of seizing control of the government and introducing fundamental and widespread social and political change. Crenshaw theorized that revolutionary terrorism has the following characteristics:

Goal. The ultimate goal is to gain state power.

Violence. Unlawful violence is used in an unpredictable fashion to impede state counterterrorism tactics and to expose the weakness of the government.

Victims. Victims are selected in order to impact a larger audience.

Intent. The intent is to attract support among a significant portion of the population.

Revolutionary terrorism is only likely to succeed when there are conditions of unrest and unhappiness among a significant percentage of the population that can be mobilized to support the rebels.

Crenshaw noted that revolutionary terrorism expands to guerilla warfare and ultimately to civil war. She cautioned that there is a risk that terrorists may provoke anger, resentment, and increased support for the regime—particularly if the terrorists are making unreasonable demands. In the 1960s and 1970s, revolutionary terrorist groups tended to be inspired by Marxist ideology.

FIGURE 5.2 Portrait of Mao Zedong

Copyright © Zhang Zhenshi (CC by 2.0) at https://commons.wikimedia.org/wiki/File%3AMao_Zedong_portrait.jpg.

Revolutionary terrorist violence has followed two models. **Mao Zedong** (1893–1976), leader of the Chinese Communist Party from 1949 until his death in 1976, commanded the Communist army that defeated the nationalist forces and captured control of what now is known as the People's Republic of China. Mao followed a three-step strategy. First, the infiltration of small bands into the countryside and the wearing down of the government through small-scale acts of violence. Second, the consolidation of control over various areas of the country and the initiation of guerilla warfare. Third, the consolidation of guerilla armies into a fighting force to defeat enemy forces and seize control of cities. Mao clearly stated that terrorism should not be used against the civilian population because of the need to maintain a popular base of support (Law, 2016).

This rural approach to revolution was followed by Fidel Castro (1926–2016) in the Cuban Revolution which in 1959 overthrew the regime of Fulgencio Batista (1901–1973). The legendary Che Guevara (1928–1967) unsuccessfully attempted to implement this model in Bolivia, where he was killed by government forces. In his own writings, Guevara advocated for the creation of a rural revolutionary vanguard comprised of the impoverished rural peasantry as the first step in the overthrow of the government.

A different approach was advocated by Brazilian **Carlos Marighella** (1911–1969) in his important *Minimanual of the Urban Guerilla* (1969). A legislator turned Communist revolutionary, Marighella died in an exchange of gunfire with the police in 1969, shortly before the publication of his manual. He advocated for relentless and chaotic urban violence by small cells against symbolically significant targets, in order to transform the political struggle with the government into a military confrontation. The resulting government response would reveal the oppressive nature of the regime and draw supporters to the rebels. The terror campaign was to be accompanied by demonstrations and strikes by students and workers and by the establishment of safe houses, stores of weapons and equipment, and medical services. As the urban population abandoned their support for the government, they would turn to the terrorists. The ranks of terrorists would grow, and the terrorist campaign would be abandoned in favor of full-scale urban warfare.

Terrorist revolutionary violence is exemplified by various Latin American movements including the Tupamaros in Uruguay, FARC in Colombia, and Shining Path in Peru which are discussed below.

In each instance, these groups were unable to develop a mass base of support and ultimately were defeated by a harsh and intense government reaction.

Uruguay

Raúl Sendic was a young activist whose efforts to organize sugarcane workers were prevented by the military, along with large landowners. He turned to violence, and in the early 1960s he organized an urban terrorist group he called the **Tupamaros**, named after the Incan leader Túpac Amaru II, who spearheaded the revolt against the Spanish in the late 18th century. The Tupamaros were a Marxist group dedicated to the creation of a socialist state and to the redistribution of wealth. The urban strategy made sense because 80% of the population was situated in cities, and an urban strategy neutralized the regime's ability to employ aerial surveillance and powerful artillery (Law, 2016).

The Tupamaros engaged in assassinations, robberies, kidnappings, and hijackings; they garnered support by distributing food and disclosing cases of government corruption. Between 1968 and 1972, they kidnapped 14 high-profile individuals—including the British ambassador to Uruguay, as well as Dan Mitrione, an alleged American CIA agent. The group, however, was unable to expand their base of support beyond young, educated students. The Uruguayan government defeated the Tupamaros by utilizing widespread detentions, torture, and targeted killings; the country degenerated into a 12-year military dictatorship (Chaliand & Blin, 2016).

Colombia

Colombia is the fourth largest country in Latin American with a population of 31 million. Three guerilla movements emerged in the 1960s; the most prominent was the Marxist **Revolutionary Armed Forces of Colombia (FARC)**. FARC originally defended peasants against the takeover of their land by ranchers and the military, and they established "liberated" zones of independence in the countryside. At the height of its military power, FARC had an army of more than 15,000 militants and posed a serious threat to the central government in Bogotá.

FARC generated substantial funds from local taxation and kidnapping, and the group raised hundreds of millions of dollars from drug trafficking. The Colombian government, assisted by the United States, gradually wore down the rebels. After 4 years of negotiations, the Colombian government reached a peace agreement with FARC in 2017. The internal conflict in Colombia has left more than 220,000 dead and has displaced roughly 7 million Colombians from their homes. Several groups loosely affiliated with FARC continue to wage a low-level terror campaign in Colombia. The future of the peace agreement was placed in doubt with the election of Ivan Duque, who as part of his platform opposed reconciliation with FARC and other terrorist groups.

Peru

FIGURE 5.3 Poster Calling for Boycott of Elections

Source: https://commons.wikimedia.org/wiki/File%3ACartelSenderoLuminosoBoycott.jpg.

The **Shining Path** (Sendero Luminoso) was founded by university professor Abimael Guzmán in 1962. Guzmán sent students into rural areas to organize peasants into a revolutionary force. The aim was to harass government forces and to break their morale and will to resist, create liberated zones, and use these areas to wage a military campaign to defeat the government. This strategy made some sense given the mass poverty in rural areas. After 10 years, the Shining Path controlled as much as one third of the country. Guzmán told his followers that Peru would have to be turned into a river of blood for the movement to emerge victorious. The Shining Path carried out an estimated 4,000 attacks, including assassinations of landowners, local mayors, and government officials. They also committed bombings. By 1988, the Shining Path had assassinated more than 200 government officials, and the next year they killed 160 members of the government. In 1992 the Shining Path ignited two truck bombs packed with 1,000 kilograms of explosives in one of Lima's most fashionable districts, killing 25 people and injuring 200, destroying homes and businesses (Capron & Mizrahi, 2016).

The Shining Path was financed by millions of dollars in drug money, which enabled the group to purchase weapons, fund social services, and bribe local officials (Law, 2016).

The government carried out a harsh counterinsurgency campaign to defeat the Shining Path which left an estimated 23,000 dead, and thousands were detained and tortured. The Shining Path was largely defunct by the late 1990s, but they continued to carry out terrorist attacks for a number of years.

Personalities and Events

Revolutionary terrorism in Guatemala, as in other Central and Latin American countries, confronted regimes that resorted to harsh and extensive counterterrorist violence.

In 1944 a civilian government committed to land reform was elected. The government of Jacobo Árbenz was removed from power in 1944 after American intervention, which ignited a civil war that only ended with a peace accord in 1996.

The conflict escalated with the election of Fernando Romeo Lucas García in 1978. In order to deny the guerillas support, the government initiated a scorched-earth campaign against the indigenous Mayan population. The number of extrajudicial killings rose from 100 in 1978 to over 10,000 in 1981.

In 1982 Efraín Ríos Montt came to power in a military coup. Between March 1982 and August 1983, an estimated 70,000 were killed or had disappeared. In this campaign of extermination, more than 600 villages were attacked, 300 of which were razed to the ground. Security forces destroyed crops, fouled drinking water, and raped, tortured, and murdered the inhabitants.

An estimated 500,000 to 1.5 million Mayan villagers were displaced before Ríos Montt was removed in a coup in 1993. A new constitution was adopted, a civilian government installed, and in 1996 a UN-sponsored peace accord was reached.

According to government sources the rebel Guerilla Army of the Poor was responsible for 1,258 guerila actions against civilians and infrastructure, including more than 200 murders, 68 kidnappings, 11 bombings against embassies, and 329 attacks.

The subsequent decades have been characterized as the "kingdom of impunity." Two truth commissions have reviewed the evidence and determined that the government carried out genocide against the Mayan people. Individuals who have worked for justice have also been assassinated. In 1998 Bishop Juan Gerardi presented *Guatemala: Nunca más*, a four-volume human rights report. Two days later he was found dead.

In 2013, Rios Montt was convicted of genocide and crimes against humanity and was sentenced to 80 years in prison. Ten days later, the Constitutional Court of Guatemala overturned his conviction. In 2015, a Guatemalan court held that Rios Montt could be prosecuted for additional crimes, although he could not be punished because of his deteriorating health.

A second UN-sponsored report, *Guatemala: Memory of Silence*, determined that 93% of the 626 massacres examined were committed by government forces and 3% were the responsibility of the guerillas. Indigenous people comprised 83% of the victims. ⬜

Revolutionary Terrorism in Europe

The Latin American revolutionary groups inspired radical left-wing movements in Europe: the Angry Brigade in Great Britain, the Red Army Faction in West Germany, and the Red Brigades in Italy.

The **Red Army Faction** in Germany (popularly referred to as Baader-Meinhof) was headed by Andreas Baader, his companion Gudrun Ensslin, and left-wing journalist Ulrike Meinhof. Analysts have viewed this movement as a product of anger at the older West German population's complicity with the Nazi regime, and by the younger generations' need to assert their own antifascist identity and as a revolt against capitalism and consumerism (Whittaker, 2012).

FIGURE 5.4 Ulrike Meihoff

Source: https://commons.wikimedia.org/
wiki/File%3AUlrike_Meinhof_als_junge_
Journalistin_(retuschiert).jpg.

The young would-be terrorists of Baader-Meinhof trained with terrorist groups abroad to develop their skills. They started with small-scale bombings of department stores and bank robberies, and later evolved into an urban guerilla campaign. A series of confrontations with the police left people dead on both sides of the conflict. Baader-Meinhof declared that it was their goal to reveal the hypocrisy of the "fascist state," and as they became increasingly radicalized they took the name the Red Army Faction (RAF) to align themselves ideologically with the Marxist and anti-Western Japanese Red Army. The RAF turned to bombing American military bases and targeting military personnel stationed in West Germany. Within several months the most prominent members of the RAF were arrested and detained in a specially constructed facility at Stammheim prison (Miller, 2013).

The RAF, however, was far from finished. The RAF next killed a federal prosecutor and the director of the Dresdner Bank. In 1977 they kidnapped prominent business executive Hanns Martin Schleyer and demanded the release of the RAF prisoners in return for Schleyer. Palestinian terrorists seized a Lufthansa airliner and unsuccessfully attempted to barter the release of the airline passengers in return for the release of the RAF detainees. After it became clear that the West German government would not negotiate, three of the imprisoned members of the RAF committed suicide. Soon thereafter Schleyer was killed and left in the trunk of a car.

Once again, many RAF members were arrested. The group continued to engage in low-level acts of terrorism. In 1985 the group bombed an American military base in Frankfurt that killed three individuals. The RAF also claimed responsibility for killing the heads of three major industrial firms before disbanding in 1985.

Between 1969 and 1987, there were nearly 10,000 terrorist attacks committed by left-wing groups in Italy (Law, 2016; Whittaker, 2012). The most prominent terrorist group was the Marxist **Red Brigades**, which was composed of students along with communism-inspired working-class individuals. The group was divided into various cells that operated independently in various cities, while a central committee loosely coordinated the cells' activities.

The Red Brigades spent the 1970s building an organization and gathering arms, funds, and recruits. In 1976 the Red Brigades launched a campaign of violence. The June assassination of the Italian prosecutor-general was followed by the March 1978 kidnapping and subsequent murder of Aldo Moro, former Italian minister and head of the Christian Democratic Party. Over the next several years, the Red Brigades carried out assassinations of police officers, federal and local officials, judges, and industrialists. In 1981 American James Dozier was kidnapped and held for ransom before being rescued by an antiterrorism squad.

Right-wing groups like the Armed Revolutionary Nuclei responded to the violence of the Red Brigade by carrying out attacks on left-wing officials and labor leaders. The Nuclei was effectively eliminated as a meaningful force because of public revulsion over the igniting of a bomb in a Bologna train station that killed 85 people and wounded 200.

The Red Brigade ultimately began to lose members and popular support as left-wing political parties began to focus on addressing working-class concerns.

PREDATORY TERRORISM

A number of groups across the globe engage in **predatory terrorism**, which is defined as the use of terrorism to accumulate wealth and power. These groups tend to be based on the cult of personality of a strong leader who preaches a utopian or semimystical ideology. Predatory groups typically recruit members by kidnapping young children or by appealing to impoverished or orphaned young people in rural villages. The members of these groups are required to swear adherence to the cult leader and to prove their loyalty by engaging in atrocious acts of abuse and murder. These groups tend to be based in rural areas and support themselves by kidnapping for ransom and by asserting control over natural and mineral resources. Their primary goal is the accumulation of wealth and power. The Lord's Resistance Army (LRA) is a Christian cult operating in northern Uganda, the Central African Republic, and the Democratic Republic of the Congo. The group lacks a clear ideology, other than the goal of administering Uganda according to the Ten Commandments, and is united by loyalty to Joseph Kony, a self-declared prophet who assures his followers that they are protected from bullets.

The LRA has carried out a campaign of mass slaughter, destroying villages and killing thousands of people. Nearly 1 million Ugandans have been displaced and tens of thousands of children have been kidnapped.

Predatory terrorism at times is combined with claims of mystical powers. The Holy Spirit Movement, led by spirit medium Alice Auma, claimed to be inspired by the Christian Holy Spirit. She called for the overthrow of the government of Ugandan government of President Yoweri Museveni as a necessary step in the purging of witchcraft and superstition from the country. Her followers smeared themselves with nut butter in order to transform bullets into water. Lakwena told her followers that the stones they threw at the government forces would be transformed into hand grenades. In the end her followers were slaughtered in a confrontation with government forces and she fled to Kenya.

5.1 You Decide

The right to self-determination is a fundamental principle of the international system; it can be traced at least to the Declaration of Independence of the United States, written July 4, 1776. The Declaration of Independence proclaimed that governments derive their "just powers from the consent of the governed" and that "whenever any Form of Government becomes destructive of these ends, it is the Right of the People to alter or to abolish it." The principle of self-determination, as we have seen in earlier chapters, was strengthened by the notion of popular sovereignty articulated in the French Revolution and by the antimonarchical philosophy of the Russian Revolution.

During World War I, Woodrow Wilson championed the notion of the self-determination of minorities in Europe to be free to express their culture and language without discrimination.

A primary principle underlying American and British policy in World War II was that all people should enjoy the right to self-government. The UN Charter (1945, Article 1(2)) provides that one of the purposes of the United Nations is to "develop friendly relations among nations based on respect for the principle of equal rights and *self-determination* of peoples, and to take measures to strengthen international peace." Article 55 of the UN Charter lists among the goals of the organization the creation of peaceful and friendly relations among nations based on the "equal rights and self-determination of peoples."

In 1960 the United Nations unanimously adopted nonbinding Resolution 1514, the Declaration on the Granting of Independence to Colonial Countries and Peoples, which recognizes the right of all peoples to self-determination. This principle has been affirmed in a number of significant human rights documents, including the Universal Declaration of Human Rights (1948) and International Covenant on Civil and Political Rights (1966).

The right of self-determination is the affirmation of the collective right of a people to control their own affairs. These laudatory sentiments raise more questions than answers. What is a "people?" How do we define "self-determination" and what means are justified to achieve self-determination? At a minimum, the right to self-determination may include the right of the people in a country to select their own form of government and may extend as far as obligating a government to provide citizens with the education and opportunity to express themselves and their culture and language.

What, if any, conditions would have to be met before individuals would be justified in undertaking terrorism to assert their "right to self-determination?" Would you place limits on what acts of terrorism would be justified? What about the terrorism engaged in by groups outlined in this chapter? Would you recognize some of these groups as "freedom fighters" rather than as criminal terrorists?

CHAPTER SUMMARY

This chapter has introduced several typologies of terrorism.

Ethnonationalist separatist terrorism. Terrorism by a group whose goal is the creation of an autonomous region within a country or the creation of a separate state. These ethnonationalist movements possess the advantage of a clearly defined, unifying goal and a natural loyalty among a portion of the general population. The groups tend to identify themselves as part of a historical tradition of struggle and tradition and are able to sustain themselves for multiple generations.

Anticolonial separatist terrorism. Terrorism by a group to obtain independence from a colonial power.

Revolutionary terrorism. Terrorism by groups to overthrow an existing government. Examples in Latin America include the Tupamaros in Uruguay and FARC in Colombia. European examples include the RAF in West Germany and the Red Brigades in Italy.

Predatory terrorism. Terrorist groups lacking a clear ideology devoted to economic accumulation and power. Groups like the LRA resemble cults with devotion to charismatic leaders.

CHAPTER REVIEW QUESTIONS

1. What are the characteristics of ethnonationalist revolutionary terrorism and some examples of ethnonationalist terrorist groups?
2. What is revolutionary terrorism? How do the strategic approaches of Carlos Marighella and Mao Zedong differ? Provide insight into why these groups generally have been successful in Latin America
3. Discuss the experience of European revolutionary groups.
4. What is unique about predatory terrorism groups?
5. Describe the primary ideas of Franz Fanon. Do you agree with him?
6. Does the discussion in this chapter support the notion that terrorist groups are "rational" and goal oriented, or are they "irrational" fanatics?

TERMINOLOGY

anticolonial terrorism
Basque Nation and Identity
  (ETA)
ethnonationalist communal
  terrorism
ethnonationalist separatist
  terrorism
Fanon, Frantz

Kurdistan Workers' Party
  (PKK)
Liberation Tigers of Tamil
  Eelam (LTTE)
Mao Zedong
Marighella, Carlos
National Liberation Front
  (NLF)
predatory terrorism

Provisional IRA
Red Army Faction
Red Brigades
Revolutionary Armed Forces
  of Colombia (FARC)
revolutionary terrorism
Shining Path
Tupamaros
Uyghur

CHAPTER 6

Religious Terrorism

TEST YOUR KNOWLEDGE

1. Understand the basis for the argument that religion-motivated terrorism is more lethal than other types of terrorism.
2. Understand the argument that religion cannot be viewed as the sole explanatory cause of terrorist violence.
3. Understand the concept of the caliphate.
4. List the basic beliefs of Salafism.
5. Understand the significance of the Mahdi.
6. Comprehend the significance and changing nature of al Qaeda.
7. Know the significance of the Islamic State of Iraq and the Levant.
8. Distinguish between Sunni and Shia Islam.
9. Understand Shia terrorism.

INTRODUCTION

Religion is customarily viewed as a force for love, peace, justice, and kindness in a world where these traits often are in short supply. The notion that religion can inspire violent terrorism is at odds with the view of religion as a positive force for good in the world.

Professor David Rapoport outlines four "waves" of terrorism. The anarchists (1870–1920) were followed by nationalist resistance to European colonialism. Leftist terrorism developed following World War II (1960s–1980s). The fourth and most recent wave is characterized by religious terrorism (1970s–present).

Rapoport writes that the rise of religious terrorism was inspired by the overthrow of the Shah in Iran in 1979 and by the successful resistance of Islamic fighters to the Soviet intervention in Afghanistan between 1979 and 1989.

Religion provides the prism through which faith-based terrorist groups view the world. As the Islamic State expanded its territorial control, Islamic State of Iraq and al-Sham (ISIS) fighters took control of the Sinjar Mountains area in Northern Iraq populated by the Yazidi in August 2014. In response to an inquiry from ISIS fighters, religious scholars that were sympathetic to ISIS's cause issued a fatwa (religious judgment) that Yazidi women were not part of any religion mentioned in the Koran and could thus be enslaved by ISIS. ISIS responded by launching a genocidal campaign against the Yazidi, a Kurdish-speaking Islamic group that practices an ancient form of religion that combines Islam with Christian influences. ISIS denounced the Yazidi as "devil worshippers." According to the United Nations, 7,000 Yazidi women and girls were abducted by ISIS and imprisoned (Taylor, 2017). Females who converted were required to marry ISIS fighters who were promised wives as part of the "spoils of war." Yazidi women who refused to convert were killed or forced into sexual slavery. Women in many instances were bought and sold repeatedly and subjected to multiple rapes and severe beatings.

According to ISIS, fornication with a slave was acceptable. ISIS theologians believed that the abolition of sexual slavery was a cause of adultery and premarital fornication; without the ability to obtain sexual satisfaction from slaves, men were tempted to engage in immoral sexual behavior (Stern & Berger, 2015). An ISIS theologian stated that it is permissible to have intercourse with a female slave who has not reached puberty, and if she is incapable of intercourse then the master may "enjoy her without intercourse" (McCants, 2015, p. 113).

Most importantly, ISIS proclaimed that the reintroduction of slavery was a "sign" that the Day of Judgment and the triumph of Islam were on the horizon. One part of this narrative is that when the forces of Islam confront the "Romans" in a battle leading to the Day of Judgment, slaves would fight on behalf of their Muslim masters (McCants, 2015).

In 2014 ISIS established a price of 200,000 Iraqi dinars ($170 in U.S. money) for children between 1 and 9 years of age who were sold; the price was reduced for each 10 additional years of age (McCants, 2015). Graeme Wood (2017) reports that the winners of a Koran-memorization competition in June 2015 were rewarded with sex slaves. ISIS takes the topic of slavery as a question of serious discussion and debate, and ISIS publications regularly consider questions such as whether an ISIS sex slave is better off than a Western prostitute, how much various prominent Western women would bring as sex slaves, or whether to use contraception in having sex with a slave before selling her.

The next section explores the link between terrorism and religion. The remainder of the chapter traces the rise of Islamic religious terrorism.

RELIGION AND THE NEW TERRORISM

As previously noted, the link between religion and terrorism can be traced as far back as 2,000 years. The Jewish Zealots employed the *sica* to attack their opponents and to cut their throats. They poisoned wells and granaries and sabotaged the water supply. The Assassins were an Islamic sect that, between 1090 and 1272, fought against the Christian crusaders and embraced suicide terrorism. Between the 7th and 19th centuries, the Hindu Thugs murdered to honor the Hindu goddess Kali. They killed an average of 800 people a year. Terrorism remained closely connected to religion until the French Revolution (Hoffman, 2006). Beginning with Pope Urban II's call in 1054 to retake the Shrine of the Holy Sepulchre in Jerusalem, Christian Europe carried out nine crusades, resulting in the death of thousands of Jews and Muslims (Juergensmeyer, 2003).

As noted by Rapoport (2012), religious terrorism reemerged on the world stage with the Islamic Revolution in Iran, which overthrew the Shah and resulted in the creation of a theocratic state. The successful Afghan campaign against the Soviet Union emboldened Muslims and revealed the weakness of secular Western nations. Most importantly, Rapoport argues that as individuals in various countries lost trust in government they began to look to religion for direction and leadership, and eventually saw adherents of other religions as the cause of their problems. Bruce Hoffman points out that during the 1990s, the number of religious terrorist groups significantly increased. In 1994 one third of the 41 identified active international terrorist groups could be classified as religion motivated, and a year later nearly 50% of international terrorist groups could be classified as religiously motivated. In contrast, nearly 30% could be classified as left wing and 20% could be classified as right wing (Hoffman, 2006). Louise Richardson (2006) notes that in 2004, of the 77 terrorist groups listed by the U.S. Department of State, 40 possessed a combination of religious and political motives (Richardson, 2006).

Bruce Hoffman is a well-known proponent of the view that religious terrorism poses a more lethal threat than terrorism based on political views. He argues that religious terrorists view themselves as agents of the divine who are carrying out their god's commands. Their war is with all nonbelievers, and their goal is the complete destruction of all existing institutions and the creation of a society based on their religious beliefs. They have little or no interest in limiting the seriousness of their attack or in moderating their goals in order to achieve a political settlement. They will select a target to kill as many as people as possible. Mark Juergensmeyer (2003) argues that acts of religious terrorism are often intended to inflict the maximum number of casualties and cause mass destruction and chaos. These attacks are designed to call attention to the religious cause and are not meant to achieve a political goal such as territorial independence. In fulfilling a divine dictate, religious terrorists are certain that, in spite of setbacks, their cause will triumph—if not now, then in the future.

Charles Townshend (2011) proposes three characteristics of contemporary religious terrorism:

Theological. Violence is a response to a theological demand.

Enemy. The violence is directed at a large number of nonbelievers who have been declared to be enemies based on their religious beliefs.

Consequences. The group has little concern for the political consequences of their actions and only are concerned about fulfilling their religious mandate.

Townshend suggests that large-scale religious terrorism is made possible by three characteristics of religious zealotry which may be found among true believers in some secular terrorist groups.

Fanaticism. The capacity to inspire devotion.

Messianism. The utopian belief in the instant transformation and reconstruction of society.

Sacred sacrifice. A belief in the virtue of an individual sacrificing his or life for a religious cause and, in some instances, a reward for this sacrifice in the afterlife.

Some analysts question whether there a direct cause between religion and terrorism. Religion is only a factor in terrorism when there are economic and political grievances that can be explained by religious differences in a society. Richardson (2006) writes that terrorism serves as a bridge that provides a justification and legitimacy for violence by individuals experiencing a sense of economic and political injustice. Religion, with its emphasis on good versus evil, has an easily understandable appeal as compared to the complexities of political ideologies such as Marxism.

These commentators question the notion of pure religion-based terrorism. Groups typically embrace both political and religious motivations—an example being the Irish Republican Army in Ireland. Although at times appearing to be a religious conflict, the primary divisions were based on what the Catholic population viewed as their limited political power and economic opportunity. In any event, individuals affiliated with terrorist groups undoubtedly differ in the strength of their commitment to religion and may have various reasons for engaging in terrorism (Jackson et al., 2011).

Richard Jackson and his coauthors (2011) question whether religious terrorists are unique in believing that they are engaged in a cosmic" of "good" against "evil" and are more violent than secular terrorists. Various secular groups exhibit the very same characteristics that are attributed to religious terrorists. The German RAF, for example, resembled a cult and demanded total loyalty and ideological purity. The RAF was contemptuous of what they viewed as the materialistic values of German society and seemingly engaged in killing for the sake of killing. Nationalist groups like FARC in Colombia and the LTTE in Sri Lanka have been far more violent than religion-motivated terrorist groups, and the LTTE demonstrated a willingness for self-sacrifice that is not unlike religious terrorists' actions.

There also is a question of the role of religion in an individual's decision to join a terrorist group. Factors such as friendship, financial incentives, and a terrorist organization's record of success appear to play an important role in an individual joining and remaining in a terrorist group. The more religious a group, the more likely it is for an individual who joins the group to develop a heightened commitment to religion and to refer to religion as an important factor in their life (White, 2017).

A more cynical view is that religion is a ploy to attract emotional, political, and financial support from believers. Identifying the enemy as a group of nonbelievers is a potent method for dehumanizing the opposition and for portraying the conflict as a religious struggle between good and evil.

Terrorism by self-identified Islamic terrorist groups, of course, is the focus of much of the discussion of contemporary terrorism and is discussed below.

THE CALIPHATE

A central concept in Islam is the oneness of God (*Tawhid*) and a strict adherence to monotheism. Muslims are guided by **sharia** (the requirements of the Koran) and by the hadith (sayings of the Prophet Muhammad). *Sharia law* refers to the legal principles contained and derived from the Koran. The Islamic aspiration historically has been an empire or **caliphate** in which the Muslim community is united by a single figure with religious and political authority. This ideal was nearly realized by the dominant role of the Ottoman Turkish Empire, which collapsed in the 1920s in the aftermath of World War I. Islamic thinkers look back on a history in which Islam was militarily powerful and was a center of intellectual thought. Salafism advocated a return to Islam as originally practiced, which is discussed below.

SALAFISM

Islam is a religion of peace and justice that spans the globe. **Salafism** is a strain of Islam which, in recent years, has been somewhat unfairly identified with inspiring terrorism. Salafists adopt a strict interpretation of the Koran and holy texts, and they reject the demands of modernity. Salafists advocate what is viewed as pure form of Islam based on the practices of the Salafi ("predecessors"), the first Muslims of the 7th century. Salafism, for example, only recognizes a narrow range of religious sources as authoritative and rejects hundreds of years of religious thinking. The extreme version of Salafism views moderate Muslims and Shia Islam as heretical, advocates the cleansing of Muslim lands of Western influences, and views the West as fighting against the religion of Islam itself. Salafists adhere to certain broad principles, including association with like-minded Muslims, a government based on Islamic law, the duty to kill nonbelievers including non-Salafist Muslims, and the duty to destroy the symbols of other religions.

There are several commentators who provided a foundation for the Salafist version of Islam. **Taqi al Din ibn Taymiyyah** (1269–1328) reflected on the slaughter of Muslims at the hands of European crusaders in the 11th century and by Mongol invaders a century later. He called for a purification of the religion and a return to Islam as practiced by the early Muslim communities. Three of his ideas profoundly impacted on contemporary Islamic movements. He interpreted **jihad** as both a spiritual struggle to follow the obligations of Islamic law and practice ("greater jihad"), as well as the duty to engage in a physical confrontation, if necessary, to protect Islam (the "lesser jihad")—both of which he claimed were central pillars of Islam. His second contribution was to declare that Muslim leaders who failed to adhere to sharia were to be excommunicated, removed from office, and killed. His third important contribution was a call for purification of the religion by a war on those he considered to be heretics.

Ibn Taymiyyah profoundly influenced **Abdul Wahhab** (1703–1792), whose thinking dominates the approach to Islam in Saudi Arabia. Wahhab denounced Muslims who had deserted the religion as practiced by the Prophet Muhammad and proclaimed that it was the responsibility of government to enforce religious norms. Wahhabism is a stringent, puritanical form of Islam rejecting music, games, arts, and alcoholism, and also confines women to a restricted life in the home. Wahhab, together with the House of Saud, conquered and united the Arabian Peninsula and established the boundaries of the modern state of Saudi Arabia.

Commentators today divide Salafism into *quietist Salafism* and *political Salafism*. Quietists focus on purifying Islam and avoid political involvement. In contrast, political Salafists believe that by working to create a more just society, they can make people receptive to their message. *Jihadi Salafism* is the militant and aggressive branch of Salafism that believes in the aggressive and violent spread of Salafism.

A number of modern Islamic commentators have combined Salafist thinking with an advocacy of militant opposition to nonbelievers and to the West. Abu Musab al-Suri is a veteran of the campaign against the Soviets in Afghanistan who was allegedly involved in the 2007 London subway attacks and in the 2004 Madrid training bombing. In *The Call to Global Islamic Resistance*, al-Suri developed the concept of "leaderless resistance" that was later advocated by American right-wing extremist Louis Beam (discussed in Chapter 7). Al-Suri urged small groups of jihadists to operate in independent cells and to attack targets throughout the world. After attacking, according to al-Suri, militants should melt into urban populations or find safe havens in rural areas. He assured Salafist fighters that there was no reason to feel guilty about killing because all non-Muslims and heretics are enemies of Islam. The key to the ultimate establishment of an Islamic state, according to al-Suri, is the destruction of the United States (Soufan, 2017)

Abu Bakr Naji, in *Management of Savagery*, endorses the killing and brutal-ization of the enemies of Islam and heretics, although he promises believers a generous and satisfying future. He advocates a three-step process of creating an Islamic caliphate—a unified religious state across the Arab world. The first is the use of violence to create chaos and to attract attention by targeting high-profile targets. The next step involves acts of extraordinary violence and the creation of "regions of savagery." Jihadists would then move into these same areas and build popular support for Salafi rule by establishing security and safety. Finally, after establishing dominance in a number of towns, these municipalities would come together in the establishment of an Islamic state. Another aspect of this strategy is to involve the United States in a series of conflicts throughout the Middle East to undermine America's all-powerful image and to motivate and to attract Islamic fighters throughout the world (Soufan, 2017).

In 2005 Jordanian Fouad Hussein published a text, *Al-Zarqawi: The Second Generation of al Qaeda*, in which he outlines a seven-step process for the estab-lishment of a Salafist state. The last step entails a confrontation between believers on the one hand, and the betrayers of Islam (apostates) and Infidels (Christians and Jews) on the other hand (Soufan, 2017).

Jihad is a central term in the discussion of Salfalism. The *greater jihad* is the spiritual struggle to live as a virtuous Muslim. The *lesser jihad* refers to armed struggle. Some commentators contend that the lesser jihad must be declared by a government, although others argue that this is an individual decision and may be directed against a government that does not follow sharia. The so-called defensive jihad requires armed struggle against nonbelievers that invade a Muslim land.

Takfir is a term used by Salafists for a nonbeliever. Salafists differ on who is categorized as takfir. The extremist version views Muslims who do not adhere to a traditional form of Islam as nonbelievers. Another central concept is of the near enemy and the far enemy. One set of strategists argues that Middle Eastern rulers that do not follow Islamic principles are the near enemy and should be the focus of attack. Other analysts argue that the focus of attack should be the far enemy—the United States and European countries that support the regimes that are viewed as the near enemy.

A point of contention is whether it is justifiable to kill noncombatant civilians. The argument for killing Western civilians is that the United States and European countries are launching attacks that kill Muslim civilians, and that given the sophisticated technology available to Western democracies, the only possible conclusion is that these civilian deaths are being inflicted in a reckless—if not intentional—fashion. These types of attacks only will come to an end when Western civilians experience the same suffering and loss of life. There also is the argument that there are no "innocents" in the War on Terror. Civilians in a democracy are viewed as responsible for the policies pursued by their governments and thus are partners in the killing of Muslim civilians. What of Muslim civilians? Killing Muslim civilians is justified on the grounds that these individuals are martyrs whose deaths are part of jihad against the near enemy. There is also seemingly little or no reluctance by Sunnis to kill Shia civilians, who are viewed by some Salafists as a heretical sect within Islam.

APOCALYPTIC NARRATIVES

Another important influence on contemporary Islamic terrorists is the belief in religious prophesies. These complicated narratives differ in their details, although public opinion surveys indicate that these beliefs exercise a strong influence on the Middle Eastern populace. These apocalyptic narratives provide a justification for the violence of terrorist groups, assist in the recruitment of fighters, and sustain the group confronted with setbacks and defeats (McCants, 2015).

The core of these apocalyptic or "end-time" beliefs is that the **Mahdi** (which translates to *the Guided One*) will appear before the Day of Judgment to lead the battle and will vanquish the Infidels. The Mahdi is a member of the Prophet's family and will emerge to create a just world. He will appear to end divisions among Muslims and to prepare the Muslim community for the second coming of Jesus Christ, who is considered to be a prophet in Islam. Jesus will appear and vanquish the forces of the anti-Christ. In personal correspondence, Osama bin Laden referred to his location as *Khorasan*—a region that encompasses portions of Iran, Central Asia, and Afghanistan—in which the Mahdi will appear.

The prophecy of the Mahdi is given added credibility by statements that alleged were uttered by the Prophet Muhammad mentioning the coming of the Mahdi. These statements can be found in the hadith—statements attributed to the Prophet and written down by his followers.

The Islamic State (ISIS/ISIL) advocated for Muslims to join them in their fight against Bashar Assad in Syria, reasoning that this was the beginning of the "Grand Battle" which will usher in the "end time" and the triumph of Islam. ISIS pointed to what they consider as small signs that the prophecy of end times was being fulfilled. The group intentionally adopted a black flag, which is associated with the Mahdi and symbolizes revenge as well as mourning. The Prophet Muhammad also flew a black flag in his war against Infidels (McCants, 2015).

Personalities and Events

Sayyid Qutb (1906–1966) has perhaps had a greater impact on contemporary Islamic Salafism than any other thinker. He progressed from a rural Egyptian village to a position in the Ministry of Education. As a young man in the 1930s, Qutb was "Westernized," enjoying European literature and classical music. He nonetheless infuriated Egypt's corrupt monarch, King Farouk, with his journalist criticism of the royal regime and thought it best to leave the country before finding himself imprisoned for crimes against the regime. In 1948 Qutb received a scholarship to study the educational system in the United States. He spent 6 months of his 2 years in the United States at Colorado State University. Qutb's experience turned him against Western culture. He was appalled by the revealing dress of women, the intermingling of the sexes, racism, the consumption of alcohol, and by American informality and superficiality. Qutb reacted against American secularism, individualism, and democracy, and he left with a view of America as a spiritually bankrupt and materialistic desert.

FIGURE 6.1 Sayyid Qutb

Source: https://commons. wikimedia.org/wiki/File:Sayyid_ Qutb.jpg.

Qutb now saw his lifetime project as turning Egypt away from Europe and the United States and toward an embrace of Islam. After returning to Egypt he published *The America That I Have Seen* in which he lashed out against every aspect of American life—including haircuts, sports, the country's "primitive" taste in music, and support for Israel.

(continues on next page)

(continued from previous page)

Qutb quickly felt out of step with the government of Gamal Abdel Nasser, which had come to power in a coup in which the military overthrew the corrupt royal regime of King Farouk. He became an editor of the newspaper of the reformist Muslim Brotherhood, which advocated for a society based on Islamic law and which rejected nationalism—considered by the Brotherhood to be a diversion from the path to Islam as practiced by the original founding fathers of the faith.

The Muslim Brotherhood was established in 1928 by Hasan al-Banna, an Egyptian primary school teacher. Al-Banna believed that West was collapsing, and that Islam would emerge as a global force. The Brotherhood engaged in religious education and established schools, clinics, and welfare societies. The Brotherhood was repressed by King Farouk, who accused the group of terrorist violence. It reemerged as a political force after the start of Nasser's military regime.

In 1954 Qutb was imprisoned by Nasser following a failed assassination attempt on the Egyptian leader, although he was released after 3 months because Nasser wished to appease Muslim and American domestic opinion. Several months later he was rearrested. Qutb would remain in a prison hospital for the next decade and while incarcerated, he wrote the eight-volume Islamic commentary, *In the Shade of the Quran*.

A prison strike by the Brotherhood led to the killing and injury of well over 50 imprisoned members of the Brotherhood. Qutb reacted by claiming that those who opposed the Brothers were not true Muslims (*tafkir* or "evil"). Qutb then wrote the manifesto *Milestones*, which circulated in the underground for years despite the fact that the work was banned in a number of countries. In *Milestones*, Qutb argued that humankind was threatened to a greater extent by an absence of values than by nuclear weapons. Neither capitalist democracy nor Communist Marxism offered a productive path; only Islam was capable of moving the Arab world forward. Qutb divided the world into Islam and *Jahiliyyah* (ignorance and barbarity), two paths which differed in virtually every area of life. Humankind could either embrace Islam or confront doom and destruction.

Qutb argued that the revival of Islam must be led by an elite vanguard ready to lead the Muslims to world domination. The obligation of this elite and of all Muslims was to oppose non-Muslim regimes, as well as Muslim regimes that deviated from the path of true Islam. The goal was to replace the "Kingdom of Man" with the "Kingdom of God."

In 1966 Nasser placed Qutb and 42 members of the Brotherhood on trial, claiming that they had plotted to overthrow his military regime. As demonstrators filled the streets, Nasser communicated to Qutb that if he appealed, that the regime would spare his life and perhaps even bring him into the government. Qutb rebuffed the offer of leniency and was executed on August 29, 1966, with the apparent realization that his words would be even more powerful following his death. ▯

AL QAEDA

The roots of **al Qaeda** are found in American support for Afghan resistance to Russian intervention intended to support a government sympathetic to the Soviet Union. The defeat of the Soviets in 1989 led to an emboldened jihadist movement which turned its focus to the removal of Western influences from Muslim countries and to the purification of Islam. In Afghanistan, the fundamentalist **Taliban** captured control of the government. The phenomenon of Muslim militants turning against the United States and Europe based on the Western powers' alleged support for semiauthoritarian governments throughout the Arab world has been termed *blowback*. A number of these authoritarian regimes were based on an oil economy, in which the rulers accumulated massive amounts of wealth and in which there was limited opportunity for young people—even those with an education. Neither Western capitalism nor Soviet communism were viewed as offering a path forward and Islam was viewed as offering the answer to the problems confronting Muslim societies.

In discussing the roots of Islamic terrorism, commentators also point to the 1979 Iranian revolution which overthrew the Shah. Although the revolution amounted to an internal upheaval in a predominantly Shia country, it demonstrated the power and ability of an Islamic-led movement to defeat a seemingly all-powerful government supported by Western powers.

As previously mentioned, Osama bin Laden was heavily influenced by Salafist thinking. As a young man, he was exposed to the teachings of Muhammad Qutb, the brother of Sayyid Qutb, and to the teachings of militant Palestinian Abdullah Azzam. Both men believed that an Islam as practiced by the founding fathers of the faith was the solution to poverty and to the return of Islam to global dominance.

Bin Laden turned on the Saudi royal family in 1991, after the Saudis joined the international coalition opposing the Iraqi invasion of Kuwait. American troops were stationed in Saudi Arabia to provide protection for the Saudi regime and to create a support structure for military attacks on Iraq. Following the war, American forces remained in Saudi Arabia. Bin Laden had argued that his fighters could protect the Saudi regime, and he was appalled that Western forces had been welcomed into sacred Saudi territory. He believed that true purpose of the United States was to seize the oil wealth of Arab countries in the Middle East. The willingness of the Islamic regimes to embrace the United States, according to Bin Laden, was a symbol of growing *Jahiliyyah*—an abandonment of Islam and a descent into darkness. At the same time, Bin Laden was convinced that the United States was a "paper tiger" and would flee and crumble when confronted with a determined Islamic opposition force.

An important event that shaped Bin Laden's view that the United States would flee if they were confronted occurred in 1993, after the United Nations authorized a humanitarian intervention in Somalia known as Operation Restore Hope. The

United States deployed 1,800 marines to the capital, Mogadishu. An al Qaeda–trained group of Islamic fighters shot down two MH-60 Black Hawk helicopters, and 18 Americans died in the ground battle and 84 were injured. In 1995 the United States, having suffered a grievous loss of fighters, withdrew its forces from Somalia.

Bin Laden was forced to leave Saudi Arabia in 1991 and along with 500 fighters, he established a foothold in Sudan. In Sudan, Bin Laden encountered terrorist figures from countries throughout the Middle East, which reportedly led him to conclude that there was the potential to form a global jihadist network. He was asked to leave Sudan after the regime was pressured by other Arab states that suspected his involvement in the attempted assassinations of Prince Abdullah of Jordan and Hosni Mubarak in Egypt. Saudi patience with Bin Laden also had reached the breaking point after he was allegedly involved in bombings in Riyadh and in Dhahran, Saudi Arabia. Bin Laden and his men left for Afghanistan, where they combined forces with Ayman Zawahiri, who had fled from Egypt after being suspected of involvement in attempting to overthrow the regime.

Afghanistan was a welcoming country. In 1996 Mullah Omar and the Taliban had seized control of two thirds of the country and subsequently emerged victorious in a civil war among competing factions; they almost immediately instituted a harsh brand of Islam. The Taliban prohibited the flying of kites, the playing of music, and pigeon and dog racing. It also banned Western hairstyles and the shaving or trimming of beards. Women were denied education and work, and they were required to wear veils. The hands and feet of thieves were amputated.

Bin Laden situated al Qaeda in Kandahar, Afghanistan, and attracted fighters from a number of countries across the Arab world. In 1996, 14 weeks after entering Afghanistan, Bin Laden, Zawahiri, and al Qaeda's security director Mohammed Atef declared war on the "Great Satan" (the United States), a statement that received little serious attention from American and European political leaders and from the media. Two years later Bin Laden and Zawahiri, along with other militant leaders, formed the Islamic Front Against Jews and Crusaders; they declared that Muslims had a religious duty to kill Americans and citizens of its Western allies wherever they were found.

In 2001 al Qaeda formally merged with Zawahiri's Egyptian Islamic Jihad forming an organization called al-Qaeda al-Jihad (Base of Jihad). At this point, al Qaeda only numbered around 400 fighters and Zawahiri, who was named second in command, brought only 10 fighters to the newly formed organization. Zawahiri had long served as Bin Laden's physician and provided medical care for Bin Laden's severe kidney and other medical problems.

Osama bin Laden's use of the media to as propaganda was a central part of his strategy to mobilize Muslims across the globe to undertake jihad. He invoked Allah in his statements to portray his struggle as divinely inspired. At times he was pictured riding a white horse which was intended to remind viewers of the Prophet who rode into battle on a white stallion. Bin Laden also carefully selected every aspect of his appearance to communicate a symbolic message. For example, he almost always was photographed with a knife at his waist, which was typical of the weapon worn by rulers on the Arabian Peninsula. This was designed to reinforce the message that Bin Laden was a legitimate authority rather than a terrorist. Osama bin Laden's calm presence was meant to portray him as a man of peace who had been provoked into responding to the onslaught of the United States and Europe.

Although al Qaeda was highly organized with committees in charge of such areas as medical care and supply along with an advisory committee to Bin Laden, al Qaeda was not a traditional hierarchical organization. The organizational core originally consisted of several hundred fighters who swore obedience to Bin Laden. However, an estimated 20,000 fighters from as many as 30 terrorist groups across the globe received sophisticated military training and ideological education from al Qaeda, returning to their homeland to create terrorist cells in far-flung locales—ranging from Chechnya to Bosnia, Algeria, the Philippines, Yemen, and Tunisia. On occasion, al Qaeda would provide needed money, arms, and technical expertise in bomb making or planning operations. Al Qaeda's relations with regional groups were handled by various regional bureaus rather than by al Qaeda central (Law, 2016).

Al Qaeda, much like organized crime syndicates, engaged in legal commercial activity to make money. These goods and services included a near monopolization of the honey trade in the Middle East, along with criminal activity such as credit card fraud. A significant source of support came from charitable organizations which directed funds to al Qaeda, and from state sponsors sympathetic to al Qaeda's aspirations (Gunaratna, 2002).

Rohan Gunaratna (2002) writes that a distinctive characteristic of al Qaeda was intensive surveillance and planning of an assault. The 9/11 attack involved more than 15 months of study. He notes that al Qaeda operatives were highly trained and disciplined, and he points to the fact that the 9/11 hijackers carried out their atrocious attack with a seeming lack of fear or panic.

Al Qaeda's first front was to wage war on Arab rulers who had betrayed their obligation to follow sharia law. The second front was to wage war on the United States and the West for occupying Arab lands, inflicting suffering on the Iraqi people, looting the oil wealth of the Middle East, and for supporting Israel. Gunaratna argues that these concerns—rather than a resentment of the lifestyle of Western democracy—were the motivating forces behind Bin Laden's declaration of war on America and his proclamation that it was the duty of Muslims to kill Americans (Gunaratna, 2002).

The first jihadist attack on American soil was a little-noticed attack by Mir Qazi, who killed two CIA employees and wounded three others during a January 1993 attack on the CIA headquarters. A month later, the World Trade Center was attacked by a small group that wanted to exact retribution for American support of Israel. The major figure involved in this attack was Kuwaiti-born Ramzi Yousef; his parents were from Pakistan and Palestine. He was influenced by Sheikh Omar Abdel-Rahman, the "blind Sheikh," an Egyptian cleric living in the United States who issued fatwas stating that Muslims had a religious duty to kill Americans and Jews and to destroy the West. On February 26, 1993, Yousef and his cell ignited a bomb in the garage of the World Trade Center, causing an estimated $1 billion in damage. He later fled to the Philippines, where a plot to bomb 11 American airliners and to assassinate the Pope was foiled when a fire led to the discovery of his bomb-making laboratory in the Philippines (Law, 2016).

Al Qaeda announced its global presence with the 1998 attacks on the embassies in Nairobi, Kenya, and Dar es Salaam, Tanzania; the USS *Cole* in 2000; the unsuccessful millennialist attack on the Los Angeles airport; and the 9/11 attack on the World Trade Center. The plan for 9/11 was to attack the symbols of American power and authority—the World Trade Center, the Pentagon, and either Congress or the White House; this third attack was diverted. It is difficult to overstate the impact of these events on the direction of American life in the subsequent decade and on the elevation of terrorism into a focus of American domestic and foreign policy.

The American intervention in Afghanistan in October 2001 led to deterioration of al Qaeda's organization. Al Qaeda found itself unable to mount large-scale attacks. The weakened al Qaeda was now operating in name only and worked through various affiliated terrorist groups across the globe. Osama bin Laden reportedly encouraged affiliates to drop the name *al Qaeda* to make themselves more acceptable to local populations. Al Qaeda central reportedly was involved with the affiliates who carried out the Madrid bombing in March 2003, the London subway bombing in July 2005, and in an unsuccessful attempt to orchestrate the simultaneous bombings of airliners and the bombing of an air cargo plane.

U.S. drone attacks have eliminated most of the original members of al Qaeda's leadership; this effort culminated on May 1, 2011, when U.S. Navy Seals raided Osama bin Laden's compound in Pakistan and killed the al Qaeda leader. The so-called new al Qaeda, led by Ayman Zawahiri, continues to present a serious threat through its affiliates across the globe; although al Qaeda has a drastically reduced capacity to provide assistance in the form of training, fighters, and expertise such as bomb making. Through its affiliates, the organization nonetheless remains a powerful inspirational force in the world of terrorism.

Zawahiri remains committed to violence and has famously stated that there is no solution other than jihad. He has managed to maintain the loyalty of most of al Qaeda's most influential affiliate organizations. Bin Laden's son Hamza is emerging as a leader who commands respect from terrorists across the globe.

The Arab Spring led to an expansion of al Qaeda groups into Egypt, Libya, and—most significantly—into Syria, where al Nusra was one of the most active groups fighting the Assad regime. Al Nusra, a faction of which merged into ISIS, was particularly noteworthy because the organization has presented itself as a nationalist, patriotic organization whose goal was to overthrow the Assad regime, and which was willing to be aligned with both religious and secular terrorist organizations.

Al Qaeda–Affiliated Groups

Al Qaeda in the Arabian Peninsula (AQAP). From 2003 to 2004, AQAP launched a terrorist campaign in Saudi Arabia, and in the next 4 years they killed nearly 300 Saudi nationals. Two years later, the group merged with al Qaeda in Yemen. AQAP supported the 2015 *Charlie Hebdo* killings in Paris. Anwar al-Alwaki was the most well-known figure affiliated with AQAP. He inspired the attacks in the United States by major Nidal Hasan at Fort Hood, Texas, and the unsuccessful bombing of a Northwest airplane over Detroit by Umar Farouk Abdulmutallab on Christmas Day 2009. These attacks were followed by the placement of chemical explosives in printers on cargo planes that were bound for the United States. The AQAP magazine *Inspire* is alleged to have played a role in motivating the Tsarnaev brothers' bombing of the Boston Marathon in 2013.

Presently AQAP is a minor military force in a civil war in Yemen and is arrayed against the forces of the weak central government sponsored by Saudi Arabia and against the Houthis, an Iran-sponsored Shia group. The big losers are the people of Yemen, whose country is devastated by starvation, disease, and death.

Al Qaeda in the Islamic Maghreb (AQIM). In reaction to the cancellation of mid-1990s elections in Algeria in anticipation of a strong showing by Islamic groups, the Armed Islamic Group (GIA) and the Armed Islamic Movement (AIM) launched brutally violent attacks, killing thousands of teachers, medical professionals, academics, and intellectuals. The government responded with a harsh crackdown, and as many as 120,000 individuals died during the conflict. A more moderate wing of the GIA, the Salafi Group for Preaching and Combat (GSPC), united with al Qaeda in 2006 and formed AQIM. AQIM engaged in bombings in Algeria, attacks in Mali, and a 2013 attack on the Israeli embassy in Mauritania, an assault on the French embassy in Mali, the kidnappings of French nationals in Niger, and an armed attack on a beach resort in Ivory Coast. A breakaway group, al Murabituom, which later rejoined AQIM, attacked a natural gas facility in Algeria, killing as many as 80 individuals. AQIM has developed links with Boko Haram and a faction, the Caliphate Soldiers in Algeria, has developed links with ISIS.

(continues on next page)

(continued from previous page)

al Shabaab. A Somali terrorist group which was first established in the mid-2000s, al Shabaab (translates to *the youth*) developed in response to an Ethiopian invasion of Somalia that aimed to displace the rule of the militant Islamic Court Union government. Al Shabaab enjoyed popular support in opposing Ethiopia, although its support rapidly declined when the forces of the African Union—a regional organization of African nations—intervened to bolster support for the newly installed Somali government. The intervention by the African Union coincided with al Shabaab's decision to affiliate with al Qaeda in 2008, shifting its rhetoric from patriotic nationalism to militant Islam and proclaiming regional and global aspirations. Al Shabaab envisioned an ethnic Somalian emirate in east Africa. The group has struck outside Somalia—most notably a 2002 attack on an Israeli-owned hotel in Kenya that killed 15 people and an attack on an Israeli jet in Mombasa, Kenya.

Kenya increasingly has come to view al Shabaab as a threat and joined the African Union, creating a buffer zone with Somalia to discourage the group from infiltrating Kenya, which has a large Somali population. Al Shabaab responded on September 13, 2015, when four young al Shabaab militants entered the campus of Garissa University College in northern Kenya and carried out the systematic killing of non-Muslim students. Two years earlier, al Shabaab attacked the Westgate shopping mall in Kenya and planted a bomb at a World Cup match in Uganda in protest over the intervention of the African Union in Somalia that killed more than 70 individuals. An American airstrike in September 2014 killed the leader of al Shabaab, Ahmed Abdi Godane. Al Shabaab has recruited fighters from Somali populations across the globe, and in 2008 the group deployed an American suicide bomber (Soufan, 2017).

Ansar Bait al Maqdis. An outgrowth of the Arab Spring in 2010, the Egyptian group Ansar Bait al Maqdis operates in the Sinai Peninsula and continues to engage in attacks on the Egyptian military and tourists.

Ansar al-Sharia (Libya). Ansar al-Sharia in Libya was founded in 2012 and was composed of Sunni jihadists seeking to create an Islamic state in Libya. The group, which is loosely affiliated with al Qaeda, is centered in eastern Libya around Benghazi. Ansar al-Sharia was reportedly responsible for the September 11, 2012, attack on the U.S. Special Mission and Annex in Benghazi that killed two security officers and the American ambassador.

Ansar al-Sharia (Tunisia). Established in Tunisia in 2011, Ansar al-Sharia has sent fighters to Syria; in the past several years the group has turned its attention to establishing an Islamic state in Tunisia. The group was likely responsible for a March 2015 attack on the Bardo National Museum, which killed 20 foreign tourists.

Boko Haram. Boko Haram in Nigeria is a much-feared group responsible for rape, murder, assassination, and the mass kidnapping of young women in 2014. The name Boko Haram means *Western education is forbidden* and is a shorthand expression for the group's actual name, "The People Committed to the Propagation of the Prophet's Teaching and Jihad." Although they view themselves as part of the global jihadist movement, Boko Haram's primary focus is on asserting their authority in a portion of Nigeria and imposing sharia law.

In 2010 Boko Haram announced its affiliation with al Qaeda. This was followed in 2011 by a car bomb attack on UN headquarters in Abuja, Nigeria, killing 23 and injuring 80. In 2014 Boko Haram kidnapped 200 young girls from a school in Northern Nigeria. Experts estimate that the group may be responsible for kidnapping as many as 500 women.

Haqqani network (HQ). The *Haqqani network* (HQ) was founded by Jalaluddin Haqqani, who commanded the Mujahideen Army (1980–1992) during the insurgency against the Soviet Union in Afghanistan. The network is centered on the Afghan–Pakistani border and at various times has been aligned with the CIA, the Taliban, and the Pakistani security services. The HQ dominates the so-called tribal regions of Pakistan bordering Afghanistan and engages in activities ranging from drug trafficking and kidnapping to terrorism. The HQ is credited with helping Bin Laden flee Pakistan during the American intervention in Afghanistan and provides crucial support to the Taliban.

Islamic Group (IG). Situated in Malaysia and in Indonesia, the IG aims to create an Islamic caliphate across Southeast Asia. In October 2002, on the second anniversary of the bombing of the USS *Cole*, the IG ignited two bombs in Bali, killing more than 200 people—including 90 mostly young Australian vacationers.

Jabhat al Nusra. Al Nusra is an al Qaeda–affiliated group that fought in Syria against the Assad regime. The group attempted to present itself as a nationalist fighting force with loyalty to both jihadist and nationalist-secular rebel forces. They were viewed as an effective force, but they lacked ties to any of the major powers involved in the conflict.

Jemaah Islamiyah (JI). The JI is a network of Southeast Asian terrorist groups whose goal is the creation of an Islamic state of Muslims in southern Thailand, Malaysia, Singapore, Brunei, Indonesia, Cambodia, and the Philippines. ⬜

Personalities and Events

Ahmad Fadil al-Khalayleh—known by his nom de guerre **Abu Musab al-Zarqawi**—was born into a working-class family and from an early age was drawn to alcohol, drugs, and prostitution. A petty criminal covered with tattoos, al-Zarqawi was imprisoned for sexual assault and drug possession. Al-Zarqawi, together with a number of men from his village, left Jordan to fight in Afghanistan. He returned to Jordan in 1993 and was incarcerated for terrorist activities. At his trial al-Zarqawi refused to recognize the legitimacy of the court and issued his own criminal indictments against King Hussein of Jordan and the judge. In prison al-Zarqawi formed a close relationship with a Palestinian sheikh Abu Muhammad al-Maqdisi, a noted scholar whose teachings inspired al-Zarqawi to commit himself to militant Salafism. Al-Maqdisi preached that the "near enemy," the Muslim regimes that were aligned with Western democracies, were the true enemy and posed a greater threat than the "far enemy." After al-Zarqawi had spent 5 years in prison, Jordanian King Abdullah II celebrated his ascendancy to the throne by granting amnesty to various prisoners, including al-Zarqawi. There was well-documented tension between Osama bin Laden (who was accustomed to being treated with reverence and respect) and the brash, opinionated al-Zarqawi. Bin Laden nonetheless approved of al-Zarqawi establishing a training camp funded by al Qaeda in western Afghanistan staffed with Jordanians, Syrians, and Palestinians. Following the American intervention in Afghanistan, al-Zarqawi and his militia fled to Iran and then to the Kurdish region of Iraq. In 2003 al-Zarqawi established al Qaeda in Iraq (AQI) which eventually evolved into Jabhat al-Nusra, an al Qaeda affiliate in Syria, a part of which later merged with ISIS.

Although the AQI was formally affiliated with al Qaeda, al-Zarqawi operated according to his own view of how to wage jihad. Following 9/11, al Qaeda concluded that maintaining popular support required limiting the number of individuals killed—at least when it came to fellow Muslims. Al-Zarqawi, however, took the opposite approach; he believed that he was fighting to spread Islam and the rule of Islamic law across the globe and advocated the killing of any and all individuals that were not firmly aligned with his cause. Despite al-Zarqawi's differences with Bin Laden, in October 2004 he swore allegiance (bayat) to Bin Laden and was named by Bin Laden as Emir of al Qaeda in Iraq. Al-Zarqawi launched a campaign of escalating violence. In 2003 he directed a bombing that destroyed the UN headquarters in Baghdad, resulting in the death of Sérgio Vieira de Mello, a globally respected figure. An online posted video in 2004 showed him severing the head of American captive Nicholas Berg. Al-Zarqawi not only relentlessly attacked Americans and Shia Muslims, but also did not hesitate to attack his fellow Sunni Muslims. In another act of violence in 2005, he directed the bombing attacks on three hotels in Jordan, killing 57 people. Al-Zarqawi believed that by attacking Shia, he could draw them into the conflict with the Sunni in Iraq and create a civil war. The AQI launched a campaign of attacks on political and religious leaders and on hundreds of scholars; they bombed markets, attacked convoys, and even killed moderate Sunnis, earning the nickname "Sheik of Slaughterers." In 2006 al-Zarqawi directed a bombing of al-Askari Mosque in Samarra, the holiest Shia mosque.

Al-Zarqawi was seemingly transforming al Qaeda in his own violent vision; this image was becoming as well-known as that of Osama bin Laden. His fighters spread into Europe and participated in the March 2004 train bombings in Spain. In July 2005, Ayman al-Zawahiri wrote al-Zarqawi, advising him to limit his attacks on Shias and to stop beheading hostages because it was harming al Qaeda's image. Former FBI agent Ali Soufan, a leading terrorist analyst, concludes that at this point al-Zarqawi stood as one of the most notorious terrorists in the world. His organization, according to Soufan, was responsible for the deaths of dozens of American soldiers and thousands of Iraqi citizens. These atrocities led to al-Zarqawi being sentenced to death four times in absentia in Jordan.

A $25 million bounty was offered by the United States for information leading to the capture or death of al-Zarqawi. In 2007 al-Zarqawi was killed when two American precision-guided bombs destroyed a house in which he was staying outside of Baghdad. Al-Zarqawi left a legacy that has animated the activities of the contemporary ISIS. Osama bin Laden believed in the golden age of an Islamic caliphate that united the Arab world could not be realistically achieved in the near future. In contrast, al-Zarqawi believed that by purifying Islam through ruthless violence and by taking and holding territory, that the caliphate could be rapidly achieved. []

THE ISLAMIC STATE OF IRAQ

In March 2003, the United States invaded Iraq and overthrew Saddam Hussein. President George W. Bush alleged that Hussein had been involved in the 9/11 attack on the United States and that his sponsorship of terrorism threatened the United States. This threat was particularly dire because of Saddam Hussein's purported possession of weapons of mass destruction. Information that emerged following the invasion revealed that none of these claims were true (Law, 2016).

The rapid end of the war did not end to the violence in Iraq. Initially, members of the military and members of Hussein's Baathist Party undertook a guerilla campaign. At the same time, Sunni tribes took up arms to assert that they were entitled to participate in the new regime despite the removal of Saddam Hussein. The long-repressed Shias responded by fighting to assert their right to control the Iraqi government and were divided into contending factions. These groups fought one another and at times fought against the Americans and the American-trained Iraqi security forces.

FIGURE 6.2 Abu Bakr Al-Baghdadi

Ayman al-Zawahiri in a eulogy to Abu Musab al-Zarqawi, the leader and inspiration behind the AQI, encouraged the organization to establish an Islamic state based on sharia law in conjunction with al Qaeda. In response, the AQI formed the **Islamic State of Iraq (ISI)** under the leadership of Abu Omar al-Baghdadi. ISI continued a policy of targeting civilians and experienced a continued inability to attract popular support from the Sunni population of Iraq, which aligned with American forces led by general David Petraeus to defeat ISI and drive the remaining ISI fighters underground or out of the country. This defeat, combined with the killing of al-Baghdadi, seemingly meant the end of al Qaeda as an effective force in Iraq. The governing council of ISI turned the leadership of the weakened organization over to Ibrahim Awad Ibrahim al-Badri whose nom de guerre was **Abu Bakr al-Baghdadi.** The scholarly al-Baghdadi appeared to be an unlikely choice, but he had made contact with a large number of insurgents during his imprisonment by American forces and claimed to be a direct descendant of the Prophet Muhammad.

Ironically, ISI was rejuvenated as a result of the miscalculation of the Iraqi regime. The government in Baghdad, headed by Nuri al-Maliki, turned its back on the Sunni tribes that had aligned with the Americans during the so-called Sunni Awakening to defeat ISI. The government did not invite Sunni participation in the governing coalition, refused to pay the salaries of Sunni militia who had aligned with the government, directed the mass arrest of Sunnis, and tolerated the mass killings of Sunnis by Shia militias. Iraq elected a more open-minded government in 2014, but the Sunnis now saw their future as one aligned with ISI.

Islamic State of Iraq and the Levant

In 2010 Abu Bakr al-Baghdadi reconstructed ISI by recruiting former Iraqi Sunni military men and experienced fighters who had lost their positions following the fall of Saddam Hussein. He also attracted former bureaucrats from the Hussein regime who were experienced in running an organization.

The Americans and Iraqis unknowingly facilitated the reconstruction of ISI. Captured Sunni fighters in Iraq were housed in a central prison called Camp Bucca. The complex, which bordered Kuwait, at one point housed as many as 24,000 inmates. The institution provided an opportunity for insurgents to meet with one another and led to the formation of a lethal alliance between jihadists affiliated with ISI and other terrorist groups, and former Sunni members of Saddam Hussein's military who had been removed from their position and had turned to insurgency. Virtually all of the Islamic State's central figures at one time were interned at Camp Bucca and following their release, they reconnected with the men they met while imprisoned.

A central ISI command established an overall strategic plan, although the details of how and when to attack were left to local leaders. Local Sunni leaders who refused to align with ISI were assassinated, which paved the way for the assertion of ISI control over cities in northwest Iraq. In 2012 ISI launched a campaign of attacking Iraqi forces in a hit-and-run campaign of assassinations and small-scale attacks. This elevated the profile of ISI by highlighting their ability to defeat the Iraqi military. The assassinations were followed by a bombing campaign targeting the central towns and cities in Iraq.

In April 2013, Abu Bakr al-Baghdadi announced the formation of a new organization, the **Islamic State of Iraq and the Levant (ISIL)**, also known as the **Islamic State of Iraq and al-Sham (ISIS)**. The Levant encompasses Syria, Jordan, Lebanon, Israel, and portions of other countries. The announcement was accompanied by the proclamation that ISIL/ISIS was joining the fight against the Assad regime in Syria. Ayman al-Zawahiri denounced the organization after it disregarded his objections to their expansion into Syria.

ISIS was distinguished from other Islamist terrorist groups by the organizations' sophisticated social media presence and well-coordinated and professional organization. Within roughly a year, ISIS had exercised military and political control over nearly one third of Syria and had asserted control over major Iraqi population centers, including Mosul and Tikrit. In June 2014, ISIS proclaimed that it had restored the caliphate with Abu Bakr al-Baghdadi as new caliph. This claim was reinforced by the announcement that the organization would henceforth be known as the Islamic State (also known as **Daesh** based on initials of the organization in Arabic). Islamic scholars questioned whether ISIS possessed the authority to declare a caliphate despite al-Baghdadi's alleged familial link to the Prophet. Nonetheless, ISIS began to attract support from the more aggressive factions in various regional terrorist groups. Al Qaeda now viewed ISIS as a rival for leadership of the global Islamic terrorist movement. Boko Haram in Nigeria went so far as to pledge loyalty to both groups.

The organization of ISIS was reminiscent of al Qaeda under Bin Laden with a consultative *shura* council that advised the caliph, along with committees concerned with security and intelligence, military affairs, finance, and media. ISIS had its own court and police force. This organizational structure was replicated in the 18 provinces in Iraq and Syria that ISIS controlled at the height of the organization's power.

At the time ISIS declared a caliphate, their forces occupied one third of Syria, one quarter of Iraq, and a small portion of Libya. This encompassed a population greater than Great Britain, Denmark, Finland, or Ireland. ISIS was sufficiently sophisticated to know that to be taken seriously as the center of the caliphate, they had to prove capable of governing. They typically ensured that in the towns they captured, public employees continued to provide basic services. ISIS fighters distributed food, repaired roads and the electrical infrastructure, and provided health care.

ISIS also continued to follow the example of al-Zarqawi, adopting a policy of ruthless violence including beheadings, crucifixions, drownings, mass rapes, kidnappings, murder, and enslavement. In many cases, these atrocities were posted on social media. As territorial control of ISIS expanded, it began filling its coffers with money obtained from smuggling seizures of property, trafficking in antiquities, extortion, robbery, taxes levied on businesses, and most importantly, the sale of oil (Soufan, 2017).

ISIS implemented a strict set of rules, enforcing the obligation to pray five times a day, strict segregation of the sexes, prohibiting women to appear in public unless fully covered and accompanied by a male relative, and loose dress codes for men. Blasphemy, homosexuality, and adultery were punishable by death; and drinking alcohol was punishable by 80 lashes and premarital sex was punishable by 100 lashes for men and stoning to death for women. In the capital city of Raqqa, the heads of individuals executed were displayed on poles with signs indicating their offense. A captured Jordanian pilot was burned alive, and photos of his charred body were distributed as a warning to others (Soufan, 2017).

These displays of cruelty and power were featured on social media to recruit foreign fighters. ISIS portrayed itself as the line of defense for Muslims confronting a Western conspiracy aimed at their extermination. ISIS recruitment and use of social media resulted in roughly 7,000 Westerners arriving in Syria to join ISIS. Many of these fighters were the sons and daughters of Muslim European immigrants or converts who lacked a detailed knowledge of Islam and were easily persuaded that as Muslims, they were responsible for protecting Islam by waging jihad against the West. ISIS was particularly attractive to the comfortable middle class who felt guilty that they had done so well for themselves and felt a desire to prove that they had not deserted Islam. Young people were attracted by the power, aggression, and seeming invincibility projected by ISIS on the Internet.

ISIS adopted a strategy of focusing on a number of jihad hotbeds across the globe. By 2014, ISIL had attracted 3,000 to 4,000 foreign fighters and the end of 2015, more than 30,000 foreign fighters were fighting as part of the terrorist group. These recruits more than replaced the average of 10,000 ISIS fighters who were killed in military operations each year (Soufan, 2017).

By 2015, ISIS found itself fighting on several fronts against the Assad regime in Syria along with its Iranian and Soviet allies; and against the U.S.-sponsored rebels and Iraqi Kurd and government forces. Between 2015 and 2016, ISIS had lost 40% of its territorial control. A number of important ISIS leaders had been killed including Mohammed al-Adnani, the group's most visible and important spokesperson. Various observers predicted the collapse of ISIS by 2016.

ISIS shifted its strategy to establishing affiliates in Afghanistan, Libya, Yemen, and in other countries and to attracting support among factions of organizations linked to al Qaeda. By the end of 2015, more than 30 terrorist groups across the globe had pledged allegiance to ISIS. Their other strategy is to attract "lone wolves"—as witnessed by a series of attacks including the Orlando, Florida, shooting in the Pulse nightclub, which resulted in the deaths of nearly 50 LGBT people and the wounding of an even greater number of individuals. In January 2016, ISIS members attacked targets in Jakarta, Indonesia, killing seven people (Law, 2016). In the first 9 months of 2017, London experienced a series of attacks on pedestrians by drivers inspired by ISIS, as well the bombings of a concert in Manchester and in the London underground subway (Soufan, 2017). In May 2018, ISIS claimed responsibility for a string of deadly suicide bombings in Afghanistan.

As predicted by most commentators, by mid-2018 ISIS had all but collapsed in Syria and no longer posed a significant threat. A number of ISIS fighters, however, have joined terrorist groups across the globe.

Other Regional Islamic Movements

Lashkar-e-Taiba (Pakistan). Lashkar-e-Taiba (LeT), meaning *Army of the Pure*, was established in 1993 and is thought to be a "proxy organization" used to further the goals of Pakistan's Inter-Services Intelligence (ISI). LeT has launched a series of assaults on Indian forces in Jammu and Kashmir. In 2001 LeT attacked the regional legislature in Kashmir; later that year they attacked the Indian parliament in New Delhi. The group launched a devastating attack on Mumbai in November 2008. Ten attackers armed with AK-47 assault rifles and hand grenades entered Mumbai by sea on dinghies. The terrorists spread throughout the city targeting hotels, a Jewish community center, and a tourist venue and killed more than 174 people and injured scores of others. Twenty police officers and members of the military were killed. Throughout the attack the assailants received direction from LeT. Only a single terrorist survived who signed a confession stating that the attackers were members of LeT. Four months later LeT attacked the Sri Lankan cricket team bus in Lahore, Pakistan. In the past, LeT has launched attacks on the Indian national parliament, and on the so-called Red Fort and on other targets in New Delhi.

Taliban. The Taliban emerged as a force following the withdrawal of Russia from Afghanistan. The Taliban, a deeply fundamentalist Muslim group, seized Kandahar in 1994 and by 1997 controlled 95% of Afghanistan. The American intervention in Afghanistan in October 2001 led to many Taliban members retreating into the bordering Pakistan Federally Administered Tribal Area (FATA). They continue to use this area as a base from which to launch attacks in Afghanistan. They receive significant support from the Pakistani security services, who view them as an instrument to prevent the creation of a stable and strong Afghan government able to assert independence from Pakistan. Keep in mind that there is a wing of the Taliban from Pakistan that is aligned with the Afghan Taliban.

Southern Thai Insurgent Groups. Although it is predominantly Buddhist, Thailand has three southern states with an Islamic population which have historically have sought autonomy. The rebellion has been taken over by jihadist groups and is spearheaded by the Barisnan Revolusi Nasional, Coordinate (BRN-C), which operates a network of madrassas (Islamic schools) that serve as a training group for jihadists. The Gerakan Mujahedeen Islami Pattani (GMIP) is another group with ties to Jamaat Islamiyya in Indonesia and the Moro Islamic Liberation Front (MILF) in the Philippines. More than 6,500 people were killed and nearly 12,000 were injured between 2004 and 2015.

Jamaat Isamiyya/Lashkar Jihad (Indonesia). Jamaat Isamiyya and Lashkar Jihad are dedicated to aligning Indonesia with a fundamentalist form of Islam based on Islamic law. Both groups have received support from al Qaeda.

Moro National Liberation Front/Moro Islamic Liberation Front Abu Sayyaf/Philippines. The Moro National Liberation Front (MNLF), the more radical Moro Islamic Liberation Front (MILF), and Abu Sayyaf dominate the islands in the south of the Philippines and have historically rebelled against the northern islands, which are dominated by a Christian population. Mindanao is a center of resistance and has been under intense siege by the Philippine armed forces. Abu Sayyaf has aligned with ISIS, and in return has received funding and fighters from Indonesia and across the Arab world. It has emerged as a powerful opposition force. []

6.1 You Decide

Stephen Paddock, a 64-year-old accountant, armed himself with semi-automatic rifles converted into the equivalent of illegal machine guns, positioned himself on the 32nd floor in a hotel in Las Vegas overlooking a country music festival attended by over 20,000 individuals, and opened fire on the concertgoers. Before Paddock took his own life, he had killed 58 people and injured more than 500. In one 31-second period he fired 280 rounds. Las Vegas sheriff Joe Lombardo rejected the notion that Paddock was a terrorist, describing him merely as a local person and a lone-wolf attacker. The shooting was the deadliest armed attack in modern American history. There was an inability to find an obvious motive, and the speculation was that Paddock must have been schizophrenic and/or a maladjusted loner (Beydoun, 2017).

Commentators noted that if Paddock were a Muslim, the atrocity in all likelihood would have been classified as terrorism despite the evidence to the contrary. The conclusion would have been that the shooter was motivated by religion and that a call would have been issued for the Muslim community to denounce terrorism. The question would be posed as to why local Muslims did not identify the individuals as a potential terrorist.

The reality is that more than 60% of mass shootings since 1982 have been carried out by White men.

Do critics who view Stephen Paddock as a terrorist fail to distinguish between mass murder and terrorism? Should mass murder be considered terrorism regardless of the perpetrator's intent and motivation? []

SHIA TERRORISM

An important aspect of contemporary Islamic terrorism is the division of Islam into two major schools of thought, each of which has distinct approaches to Islam. The primary division is between the majority **Sunni** tradition and the minority **Shia** tradition. Shias are represented in Iran, by Hezbollah in Lebanon, and by the ruling Syrian Assad government. There also are pockets of Shias throughout the Middle East, including Bahrain and Saudi Arabia, where the Shia confront a lack of opportunity and, in some instances, overt discrimination and even repression. The original division between the Sunni and Shia traditions was based on the line of legitimate succession to the Prophet Muhammad (570–632) along with some theological disagreements.

Following Muhammad's death, the decision was made that the community should be led by a caliph, who was thought of as a leader rather than as a religious figure. The first four caliphs were known as the Rightly Guided Caliphs (they ruled from 632–661) and consolidated the policies of Muhammed.

The death of the third caliph sparked a division within Islam. One view held by what has become known as the Sunni tradition (meaning *people of the tradition and community*) who argued that the caliph could be selected from any male member of Muhammad's Quraysh tribe. This view was opposed by the Shia tradition (followers of Ali, the son-in-law and cousin of Muhammad), which contended that the leader should be a direct male descendant of Muhammad. Ali was named the fourth caliph but was assassinated after 5 years of rule. His adherents claimed that Ali's rightful successors were his son Hasan or his son Husayn. Husayn, however, was killed in 680 in a battle at Karbala and his family was assassinated. Subsequent caliphs were not selected from the direct descendants of Muhammad, creating a permanent division among Muslims.

Shias have a much more formal and hierarchical religious structure than Sunnis. There is significant complexity of sects within both of these two broad groupings of Muslims. The Sunni–Shia divide is a political as well as a religious rivalry, with Saudi Arabia embodying Sunni Islam and Iran representing Shia Islam.

FIGURE 6.3 Ruholllah Khomeini

Source: https://commons.wikimedia.org/wiki/File:Portrait_of_Ruhollah_Khomeini_By_Mohammad_Sayyad.jpg.

A radical school of Shiism emerged in Iran in the 20th century. Ali Shariati (1933–1977) preached a doctrine that integrated a heavy dose of Marxist social redistribution of wealth, along with the social reform aims of Catholic liberation theology. This interpretation of Shia Islam provided the foundation for the Iranian revolution of 1979 and for the coming to power of **Ayatollah Ruhollah Khomeini**. Ayatollah asserted that there was no separation between religious and political authority. Iran was accused of exporting terrorism abroad, sponsoring an attack on the Jewish community in Argentina, and openly supporting the state terrorism of the Assad regimes in Syria. Iran has also sponsored Hezbollah in Lebanon, which has been transformed from a terrorist group into a powerful political power and remains strongly connected with the majority-Shia regime in Iraq.

A central event following the Iranian revolution was the hostage crisis, in which young militants forced their way into the American embassy and took 63 hostages, 52 of whom were detained for 444 days before being released. This event demonstrated that a small group of highly motivated individuals could impact the American political system and capture global attention.

The Iranian revolution helped to inspire the Shia in southern and eastern Lebanon. In 1982 Iran began providing weapons and advisors to the forces of Ayatollah Muhamad Hussein Fadallah, which adopted the name **Hezbollah** ("the Party of God"). Hezbollah provided education, health, and social services, and they organized a militia which provided security to the Shia population. Hezbollah also promotes Iranian interests throughout the Middle East.

In the early 1980s, Hezbollah carried out a number of deadly attacks intended to force Israel to withdraw its military from Lebanon and to push out the United States and European peacekeepers who had arrived to maintain peace between Christian and Muslim militias. The most infamous attack was on October 23, 1983, when simultaneous car bomb attacks resulted in the death of 241 U.S. Marines, the largest single-day loss of American military personnel since World War II. France suffered the loss of 58 paratroopers in the attack, its heaviest loss of military life since the Algerian Civil War.

Hezbollah also has initiated attacks on behalf of Iran abroad. Hezbollah initiated six suicide bombings on targets in Kuwait in 1983 including the American and French embassies. Most recently Hezbollah has been an effective fighting force in support of the Assad regime in Syria.

In 2008 Hezbollah translated its formidable military power into a role in the coalition government of Lebanon and continues to balance the identity of a conventional political party with role of a terrorist military force.

6.2. You Decide

The Rohingya (pronounced ROH-hihn-juh) have been labeled as the "world's most friendless people." They have been persecuted and denied citizenship in Buddhist-dominated Myanmar (also called Burma) since 1982. Although Myanmar made a transition from military rule to democracy in 2011, the situation of the Rohingya has not improved. Nearly 1 million Rohingya populate the Rakhine state in Myanmar, which is located on the western border with Bangladesh and India.

The Rohingya have lived in Myanmar for generations—perhaps centuries. Historical records indicate a Muslim presence in Myanmar before the British began encouraging Muslim laborers to immigrate to its Southeast Asian colony in 1823. The Rohingya nonetheless continue to be officially categorized by the Myanmar government as "Bengali" based on their use of Bengali language. Semantics are important. The term Bengali reflects the belief that the "Bengalis" fled from Bangladesh (West Bengal) in 1971 when the country declared independence.

Rohingya fought for the British against the Japanese during World War II. After the war, the Rohingya hoped to be independent or join East Pakistan (today Bangladesh). The British, hoping to appease the Buddhist majority in Myanmar, decided that the Rohingya regions would become part of the newly independent Myanmar. Myanmar's leaders immediately began persecuting the Rohingya to drive them out of the country.

It was hoped that discriminatory attitudes towards the Rohingya would change with the ascendancy of the party led by Nobel Prize laureate Aung San Suu Kyi, who holds a position roughly equivalent to that of a prime minister. During the fight against military dominance in Myanmar, Suu Kyi was called the Nelson Mandela of Asia and was embraced by democratic leaders throughout the world. Despite pleas that Aung San Suu Kyi speak out against the military's violent repression of the Rohingya, she has remained largely silent on the topic and reportedly has asked the United States not to use the term Rohingya. Her critics were somewhat quieted when in collaboration with former UN Secretary General Kofi Annan, Aung San Sun Kyi warned that if Myanmar did not extend basic rights to the Rohingya that the country risked additional "violence and radicalization."

Fundamentalist Buddhist monks have performed a central role in mobilizing support for the cleansing of the Rohingya from Myanmar. They fear the spread of Islam in the country and have advocated restrictions on Muslim procreation, marriage, and religious practices. Fundamentalist Buddhist monks compared the Rohingya to snakes and insects who should be exterminated.

In recent years, wealthy Saudi and Pakistani Muslims have funded a Rohingya insurgent movement called Harakah al-Yaqin (which translates to *faith movement*), now known as the Arakan Rohingya Salvation Army (ARSA). The group dresses in black and motivates themselves by invoking the power of God. In October 2016 and then in August 2017, ARSA killed roughly a dozen police officers at a border post. The group also has been accused of killing suspected collaborators as well as Buddhist and Hindu civilians. With a small and largely underequipped fighting force, ARSA called a ceasefire in October 2017. The ceasefire was not recognized by the Myanmar government, which has adopted a "clearance option" involving a "scorched-earth" policy entailing the destruction of villages, blocking of humanitarian aid, and has engaged in mass murder, rape, and torture.

Nearly 7,000 Rohingya have been killed, including close to 800 children under the age of five; hundreds of villages have been destroyed, the crops burned, and livestock killed. Eyewitness testimony recounts unspeakable acts of rape and violence against women, infants, and children.

There is only one instance in which members of the military have been prosecuted for carrying out massacres. The two Reuters journalists who investigated the killings were jailed by Myanmar authorities.

Muslims throughout the world have grown aware of what has been described by Turkey as a genocide confronting the Rohingya and have threatened military intervention on behalf of the Rohingya. Bangladesh reluctantly opened its borders to nearly 700,000 refugees, 100,000 of whom are living in hastily constructed camps prone to flooding and landslides. Other Rohingya have been forced out of their villages by violent mobs and live in crude camps within Myanmar. Many other Rohingya have died attempting to flee Myanmar by boat.

As early as 2014, the United Nations special rapporteur Tomás Ojea Quintana concluded that the policy of "discrimination and persecution against the Rohingya community ... could amount to crimes against humanity" (United Nations Office of High Commissioner for Human Rights, 2014, para. 2). Two years later the U.S. Holocaust Memorial Museum warned that there are early warning signs of possible genocide (United States Holocaust Museum, 2015).

What lessons do events in Myanmar have for understanding the relationship between religion and terrorism?

CHAPTER SUMMARY

Religion, which commonly is viewed as a force for peace and reconciliation, has provided a source and inspiration for terrorism. Because of the power of belief and faith, religious terrorism is thought to inspire greater death and destruction than other forms of terrorism. Various commentators, however, question whether religion is a direct cause of terrorist violence.

The growth of contemporary Sunni terrorism originated in the struggle against the Soviet Union in Afghanistan and has been heavily influenced by the thinking of Salafist Muslims. Osama bin Laden and al Qaeda were central in demonstrating the ability of Islamic terrorists to seriously challenge Middle Eastern regimes and the United States. Al Qaeda spread terrorism by training and assisting affiliates across the globe which identified with al Qaeda. Al Qaeda in Iraq evolved into the Islamic State of Iraq and combined jihadists and former members of Saddam Hussein's Iraqi army into the Islamic State of the Iraq and the Levant and declared a caliphate. By mid-2018, ISIS was largely defeated.

Iran is the center of Shia terrorism and exerts influence in countries across the Middle East, including Iraq and Syria, and is in competition with Saudi Arabia to dominate the region.

CHAPTER REVIEW QUESTIONS

1. Discuss the theory that religious terrorism is more violent than other types of terrorism.

2. Outline the distinguishing characteristics of Sunni terrorism.

3. What is the significance of the Mahdi and of apocalyptic narratives?

4. Describe the rise and decline of al Qaeda.

5. Discuss the significance of Abu Musab al-Zarqawi and trace the development of al Qaeda in Iraq to the Islamic State of Iraq and the Levant.

6. Outline the evolution of Shia terrorism.

TERMINOLOGY

al-Baghdadi, Abu Bakr
al Qaeda
al-Zarqawi, Abu Musab
caliphate
Daesh
Hezbollah
ibn Taymiyyah, Taqi al Din

Islamic State of Iraq (ISI)
Islamic State of Iraq and
    al-Sham (ISIS)
Islamic State of Iraq and the
    Levant (ISIL)
Khomeini, Ayatollah Ruhollah
Mahdi

Qutb, Sayyid
Rohingya
Salafism
sharia
Shia
Sunni
Wahhab, Abdul

CHAPTER 7

State Terrorism

TEST YOUR KNOWLEDGE

1. Distinguish subnational terrorism from national terrorism.

2. Understand whether most terrorism scholars focus their attention equally on state terrorism and subnational terrorism.

3. Understand the reasons that some analysts do not include violence by governments as part of the concept of terrorism.

4. Provide the definition of state-sponsored terrorism and the conditions under which a state will engage in terrorism.

5. List the different categories of state terrorism.

6. Comprehend the distinction between direct domestic state-sponsored terrorism and indirect domestic state-sponsored terrorism.

7. Understand the difference between direct state-sponsored interventionist terrorism and indirect state-sponsored interventionist terrorism.

8. Describe the methods of state terrorism at home and abroad.

9. Provide examples of state domestic and foreign terrorism.

INTRODUCTION

Terrorism experts continue to disagree on whether it is accurate and useful to use the term **state terrorism**. Bruce Hoffman notes that there is a difference between the situation of states and of terrorists. He notes that states are subject to the law of war and to the requirements of international agreements. Violating these rules is tantamount to committing war crimes or crimes against humanity.

States that violate these rules recognize their legitimacy and either deny that the attack occurred or argue that they possessed a legal justification for the attack, such as self-defense.

State civilian and military officials and combatants who violate the internationally recognized rules for armed conflict are subject to criminal prosecution and the states responsible may be required to pay monetary compensation. In contrast to nation-states, terrorists do not recognize legal or moral restraints on their use of violence and disregard these restraints (Hoffman, 2006). Although states may commit significant acts of violence, Louise Richardson (2006, p. 5) argues that it is important to define terrorism as "sub-national violence" so as to ensure "analytical clarity" and to focus time and attention on the phenomena that we need to understand, combat, and deter.

Richard Jackson and his colleagues (2011) in the United Kingdom surveyed articles published in two leading counterterrorism journals between 1990 and 1999 and found that only 2% addressed state terrorism. This finding was confirmed in an examination of the number of pages devoted to state terrorism in leading books on terrorism. They conclude that analyses focusing on state terrorism are uncommon, and that this imbalance contributes to the inaccurate view that states—particularly western democracies—are the victims rather than the perpetrators of terrorism. The bottom line, according to the **critical terrorism scholars**, is that the omission of states from the definition of terrorism seems to be based on political considerations rather than on logic.

The distinction between acts undertaken by state officials and acts undertaken by subnational groups in defining terrorism makes little sense, according to critical scholars. Violence undertaken for political motives—no matter the perpetrator—is terrorism. Why should the bombing of a plane over Lockerbie, Scotland, not qualify as terrorism (the bombing was carried out by Libyan agents), while the bombing of an Air India flight in 1989 is considered terrorism (this bombing was carried out by Sikh militants) (Jackson et al., 2011)? Alex P. Schmid (2011) asks why, before Adolf Hitler came to power, the use of his paramilitary Brown Shirts to attack and to intimidate opponents constituted terrorism; the same acts undertaken by the regime after Hitler came to power in 1933 committed on a larger scale do not constitute terrorism.

The notion that states are entitled to use violence and that subnational (nonstate) terrorist groups do not erroneously assumes that all violence by states is both legal and justified. On June 4, 1989, the Chinese government was internationally condemned for assaulting peaceful, prodemocracy student demonstrators in Tiananmen Square with assault rifles and tanks, killing anywhere from several hundred to 1,000 demonstrators.

Yet another argument against the concept of state terrorism is that unlike subnational terrorists, state agents do not seek publicity and typically attempt to conceal their involvement in terrorism. In other words, state terrorism—unlike subnational terrorism—does not create fear and apprehension of state-sponsored violence among the population. This overlooks the fact that, in most instances, there is little doubt that is the government that is behind a kidnapping and mutilation of a body left on the street. There is no need to publicize government involvement. In the Philippines, the government of Rodrigo Duterte has carried out thousands of extrajudicial killings, leaving the bodies on the streets wrapped in masking tape—creating no doubt that they were killed because they were suspected drug traffickers, users, criminals, or opponents of the regime.

Another argument is that states use violence selectively against individuals and that individuals in the country are aware of how to act to avoid being targeted by government forces. Terrorists, in contrast, target individuals without rhyme or reason. On the other hand, subnational terrorist violence may be "unpredictable," but that the individuals who are the focus of terrorist attacks, like government officials and the police, are not selected without reason. In any event, governmental mass violence in countries like the Philippines can be as irrational and unpredictable and may mistakenly target individuals.

Jackson and his colleagues (2011) reject the argument that state terrorism already is encompassed by terms like *repression* and *human rights abuses*, and that there is no reason to introduce the additional analytical category of state terrorism. It is true that acts of terrorism also already are encompassed in existing analytical categories such as murder, assassination, and hijacking. Nonetheless, the use of the term *terrorism* to describe the criminal acts of a state clarifies and highlights that acts of terror—whether committed by governments or by subnational groups—are morally reprehensible and involve the unjustified infliction of widespread harm and human suffering for political purposes. The term *state terrorism* is important because it helps to highlight the fact that official violence is the cause of much of the pain and violence in the world and encourages individuals to think twice before accepting the arguments of government officials that their use of violence is both necessary and justified.

In sum, there is a continuing question as to whether subnational terrorism and state terrorism should be viewed as a single concept. Keep in mind that state terrorism is committed by governments of all types and varieties and is not limited to right-wing or to left-wing regimes. In considering whether the actions of states should be considered terrorism, consider events in Kampuchea in Southeast Asia between 1975 and 1978.

Genocide in Kampuchea

The United States intervention in South Vietnam (SVN) in 1965 led the North Vietnamese to send assistance to the National Liberation Front (NLF), an insurgent movement mobilized to overthrow the South Vietnamese regime. The NLF, in addition to controlling territory in SVN, occupied the border between SVN and Cambodia. In pursuit of a strong Cambodian ally in the struggle against the NLF, the United States supported a coup against Prince Sihanouk and facilitated his replacement by Lon Nol, head of the armed forces. Lon Nol welcomed the American bombing of NLF sanctuaries and in 1973, the United States dropped more than 11 times more explosives in 6 months than was dropped on Japan during the entirety of World War II. The devastation resulted in the death of as many as 150,000 people, the killing of livestock, the displacement of village populations, and the acreage devoted to rice cultivation decreasing from 6 million to 1 million by the end of the bombing campaign. This combination of factors created mass starvation which only was partially alleviated by assistance from American humanitarian organizations (Jones, 2017).

Although the NLF agreed to leave Cambodia in 1973, they left behind a well-armed and highly trained domestic insurgent group, the Khmer Rouge, which was embraced by the rural population that had suffered under the Lon Nol regime.

The Khmer Rouge swept into power in 1975 and renamed the country Kampuchea in recognition of the country's ancient Angor Empire that stretched across Southeast Asia during the 12th to 14th centuries. The new regime declared that the calendar was reset to "year zero" in recognition that a new day had dawned. Their goal was to immediately create the first pure Communist state. The Khmer advocated an extreme nationalism combined with an antiurban philosophy, introduced collective land ownership, and forced slave labor, the abolition of money, and rejection of Buddhism and other religions.

Food was distributed in collective kitchens, and it was prohibited to forage for food or to share food with one another. Families were often divided, and individuals were subject to intense surveillance of their daily life. Despite starvation, disease, and the lack of medicine the regime refused foreign assistance.

Two million inhabitants of the capital city of Phnom Penh and the inhabitants of other cities were deported by foot to rural areas. They were labeled the "new people" because, unlike the rural "old people" population, they were "late" to the revolution and were targeted for mass executions along with their families. Intellectuals in particular were summarily killed. In the Tuol Sleng prison, an estimated 17,000 "class enemies" were subjected to internment, torture, and to death. Prisoners were abused until they revealed the names of family, friends, and neighbors who were involved in the complex conspiracies concocted by interrogators.

At the end of the Khmer Rouge regime, only an estimated 3,000 Buddhist monks remained out of an original population of 60,000 monks. The country's entire Vietnamese population appeared to have been exterminated, along with one third of Muslims and more than 50% of the Thai population.

A combination of direct killings, starvation, and disease resulted in the death of as many as 2 million people out of a total population of 8 million between 1975 and 1978. As many as 50% of these individuals were directly killed by the Khmer Rouge. Although the Khmer regime was removed in 1979 following a Vietnamese invasion, only a handful of officials in the Khmer regime have been prosecuted and convicted before an international tribunal established in Kampuchea by the United Nations.

The Khmer Rouge illustrates that regimes are able to engage in much more far-reaching violence over an extended period of time than a terrorist group. Although governments are theoretically restrained by domestic law—and subject to international law and norms of conduct—they are actually subject to little restraint. Regimes typically claim that they are acting against individuals and groups who are enemies of the regime and who pose a terrorist threat. Individuals in the general population who might ordinarily protest the government's terrorist acts are silenced by the threat that they will be prosecuted for supporting the terrorists. []

DEFINING STATE TERRORISM

There are several definitions of state terrorism. Richard Jackson and his colleagues (2011, p. 177) define state terrorism as the "intentional use or threat of violence by state agents or their proxies against individuals or groups for the purpose of intimidating or frightening a broader audience."

David Claridge (1996) argues that state terrorism is comprised of the following elements:

1. The threat or commission of organized violence.
2. A political (rather than personal) motivation.
3. The violence is committed by individuals affiliated with the state or by individuals acting on behalf of the state who are supplied and/or directed by the state.
4. The violence is carried out to eliminate the targets of the attack, as well as to create fear in the general population.
5. The purpose is to target the immediate victim as well as the wider audience of potential targets.
6. At the time of the attack, the victims are not armed or organized for aggression at the time they are targeted.

As suggested in the above elements of state terrorism, states rely on terrorism to eliminate, punish, or deter individuals or regimes that states view as posing an actual or potential security threat. In other instances, opponents or critics of the government are targeted to allow the government to carry out policies at home or abroad free from criticism. Both Jackson and Claridge stress that state terrorism is directed at the immediate victims as well as at deterring opposition from a wider audience. Of course, claims that a state is engaging in violence to protect national security may in some instances be a convenient excuse for attacking individuals or groups that threaten the government's grip on power. Keep in mind that acts of state terrorism, however violent, are typically endorsed and embraced by individuals who support and who benefit from the regime.

Duvall and Stohl (1988) theorize that state terrorism involves a calculation of costs and benefits. A government will use terrorism when it enables the regime to achieve goals more effectively than other policies; and when the regime believes that the costs of state terrorism are lower than the costs of other policies. In other words, the greater the threat to the government, the more likely a government will resort to violence to maintain power.

Ted Gurr (1989) lists a number of factors that determine whether a regime will resort to terrorism. A government that lacks popular support that confronts a serious threat, and which has relied on force in the past to maintain power, is likely to resort to terrorism. A government composed of individuals from a different ethnic and economic background than the individuals who are viewed as posing the threat also is likely to resort to violence. McAllister and Schmid (2011) note that state terrorism is of greater intensity when there is unequal distribution of income in a society.

Stohl (2006) theorizes that a regime will use state terror against their own populations to consolidate power; to repress demands for political, social, or economic reform; to defeat insurgents; and in furtherance of a program of domestic repression.

Part of the calculation of a regime in deciding whether to use violence is the reaction of the international community. A strong state can act with little concern about the reaction of other governments. On the other hand, states that depend on the United States or Europe for arms, foreign assistance, trade, and tourism need to determine whether they will be subject to a cutoff of foreign aid and/or a trade boycott if they engage in state terror. Israel is an example of a country that is constantly balancing what it views as the need to undertake violence to protect itself against what it considers the threat posed by Palestinian terrorists and by rogue regimes in the Middle East versus the costs of international condemnation by other governments and boycotts by nongovernmental organizations.

There are a number of types of state terrorism that can be categorized by whether the violence or threat of violence is committed by the government or by individuals who are not formally part of the government, and whether the violence is committed at home or aboard. Direct state terrorism is thus distinguished in this chapter from **state-sponsored terrorism**, or terrorism carried out by individuals who are acting in the interests of the government and are trained, funded, or encouraged by a government but not formally affiliated with the government. Domestic terrorism within a state's national territory is differentiated from external terrorism carried out abroad (McAllister & Schmid, 2011).

Domestic state terrorism. Government attacks against unarmed civilians in a so-called "dirty war" against terrorism.

Domestic state-sponsored terrorism. Supporting, encouraging, or condoning domestic, private paramilitary groups to target dissidents.

External state terrorism. A state's direct use of force or the threat of force against civilians and unarmed individuals in another country.

External state-sponsored terrorism. A state's support for a terrorist group that is fighting to disrupt or overthrow a foreign government and/or support for the new government's use of force against a domestic population.

States rely on various methods of state terrorism at home and abroad against individuals perceived as posing a threat to the government.

Capital punishment. The use of the criminal justice system on a systematic basis to convict and to execute opponents of the regime.

Extrajudicial execution. The murder of regime opponents without trial.

Torture. The infliction of severe pain and punishment on individuals.

Disappearance. The kidnapping and secret detention of individuals who are subjected to abuse.

Sexual violence. The use of sexual violence against detainees.

Internment. The mass imprisonment of opponents of the regime.

Imposition of life-threatening conditions. The imposition of poor conditions that are calculated to eliminate individuals. This may entail starvation, along with an absence of basic hygiene, medical care, and adequate shelter.

Genocide. The mass extermination of a religious, national, ethnic, or racial group with the intent to exterminate the group is categorized as the international crime of **genocide**.

War crimes. A state may engage in the commission of unlawful acts of war, such as the bombing of civilians or objects required for human survival.

Consider some of the death tolls from state terrorism listed below (McAllister & Schmid, 2011).

Guatemala (1965–1995) 200,000

El Salvador (1979–1992) 70,000

Iraq (1989–1990) 200,000

Algeria (1992) 100,000

(Former) Yugoslavia 110,000

An interesting aspect of state terrorism is that government officials invariably use terminology in communicating among themselves that obscures the reality of their actions. Killing, for example, may be termed *neutralization* or *special treatment*; torture may be termed *enhanced interrogation*. The use of these types of terms allows decision makers to psychologically distance themselves from the consequences of their policies. Another distancing technique is to view the individuals who are attacked as evil or as deserving of their fate. The Nazi extermination squads were able to persuade themselves that they had the strength of character to cleanse Germany of Jews and minorities, and that only a small elite possessed that same capacity to kill. In other instances, individuals rationalize that they are following orders and that their superiors are ultimately responsible.

The next sections sketch four types of state terrorism.

TYPES OF STATE TERRORISM

Domestic State Terrorism

A democratic government maintains power by attracting support from the majority of the population and tailors its policies to maintain that support. The hallmark of an effective democracy is the peaceful settlement of disputes in accordance with the law and the acceptance of the outcome of the dispute. A government that resorts to violence against a domestic population risks losing popular support and its governing majority. A democratic government, in addition to depending on popular support, is typically limited by the legislative branch and by the law as interpreted by the judiciary. The position of an authoritarian regime is very different. The executive power of the president or dictator is unlimited and unrestrained by the law or by the other branches of government. A democratic government may find itself in a state of emergency and revert to an authoritarian-style government. In a totalitarian government, power is centralized—much like in an authoritarian government. The difference is that in a totalitarian regime the state dominates every aspect of life and there is no room for private organizations, businesses, or individual decisions about matters ranging from what profession to pursue to the number of children in a family.

The modern origins of the concept of state terrorism, according to some historians, can be traced to the **French Revolution of 1792** and to the execution of Louis XVI. The Jacobins established a revolutionary dictatorship headed by Maximilien Robespierre. The Convention (the French legislative assembly) on September 5, 1794, proclaimed the country to be in a state of terror. On September 17, the Convention adopted the Law on Suspects which authorized the arrest of individuals who by their conduct, associates, words, or writings, demonstrated themselves to be enemies of the state. In a 10-month period beginning in September 1793, an estimated 16,000 people were killed, although the number easily could be double that figure. Individuals were rounded up by revolutionary mobs and brought before local committees. These committees conducted hurried hearings and condemned individuals to be executed by guillotine or by firing squad. Terror in the latter phases was used to ensure civic virtue and targeted individuals suspected of disloyalty to the homeland (Law, 2016).

Randall Law (2016, pp. 158–161) writes that the second third of the 20th century ushered in an "era of state terror." In the Soviet Union **Josef Stalin** emerged as premier and instituted the "Great Terror," designed to eliminate the "wreckers, saboteurs, double-dealers, and terrorists" who conspired with the country's international enemies to undermine Stalin's plans to create a Communist paradise. Stalin established a quota in July 1937 for the security police to arrest 268,950 individuals—of whom 75,950 were to be executed. Between 1934 and 1953, Stalin executed more than 786,000 individuals for counterrevolutionary crimes. Roughly 680,000 of these individuals were executed at the height of the terror between 1937 and 1938. An estimated 17 million individuals were incarcerated, many of whom were interned in the Siberian Gulag where they were subjected to forced labor and to near starvation.

Adolf Hitler was named German chancellor by Weimar president Paul von Hindenburg in January 1933. Hitler blamed a fire ignited at the Reichstag (the German parliament) on a Dutch immigrant, Marinus van der Lubbe, a former Communist who had become aligned with anarchists. Hitler issued emergency decrees to combat Communist terror, which suspended civil liberties and expanded police powers. Thousands of Communists, socialists, anarchists, and trade unionists were interned. Members of the Reichstag, frightened and in a panic, vested all authority in Hitler—who proclaimed himself Führer, or leader of Germany. Opposition parties were abolished, and German Jews were gradually stripped of their rights and possessions and either forced to emigrate or be interned in concentration camps. The mentally and physically challenged were marginalized and eventually subject to sterilization—and in some instances, to euthanasia (Law, 2016).

The German expansion across Europe was accompanied by the establishment of extermination camps. As many as 6 million Jews and 5 million others—including religious minorities and nonbelievers, Roma, and political dissidents—were exterminated.

Following the war, 22 Nazi officials were prosecuted by the Allied Powers at Nuremberg. The tribunal—in convicting the defendants of war crimes, crimes against humanity, and crimes against peace—condemned the Nazis' terroristic policies and use of terrorism against civilians across Europe.

A third wave of state-sponsored terrorism took place in the 1950s, when European countries used force in an unsuccessful effort to maintain control over their colonies. In 1953 the British declared a state of emergency in Kenya in response to the Mau Mau Uprising. In a 10-year struggle for independence, nearly 80,000 individuals were subjected to detention, beatings, torture, starvation, and rape (Blakeley & Raphael, 2016).

A fourth wave of state-sponsored terrorism against a domestic population took place in the 1970s and 1980s, in Central and Latin America and in Communist Eastern Europe. In Argentina, a coup brought a military government to power which, between 1976 and 1983, waged a war against a guerilla threat that resulted in virtually unrestrained violence against leftists, students, intellectuals, and religious minorities. An Argentinian national commission estimated that more than 8,000 individuals were detained and disappeared, although human rights groups place this figure closer to 30,000.

In this same period, authoritarian regimes in Uganda, Ethiopia, Haiti, and Rhodesia (Zimbabwe) employed violence against domestic populations. Idi Amin in Uganda killed over 200,000 individuals in an effort to seize power and forced Asians to leave the country then confiscated their property. Somewhat earlier, in the mid-1960s, as many as half a million suspected Communists were killed by the Indonesian government.

Middle Eastern states have engaged in terror campaigns against their domestic populations over the past 30 years. In March 1988, Iraqi dictator Saddam Hussein, in what has become known as the "Black Friday," launched a chemical-weapon attack against the Kurdish population in Halabja in Northern Iraq. Between 3,200 and 5,000 people were killed, and between 7,000 and 10,000 were injured. Those affected by the attack suffered from increased rates of cancer and birth defects. The Iraqi attack likely is the most lethal chemical-weapon attack directed against a civilian population.

The catalogue of countries that have employed terrorism against their domestic populations are too numerous to mention. Another tactic of state terrorism discussed below is the government's reliance on paramilitary groups that are not formally affiliated with the government to attack individuals viewed as internal enemies of the regime.

7.1 You Decide

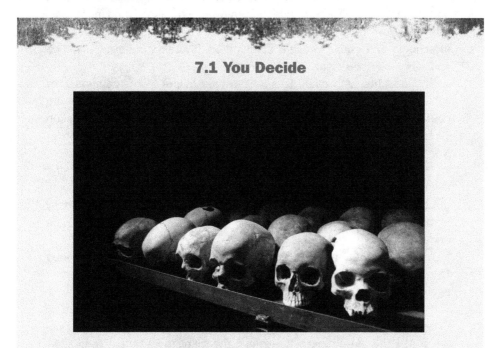

FIGURE 7.1 Memorial to Victims of the Rwandan Genocide

Copyright © Sergejpinka (CC BY-SA 3.0) at https://commons.wikimedia.org/wiki/File%3ATeschi.jpg.

Rwanda is comprised of two dominant ethnic groups: the majority Hutu comprise roughly 85% of the country's estimated 2 million inhabitants. The Hutu cultivated the land and provided the labor; the minority Tutsi raised cattle. Although there has been an intermingling of the two groups, and economic distinctions between the two groups are no longer significant, the Hutu traditionally have been portrayed in the popular imagination as stocky and oval-faced. The Tutsi are characterized as the exact opposite—tall and thin with sharp features. The two groups share a common language, religion, and national culture.

The perceived differences between the two groups provided an opportunity throughout the latter part of the 20th century for Hutu politicians to consolidate power by engaging in nationalistic rhetoric. In 1990 a leading newspaper published the "Hutu Ten Commandments" which warned that Hutu who befriended or engaged in business with Tutsi would be killed and that no mercy should be shown to the Tutsi.

(continues on next page)

(continued from previous page)

In August 1993, President Juvénal Habyarimana, the Hutu head of Rwanda who had sought to put an end to the smoldering violence between the Hutu and Tutsi, was killed when his plane was shot down as it landed in Rwanda. Hutu extremists in the government immediately employed youth gangs armed with machetes and hammers and scythes to kill Tutsi and moderate Hutu leaders. Roadblocks were established, and individuals with Tutsi government identity cards were killed; individuals taking shelter in schools and churches were slaughtered. Systematic sexual violence and rape was used against Tutsi women.

The slaughter only came to a halt when a military force comprised of Tutsi living in exile in neighboring Uganda managed to take control of the country. It is estimated that beginning on April 4, 1994, half a million Tutsi were killed in 13 weeks—roughly 75% of the Tutsi population of Rwanda.

The Rwandan genocide was unique because for the most part, the killing was carried out in a face-to-face fashion using crude farm and construction tools. The primary perpetrators were youth gangs who in many instances pressured ordinary Hutus to participate in killing their friends and neighbors.

A special UN international criminal tribunal for Rwanda was established following the genocide. The tribunal convicted 61 individuals of crimes against humanity and of genocide.

The events in Rwanda illustrate how ethnic differences can be used by extremists to mobilize popular support and involvement to inflict mass violence. The U.S. government, throughout the killing in Rwanda, intentionally avoided the use of the term *genocide* and refused to intervene to stop the killing. American lives and resources were considered too precious to be spent on calming the situation in Rwanda (Power, 2002).

The UN International Convention on the Prevention and Punishment of the Crime of Genocide in the preamble notes that "international co-operation" is required to liberate humanity from the "scourge" of the crime of genocide. In Article One, signatories "undertake" to cooperate in the prevention and punishment of genocide. In 2005 the United Nations adopted a document imposing a "responsibility to protect" on all countries when a state does not act to prevent genocide within its territory (Jones, 2017, pp. 17–22, 764–765).

In Rwanda today "genocide denial" is prohibited: It is a crime to deny that the killings in 1993 constituted genocide.

Should the United States intervene across the globe to prevent and punish the crime of genocide? Do you believe that genocide denial should be a crime in Rwanda? In other countries? ⬚

Domestic State-Sponsored Terrorism

At times, regimes use **death squads** to conduct kidnappings, assassinations, and detention of individuals in secret locations. These secret squads are typically comprised of nonuniformed security forces and private paramilitary groups. Countries want to avoid being accused of carrying out a terrorist campaign against their own population. The government typically claims to have no knowledge of the fate of the individuals targeted by these squads and claims to respect human rights. In effect, there are two systems of justice. The formal criminal justice system that functions in accordance with due process, and an informal terror system of justice. The reliance on death squads enables a government to quickly and efficiently eliminate dissidents and suspected terrorists without needing to employ the procedures of the criminal justice system.

In the 1980s in El Salvador, wealthy landowners supported death squads, including the infamous "Squadron of Death." This squad was responsible for the assassination of the inspirational archbishop Romero and for the rape and murder of three American nuns and a lay worker. These groups, which were comprised of members of the military, were responsible for the killing of thousands of peasants and leftists.

Death squads in countries throughout the world have been responsible for the killing of as many as 300,000 individuals. Death squad activity was at its height during the 1970s and 1980s, when authoritarian regimes employed these types of units to eliminate dissidents and to intimidate the population into accepting the government. Death squads were most active in Central and South America in Argentina, Colombia, El Salvador, Guatemala, and Honduras.

Because of its significant oil resources and massive Chinese investments, Sudan experienced enormous economic growth in the early 2000s. In the western Darfur region, African tribes expressed anger at the failure of the Arab government to make investments in regions populated by Africans.

The Sudanese government responded by organizing, training, and supporting Arab militias comprised of nomadic camel-herding tribes that were resentful over the Africans' monopolization of land for agriculture. The so-called *Janjaweed* ("men on horseback") burned and looted villages, raped women, and killed young men and livestock. The death toll numbered between 250,000 and 400,000, and as many as 2.5 million people have been pushed into refugee camps or into internally displaced person camps. President Omar al-Bashir has been charged with genocide by the international criminal court (Lippman, 2007).

State Sponsors of External Terrorism

The Bureau of Counterterrorism, in the 2015 *Country Reports on Terrorism*, lists Iran and Syria as the leading state sponsors of terrorism. In the past, Cuba has also been included on the list. A country is designated as a State Sponsor of Terrorism if it has "repeatedly provided support for acts of international terrorism." A country remains on the list and only is removed if certain statutory standards are satisfied. Designation as a State Sponsor of Terrorism results in various penalties including a ban on American arms-related exports and sales; controls over Americans exports of dual-use items that may have both civilian and military uses; prohibitions on economic assistance to the country; and various other financially related penalties.

The president can remove the designation of State Sponsor of Terrorism by certifying to Congress that the country is no longer supporting terrorism, has provided assurances that it will not support terrorism in the future, and that there has been a fundamental change in leadership and policies. The president also can report to Congress at least 45 days before removing the designation that the country has not supported international terrorism for a 6-month period and that the country has provided assurance that it will not support international terrorism in the future.

Iran has been designated a State Sponsor of Terrorism since 1984, based on its support for the Palestinian group Hamas, the Shia group Hezbollah in Lebanon, and support for various Iraqi Shia terrorist groups in Iraq. Iran, along with Russia, has been the primary supporter of the Assad regime in Syria. In 2015 Iran provided weapons, funding, and training to Shia militants in Bahrain working to overthrow the government. The Iranian Islamic Revolutionary Guard Corps-Quds Force (IRGC-QF) is the regime's primary vehicle for supporting terrorism abroad. In July 1985, an Iran-sponsored suicide bomber ignited a bomb outside the Jewish community center in Buenos Aires, Argentina, killing 85 people and injuring hundreds. In May 2018 President Trump withdrew the United States from the multilateral nuclear arms agreement with Iran.

Sudan was designated a State Sponsor of Terrorism in 1993 because of its support for various terrorist groups—including al Qaeda. The country provided a meeting site for various groups and allowed members of the Palestinian group Hamas to live in the country, train, and raise money. The Trump administration withdrew Sudan from the list of state sponsors of terrorism.

Syria was designated as a State Sponsor of Terrorism in 1979. President Bashar Assad's Baathist regime is aligned with Hezbollah in Lebanon and with Iran. The Assad government has a history of using chemical weapons against its population and has illegally stockpiled chemical weapons in violation of its responsibilities under the international Chemical Weapons Convention (CWC). The Assad regime also has engaged in the systematic torture and mass extermination of opponents of the regime and has violently suppressed peaceful demonstrations, provoking the current civil war.

Syria has a long history of state terrorism. In 1982 the government of patriarch Hafez al-Assad suppressed a revolt by the Muslim Brotherhood, a Sunni Muslim opposition group, killing more than 25,000 civilians and destroying a large section of the city of Hama.

In the past the United States has listed Cuba as a State Sponsor of Terrorism based on its support for the Basque Nation and Identity (ETA) and providing safe haven to ETA members, along with harboring known American terrorists.

The state department's report identifies 13 terrorist safe havens around the world, where "terrorists are able to organize, plan, raise funds, communicate, recruit, train, transit and operate" (Bureau of Counterterrorism, 2016). These safe havens are located isolated regions in Southeast Asia, the Middle East, and South America. There are also 58 "Foreign Terrorist Organizations" listed, including the Islamic State, al Qaeda, and their affiliates and branches.

External State Terrorism

The law of war is set forth in various international agreements and establishes various types of violations that are subject to criminal punishment. These include attacks on civilians and civilian objects, the mistreatment of prisoners of war, and the use of prohibited weapons. War crimes—when undertaken in a systematic, violent fashion with the specific intent to intimidate an enemy government or population—constitute state terrorism.

FIGURE 7.2 Photo From the Rape of Nanking

Source: https://commons.wikimedia.org/wiki/File:Chinese_captives_in_Nanking.jpg.

The law of war also sets forth the obligations of an occupying power—a state which takes control of the territory of a defeated country. An occupying power has an obligation to treat the domestic population with dignity and respect, and to respect human and property rights.

There is perhaps no more tragic example of war crimes committed by an occupying power than the **Nanking Massacre**. As part of its drive to expand its borders for resources, Japan provoked a war with China in 1937. The Japanese troops encountered unanticipated difficulties and by the time they arrived at the gates of the Nanking, they were primed to exact retribution. Civilians were massacred, buried alive, thrown into burning pits, frozen to death, decapitated and dismembered, nailed to boards, ripped apart by dogs, and run over with tanks and crucified on trees and posts. Men had their eyes gouged out and their noses and ears cut off before being set on fire.

The number of Chinese killed within a 6-week period are estimated to range from 260,000 to 300,000 individuals. Women were gang raped, tortured, and killed in unspeakable fashion. The estimates on the number of rapes range from a staggering 200,000 to over 400,000.

The United States in Vietnam combated guerilla warfare using a "scorched earth" policy. By the end of 1969, American pilots had dropped "seventy tons of bombs for every square mile of North and South Vietnam; and five hundred pounds of bombs had been dropped for every resident of Vietnam" (Lippman, 1993, pp. 383–384). "The use of herbicides contaminated six and one-half million acres of arable land in South Vietnam and contaminated the food chain and caused fetal death and birth defects" (Lippman, 1993, p. 388). Military operations resulted in the maiming or killing of between 20% and 25% of the South Vietnamese civilian population.

Other notable foreign invasions include the Soviet Union's 1956 invasion of Hungary and its 1968 intervention into Czechoslovakia—two countries that the Soviet Union considered to be within its sphere of political influence. In 1990 Iraq invaded Kuwait, provoking the first Gulf War.

A state that directly intervenes abroad may also engage in a joint operation, in which the government collaborates with another regime in carrying out a collective campaign of terror. A classic example is the **Phoenix Program** in South Vietnam, in which Americans, Australians, and allied South Vietnamese intelligence units assassinated suspected Viet Cong guerilla fighters and sympathizers. Over 20,000 individuals were killed, and roughly 60,000 were interned and subjected to harsh interrogation—and in some instances, torture. The program is credited with creating a significant dent in the NLF in South Vietnam, although it was ultimately disbanded because of the brutal tactics that were employed to gather information.

A more typical pattern is for a state to sponsor terrorism abroad, concealing its involvement by directing support to a foreign regime or sponsoring paramilitary groups operating abroad.

External State-Sponsored Terrorism: Coup D'état

States that invade and seize the territory of another nation risk condemnation for failing to respect the core principle of international law, which requires respect for the territorial integrity of another country. In invading another country, a state also confronts the challenge of occupying a foreign territory. It makes a great deal of political sense for a state to support the overthrow of an enemy government and to install a friendly government that can ensure domestic stability and support the national security interests of the dominant state in the partnership. The sudden rebellious replacement of a government by an internal opposition group is termed a **coup d'état.**

In the latter part of the 20th century, the United States protected its national security interests by supporting and in some instances installing anticommunist governments in Central and Latin America to combat the threatened spread of communism.

In 1954 the United States sponsored a military coup to overthrow the democratically elected government of Jacobo Árbenz in Guatemala. The Central Intelligence Agency (CIA) installed the military government of Carlos Castillo, which carried out a campaign of mass repression. This ultimately led to a 36-year civil war, which resulted in the deaths of more than 200,000 individuals. In 1999 President Bill Clinton apologized for the role of the United States in the war.

A year earlier, the United States and Great Britain organized a coup against the democratically elected Iranian government of Prime Minister Mohammad Mosaddegh. Great Britain feared that Mosaddegh would nationalize its oil interests in Iran. The monarchical government of Shah Mohammad Reza Pahlavi was installed, which ruled through the use of secret police known as SAVAK. The Shah may have been responsible for as many as 30,000 deaths before being overthrown by a popular revolution in 1979. Rather than ushering in true reform, the revolution resulted in the repressive Islamic government of Ayatollah Ruhollah Khomeini.

Between 1970 and 1973, the United States spent more than $8 million to prevent the election of socialist Salvador Allende to the Chilean presidency, and then to create chaos in the country to prevent Allende from succeeding in implementing his reform agenda. The United States feared that Chile would become a Communist country aligned with Fidel Castro's Cuban dictatorship and spread Communist ideology throughout Latin America.

A Senate investigation in 1975 (the Church Committee) found that the United States provided money and weapons to military officers who assassinated the army commander, who was a supporter of Allende. The evidence is subject to dispute, although at a minimum, the United States was aware of the planned coup and murder of Allende and did not discourage the military takeover. President Nixon and Secretary of State Henry Kissinger privately took credit for creating the conditions for the coup.

Following the overthrow of the Allende regime, president-general Augusto Pinochet interned an estimated 5,000 Allende supporters; roughly 3,000 individuals were killed or had disappeared, and thousands were tortured. The Chilean regime, together with other Latin American dictatorships, implemented "Operation Condor" with the support of the United States, which cooperated in the assassination of left-wing dissidents throughout Central and Latin America, including Argentina, Bolivia, Chile, Paraguay, and Uruguay. Estimates of the number of individuals killed range from several thousand to the tens of thousands.

7.2 You Decide

In his 2015 address to Congress, Pope Francis denounced the international arms trade and the "shameful and culpable silence" that surrounds the "economy of death" (Gaetan, 2016). The address may have been directed at President Barack Obama, who sold more weapons to foreign governments while he was in office than any U.S. president since World War II. During his first 5 years in office, President Obama sold $169 billion in arms—when adjusted for inflation, that is more than the total arms sales under President George W. Bush (Human Rights First, 2013).

These arms sales partially result from the fact that the United States has depended on allied nations to fight the War on Terror. These sales also provide a boost to the U.S. economy. Sixty percent of these arms sales went to Middle Eastern governments with questionable human rights records. The biggest recipient of arms sales was Saudi Arabia, which has used American weapons to carry out a bloody war in Yemen and implement a repressive regime at home. Another benefactor was Bahrain, which has a well-documented record of human rights abuses in repressing its Shia minority. This pattern has continued under President Donald Trump, whose administration has announced a billion-dollar arms sale to Saudi Arabia and an even larger sale to Bahrain. Note that these sales all have been approved by the U.S. Congress.

American arms sales include military weapons as well as technology used for internal crowd control, such as riot batons and tear gas. The United States, of course, is not alone in selling arms abroad. The United Kingdom is the second largest seller of arms and has sold arms to 39 of the 51 countries listed by the nongovernmental organization Freedom House as the leading human rights violators in the world, and the United Kingdom has sold arms to 22 of the 30 countries on the its own watchlist of human rights violators.

Russian arms sales have reached record levels as a result the proven effectiveness of Russian armaments in the Syrian War, and Russia has become a major competitor to the United States.

Sweden recently announced that it will not sell arms to nondemocratic regimes.

Should the United States limit arms sales abroad?

External State-Sponsored Terrorism: Terrorist Groups

A state can achieve foreign policy goals with the support or encouragement of paramilitary groups operating in another country. This enables the sponsoring government to achieve foreign policy goals without direct involvement. The sponsoring government can deny involvement with the paramilitary group and claim that the regime being attacked has provoked the armed attack by its polices and can praise the insurgents as national liberation fighters. Sponsorship may involve training, providing equipment and arms, money, enlisting support from other states, and public political endorsement of the insurgents. The sponsoring state also may provide nonuniformed fighters; an example is Russia in the Ukrainian conflict. The negative aspect of this policy is that the sponsoring state risks embarrassment if its involvement comes to light. A classic case is the Bay of Pigs crisis when a CIA-sponsored invasion of Cuba failed, and American involvement was revealed.

State-sponsored terrorism may involve an ongoing campaign or a single episode.

In 1979 the Sandinista guerillas overthrew the corrupt Nicaraguan government of Anastasio Somoza and established the left-wing Sandinista Junta of National Reconstruction as the ruling regime. The United States funded and armed a number paramilitary guerilla groups, collectively referred to as the Contras. The disclosure of Contra acts of terrorism against civilians, a Contra assassination manual, and the revelation that the United States had mined the Managua Harbor led Congress to pass the first Boland Amendment in 1982, which prohibited the expenditure of American funds to overthrow the Nicaraguan government. The subsequent versions of the Boland Amendments in 1983 and 1984 reaffirmed the Congressional intent to end support for the Contras and closed loopholes in the legislation.

The Reagan administration was intent on removing the Sandinista regime, which it feared would spread communism throughout neighboring states. The administration circumvented Congress's failure to support the Contras by using $30 million in profits from a secret arms deal with Iran, a sworn enemy of the United States, to secretly fund the Contras.

In 1989 in summarizing the activities of the Contras, the international non-governmental organization Human Rights Watch reported that the Contras had engaged in the regular and systematic violation of human rights including kidnapping, torture, rape, and execution of civilians, destruction of civilian property, and the targeting of health clinics. In recent years the Sandnesta government itself has engaged in repressive policies to suppress popular protests.

A state also may provide support by tolerating the activities of a terrorist group that it has the power to influence. In July 1995, the forces of the Bosnian Serb Army of Republika Srpska (VRS), under the command of General Ratko Mladić, attacked Srebrenica in northeast Bosnia. The area had been declared a safe haven by the United Nations and was guarded by Dutch peacekeepers, who provided protection for the Muslim population.

The Bosnian Serbs had declared independence from the newly established multiethnic Bosnian state and aspired to link their territory with Serbia to create Greater Serbia. This required that the Bosnian Serbs cleanse the area surrounding Srebrenica of the local Muslim population. Although Serbia did not control the Bosnian Serb forces, government officials allowed Serb soldiers and citizens to freely fight alongside their Bosnian brothers and sisters. The Serbs also were kept informed of the strategic plans of the Bosnian Serb military.

The Serbian forces disregarded the declaration that Srebrenica constituted an international safe haven and easily overcame the Dutch peacekeepers, deported more than 30,000 women, children, and elderly, and proceeded to engage in the mass murder of more than 8,000 Muslim males. In 2004 an international criminal tribunal for the (former) Yugoslavia found that the events in Srebrenica constituted genocide. The UN International Court for Justice later found that Serbia did not take adequate action to prevent the genocide, and later failed to bring to trial its own nationals involved in the massacre. In April 2013, Serbian president Tomislav Nikolić apologized for his country's involvement in the Srebrenica massacre.

Another infamous incident is the Sabra and Shatila massacre in Lebanon. In September 1982, the Phalange, a Christian Lebanese group allied to the Israel Defense Force (IDF) in occupied Lebanon, launched an operation to clear the Sabra and Shatila refugee camp of Palestine Liberation Organization (PLO) fighters. The Phalange was eager for a fight to avenge the assassination of Bachir Gemayel, the head of their party and newly elected president of Lebanon. The IDF monitored the activities of the Phalange fighters as they killed between 762 and 3,500 civilians in the camp. In 1983 the Israeli Kahan Commission found that Israeli military officials were aware of the ongoing massacre and failed to take steps to halt the killings.

Personalities and Events

In 2014 a UN committee of inquiry characterized the Democratic People's Republic of North Korea as the most repressive government in the world. Kim Jong Un, the 34-year-old Supreme Leader, succeeded his father as leader of the so-called hermit kingdom. The country is ruled as a total-itarian police state in which there is no freedom of expression, religion, movement, or private enterprise and unionization; only a small elite has Internet access. Individuals are subject to continuous propaganda cam-paigns in which they are told that Kim is a divine and perfect being.

Individuals are under constant surveillance by informants, and children are encouraged to inform officials on the activities members of their family. The population is divided into "loyalists," "wavering," and "hostile." Individ-uals considered hostile are labeled as enemies of the regime and, along with their family and friends, are singled out for persecution. The government operates at least 10 prison camps, in which between 200,000 and 250,000 individuals are imprisoned. Prisoners are starved and enslaved, and the death rate is said to be as high as 25% each year. Executions of individuals are regularly carried out in public to deter dissent.

FIGURE 7.3 Grand Monument to Kim Il Sung at Mansudae, North Korea

Copyright © John Pavelka (CC by 2.0) at https://commons.wikimedia.org/wiki/File%3APaying_Their_Respects.jpg.

North Korea also sponsors a sophisticated program of cyberterrorism and in retribution for a satirical film about Kim Jong Un, Korean nationals hacked into Sony Pictures' computer system and, on at least one occasion, hacked into computers around the world to spread ransomware.

Kim Jong Un views North Korea as constantly under the threat of invasion. The country has a military of more than 1 million men, has stockpiled chemical weapons, and has developed missiles capable of reaching South Korea and Japan.

North Korea has at least 10 nuclear weapons and has developed the missile technology to strike the United States with a nuclear weapon. Kim Jong Un has insisted on the right to develop nuclear weapons and to possess nuclear armed missiles capable of reaching the United States. North Korea's domestic policies and the threat to deploy nuclear weapons has made the country both an internal terrorist regime and an international nuclear terrorist regime.

(continues on next page)

(continued from previous page)

Pressure on the North Korean regime to abandon its nuclear program has thus far proven unsuccessful and the United States has a long-established policy of striking North Korea before the regime develops a missile capable of striking the United States. In 2018 President Donald Trump took the bold step of meeting with Kim Jong Un.

Any effort to attack North Korea is complicated because hundreds of thousands of individuals in South Korea would likely suffer as well. China opposes any use of force because the collapse of North Korea could cause a flood of refugees into China.

In 2017 while visiting North Korea University of Virginia student Otto Warmbier attempted to take a poster off a wall and was criminally convicted and sentenced to 15 years of hard labor. In June 2017 he was returned home to the United States in a coma and died within a few days because of injuries resulting from head trauma. Critics asserted that this was emblematic of North Korea's disregard for human life.

CHAPTER SUMMARY

There is a continuing debate over whether the term *state terrorism* is useful and appropriate. Some commentators assert that there already are categories of criminal conduct available to describe the unjustified—if not illegal—actions of states, and that the focus should be on subnational terrorism. On the other hand, according to critical terrorism scholars, state violence inflicts much greater harm than the actions of subnational groups and thus fits the definition of terrorism. There are a wide variety of types of state terrorism, ranging from killing to torture. Genocide is the most extreme form of state terrorism.

States typically attempt to justify or deny terrorism or use terms that obscure their acts of terrorism.

There are various approaches to categorizing acts of state terror. One approach is to focus on who is carrying out the terror and on the location of the terrorism.

Domestic state terrorism. Government attacks against unarmed civilians in a so-called dirty war against terrorism.

Domestic state-sponsored terrorism. Supporting, encouraging, or condoning domestic private paramilitary groups to target dissidents.

External state terrorism. A state's direct use of force or threat of force against civilians and unarmed individuals in another country.

External state-sponsored terrorism. A state's direction or support for the internal replacement of a foreign government and support for the new government's use of force against the domestic population. Foreign state-sponsored terrorism also may involve support for a terrorist group acting against a foreign government.

The next chapter focuses on terrorism in the United States.

CHAPTER REVIEW QUESTIONS

1. Discuss the arguments for and against recognizing the concept of state terrorism.
2. Outline the elements of the definition of state terrorism.
3. Under what conditions will a state resort to terrorism?
4. List various methods of state terrorism.
5. Discuss how governments engaging in terrorism modify the use of language to refer to the regime's terrorist activities.
6. Define and distinguish between the various categories of state terrorism and provide examples of each type of terrorism.
7. Should the United States government negotiate with North Korea?

TERMINOLOGY

coup d'état
death squads
Democratic People's Republic of North Korea
domestic state terrorism
domestic state-sponsored terrorism

external state terrorism
external state-sponsored terrorism
French Revolution
genocide
Hitler, Adolf

Phoenix Program
Rwandan genocide
Stalin, Joseph
state-sponsored terrorism
state terrorism

CHAPTER 8

Terrorism in the United States

TEST YOUR KNOWLEDGE

1. State whether right-wing terrorists and terrorist groups tend to support centralized government or local control.

2. Understand the origins and ideology of the Ku Klux Klan.

3. State the ideology of Posse Comitatus.

4. Know the principles of Christian Identity.

5. Know the importance of *The Turner Diaries*.

6. Understand "leaderless resistance."

7. Know the significance of the Branch Davidian Compound, the Murrah Federal Building, and Ruby Ridge for right-wing terrorist groups.

8. Distinguish between the membership of left-wing and right-wing terrorist groups.

9. Understand the origins of the Weather Underground.

10. Understand the background of the Black Panthers.

11. Identify the importance of the Symbionese Liberation Army and Patty Hearst.

12. Understand the motivations of Puerto Rican terrorist groups.

13. State the significance of the May 19 Communist Organization.

14. Understand the philosophies of the Animal Liberation Front and the Earth Liberation Front.

15. State the intended targets of the four plane hijackings on 9/11.

16. Identify some of the major jihadist attacks against the United States in recent years.

INTRODUCTION

Americans historically have viewed the United States as an exceptional country blessed with freedom, natural resources, and a relatively stable, democratic political system. In the past, Americans seemingly shared common values and were able to solve their disagreements through the ballot box rather than on the battlefield. The United States, according to this narrative, was the "gold standard" that other countries sought to emulate and analysts celebrated what is termed American "exceptionalism." This narrative often fails to recognize that historically there have been individuals and groups in the United States who have believed that their grievances only could be effectively addressed through the use of terrorist violence (Gurr, 1989). Some commentators have gone so far as to view America as a country established through conflict—the use of violence against Native Americans, the enslavement of African Americans, and the exploitation of workers (Combs, 2013).

William J. Crotty (1971) finds that for the 50-year period from 1918 to 1968, the United States ranked 13th out of 89 nations in terms of political assassinations and attempted assassinations. Another study found in the 2 decades immediately following World War II, the United States ranked fifth among

FIGURE 8.1 Timothy McVeigh

84 nations in terms of political assassinations. The only established democratic country that had a comparable number of high-ranking public figures assassinated was France.

Timothy McVeigh (1968–2001) was responsible for the bombing of the **Murrah Federal Building** in Oklahoma City, Oklahoma, on April 19, 1995—an explosion which killed 168 and injured over 680. The victims included 19 children in a daycare center on the second floor of the building. The 4,800-pound ammonium nitrate and nitromethane bomb was packed into 55-gallon drums in a rental truck, and it decimated the building and damaged over 300 nearby structures. This was the deadliest domestic-terrorist assault in the United States prior to the 9/11 attacks.

McVeigh was convicted of 11 federal felony charges and executed. His coconspirator Michael Fortier was sentenced to 12 years in prison, and coconspirator Terry Nichols was sentenced to 181 life terms.

McVeigh was born in Lockport, New York. At age 20, McVeigh graduated from the U.S. Army Infantry School and while in the army, he maintained an avid interest in firearms and explosives—along with a commitment to White nationalism. He served in both the Persian Gulf War and Operation Desert Storm in the Middle East and earned several service medals. After failing to be admitted to the Special Forces, McVeigh was honorably discharged from the military in 1991.

McVeigh found it difficult to adjust to life outside the military. He drifted from one dead-end job to another, grew frustrated over his inability to maintain a romantic relationship, complained about taxes and his mistreatment by the military, and accumulated significant gambling debts.

In 1993 McVeigh drove to Waco, Texas, to support the **Branch Davidians**, a religious cult, suspected of federal weapons violations. He watched as 82 cult members—including 18 children—and four federal agents were killed during a 51-day federal siege of their compound. The bombing of the Murrah Federal Building took place on the 2-year anniversary of the federal action against the Branch Davidians.

McVeigh found a purpose in his life when he began selling firearms and antigovernment literature on the gun show circuit. He met individuals who encouraged his view of the U.S. government as a threat to the liberty of the American people. McVeigh increasingly began to refer to the government as "tyrannical fascists" and to federal authorities as Nazi storm troopers.

As McVeigh's fear of the government reached its height, he asked Nichols to teach him to construct a fertilizer bomb. On April 19, 1995, McVeigh drove a truck to the Alfred P. Murrah Federal Building and ignited a fertilizer bomb that destroyed the northern half of the building. On June 2, 1997, McVeigh was found guilty on all 11 counts of his federal indictment (Bellew, 2018).

McVeigh was not connected to a specific terrorist group, although he seemed to have been influenced by Christian Identity, a White nationalist ideology that advocated the overthrow of the U.S. government. He rationalized that his actions were no more violent than those committed by the United States abroad. McVeigh proclaimed that he had acted in revenge for the attack on the Branch Davidians and a federal attack on Randy Weaver and his family at **Ruby Ridge**, Idaho, in 1992 (Bellew, 2018).

The larger lesson of Timothy McVeigh is that homegrown American terrorism from the right wing as well as the left wing poses a threat that should be regarded as seriously as international terrorism.

RIGHT-WING TERRORISM

Right-wing extremist terrorism in the United States historically has been carried out by relatively small groups that possess differing beliefs. For the most part, these groups do not participate in conventional politics like elections and have experienced limited success in achieving their goals. However, they historically have proven to be extremely violent and to pose a threat to social stability. There are various views that are common to most right-wing terrorist groups. These views include White supremacy, a distinctive version of Christianity, distrust of government institutions and policies, local political control, a rejection of international institutions, and a belief in absolute individual freedom. In general, there is an underlying psychological desire among right-wing terrorists to maintain an idealized way of life that existed in the past and that is viewed as threatened by immigration, diversity, feminism, and the changing economy. The core views of most right-wing terrorists include:

Racism. There is a belief in White supremacy and a demonization of Jews, African-Americans, Hispanics, and immigrants, as well as a rejection of diversity.

Religion. There is strong adherence to a distinctive form of Christianity.

Social conservatism. The groups for the most part are strongly opposed to abortion, homosexuality, and feminism, and other "liberal" policies.

Local control. There is a belief in some form of local control or decentralized governance and opposition to the federal government and to federal policies.

Second Amendment. The Second Amendment protection of the right to bear arms is vital to protect individuals against the threat posed by "big government" and as essential to the protection of other fundamental rights.

Globalism. There is a distrust of international organizations and treaties and a belief in a global conspiracy of Jews, bankers, and the United Nations. International trade is blamed for the loss of jobs and for the decline of local communities.

Conspiracy theories. Most groups believe in various government conspiracies that are intended to threaten individual freedom. This ranges from the belief that the U.S. government was responsible for the 9/11 attacks to the belief that the government is planning to seize individuals' firearms.

Groups place differing degrees of emphasis on these aspects of right-wing ideology and the emphasis has shifted depending on the issues that are at the center of public debate. During the 1950s the focus was on the threat posed by "godless" Communism and with the decline of the Soviet Union, this was replaced by a fear of the so-called New World Order imposed by Jews, bankers, and international organizations. More recently, the primary threat is perceived by right-wing groups as coming from immigration and Islamic extremists.

In his book on U.S. terrorism, Brent Smith (1994)observes that members of right-wing terror groups tend to draw support from older, rural White males who are not college educated and who are lower income workers or are unemployed. Right-wing groups tend to be headquartered in rural training camps and organized in a hierarchical fashion. The groups support themselves through criminal activity and although they have committed significant attacks against the government, most of their violence is directed against racial and religious "enemies."

In the 1980s two thirds of individuals indicted for federal terrorism offenses were right-wing extremists; in the 1990s 44% of federal terrorism indictments involved right-wing extremists. In the 5 years following the bombing of the Murrah Federal Building in 1995, the Southern Poverty Law Center found that 35 terrorist plots were planned or carried out by right-wing groups. Other analysts report that more than 150 far-right-wing motivated homicides were committed between 1990 and 2014 (Simi & Bubolz, 2017).

Ku Klux Klan

Resistance and revolts by African American slaves in the South prior to the Civil War were met with harsh retribution. In 1800 a group of 25 slaves suspected of conspiring to escape and to join the Catawba Native American tribe in a revolt were executed. Two years later an unsuccessful slave rebellion led by Denmark Vesey in South Carolina resulted in his execution and that of 30 others.

This type of violence continued during the Reconstruction period following the U.S. Civil War. Institutions like the Freedmen's Bureau were established by the federal government to ensure that African Americans were registered to vote, provided with property rights, and guaranteed access to education and to medical care. Southern White vigilantes responded by burning down hospitals and schools that admitted African Americans, and African Americans were singled out for killing, maiming, and torture (Miller, 2013).

In 1866 a meeting was convened by Confederate veterans in Pulaski, Tennessee, to form an organization to maintain White privilege. They called their secret society Kuklos (after the Greek word for group, circle, or band). The attacks against African Americans around Pulaski inspired attacks across the South and were attributed to what would become known as the **Ku Klux Klan (KKK)**. Operating across mostly southern states, the Klan dressed in White robes, took on local names (like the Constitutional Union Guard in North Carolina), and held rallies around the symbol of a burning cross. The KKK was dedicated to keeping African Americans from the polls; attacks escalated around election time. A federal undercover agent who infiltrated what was known as the Knights of the White Camelia in Louisiana reported that 200 African Americans had been killed in a single day to keep them from voting. State governments cooperated in these efforts by creating impediments to the voting booth—including literacy tests, property requirements, and prohibitive poll taxes (Miller, 2013).

A White mob went on a rampage through the majority–African American city of Wilmington, North Carolina. They burned down the African American–owned newspaper, destroyed homes, and killed more than 100 persons. The White population declared the election that had brought African Americans to power null and void and elected an all-White city government. These types of attacks largely went unpunished because the entire criminal justice system in most states was aligned with the KKK (Miller, 2013).

The passage of a federal anti-Klan law in 1871 gave federal courts jurisdiction over Klan cases and marked the beginning of the end for the first phase of the KKK, which all but disappeared in the early 1880s. The second phase of the Klan was initiated in the 20th century. The so-called new Klan was formed by Methodist minister William Simmons who declared himself "Imperial Wizard." A celebratory ceremony at Stone Mountain, Georgia, in addition to attacking African Americans, targeted Communists, gays, Catholics, Jews, immigrants, and organized labor (Law, 2016).

The new Klan attracted support in the Midwest and in Oklahoma, Colorado, and Oregon. At the height of its power in 1923, the membership of the so-called invisible empire was between 3 million and 6 million; that same year, 30,000 Klansmen marched down Pennsylvania Avenue in Washington, D.C. Five U.S. senators and one governor were members of the Klan (Law, 2016).

Between 1889 and 1932, there were as many as 3,753 lynchings of African Americans by Whites; most were carried out as public spectacles. Although violence by the KKK largely came to an end by the early 1930s, between 1936 and 1946 there were more than 40 lynchings of African Americans—none of which resulted in a criminal conviction (Miller, 2013).

FIGURE 8.2 Civil Rights Workers

Source: https://commons.wikimedia.org/wiki/File:Civil_Rights_Workers.jpg.

The Klan, which by the 1950s was in decline, was reinvigorated by the Civil Rights Movement in the South in the late 1950s and 1960s which relied on marches, rallies, and sit-ins to desegregate public accommodations and schools and to ensure access to a quality education. African Americans ultimately succeeded through federal legislation and federal court decisions in desegregating the schools and public facilities and in gaining the right to vote free from discrimination. The Klan now was organized into various independent factions such as the White Knights of Mississippi and the United Klans of America. These groups were united in violently opposing African American empowerment. The Klan was responsible for more than 130 bombings between January 1956 and June 1963 and was involved in shootings, lynchings, and torture. Klansmen perpetrated the notorious 1963 bombing of the Sixteenth Street Baptist Church in Birmingham, Alabama, in which four young African American girls were killed; the "Mississippi Burning"—the murder of civil rights workers Andrew Goodman, James Chaney, and Michael Schwerner near Philadelphia, Mississippi; the assassination of civil rights leader Medgar Evers in Fayette, Mississippi; and the killing of Lemuel Penn in Athens, Georgia, in 1964; and the murder of Detroit native Viola Liuzzo.

The Klan has also emerged to attack civil rights demonstrators. In 1979 Klan members attacked a group of demonstrators in Greensboro, North Carolina, killing five individuals and wounding eight. The assailants were acquitted at trial (Simi & Bubolz, 2017).

The Klan group called the Invisible Empire, was dissolved by court order in 1993 after having been found civilly liable for a 1987 attack on civil rights workers in Georgia. In 1997 members of the True Knights of the KKK were arrested for a plot to bomb gas storage tanks that would have killed between 10,000 and 30,000 individuals (Simi & Bubolz, 2017).

Klan membership has continued to decline and today largely has been replaced by the so-called "clean-cut Klan" led by David Duke. The Klan now portrays itself as middle class and socially acceptable and has discarded white robes and cross burnings for business suits. A small group of traditionalists cling to the Klan's historical roots.

Neo-Nazi Extremists

The post–World War II American neo-Nazi movement was established in 1958 by George Lincoln Rockwell, a former navy pilot. The movement collapsed when Rockwell was shot and killed by a member of the Nazi party in 1967. Rockwell and his small group of followers distributed Nazi literature, picketed and protested civil rights leaders, and drove a "hate bus" though the southern states. Hitler and the Nazi Party continue to inspire lone-wolf terrorists to commit violence. Tom Metzger, a former adherent to the KKK, advocated a neo-Nazi ideology to organize young White working-class skinheads. In the early 1990s the group had as many as 144 chapters and 3,500 members. The skinheads engaged in a string of murders and robberies but began to decline when three members in Seattle were criminally convicted of murdering a young Ethiopian man and were held liable for $10 million in damages.

Inspired by neo-Nazi racist ideology, Richard Baumhammers formed the Free Market Party which opposed non-White immigration. In April 2000 Baumhammers murdered five persons and wounded one other individual. He intentionally targeted Jews, Asians, Indians, and African Americans, among other minority groups (Bennett, 1988).

Minutemen and Posse Comitatus

Robert Bolivar DePugh founded the Minutemen in 1960. Until DePugh's arrest on federal gun charges, his group of a few thousand men formed a fanatically anti-communist and pro–gun rights militant group (Bennett, 1988). The Minutemen's focus on waging guerilla warfare and its contempt for federal law laid the foundation for **Posse Comitatus** (meaning "power of the county"). Posse Comitatus was comprised of small groups that combined tax protestors, farmers, and survivalists.

They believed that county law and a county sheriff is the only acceptable source of governance. If the sheriff does not follow the will of the people, the proper response is for the people to execute the sheriff.

The name Posse Comitatius is derived from an 1878 Congressional piece of legislation that prohibits the military from engaging in local law enforcement, and authorizes local sheriffs to deputize citizens to assist in maintaining law and order.

Adherents to Posse Comitatus refused to pay taxes and to apply for driver's and hunting licenses. The Posse Comitatus movement became a powerful force in the farm states in the early and mid-1980s when hundreds of thousands of farmers confronted the prospect of banks seizing their lands because of an inability to meet their monthly mortgage payments. The most infamous incident involving Posse Comitatus occurred in 1983, when Gordon W. Kahl shot and killed two federal marshals in Medina, North Dakota. Kahl subsequently died in a gun battle with authorities (Toy, 1989).

The **sovereign citizens movement** is an outgrowth of Posse Comitatus. Sovereign citizens believe that they are not subject to state or federal laws. They engage in "paper terrorism"—such as filing false tax returns, using counterfeit money, creating in fraudulent drivers' licenses, and relying on fake deeds to claim a right to property. Sovereign citizens have been convicted of tax and document fraud, and they have engaged in a series of violent confrontations with law enforcement. In May 2010, Jerry Kane and his teenage son, Joseph, were pulled over by the police in West Memphis, Arkansas. Joseph exited the car firing a pistol, and he killed two police officers. The Kanes then fled to a parking lot where they were killed after wounding two officers.

Christian Identity, Aryan Identity, and the Order

In 1946 in his California church, Wesley A. Swift established the foundation of the **Christian Identity (CI) movement**. He revived a 19th-century belief called Anglo-Israelism that views Christ as an Anglo-Saxon and believes Anglo-Saxons—rather than Jews—are the Lost Tribes of Israel. Anglo-Saxons, according to Anglo-Israelism, are God's chosen children and Jews are the product of an illicit relationship between Cain and Eve and are the sons and daughters of Satan. The CI doctrine is augmented by a heavy dose of racism and is combined with opposition to taxes, gun control, environmental regulation, and public education and a belief in one-world global conspiracy comprised of Jews, wealthy bankers, and the United Nations. Swift established the Christian Defense League as the military arm of the church (Toy, 1989).

CI ideology is incorporated into the belief systems of a broad range of right-wing groups.

Smith's disciple William Potter Gale created the paramilitary California Rangers, which state officials characterized as a threat to public order. A competing CI church was established in Hayden Lake, Idaho, by aerospace worker Richard G. Butler. Butler organized an Aryan Nation Congress in 1983. Robert A. Miles of the Mountain Church of Cohoctah, Michigan, speaking at the Congress, advocated racial separation as the first step in creating an Aryan nation and demanded that the purported Zionist Occupied Government (ZOG) hand over the five states of the Pacific Northwest to White Aryan people. According to Miles, there was no obligation to pay taxes to or respect federal authorities because they were part of ZOG (Toy,1989).

Aryan Nations is a broad movement that includes a number of groups that believe in White supremacy and anti-Semitism. Aryan Nations shares the CI view that the American government is a tool of an international Jewish–banker conspiracy and should be resisted by armed force. The Aryan Nations declaration of independence includes the **Fourteen Words** which reads as follows: "We must secure the existence of our people and a future for White children." The words typically are written or tattooed as *14*. Groups identifying with Aryan Nations include the Order; the Silent Brotherhood; the Covenant, the Sword and the Arm; and the White Patriot Party (Bennett, 1988).

The **Order** (Bruder Schweigen—German for *silent brotherhood*) was formed by younger Aryan activists. It engaged in a series of bank and armored car robberies that netted $4 million. Members of the order also created counterfeit currency and conspired to commit murder and bombed a synagogue in Boise, Idaho. The Order fragmented after federal agents killed the group's leader, Robert Jay Matthews, in December 1983. Twenty-three members of the Order, most of whom were connected to Butler's CI church, were criminally convicted in 1985. It was disclosed at trial that the group was responsible for the assassination of outspoken Denver, Colorado, talk show host Alan Berg because he was Jewish, and also had plans to assassinate political leaders and the heads of American television networks and to wage war on the U.S. government (Bennett, 1988).

Prosecutors in the trial of those responsible for killing Alan Berg demonstrated that the Order was following the blueprint for racial revolution outlined in ***The Turner Diaries***, a novel written by William T. Pierce that Pierce describes as a "handbook for White Victory" (written under the pseudonym Andrew Macdonald). *The Turner Diaries* received a great deal of notoriety when following the Oklahoma City bombing it was reported that Timothy McVeigh regularly carried a copy of *The Turner Diaries* and sold the book at gun shows.

The Order continues to inspire various lone wolves. In August 1999, Buford O'Neal Furrow, married to Matthews's widow, went on a shooting rampage in Los Angeles at a Jewish community center and wounded five persons (Toy, 1989).

The **Covenant, the Sword and the Arm (CSA)** was one of the most lethal right-wing groups. The group established its headquarters at a compound on the Arkansas–Missouri border and planned to bomb the Murrah Federal Building in Oklahoma City years before it was bombed by Timothy McVeigh. The group planned to attack FBI agents and federal judges and to poison local water supplies. The CSA successfully bombed a Missouri church that supported LGBT civil rights and a Jewish community center, and they murdered a Jewish businessman and an African American state trooper in Missouri. A federal raid on the CSA compound uncovered land mines, a supply of cyanide, and hundreds of firearms. More than 20 members were sentenced to lengthy prison terms (Simi & Bubolz, 2017)

Militia Groups

In the past few decades there has been a proliferation of armed local **militia groups** or patriot groups. These paramilitary groups are inspired by the American Revolution and are dedicated to restoring the values that they believe inspired the struggle against Great Britain. Following the events at Ruby Ridge in October 1992, militia members across the country gathered to form a national movement dedicated to White supremacy, gun rights, and opposition to the federal government and to immigration. The militia movement notes Timothy McVeigh and Randy Weaver as their inspirations.

Militia leader Louis Beam called for **leaderless resistance** against the American government. This involved the formation of decentralized "phantom cells" independently engaged in terrorist attacks. The thinking was that this strategy would prevent federal infiltration of the movement. Beam also proposed that individuals be awarded "points" based on the importance of their terrorist targets. Following the 1995 explosion at the Murrah Federal Building, the movement began to decline in numbers. This trend accelerated after the 1995 and 1996 arrests of militia members in Arizona and West Virginia for conspiring to bomb a government building and arrests of militia members in Oklahoma for conspiring to bomb gay bars and abortion clinics. After nearly 90% of the armed militias was dissolved, the number of militia groups began to dramatically increase following the election of Barack Obama in 2008 (Bennett, 1988).

The militia movement introduced the belief that the United Nations was preparing to invade and to take control of the U.S. government. They reportedly saw "black helicopters" ferrying troops that when ordered to attack would seize power, create concentration camps, and rule America as part of a one-world government. The militia movement denounced issues like global warming, abortion, and same-sex marriage as an expression of the **New World Order** that they were committed to combating. They viewed the attack on the World Trade Center on 9/11 as an "inside job" by the American government designed to enable the federal government to consolidate power. At the extreme end, the militia groups warned that the federal government was inserting computer chips into Americans' skin to keep them under continuous surveillance.

Armed militia groups in the western states bordering Mexico—groups like Three Percenters, Patriots, and Oath Keepers are strongly anti-immigration and patrol the border to prevent undocumented individuals from entering the United States.

Some self-anointed *constitutionalists* pride themselves on demonstrating that the text and history of American Constitution prohibits federal regulation, environmental protection, taxation, gun control, abortion, public schools, and antidiscrimination laws.

Groups like the Militia of Montana (MOM), formed by David John Trochman, combined the militia's patriotic ideology with the CI movement. MOM engaged in armed conflict with law enforcement officers, prosecutors, and judges (Bennett, 1988).

Militia groups in some instances include **survivalists**—individuals who arm themselves and take extreme measures (including building underground shelters) to prepare for a global nuclear exchange or race war. In some instances, these individuals live *off the grid*, refusing to use the Internet, register for Social Security, or obtain driver's licenses and avoid noncash payments, as well as bank accounts and other activities that would permit the government to identify and to monitor them.

The invasion of the Branch Davidian compound near Waco, Texas, in 1993 and the Oklahoma bombing in 1995 are two important events on the militia movement calendar. A third event of continuing importance is **Ruby Ridge**. Ruby Ridge, along with Waco, are right-wing symbols of the federal abuse of power. Randy Weaver was alleged to have been selling illegal firearms. He failed to appear for a court hearing and hid with his family in a remote cabin in Idaho. Weaver and a codefendant exchanged gunfire with federal agents who were attempting to arrest him, and his wife and son were killed during the 11-day siege. Both Weaver and a codefendant were acquitted for the killing of a federal marshal during the fight (Bennett, 1988).

Moralist Movements

The **Army of God** and Phineas Priesthood are two loosely organized coalitions of lone-wolf terrorists who are inspired by fundamentalist interpretations of biblical texts and/or by the CI movement to violently combat abortion, LGBT rights, and feminism, which they view as contrary to Christian teaching. Individuals identifying with these groups have committed a string of abortion-clinic bombings, the killing of doctors performing abortions, and bombing gay bars.

The violent antiabortion movement firmly established itself as a threat in 1984 when 30 abortion clinics were damaged by arson. Michael Bray, one of the chief spokespeople for the Army of God, described America as an immoral society which by tolerating homosexuality, fornication, and abortion had abandoned God's law. He characterized violence against abortion providers as acts of self-defense against "baby killers" (Law, 2016).

Eric Rudolph is the most notorious individual identifying with the Army of God and the CI movement. He was responsible for the bombing at the Atlanta Olympic Park and for bombing a gay nightclub and abortion clinics in Atlanta, Georgia, and Birmingham, Alabama, in 1998. Rudolph is responsible for two deaths and the injury of 119 others. In 2003 Paul Hill shot and killed a Florida doctor who provided abortions. Hill was sentenced to death and executed.

In 2009 Dr. George Tiller, a Kansas abortion provider, was gunned down in his church by Scott Roeder. In 2015 Robert Lewis Dear killed two individuals and wounded nine others who worked at a Planned Parenthood in Colorado Springs, Colorado, and killed a police officer during a standoff with the police.

Lone Wolves

The majority of far-right attacks between 1990 and 2012 were lone-wolf attacks (Simi & Bubolz, 2017). These attacks include neo-Nazi James von Brunn's armed attack in 2009 at the Holocaust Museum in Washington, D.C., which killed a security guard; and Wade Michael Page's 2012 shooting rampage at a Sikh Temple in Oak Creek, Wisconsin, in which six died and four were wounded. Two years later during Passover, Frazier Glen Miller killed a 14-year-old boy, his grandfather, and a woman outside a Jewish retirement community. After being apprehended, Miller shouted "heil Hitler." In June 2014, Jerad and Amanda Miller shot and killed two Las Vegas police officers and covered their bodies with a far-right terrorist symbol. Following this attack, Eric Frein killed one police officer and wounded another in an attack on a police barracks in Blooming Grove, Pennsylvania. Frein was found in possession of firearms and pipe bombs. In January 2017, White supremacist Jeremy Joseph Christian attacked two Muslim women on a commuter train in Portland, Oregon, and killed two individuals who were attempting to subdue him (Simi & Bubolz, 2017).

LEFT-WING TERRORISM

Labor Violence

The most violent American labor group in the 1870s were the Molly Maguires. A group of Irish immigrants, they worked under brutal and dangerous conditions in the anthracite coal fields of eastern Pennsylvania. The dangers that the Molly Maguires confronted are illustrated by a fire in 1869 that took the life of 110 workers. Tension in the mines was enhanced by the fact that most of the owners, supervisors, and skilled workers were English or Welsh; the Irish miners had long-standing ethnic, religious, and economic antagonisms with these groups. Powerful mine and railway owner Franklin B. Gowen blamed the Molly Maguires—without persuasive evidence—for the deaths of a number of mine supervisors and undertook a campaign to eradicate the Mollies. Between 1876 and 1879 20 members of the Molly Maguires were prosecuted, convicted, and executed, eliminating the group as a political (Law, 2016).

Anarchism

American **anarchism** was introduced and popularized by European immigrants who fled from repression in their own countries. They viewed the entire political and economic structure as corrupt and exploitative of the working class; according to these groups, violence was justified to liberate people from these tyrannical structures.

In the late 19th and early 20th centuries, anarchism found a fertile ground among the large immigrant population in the United States. German immigrant and anarchist Johann Most in the 1880s promoted anarchist ideas to working-class populations and advertised bomb kits in his self-published newspaper. Chicago factories subjected workers to appalling conditions, and labor resistance was met by harsh police reaction. On May 1, 1886, workers at the McCormick plant went on strike to demand an 8-hour day and to improve their working conditions. The police were called to the factory and shot and killed two strikers. Two days later the police intervened to break up a rally in support of the workers in Haymarket Square near the north side of the city. As the police opened fire on the crowd, someone threw a small bomb into the middle of the police squadron, killing seven officers and five protesters. Eight anarchists were convicted of conspiracy and murder and were sentenced to life imprisonment. One defendant committed suicide; four were executed and three were pardoned (Miller, 2013). Keep in mind that the precise facts surrounding the Haymarket incident remain uncertain and the defendants' guilt is far from clear (Carr, 2007).

Industrialists contributed money to the Chicago police to support the campaign against the anarchists. In 1892 Alexander Berkman, the romantic partner of famed anarchist Emma Goldman, exacted revenge for Haymarket by seriously wounding Clay Frick, the head of the Carnegie Steel Corporation during a strike for higher wages at the Homestead, Pennsylvania, steel plant. Berkman was convicted and sentenced to 14 years in prison. In 1901 Leon Czolgosz, a self-proclaimed anarchist, assassinated President William McKinley. Czolgosz proclaimed at his execution that his purpose in killing McKinley was to liberate the American people from the yoke of political oppression. Anarchism, however, was far from dead. In 1914 three associates of Berkman were killed when a bomb exploded in their Harlem apartment. They had planned to use the bomb to assassinate prominent industrialist John D. Rockefeller in retribution for his suppression of a Colorado mine strike (Miller, 2013).

Labor resistance continued, and events culminated in October 1910 when a bomb damaged the *Los Angeles Times* building during a bitter labor strike, killing 21 employees of the newspaper. Six years later a bomb exploded during a San Francisco parade that was sponsored by local business leaders (Law, 2016).

The Russian Revolution in October 1917 was viewed as a threat to the United States, and government authorities began to use the Immigration Act of 1917 to deport politically suspicious immigrants. In April 1919, more than 30 bombs were sent by unknown individuals through the U.S. mail to federal law enforcement agents, industrialists, and members of Congress involved in passage of the Sedition Act of 1918 which prohibited subversive, antigovernmental speech. The Sedition Act was used to prosecute anarchists, socialists, and labor activists. Leftists responded by igniting bombs outside the homes of eight officials involved in the passage of the Sedition Act. Authorities subsequently traced the bombs to adherents of Luigi Galleani, a prominent anarchist who was spiritual leader of a "cult of dynamite" (Law, 2016).

In 1920 a bomb attack on the J. P. Morgan Bank in New York City killed 38 individuals, wounded more than 200, and resulted in $2 million in property damage. Attorney General A. Mitchell Palmer initiated the arrest of thousands of immigrant anarchists, Russian union activists, Wobblies, and other left-wing activists. More than 500 of these detainees were deported (Law, 2016).

MODERN LEFT-WING TERRORISM

Left-wing terrorists range from White radicals to African-American reformists, nationalists, and revolutionaries, and to Puerto Rican groups advocating for independence. Organized left-wing terrorism in the United States has largely disappeared in recent years. These leftist groups to a greater or less extent share certain ideological beliefs (Smith, 1994).

Economy. These groups are skeptical of capitalism, believe in the redistribution of wealth, and advocate for a society that provides equal access to quality education, medical, care and housing.

Diversity. There is a commitment to the eradication of racism and to support ethnic and racial diversity.

Feminism. These groups believe in gender equality and women's rights.

Local control. There is a belief in the need for local community involvement in decision making in education, policing, transportation, and health care and in other areas.

Internationalism. These group identify with foreign terrorist groups struggling for national autonomy and with what they view as progressive foreign governments.

Leadership. Left-wing groups in the past have endorsed the notion that there is a potential for revolutionary violence by students, minorities, and a portion of White youth. They believed that by acting as a violent vanguard that they would inspire mass revolt.

Various single-issue groups have a strong commitment to the protection of the environment and to the rights of animals.

As previously noted, left-wing groups tend to have a younger, better educated, and more racially diverse membership than right-wing groups. About 25% of the members of left-wing groups are women. Left-wing terrorists are also frequently from white-collar backgrounds. They tend to be organized in small, decentralized urban cells rather than in a "top-down" structure; and like right-wing groups fund themselves through criminal activity. Left-wing groups tend to focus their attacks on political institutions and large corporations and avoid targeting individuals and the general populace. Two thirds of the attacks by left-wing groups, according to one study, were directed at property and roughly 18% resulted in fatalities or injuries (Carson, 2017).

Between 1960 and the mid-1980s, roughly 45% of all terrorism was committed by left-wing groups—although some analysts believe the figure was as high as 75%. This violence centered on opposition to the Vietnam War and income inequality (Carson, 2017).

The next sections survey various left-wing groups, most of whom were active in the 1960s and 1980s:

Weather Underground

African American liberation movements

Puerto Rican nationalist groups

Symbionese Liberation Army

United Freedom Front

M19CO

Animal Liberation Front and Earth Liberation Front

Youth Violence: The Weather Underground

The **Students for a Democratic Society** (SDS) was a group of college students that organized on college campuses across the country and advocated fundamental change in America. In 1962 the SDS agreed on a set of principles in the Port Huron Statement which included opposition to militarism, foreign interventions, and capitalist exploitations, and also articulated a strong commitment to social equality. The statement strongly condemned violence and advocated peaceful reform through the building of a mass movement of students, minorities, and the White working class.

The SDS burst onto the national scene when students occupied buildings at Columbia University to protest the university's policies toward the local community. Reserve Officer Training Corps (ROTC) facilities were burned at a number of campuses to protest the Vietnam War. The SDS also played a significant leadership role in the anti–Vietnam War movement and in organizing the protests at the 1968 Democratic Convention, which led to violent clashes between demonstrators and the police. The SDS was divided over how to support the diverse group of antiwar leaders charged and prosecuted (and ultimately acquitted on appeal) in the Chicago Seven trial for a conspiracy to cross state lines to incite a riot at the convention. The majority of the group favored building a mass movement to protest the trial. A faction of the SDS, however, was disillusioned with the possibility of democratic change and believed that violence was the only avenue to achieve social change. There also was the belief among this faction that the United States was committing war crimes against the Vietnamese and that it was necessary to "bring the war home" to make America realize the violence being practiced against the Vietnamese.

Individuals advocating violence invoked the words of a Bob Dylan song "you don't need a weatherman to tell you which way the wind is blowing" and adopted the name the Weathermen. The Weathermen organized four "Days of Rage" in Chicago, which resulted in extensive property damage and confrontations between the Weathermen and the police. Following the "Days of Rage," a group within the Weathermen decided to form small revolutionary cells and named themselves the Weather Underground. They viewed themselves as fighting behind enemy lines to bring down the "American Empire" and drew inspiration from international revolutionary movements such as the Cuban Revolution.

During the next 5 years, the **Weather Underground** was responsible for at least 19 bombings—including the police headquarters in New York City, the National Guard Headquarters in Washington, D.C., the Presidio army base in San Francisco, the U.S. Capitol, and the Pentagon. Three members of the group died in 1970 when a bomb they were constructing ignited. In another incident, an innocent graduate student working late at night in the Army Math Research Center at the

University of Wisconsin was killed when the building was bombed by a group of radicals inspired by the Weather Underground (Law, 2016).

African American Liberation Movements

By the mid-1960s, American society could celebrate at least some racial progress. Public facilities had been desegregated throughout the country, the right to vote was guaranteed and enforced by the Department of Justice, and schools throughout the South had been desegregated. However, a considerable gap remained in income between Whites and African Americans, and subtle forms of discrimination persisted in housing, employment, and education. The criminal justice system continued to single out African Americans for arrest, prosecution, and incarceration. The notion that civil rights had been achieved and that American could rest on its laurels was shaken in August 1965 when a violent protest erupted in the Watts neighborhood of Los Angles. By 1970 roughly 500 so-called urban rebellions had taken place in cities across the United States. The Kerner Commission was appointed by President Lyndon Johnson to report on the causes of civil disorders. Their reports captured the reality that America was moving toward two separate and unequal societies, and that American society both maintained and condoned African American inequality (National Advisory Commission on Civil Disorders, 1968).

The Black Panther Party

The **Black Panther Party for Self-Defense** was founded in 1968 in Oakland, California. The name was taken from an African American voting rights organization founded in Lowndes County, Alabama, by civil rights activist Stokely Carmichael.

At the height of the organization's influence, the Black Panthers had more than 40 chapters and 2,000 members and very quickly became the most visible and influential radical African American organization. The Black Panthers 10-point program called for full employment, quality housing and education, and criminal justice reform. They were involved in local efforts to support and strengthen their communities, including breakfast, health, and educational programs. The Panthers also would appear at the scene of an arrest to monitor police behavior. They directly challenged the police with the slogan "off the pig (police)." At the time it was lawful to openly carry a weapon in California, and the Panthers caused a national panic when they appeared armed at the state legislative assembly.

The Black Panthers, led by Huey P. Newton and Bobby Seale, were viewed as the single most dangerous group in the United States by the FBI; most of the significant figures in the party were shot and killed in confrontation with law enforcement or were imprisoned. Although influential, by 1969 the Black Panthers had ceased to be a powerful force—Huey Newton was criminally convicted of manslaughter, Bobby Seale was indicted in the Chicago Seven Trial, and Eldridge Cleaver, the charismatic Minister of Information, fled the country. In 1969 the Chicago police raided the apartment of Fred Hampton and Mark Clark and shot and killed the two Black Panthers under suspicious circumstances, driving the remaining members of the organization underground (Burrough, 2015).

Black Liberation Army

The Black Panthers were responsible for a number of terrorist incidents, most of which were committed by a breakaway militant wing, the **Black Liberation Army (BLA)**. The BLA was inspired by Eldridge Cleaver's call for the Panthers to engage in armed revolutionary violence. The BLA was a violent underground organization headquartered in New York City led by Lumumba Shakur and Sekou Odinga, and undoubtedly was the most violent and dangerous African American terrorist group in American history. Between 1970 and 1985, the BLA was responsible for more than 30 attacks—almost half of which resulted in at least one death. Most of their attacks focused on the police, including the murder of two New York officers and the serious wounding of two other officers in May 1971. The New York cells supported themselves by engaging in a string of violent robberies (Carson, 2017). A West Coast wing of the BLA was responsible for a number of minor bombings and the killing of a police officer. Yet another cell in Atlanta murdered a police officer (Burroughs, 2015).

In January 1972, three members of a New York cell brutally assassinated two New York police officers, shooting one between the eyes and the other in the groin as they lay wounded on the ground. The individuals responsible were later apprehended after exchanging gunfire with the police and the BLA, although continuing their attacks, was greatly diminished (Burroughs, 2015).

The Republic of New Afrika (New Afrikan Freedom Fighters)

The **Republic of New Afrika (RNA)** was formed by former Black Panthers and BLA members. The aspiration was to create an African American nation in the southern part of the United States. The group was severely disrupted when a number of former members of the Black Panthers and the BLA that were active in the RNA were convicted for involvement in the 1981 Brink's robbery. The remaining militants regrouped and formed the New Afrikan Freedom Fighters (NAFF) as an underground wing of the RNA.

The NAFF was headed by Randolph Simms (also known as Coltraine Chimurengo), a Harvard doctoral student. The police penetrated the organization and arrested the core leadership before they were able to carry out a plan to attack the Brooklyn courthouse, intended to free Donald Weems (who was standing trial for the Brink's robbery) and Nathaniel Burns (who had been convicted of involvement in the robbery). The Brink's robbery is discussed below. The police were startled to find that a number of the members of the NAFF were successful middle-class professionals (Smith, 1994).

Nationalist Violence: Puerto Rican Independence

Puerto Rico is a commonwealth of the United States, rather than one of the 50 states. The United States acquired Puerto Rico from Spain following the Spanish-American War. As a territory of the United States, Puerto Rico does not have a voting member in the U.S. Congress and does not participate in the November presidential elections. Although Puerto Rico enjoys considerable self-governance, the island is subject to the decisions of the U.S. Congress. A majority of Puerto Ricans have voted as recently as 2017 in favor of statehood and have rejected independence. There has nonetheless been a strong *independencia* movement that advocates for Puerto Rico becoming an independent country.

There have been several terrorist acts carried out against the American government by Puerto Rican groups advocating nationhood. In 1950 there was an attempt to assassinate President Harry S. Truman. The gunman and a Secret Service agent died during the exchange of gunfire at Blair House across from the White House. Four years later four Puerto Rican nationalists entered the gallery of the U.S. House of Representatives and opened fire, wounding five members of the House. All five were apprehended and criminally convicted (Burroughs, 2015). Between 1985 and 1990, Puerto Rican terrorists were responsible for over 60% of terrorist acts in the United States and Puerto Rico (Smith, 1994).

The Puerto Rican terrorist groups opposed American control and military presence on the island. Most also believed in socialist economics and rejected capitalism, and they were closely aligned with the Castro brothers in Cuba. These groups generally worked together, and members were often affiliated with more than one group. The primary Puerto Rican terrorist groups that are generally no longer active include the following (Smith, 1994):

Armed Forces of National Liberation (FALN)

the Organization of Volunteers for the Puerto Rican Revolution (OVRP)

Boricua Popular Army (Los Macheteros)

the Armed Forces of Popular Resistance (FARP)

the Guerilla Forces of Liberation (GFL)

the Pedro Albizu Campos Revolutionary Forces (PACRF)

These groups in past years have focused their attacks on Puerto Rico, although the FALN also operated in the United States; in the late 1970s they launched a number of attacks in Chicago and in New York. Between 1974 and 1980, the FALN carried out 100 bombings in the territorial United States. In 1975 the group bombed Fraunces Tavern—one of the oldest buildings in New York City, the tavern opened in 1762 and was regularly visited by George Washington. Four individuals were killed and 54 were wounded in the attack. On the anniversary of the bombing of Fraunces Tavern, the FALN ignited 10 bombs in Washington D.C., New York, and Chicago. The year before these bombings, the FALN had ignited 15 bombs (Burrough, 2015).

In 1977 William Morales, the leader of the FALN, suffered severe injuries while constructing a bomb in New York City. He lost most of his fingers, teeth, and jaw and fled to Mexico. In 1983 Morales was arrested along with several other FALN terrorists in Chicago (Smith, 1994).

Los Macheteros, the FARP, and the OVRP established themselves as organizations to be feared when they engaged in a coordinated ambush attack in 1979 on a U.S. Navy bus, killing two soldiers and wounding nine others. In 1981 Los Macheteros blew up nine Puerto Rican National Guard planes at Muniz Airport on Isla Verde, Puerto Rico. Later in the same year Los Macheteros killed one navy soldier and wounded three others who were on shore leave from the USS *Pensacola* (Smith, 1994).

In 1985 Los Macheteros and the OVRP combined to fire a light antitank weapon at the federal courthouse in Old San Juan. They later shot an army major; the next year, the two organizations, together with the FARP, were responsible for 10 terrorist incidents in Puerto Rico. The most daring of these was carried out primarily by the OVRP—the assassination of former police officer Alejandro Malavé. On October 28, 1986, in a joint action intended to discourage young Puerto Ricans from joining the military, the three groups planted 10 pipe bombs at military targets throughout Puerto Rico. These actions were funded by various robberies carried out by Los Macheteros on the mainland United States, including a September 1983 Wells Fargo robbery in which the organization seized $7 million (Smith, 1994).

In 1987 the GFL committed several acts of domestic terrorism in the United States—they bombed banks, a department store, and government buildings (Smith, 1994).

8.1 You Decide

In January 2016 President Barack Obama commuted the prison sentence of Oscar López Rivera, age 74, leader of the FALN. López Rivera had served 35 years of his 55-year prison sentence (and 15 additional years for an unsuccessful escape) for seditious conspiracy and armed robbery. The plan of the organizers of the Puerto Rican Day parade in New York City to honor López Rivera as a "National Freedom Hero" was roundly condemned by individuals who viewed him as a criminal killer who never should have been released from prison. López Rivera responded by stating that he would forego the honor and would participate as a citizen because the focus should be on the plight of the Puerto Rican people—roughly 45% of whom on the island live in poverty—rather than on him. JetBlue Airways, AT&T, and other advertisers nonetheless decided against serving as sponsors, and the New York Police Benevolent Association called for a boycott of the parade because of López Rivera's inclusion on a float in the parade.

Joseph Connor, who was 9 years of age when his father was killed in the Fraunces Tavern bombing had earlier called López Rivera's commutation a "travesty" and a "mistake" and pointed out that López Rivera had never expressed contrition. In 1999 President Clinton offered clemency to 16 imprisoned Puerto Rican nationalists—none of whom had been convicted of direct involvement in violence. López Rivera refused clemency for various reasons, including the fact that he refused to renounce violence.

López Rivera's supporters, including *Hamilton* playwright Lin Miranda, view him as a national hero who had fought against Puerto Rico's colonial status as an American commonwealth.

López Rivera was honored as a grand marshal in a People's Parade celebration sponsored by activists in Chicago, a city in which he lived before serving in Vietnam.

Was it appropriate to honor López Rivera in the New York Puerto Rican Day parade? Should López Rivera have been permitted to ride a float on the parade? Do you agree with the sponsors who withdrew support from the parade? ☐

Left-Wing Revolutionary Violence: Symbionese Liberation Army

The **Symbionese Liberation Army (SLA)** was a small independent terrorist group that was active between 1975 and 1976. The SLA was headed by a an escaped inmate named Donald DeFreeze (who took the alias of "Cinque" after the leader of the revolt on the slave ship *Amistad*). The organization was committed to anticapitalist revolutionary violence and as their first act, they assassinated the African American superintendent of Oakland, California, public schools, Marcus Foster, and later shot and killed a police officer (Burrough, 2015).

The group received considerable notoriety in February 1974 when members of the SLA kidnapped newspaper heiress Patty Hearst from her apartment at the University of California at Berkeley. The SLA kept Hearst in a closet for 50 days and subjected her to psychological abuse and to political indoctrination. They demanded a ransom for Hearst's return, involving free food for the community 3 days a week for 4 weeks, along with a payment of several million dollars.

Hearst subsequently adopted the name "Tania" and took part in a bank robbery. A widely distributed photo portrayed her in a beret wielding a firearm. She was prosecuted, unsuccessfully claiming that she was brainwashed. Most of the members of the SLA were killed after the house in which they were hiding caught fire during a fight with the police.

The remaining members of the SLA formed the New World Liberation Front (NWLF) and ignited over 64 bombs in the Bay Area, aimed at the military and corporations. In a single evening the NWLF sabotaged as many as 500 parking meters in San Francisco. In February 2003, four NWLF members were criminally convicted for a bank robbery in Carmichael, California, in which a mother of four was killed (Burrough, 2015).

Left-Wing Revolutionary Violence: The United Freedom Front

The United Freedom Front (UFF) was a small underground ideological group that was active for roughly a decade. The group was composed of former members of the SDS who devoted their efforts to developing a revolutionary consciousness among inmates. The UFF detonated a bomb in 1975 at the Boston Courthouse. In 1983 the group bombed the U.S. Capitol to protest the American invasion of Grenada. The UFF focused its attacks on the East Coast, and in a 2-year period they bombed an IBM office, army reserve center, army recruiting center, and the offices of General Electric and Union Carbide (Burrough, 2015).

Left-Wing Revolutionary Violence: May 19 Communist Organization

Perhaps the most lethal terrorist organization in the 1970s and early 1980s was the **May 19 Communist Organization (M19CO)**. The organization derived its name from the birthdays of the inspirational African American activist Malcolm X and the Vietnamese leader Ho Chi Minh. The organization thus was inspired by both domestic and international resistance to American racial and international policies. M19CO brought together members of the RNA, the BLA, the Weather Underground, and the Black Panthers. The organization used various names in claiming credit for attacks and remained a threat until the last members were arrested in May 1985.

M19CO's most daring attacks occurred in 1979 when the group managed to free BLA leader JoAnne Chesimard from a New Jersey prison and helped her escape to Cuba. The same year they arranged for FALN leader William Morales to escape from police custody in a New York hospital and flee to Mexico. M19CO also was responsible for one of the most high-profile terrorist attacks when in October 1979, the group killed a security guard during the robbery of a Brink's armored truck in Nyack, New York. The group fled, and two police officers were killed during a gunfire exchange at a roadblock (Smith, 1994).

Fourteen months after the Brink's robbery, M19C0 bombed a federal building in Staten Island, New York, and later bombed the National War College in Washington, D.C, the Washington Navy Yard Computing Center, and the U.S. Capitol. The group carried out a bombing roughly every 3 months until the last members of M19C0 were apprehended in May 1985 (Smith, 1994).

8.2. You Decide

In 1983 Judith Clark, age 33, was sentenced to 75 years in prison for her role as a getaway driver in the Brink's robbery. Clark was unapologetic at her sentencing and called herself a freedom fighter, proclaiming that "revolutionary violence is necessary." The two police officers and the security guard killed during the robbery, whom Clark denounced as "fascist dogs," left behind grieving families and a total of nine children.

In 2016 New York governor Andrew Cuomo commuted Clark's sentence to 35 years in prison (time served), resulting in her immediate eligibility for parole. He based this decision on her sincere remorse, acceptance of responsibility, the number of people who wrote on her behalf, and her positive record in prison. Governor Cuomo noted that the prison system is meant to be a correctional system, and that Clark had demonstrated that she had been rehabilitated.

Elaine Lord, former superintendent of the maximum-security Bedford Hills Correctional Facility where Clark had spent her sentence, wrote that she had witnessed Clark change into one of the most "perceptive, thoughtful, helpful and profound human beings that I have ever known, either inside or outside of a prison." Thirteen former presidents of the New York City Bar Association wrote to endorse Clark's clemency.

Ed Day, county executive of Rockland County, the site of the Brink's robbery, called Clark a domestic terrorist whose only place in a civilized society is behind bars. He stated that the blood of the two officers and the Brink's guard were on Clark's hands and conscience.

Clark was slow to change once incarcerated and spent 2 years in solitary confinement. She eventually transformed herself, earning bachelor's and master's degrees. She also led educational programs for inmates including prenatal and HIV/AIDS programs, served as a chaplain's assistant, and trained service dogs.

Three members of the New York State parole board following a 7-hour hearing voted unanimously against granting Clark parole and releasing her from prison. The parole board, although agreeing with Governor Cuomo that Clark had demonstrated regret and had been rehabilitated, was unwilling to overlook the petitions by police unions that given the seriousness of Clark's crimes, her release would undermine the rule of law. A new parole hearing was subsequently ordered by a judge who found that the parole board had improperly based their decision to deny Clark parole on the severity of Clark's crimes rather than on her rehabilitation (Dwyer, 2017; McKinley, 2018).

Should Judith Clark be released from prison? []

SINGLE-ISSUE TERRORISM
Radical Environmental and Animal-Liberation Groups

There are countless groups engaging in lawful political efforts to protect the environment or animals. The **Animal Liberation Front (ALF)** and the **Earth Liberation Front (ELF)**, however, are an exception and have collaborated to commit arson and vandalism under the banner of what calls *animal liberation* and what the ELF call *monkey-wrenching* or *eco-tage*. These groups generally avoid attacking people, instead directing their attacks toward animal research laboratories and property developments that they view as posing a threat to animals or to the environment.

The ALF was founded in 1963 in Great Britain and engaged in the sabotage of animal research and fox hunts. The ALF is based on the philosophy that human beings have no right to treat animals as property, and that animals have rights that should be respected. In the view of the ALF, the mistreatment of animals is as serious an ethical violation as racism or sexism. The "liberation" of animals from their cages is not vandalism or theft because human beings have no right to restrain or abuse them. The term *extensional self-defense* is used to justify the right of human beings to defend animals.

The ALF, along with the ELF, has been condemned as a terrorist organization by the FBI and other federal law enforcement agencies. ALF actions include releasing dolphins from the University of Hawaii Marine Mammal Laboratory in 1977 and removing 468 animals from a laboratory at the University of California, Riverside. At times, ALF actions have endangered individuals. In June 2006, the ALF claimed responsibility for a firebomb attack on a house owned by

UCLA researcher Lynn Fairbanks which, had it been successful, was sufficiently powerful to kill the occupants.

The ELF was established in 1992 in Great Britain by members of Earth First!, whose symbol is a monkey wrench and stone hammer. The American movement was launched on Columbus Day in 1996 when activists spray painted "504 years of genocide" and "ELF" on a McDonald's restaurant in Oregon. On Christmas Day of that year, 150 minks were released from a Michigan farm by the ELF.

One of the ELF's next actions was to burn down a ski resort in Vail, Colorado, in protest of plans to expand the resort because the expansion would destroy a lynx habitat in Colorado. Other actions included the burning of an SUV dealership and the burning of a logging company's headquarters.

In 2001 the Center for Urban Horticulture at the University of Washington was destroyed by arson committed by members of the ELF. This resulted in the loss of 20 years of research, and of valuable plant and book collections. Six months later, bombs failed to ignite on the campus of Michigan Technological University. In 2003 a 206-unit condominium in San Diego, California, was burned, causing $20 million in damages. A banner was left proclaiming, "If you build it, we will burn it," signed "The E.L.F.s are mad." In 2008 a bombing set fire to four multimillion-dollar homes in Echo Lake, Washington, causing $7 million in damages.

The FBI records more 1,200 criminal acts by the ELF since 1996, causing roughly $100 million in damages. In 2006 American and Canadian activists pled guilty to 20 counts of arson committed between 1996 and 2001, which resulted in $40 million in damages.

Lone Wolves: Biological Terrorism

Following the 9/11 attacks, shockwaves resonated throughout the United States when anthrax was sent through the mail, gravely threatening postal workers and recipients. When the envelope was opened, the powdery mixture was released into the air and absorbed into people's lungs. Once in the lungs, the spores released a deadly toxin and caused an infection.

The perpetrator of the anthrax attacks eventually was identified as Dr. Bruce Ivins, a researcher at the U.S. Army Medical Research Institute of Infectious Diseases (USAMRIID), which engages in medical research to counter biological warfare threats. After arriving at USAMRIID, Ivins was assigned to research anthrax, which had become a high priority after an accidental release of the agent at a Soviet military facility killed 66 individuals. Ivins allegedly sent anthrax through the mail to create a crisis and to increase funding for the anthrax program, which he thought was going to lose budgetary support. Ivins committed suicide in 2008 when he realized that the FBI had traced the anthrax to his laboratory (Simon, 2016).

Ivins sent the anthrax through the mail to television anchor Tom Brokaw at NBC news and to the editor of the *New York Post*. A second round of letters was sent to members of the U.S. Senate and to a Florida newspaper. Five people died from inhaling anthrax spores, and 17 others were infected. Many more people had potentially been exposed to anthrax—10,000 people went through medical treatment following the incidents—and a number of postal facilities were closed for decontamination.

The anthrax attack illustrates the difficulty of defending against a biological attack and locating the perpetrator. A federal investigative task force interviewed 10,000 witnesses on six continents, conducted 80 searches, and seized 6,000 items of evidence. More than 5,750 subpoenas were issued to individuals to appear before a grand jury, and 5,730 environmental samples were taken from 60 locations.

INTERNATIONAL TERRORISM IN THE UNITED STATES

Attacks by international terrorist groups in the American homeland aimed against the U.S. government before the 1990s were relatively infrequent as compared to Europe. The attacks that were initiated generally involved conflicts that originated outside the United States. A tragic example was the Chilean secret service's assassination in 1976 of former Chilean foreign minister Orlando Letelier and his American assistant Ronni Moffet in Washington, D.C.

Croatian terrorists engaged in sustained terror within the United States as part of their global struggle to obtain independence from former Yugoslavia. Croatian nationalists reportedly were responsible for 21 acts of terror in the United States between 1976 and 1980. These attacks included the bombing of the Yugoslav mission to the United Nations, the hijacking of a commercial airliner, the bombing of a travel agency, and the death of a New York City police officer while he was attempting to defuse a bomb.

Omega 7 was composed of Cuban exiles living in the United States and actively attacked Cuban interests in America. The first Omega 7 attack was the 1975 bombing of the Venezuelan Consulate in New York City because of Venezuela's support for Fidel Castro. The next year a Soviet ship was bombed in Port Elizabeth, New Jersey, and a Cuban diplomat attached to the Cuban Mission to the United States was assassinated. In 1984 the leader of Omega 7, Eduardo Arocena, was sentenced to life imprisonment for the murder of a diplomat and for other crimes carried out by Omega 7. Three other members of Omega 7 pled guilty and were sentenced to 10 years in prison for conspiracy to murder a diplomat (Smith, 1994).

Sixteen members of the provisional wing of the Irish Republican Army (IRA) were criminally convicted for terrorist activity in the United States. Several men were also arrested for drug trafficking—the proceeds from which were used to purchase weapons and ammunition that was smuggled abroad to the IRA.

During the 1980s, terrorist groups affiliated with Libya and Syria as well as the Japanese Red Army and Lebanese Shia were active in planning violence within the United States and more recently, a number of individuals have been prosecuted for raising money in the United States to support foreign terrorist groups (Smith 1994).

Jihad in America

In the 1990s America suffered the first of what would become a series of attacks by **jihadist groups**. Jihad, as noted earlier, means *struggle* and the term has traditionally been interpreted as a religious term meaning the struggle to adhere to the requirements of the Koran. Jihad was also historically meant as a duty to defend Muslim lands against invaders. The term, as interpreted by Osama bin Laden and other terrorists, is interpreted as a duty of Muslims to fight against enemies of Islam—wherever they may be found. Osama bin Laden and Ayman al-Zawahiri declared that America and its allies had declared war on Islam by way of their military presence in Saudi Arabia, military actions across the Middle East, and support for Israel. Bin Laden declared that every Muslim had a duty to kill Americans and their allies—whether civilian or military—wherever they may be found.

A hint of what was to come in the future occurred in 1990 when El Sayyid Nosair, later implicated in a New York City terrorist cell, assassinated the militant rabbi Meir Kahane, founder of the extremist Jewish Defense League in New York.

In February 1993, Palestinian–Pakistani militant Ramzi Yousef, who had come to the United States to supervise an attack on the World Trade Center, drove a van into the basement parking garage of the building and lit four 20-foot long fuses meant to detonate a dirty bomb. Yousef hoped to bring down one of the twin towers and to kill 250,000 people. The blast penetrated six stories of structural steel and cement, created a 200-foot-wide crater and could be felt more than a mile from the site of the explosion. In the end, six people were killed and 1,042 were injured, and engineers concluded that the center would stand forever (Wright, 2006).

In 1995, 10 individuals, including the now-deceased radical Egyptian cleric Omar Abdel-Rahman (also known as the blind Sheik), were convicted of a seditious conspiracy to ignite five bombs in 10 minutes against the UN building and other structures in New York City. Abdel-Rahman and a cell of militants were linked to Nosair and Yousef.

These attacks were a prelude to the 9/11 attacks.

September 11, 2001 Attacks

On **September 11, 2001,** 19 al Qaeda terrorists on a suicide mission hijacked four American airliners and crashed them into the Pentagon in Washington, D.C., and into the World Trade Center (WTC) in New York City. This terrorist attack was one of the most lethal in history, killing close to 3,000 people and injuring roughly 6,000. This included 265 on the four hijacked planes, 2,606 in the WTC and in the adjacent area, and 125 at the Pentagon. The death toll also included 343 firefighters, 72 law enforcement officers, 55

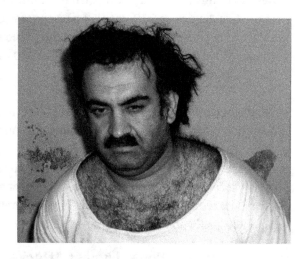

FIGURE 8.3 Khalid Sheikh Mohammed

Source: https://commons.wikimedia.org/wiki/ File:Khalid_Shaikh_Mohammed_after_capture.jpg.

military personnel, and 19 terrorists. New York and New Jersey lost more residents than any other states, and people from 90 countries lost their lives, including 67 from the United Kingdom. This was the most lethal attack on American territory since the attack on Pearl Harbor on December 7, 1941.

The 9/11 attacks demonstrated that America was not immune to international terrorism and that America confronted an enemy capable of inflicting mass casualties on the United States. There is a great deal that is unknown about the unfolding of events, which are sketched below (National Commission on Terrorist Attacks Upon the United States, 2012).

American Airlines Flight 11. Eighty-one passengers—including five terrorists— boarded American Airlines Flight 11 from Boston to Los Angeles. The plane took off at 8:14 a.m. Mohamed Atta and the other attackers gained control of the cockpit and using mace and pepper spray, they forced the passengers and flight attendants towards the rear of the plane and claimed to have a bomb. One first-class passenger had his throat slashed and two flight attendants were stabbed. At 8:46, Flight 11 crashed into the north tower of the WTC, instantly killing all aboard the plane.

United Flight 173. United Flight 173 left Boston Logan Airport at 7:58 a.m. for Los Angeles with 56 passengers aboard. The hijackers killed the pilots, stabbed flight attendants and a number of passengers, and at 9:03 crashed into the south tower of the WTC.

American Flight 77. American Airlines Flight 77 departed from the Dulles airport for Los Angles at 8:10 with 58 passengers. The terrorists used knives and box cutters to take control of the plane and to move passengers to the rear of the airplane. At 9:37 a.m. the plane, traveling at 530 miles per hour, crashed into the Pentagon killing all aboard the plane.

United Flight 93. United Airlines Flight 93 from Newark, New Jersey's Liberty International Airport left at 8:32 a.m. (it was 15 minutes late) for Los Angeles. The flight had 33 passengers and four hijackers aboard. After the plane had been taken over by the hijackers, the passengers became aware that other flights had been seized by terrorists and a number of passengers charged the cockpit. The hijackers likely panicked and crashed the plane into an empty field in Shanksville, Pennsylvania, killing all aboard. The plane appeared to be headed for the White House.

Post-9/11 International Jihadist Attacks

Following the 9/11 attacks a number of other international terrorist attacks were launched against the American homeland. Below are some of the most lethal attacks.

Zacarias Moussaoui, a French citizen, was sent by al Qaeda to the United States to serve as the "20th 9/11 hijacker." He was convicted of conspiracy to kill citizens of the United States.

Jose Padilla, an American trained by al Qaeda, was arrested in 2002 at O'Hare Airport in Chicago. Padilla was attempting to enter the United States with the intent of exploiting natural gas leaks to destroy high-rise buildings.

Ahmed Ressam, an Algerian member of al Qaeda and the so-called Millennium Plot bomber, was convicted of plotting to bomb Los Angeles International Airport in December 1999.

Richard Reed, an English national, attempted to detonate a bomb in his shoe on a flight from Paris to Miami December 2001.

Umar Farouk Abdulmutallab, age 22, was convicted of attempting to ignite a bomb hidden in his underwear on a flight between Amsterdam and Detroit.

Post-9/11 Domestic Jihadist Attacks

A number of attacks have been committed by individuals who were legal residents of the United States and affiliated with jihadist groups.

In 2003 Lyman Faisal was arrested as part of an al Qaeda plot to blow up the Brooklyn Bridge.

In 2009 Najibullah Zazi, an American trained by al Qaeda, was arrested for plotting a suicide bombing attack on the New York subway.

In 2009 Major Nidal Hasan shot and killed 13 individuals at Fort Hood, Texas, and wounded more than 30.

In 2010 Faisal Shahzad unsuccessfully ignited a car bomb in Times Square in New York City.

In April 2013, two Chechen-American brothers, Dzhokhar and Tamerlan Tsarnaev, ignited two pressure-cooker bombs at the finish line of the **Boston Marathon**, killing 3 people and injuring several hundred. The brothers fled the scene and killed a Massachusetts Institute of Technology police officer and severely wounded two other officers in a shootout.

In May 2016 Syed Rizwan Farook (born in the United States) and his wife, Tashfeen Malik, a permanent resident of Pakistani descent, killed 14 people and wounded at least 22 in an attack on a San Bernardino, California, County Public Health training session and Christmas party. The terror group ISIS identified them as "soldiers of the caliphate."

FIGURE 8.4 Boston Marathon Bombing Memorial

In June 2016 **Omar Mateen** entered the Pulse nightclub in Orlando, Florida, and killed 49 individuals in a mass shooting at the club; 90% of the victims were LGBT. The Pulse shooting is discussed below.

Personalities and Events

Omar Mateen, aged 29, fatally shot 49 individuals and wounded scores more in an armed attack with an assault rifle and pistol on the patrons of the Pulse nightclub in Orlando, Florida, on June 13, 2016. After negotiating for 3 hours with Mateen, police stormed the building and killed Mateen after he threatened to ignite a bomb and to kill those he had taken hostage.

The Pulse was known as a gay club, frequented by Hispanics. The FBI later categorized the attack as both a hate crime (in this case, killing individuals because of their sexual orientation) and as a terrorist attack based on Mateen's calling 911 during the attack, declaring his allegiance to ISIS, and referring to the 9/11 bombers as his "homeboys." He also announced his allegiance to ISIS during a call to a local television station and in his final Facebook postings.

FIGURE 8.5 Pulse Nightclub Memorial

Copyright © Walter (CC by 2.0) at https://commons.wikimedia.org/wiki/File%3APulse_fence_memorials.jpg.

Mateen was born in the United States to parents who had emigrated from Afghanistan. He grew up in Florida. As a high school student, he was a disruptive bully, applauded the 9/11 attack, and claimed that Osama bin Laden was his relative who had taught him to handle a firearm. He held down various jobs, including as a grocer and a salesman, then earned an associate's degree in criminal justice and worked in a correctional facility before obtaining employment with a private security company.

Mateen had been interviewed three times by the FBI, and at one point had been placed under surveillance for 10 months in response to complaints by coworkers at the private security firm that he boasted of ties to terrorist groups. An undercover informant befriended him for a year in an effort to determine whether he posed a danger. In 2014 the FBI concluded that Matten did not pose a threat and removed him from the domestic terrorist watchlist.

At any given time, the FBI may have as many as 10,000 individuals under investigation and did not follow up on additional complaints about Mateen—including a report that he had tried to purchase military-grade body armor and more than 1,000 rounds of ammunition. On May 22, 2016, ISIS called for attacks on the United States. Two weeks later, Mateen passed the background check and purchased the assault rifle and Glock pistol, both of which he used in the attack at Pulse.

Before entering Pulse, Mateen posted his adherence to ISIS on Facebook and expressed his support for the suicide bomber Moner Abu-Salah and denounced American bombing strikes against ISIS.

There were rumors that Mateen, who was married, may have been gay himself, used a dating app, and had visited Pulse in the past. According to this line of thinking, Mateen committed the attack because of self-hatred or in reaction to mistreatment by a lover. His first wife divorced him after 4 months and said that he harbored extreme prejudice against LGBT people and also described him as mentally unbalanced and violent.

President Barack Obama characterized the mass shooting at Pulse as an act of homegrown extremism inspired by the Internet, and that there was no evidence of a wider plot. Then-FBI-director James Comey was confident that Mateen had been radicalized on the Internet. Donald Trump, despite Mateen's lack of established ties to ISIS, declared that the attack was an example of radical Islamic terrorism as well as of the threat posed by continued Muslim immigration into the United States. Other commentators argued that the attack was best described as a hate crime directed against the LGBT community—particularly LGBT people of color. Yet another narrative viewed the attack as an example of the need for stricter gun laws that denied firearms to people like Mateen with a history of mental instability and domestic violence. In 2018 Noor Salman, Mateen's second wife, was acquitted of assisting him in carrying out the Pulse shooting.

Was Omar Mateen's armed assault on Pulse a hate crime or an act of terrorism? Are we too quick to label crimes committed by Muslims as terrorism? Does it matter how we characterize the attack? []

CHAPTER SUMMARY

Despite the fact that the United States is a functioning democracy, the country has experienced both right-wing and left-wing violence.

Right-wing groups tend to endorse White supremacy and social conservatism, and they are strong proponents of the Second Amendment. They reject diversity, immigration, and globalism. The KKK is perhaps the most well-known domestic right-wing terrorist group because of the Klan's historic resistance to African American civil rights. Neo-Nazis, in contrast, have been a relatively insignificant group.

Posse Comitatus is known for a strong commitment to local control and opposition to the federal government. This was extended by the sovereign citizens movement's refusal to recognize the force of state and federal law. The CI movement has proven a highly influential group, with a belief system based on Anglo-Israelism. Various Aryan Nations groups have embraced CI and endorse racial separation and violent opposition to the government.

Armed paramilitary militia groups view themselves as the inheritors of the American revolutionary tradition and have focused on self-defense against the federal government, the New World Order, and the threat posed by immigration.

Moralist movements like the Army of God have undertaken a series of attacks on abortion providers and clinics.

Left-wing terrorist groups trace their roots to labor and anarchist violence in the 19th and early 20th century. Modern left-wing terrorist groups tend to embrace socialism, diversity, feminism, and internationalism. In contrast to right-wing groups, left-wing groups are organized on the basis of small cells rather than on the basis of strong hierarchical control.

The Weather Underground was comprised of radical students disillusioned with the possibility of democratic change and committed to the resistance to what they viewed as American imperialism in Vietnam and in the developing world. The Black Panthers were a self-styled community defense organization that endorsed a program of social reform. The Panthers engaged in violent confrontations with law enforcement and were significantly weakened when most of the group's leadership was imprisoned or killed. The Panthers were succeeded by smaller, less influential African American groups such as the BLA and the RNA. A number of Puerto Rican terrorist groups supporting independence have carried out violent attacks both in Puerto Rico and in the United States.

The SLA was a small revolutionary group best known for kidnapping newspaper heiress Patty Hearst. Perhaps the most violent left-wing revolutionary group was the M19CO. ALF and ELF are two single-issue groups considered to pose a significant threat by law enforcement. The anthrax attack on the United States illustrates the country's vulnerability to an attack by a biological weapon.

The United States has a history of international terrorist groups with grievances against foreign governments committing terrorist acts in the United States. Following the 9/11 attacks on the World Trade Center and Pentagon, the United States experienced a number of jihadist attacks.

CHAPTER REVIEW QUESTIONS

1. Discuss the core beliefs of right-wing terrorist groups.
2. Trace the history and significance of the Ku Klux Klan.
3. Describe the philosophies of Posse Comitatus and the sovereign citizens movement.
4. Outline the elements of the Christian Identity movement.
5. Describe the significance of the Branch Davidians, the Oklahoma City bombing, and Ruby Ridge.
6. Discuss the core beliefs of left-wing terrorist groups.
7. Describe the development and importance of the Symbionese Liberation Army and the Weather Underground.
8. Discuss the significance of the Black Panthers and explain how the Panthers created a foundation for other African American liberation groups.
9. Outline the philosophy and activities of Puerto Rican terrorist groups.
10. Discuss the activities of the Symbionese Liberation Army.
11. Describe the philosophy and activities of the Animal Liberation Front and the Earth Liberation Front.
12. What are some of the significant jihadist attacks in the United States? What has been the impact of these attacks?
13. Describe the anthrax terrorist attacks.
14. Does America have as much to fear from right-wing terrorist attacks as from left-wing terrorist attacks?
15. Should Americans be concerned about the danger posed by domestic terrorist attacks? What of attacks from groups headquartered abroad?

TERMINOLOGY

Animal Liberation Front (ALF)
Armed Forces of National Liberation (FALN)
Army of God
Aryan Nations
Black Liberation Army (BLA)
Black Panther Party for Self-Defense
Boston Marathon
Branch Davidians
Christian Identity (CI) Movement

Covenant, the Sword and the Arm (CSA)
Earth Liberation Front (ELF)
jihadist groups
Ku Klux Klan (KKK)
leaderless resistance
Mateen, Omar
May 19 Communist Organization (M19CO)
McVeigh, Timothy
militia groups
Murrah Federal Building

New World Order
Order
Posse Comitatus
Republic of New Afrika (RNA)
Ruby Ridge
sovereign citizens movement
Symbionese Liberation Army (SLA)
Turner Diaries, The
Weather Underground

CHAPTER 9

The Media and Terrorism

TEST YOUR KNOWLEDGE

1. State the definitions of old media and of new media.
2. Understand the issues surrounding the media's use of the terms *terrorist* and *terrorism*.
3. Know what is meant by mass-mediated terrorism, and understand the interdependence between the media and terrorism.
4. List the countries in which terrorist attacks receive the most and least amount of attention by the American media, and understand the difference between the news coverage of terrorist attacks in the United States by Muslims and by non-Muslims.
5. Understand the coverage devoted to terrorism by the media as compared to other public policy issues.
6. Understand media contagion.
7. Understand how the media covers counterterrorist policies.
8. Understand the how terrorism is presented by the new media.
9. Understand the arguments for and against censoring the media.

INTRODUCTION

The media includes two primary means of disseminating information. Newspapers and magazines are called *print media*. Radio and television sources are termed *electronic media*. These established media outlets—like your local paper or television station, along with national networks, cable stations, and national newspapers

FIGURE 9.1 Anarchist Bombing of a Paris Café

Source: https://commons.wikimedia.org/wiki/
File%3ALe_Progr%C3%A8s_illustr%C3%A9_-_
Explosion_au_caf%C3%A9_V%C3%A9ry.jpg.

like the *New York Times* and *Washington Post*—are commonly referred to as the **old media**. The old media may appear in a paper edition or in an online version. The old media tends to be owned by wealthy and powerful news organizations that combine control of several news outlets. The old media prides itself on objective and balanced reporting, and in separating the reporting of the news from opinion—which is confined to the editorial page and to columnists. A reporter may be assigned to cover a story or to a particular area. Stories are edited and checked for accuracy. The old media also includes the *entertainment media* which refers to movies, television sitcoms and series, and magazines. These forms of popular entertainment are proven to play a significant role in shaping public perceptions of terrorism.

The **new media** is used to describe social media, blogs, Internet postings, and alternative online publications. New media exists solely in cyberspace and typically allows online interaction between readers. Another important characteristic of the new media is that it does not rely on specialized experts—instead allowing for a broad range of views to be represented by individuals from diverse backgrounds. The new media is able to rapidly respond to events and unlike the old media, it includes a heavy dose of personal opinion and uncorroborated facts. The new media has grown at a rapid rate as the Internet has become more accessible. People can take their phones with them wherever they go, which permits them to be in constant communication. In the past, many fewer people had access to the media because of cost and the lack of mobility of these forms of communication. In terms of terrorism, the old media is primarily concerned with investigating and reporting events that executive decision-makers consider newsworthy. The new media is employed by ordinary citizens to report on ongoing events. Terrorist groups use the new media for various purposes including recruitment of individuals, providing instructions on terrorist tactics, inspiring acts of terrorism, and transmitting information to members of the group. In response, governments have begun to counter the proliferation of terrorist groups online.

This chapter focuses on the Western media—media largely based in the United States and in Europe. Keep in mind that the Western monopoly on the old media in recent years has been challenged by Middle Eastern networks such as Al Jazeera and Al Arabiya. These two media organizations are aimed at an audience in the Arab world and thus communicate different stories and perspectives than the Western media.

The coverage of terrorism presents the "old media" with various challenges. For example, journalists must balance reporting on terrorist attacks with the risk that the account will help the terrorists spread fear and anxiety, promoting an image of strength that will attract recruits and encourage lone wolves. In objectively reporting on terrorism or repeating the claims of terrorist groups, the media runs the risk of being labelled as "unpatriotic" and "disloyal." On the other hand, the media is sensitive to allowing their coverage of a terrorist attack to be dictated by the government which, for example, might falsely claim that the security services were unaware of the possibility of a terrorist attack.

A controversial issue involves the media's use of the terms *terrorist* and *terrorism* in reporting a story. The fact is that some people in the world sympathize with and support groups that are labeled as terrorist groups in Western industrialized countries. These people argue that the media is taking sides—rather than remaining neutral—in reporting a story when using the terms *terrorism* or *terrorist*. Following the 9/11 attacks, Reuters began referring to the attackers as *hijackers* rather than *terrorists*. Stephen Jukes, the former head of global news for Reuters, wrote that the news service reports on the actions, identity, and backgrounds of those involved in an event and does not attempt to characterize them (Seib & Janbeck, 2011).

The British newspaper the *Guardian* addressed the use of the terms *terrorism* and *terrorist* in their style guide, which establishes the rules that reporters are to follow in drafting their stories. The style guide stressed that the stories should be written in a way that avoids taking sides. The guide recognized that the use of the terms *terrorist* and *terrorism* was appropriate in various instances—such as in suicide bombings—although at times alternative terms such as "militants, radicals, separatists ... may be more appropriate and less controversial" (Seib & Janbeck, 2011, p. 8). Other terms, such as *resistance*, may convey more sympathy than is intended by the writer.

The *New York Times* does not have a formal policy on the use of the terms *terrorism* and *terrorist*. Following the Mumbai attacks, the newspaper's then–public editor Clark Hoyt (the public editor is responsible for examining the newspaper's accuracy, objectivity, and ethics), was critical of newspaper reports' usage of the terms *militants, gunmen, attackers*, and *assailants*—and the omission of the term *terrorist*. He argued that language matters and that these terms do not adequately describe *terrorist*s and the nature of terrorism: Terrorists are the enemy of humankind, who spread fear through acts that shock the conscience. Hoyt concluded by asking whether in avoiding the appearance of "taking sides" by failing to use the term *terrorism*, the *New York Times* had in fact made a political choice in support of terrorism.

The *Washington Post* (along with most other newspapers) has adopted a policy of avoiding the term *terrorism*, instead simply presenting the facts and allowing readers to draw their own conclusion (Seib & Janbeck, 2011). Several foreign media organizations reportedly do not use the term *terrorism* when describing foreign terrorist groups in order to avoid attacks on their correspondents (Nacos, 2016).

An additional issue is the selective use of the term *terrorism* when covering domestic acts of violence. One study of more than 500 print and broadcast stories found that coverage of the killing of Barnett Slepian, a medical abortion provider, by an antichoice extremist was labeled as *terrorism* only six times. On the other hand, the arson attack on a Vail, Colorado, ski resort by earth liberation activists was labeled as *terrorism* 55 times in the 300 articles and newscasts in the study (Nacos, 2016).

Another much-cited example is the tendency to characterize violent acts committed by Muslims inside the United States as *terrorism*—even though the 2015 killings by Dylann Roof (a 22-year-old White man) of nine African American members of the Emanuel African Methodist Episcopal Church while he was attending a bible study class in Charleston, South Carolina, is considered a hate crime. According to some commentators, the media is quick to label non-Muslims who engage in mass violence (like Devin Kelley, who killed 26 parishioners in Sutherland Spring, Texas) as mentally unbalanced or as seeking revenge—rather than as terrorists (Nacos, 2016).

Journalists pride themselves on their role in informing the public, and they view governmental restriction on their reporting as a violation of their First Amendment rights to freedom of expression. The question nonetheless continues to be asked: At what point does media objectivity assist terrorists? Following the 9/11 attack Osama bin Laden distributed a videotape to Al Jazeera. Shortly after President George W. Bush announced the initial air attacks against targets in Afghanistan, five major American networks ran an unedited copy of the videotape, providing Bin Laden with an international platform from which to articulate his views and to attract followers. Two days later, three cable channels ran a statement by al Qaeda spokesperson Sulaiman Abu Ghaith threatening America and calling on Muslims to launch attacks. The media's logic was that Americans needed to learn about al Qaeda and understand their motivation in launching the 9/11 attacks. The Bush administration pressured the networks into agreeing to edit tapes in the future and to limit passages calling for violence against Americans (Nacos, 2016). What is your view—should television networks have broadcast Bin Laden's tapes?

Regardless of the technology they use, the terminology that print and electronic media use to describe terrorists and acts of terrorism are a central aspect of terrorism.

MASS-MEDIATED TERRORISM

Brigitte L. Nacos (2016) defines **mass-mediated terrorism** as political violence against civilians and noncombatants that is committed with the intent to garner public and government attention. She argues that terrorist groups rely on the mass media to communicate their message, spread fear, and elevate their profile. They are aware that a media that depends on entertainment to attract viewers will cover violence. These reports and images will in turn be broadcast (or conveyed via electronic media and cyberspace) around the world. An event like the attack on the magazine *Charlie Hebdo* in January 2015 was first broadcast in France and quickly dominated the screens in Europe, the United States, and Canada (Nacos, 2016).

Paul Wilkinson (2011), a now-deceased important terrorism scholar, wrote that terrorism and the media are inseparable. Terrorism is primarily a psychological weapon, and the media is central in communicating the terrorist cause and threat to a large audience. In other words, as Nacos (2016) notes, although terrorists' objectives are political, their attacks are consciously shaped and planned to attract media interest.

The media thus amplifies and accelerates the impact of terrorist acts and is a central component of terrorism. At the same time, the media finds itself unavoidably dependent on terrorism. Terrorism provides content to fill the pages of newspapers and broadcast time for newscasts which, in turn, attracts views and generates advertising revenue. The pictures of bomb explosions, damaged buildings, first responders, and shaken civilians are the type of visual images that are tailor made for television. The careers and reputations of young journalists and veteran commentators are advanced by reporting and commenting on terrorism (Matusitz, 2015).

Nacos (2016) states that when designing their attacks, terrorists have a number of communication-related goals:

Public attention and intimidation. Terrorists and terrorist groups desire to promote their name, highlight their military capacity, and spread fear among the target population.

Recognition of grievances and demands. Terrorists want to advance knowledge of the issues that motivate their attack.

Respect. Terrorists aspire for their demands and motivations to be taken seriously.

Legitimacy. The terrorists desire to become equals with nation-states and want to be seen as a group whose demands should the subject to negotiation with leaders of nation-states.

There are numerous examples of terrorists and terrorist groups designing attacks to attract media coverage and publicity. Following the 9/11 attack, al Qaeda boasted that the attack shattered records for media coverage of a terrorist attack. In an al Qaeda training guide, Osama bin Laden advocated for attacks on landmarks such as the Statute of Liberty in New York, Big Ben in London, and the Eiffel Tower in Paris because these attacks would result in widespread publicity with minimal loss of life.

Prior to his execution in 2001 for the 1995 Oklahoma City bombing that killed 168 persons and injured several hundred, Timothy McVeigh expressed satisfaction that the explosion was heard around the world. He noted that he targeted the Alfred P. Murrah Federal Building because the open space surrounding the structure would make it easier for television to cover the impact of the attack. In November 2008, terrorists attacked a dozen targets in Mumbai, India, killing 175 people and wounding hundreds over a 60-hour period. Transcripts of a phone conversation between two terrorists monitoring the attack in Pakistan and two hostage takers in Mumbai record the Pakistani monitors expressing excitement that the media was covering the events and comparing the media coverage to the 9/11 attacks (Nacos, 2016).

In addition to looking to the mass print and electronic media for publicity, terrorists have traditionally relied on their own methods of communication. Al Qaeda developed an online magazine and the Palestinian group Hamas established its own radio station. The Yemeni cleric Anwar al-Alwaki, the so-called Bin Laden of the Internet, spread his message through Facebook, YouTube videos, blog posts, and an online magazine. Alwaki's use of social media later inspired the massive reliance on social media by ISIS.

Terrorists will sometimes post videos on the Internet, knowing that the videos will be covered by conventional media outlets. In August 2014, ISIS posted a four-minute "execution video" on YouTube. The video pictured American journalist James Foley dressed in an orange jumpsuit similar to those worn by Muslims interned by the United States at Guantánamo Bay. Foley kneels next to a black-clad ISIS terrorist, who pulls out a knife and decapitates the American journalist. Two weeks later a video captured the beheading of another American, Joesh Sotoloff, and 10 days later a video was posted of the beheading of British aid worker David Haines. A carefully produced video in February 2015 showed the immolation of Moaz al-Kasabeh, a captured Jordanian fighter pilot. ISIS later posted a clock ticking down to the day and time at which two Japanese hostages were to be executed. Social media blocked the videos, although both the old media and some new media outlets broadcast portions of the videos. Fox News decided to present the entire video of the burning alive of the Jordanian pilot, reasoning that its viewers should be exposed to the barbarity of ISIS.

ISIS succeeded in spreading its propaganda and was also able to enhance its reputation by drawing commentary and criticism from Western political leaders. Both U.S. president Barack Obama and English prime minister David Cameron denounced ISIS as "pure evil." President Obama announced that the United States would expand its bombing campaign in Syria, while Cameron announced that England would join the fight against ISIS in Iraq. President Obama, in turn, was criticized by his critics for failing to act earlier to blunt the growing power of ISIS (Nacos, 2016).

The success of ISIS propaganda was further enhanced by the terrorist group's continual posting of videos of successful attacks against government forces in northern Iraq.

The next section examines the type of terrorist attacks that receive the most coverage by the old media.

10.1 You Decide

On March 11, 2004, 10 explosions were ignited by an al Qaeda–affiliated group on four passenger trains in Madrid, Spain, killing nearly 200 people and injuring more than 1,800. Pablo Torres Guerrero of the Spanish newspaper *El País* captured a remarkable photo of the bombing moments after the explosion. The photo included the image of a severed, bloody arm on the train tracks. Four major English newspapers modified the photograph and replaced the arm with stones. The *Guardian* changed the arm from red to grey to obscure the image of the severed arm. Two other English newspapers printed the photo in black and white, so as to obscure the blood on the arm. A leading online magazine for photographers objected to these modifications, arguing that newspapers are to present the news in an objective fashion. If the newspapers believed that the photo would cause readers distress, a better option would be to print another photograph. According to the magazine editors, a newspaper should not modify photographs because of the sensitivity of readers.

FIGURE 9.2 Memorial to Victims of the Madrid Bombing

Copyright © Benjamín Núñez González (CC BY-SA 4.0) at https://commons.wikimedia.org/wiki/File%3AMonumento_a_las_v%C3%ADctimas%2C_Coslada%2C_Madrid%2C_Espa%C3%B1a%2C_2015.jpg.

As a newspaper editor, would you print the photograph? Would you modify the photograph or decide against printing the photograph altogether? ☐

THE FOCUS OF MEDIA COVERAGE OF TERRORISM

Milo Beckman, in a July 2017 article for *FiveThirtyEight*, analyzed *New York Times* coverage of terrorism and finds that acts of terrorism in the United States, Europe, and American-allied countries like Saudi Arabia and Israel were overreported when compared with similar attacks in other parts of the world. Beckman notes that while the American media focused on a terrorist who drove a truck through a crowd in Nice, France, relatively little attention was paid to attacks in Beirut, Lebanon; Baghdad; and Dhaka, Bangladesh.

It is understandable that terrorism in France receives attention. The country is similar to the United States in terms of history, culture, kinship, and economic development than countries in Asia, Africa, and the Middle East. Others point out that by focusing on some countries rather than others, the media is failing to fulfill their responsibility to fully inform the American public about world events and to help Americans learn about where their country may find itself militarily involved in the future.

Kearns, Betus, and Lemieux (2017), in a paper posted online, find that the news media devotes significantly more coverage to attacks in the United States by Muslims—specifically foreign-born Muslims—although these attacks are much less frequent and destructive than terrorist attacks committed by non-Muslim terrorists. The authors of the study examined 89 attacks committed in the United States between 2011 and 2014, which were discussed in 2,413 articles in American print media and covered by CNN. The 12% of attacks committed by Muslims received 44% of the news coverage. Only 5% of terrorist attacks in the study were committed by a perpetrator who was a foreign-born Muslim resident of the United States. These attacks received 32% of all media coverage. An attack by a Muslim was covered, on average, in 90.8 articles; an attack by a foreign-born Muslim was covered, on average, in 192.8 articles; and attacks by other individuals were covered in, on average, 18.1 articles. When comparing an attack by a Muslim perpetrator with an attack by a non-Muslim perpetrator, the attack by the Muslim was 4.5 times likely to receive a greater amount of coverage. The authors note that the research indicates that people are more likely to consider at attack committed by a Muslim to be an act of terror when compared with an attack committed by a non-Muslim (Kearns, Betus, & Lemieux, 2017).

The next section discusses how the coverage of terrorism compares to coverage of other types of newsworthy events.

THE EXTENT OF MEDIA COVERAGE OF TERRORISM

The available evidence indicates that the media devotes more coverage to terrorism than to virtually any other issue. One study found that over a 6-year period in the 1980s, the three major old media networks (ABC, CBS and NBC) broadcast more stories about terrorism than about crime, poverty, racial equality, and unemployment. Nacos (2016) analyzed articles in the *New York Times* and the *Washington Post* that were published in 2014. These two influential newspapers published more articles on terrorism than health insurance, medical insurance for the retired and elderly, and poverty. The greatest concentration was on ISIS.

By focusing attention on beheadings, ISIS significantly increased the media coverage the group received. Beginning in mid-2014, these beheadings featured a masked executioner with an English accent called "Jihadi John" by media around the world. At one point, a Google search of the name *Jihadi John* yielded more than 6,280 results. The *New York Times* archives contain 266 stories on "Jihadi John," the *Washington Post* published 78 articles, and 299 results appeared on a search of CNN coverage.

Media coverage of ISIS significantly increased following the execution of American journalist James Foley in July 2014. Nacos (2016) reports that the number of articles about or mentioning ISIS tripled in the month following the release of the video when compared with the month before the release of the video. Headlines that included ISIS in the *New York Times*, *Newsweek*, and CNN also dramatically increased. *New York Times* headlines in the month following the release of the Foley video increased from three in the month before release to 99 in the month following release.

A dilemma for the media is that in the interest of covering important stories, they may be providing publicity for terrorists. In June 1985, Lebanese Shia terrorists hijacked TWA Flight 847 and diverted the Rome-bound flight to Algiers, Algeria and then to Beirut, Lebanon. The passengers were released during the crisis, although American Navy diver Robert Stethem was brutally murdered. The American television networks ABC, CBS, and NBC broadcast a combined average of 28.8 reports per day and during the 16-day crisis, the networks devoted more than 60% of their nightly news broadcasts to the hijacking. During the hijacking, the terrorists offered interviews with themselves and with the hostages to news organizations willing to pay for access. The publicity created pressure on the Reagan administration which, in turn, persuaded Israel to release 756 prisoners. The larger impact of the intense media coverage was to communicate that terrorism was an effective tool for a group to accomplish their goals and may have had the unanticipated impact of leading to additional acts of terrorism. The phenomenon of *media contagion* is discussed below.

MEDIA CONTAGION

The question arises whether media coverage of terrorism inspires other terrorist acts. Terrorist attacks seem to inspire terrorists across the globe to commit similar types of acts. Consider what seemed like an epidemic of knife and hatchet attacks in Israel and in Europe and the sudden spread of the use of trucks and automobiles to target pedestrians in London, Paris, and Nice, France. A number of commentators reject the notion of **media contagion**—that coverage of terrorism inspires other terrorist acts. Other commentators, on the other hand, conclude that media contagion is supported by anecdotal evidence as well as systematic research.

Alex P. Schmid and Janny de Graaf (1982), two prominent terrorist specialists, write that media coverage of terrorism can reduce inhibitions against the use of violence, inspire others to emulate and to imitate the attacks, and can provide insight and technical details into how to carry out a terrorist attack. They later note that South Moluccan nationalists who hijacked trains in the Netherlands in the 1970s reported that they were inspired by the attacks on trains carried out by Islamic terrorists. Brian Jenkins (1981) concludes that initial research indicates that intense media coverage of a terrorist event enhances the likelihood that similar acts will occur in the future. He goes on to note that embassy seizures took place in clusters, which is consistent with a contagion effect. Between 1971 and 1980 there were 43 successful embassy takeovers (an additional five attempts were unsuccessful) in 27 countries. The most prominent attack was the 1979 takeover of the American embassy in Tehran, in which embassy personnel were held hostage. The wave of beheadings and suicide bombings are two other examples of a terrorist tactic being adopted by various "copycat" lone wolves and groups (Nacos, 2016).

Michael Jetter (2017) undertook a complex economic analysis and finds that television and *New York Times* coverage of a terrorist attack are directly associated with additional attacks. He finds that media attention on a terrorist attack increased the likelihood of another attack within the same country and reduced the time frame between terrorist attacks. He speculates that suicide bombings receive the most publicity, which encourages terrorist groups to undertake similar—although more lethal—attacks. Other studies find that deaths caused by terrorist violence receive more coverage than deaths resulting from other causes, which inspires other groups to undertake attacks. Jetter reflects on the findings of his study and questions the decision of the media to cover terrorist deaths so intensely, given that an average of 42 people die every day from terrorist attacks as compared with 7,123 children who die from hunger-related causes.

Nacos (2016) speculates that McVeigh's 1995 attack on the Murrah Federal Building in Oklahoma City may have inspired Theodore Kaczynski, the so-called "Unabomber," to send a lethal letter bomb 5 days later to Gilbert Murray, director of the California Forest Association. The same day as the Oklahoma City bombing, the *New York Times* received a note from the Unabomber threatening to bomb their headquarters unless the newspaper published his 35,000-word manifesto explaining the reasons for his attacks. This was quickly followed by threats and demands to a number of other newspapers. Nacos speculates that Kaczynski may have been upset because McVeigh had displaced him as the preeminent terrorist in America and that he acted to focus attention on his attacks.

In another example of contagion, the shootings at Columbine High School in 1999—which killed 12 students and a teacher and injured 23 students—was followed by more than 400 school shootings, including the 2007 attack at Virginia Tech University.

This type of anecdotal evidence is reinforced by various studies on the contagion of terrorism. In an early study, Gabriel Weimann and Conrad Winn (1994) found that their data indicated a significant relationship between media coverage of terrorist acts and the subsequent commission of similar types of acts. Television coverage in particular encouraged "copycat" attacks.

Commentators speculate on the causes of media contagion. First, the more prolonged and intense the coverage of a terrorist attack, the more likely that the attack will inspire a similar attack in the future. Another explanation for contagion is that media coverage that portrays an attack as relatively uncomplicated to undertake will likely inspire other groups and lone wolves to commit acts of terrorism. Media coverage that devotes attention to the perpetrator will also likely provoke others that are seeking notoriety to engage in terrorism. Of course, it is almost impossible to determine whether follow-up attacks would have occurred without that coverage. Various commentators who do not accept the contagion theory appear to be apprehensive that, if this theory is accepted, it will lead to calls for government censorship of the media.

Even if it does not lead to a contagion effect, media coverage of terrorism can provoke fear and anxiety. Following the death of a Florida man from anthrax in October 2001, print and electronic media carried hundreds of stories of biological, chemical, and nuclear war (BCN), and thousands of people rushed out to purchase the items recommended by the government to assist them to survive a BCN attack. Media commentators raised additional anxiety by speculating that attacks involving smallpox, measles, and nuclear weapons would be quick to follow. On the other hand, media coverage served to educate and mobilize individuals, enabling them to take protective measures.

The next section explores media coverage of government counterterrorism efforts.

MEDIA COVERAGE OF COUNTERTERRORISM

The old news media is often termed the fourth branch of government and is referred to as the "fourth estate." The media, particularly in times of crisis finds itself, playing the role "cheerleader" for the government. This is the so-called "propaganda" model of news coverage. There is a natural tendency for reporters to "rally" support for the government when the government is confronted by a terrorist threat.

The elite-opinion approach assumes that journalists are cautious and conservative, wanting to be accepted by people who are powerful in politics. According to this view, reporters seek out elite opinions before endorsing or distancing themselves from a given policy. The entertainment approach argues that the media is interested in ratings, highlighting dramatic news that will draw an audience.

There is what researchers term *symbiosis*—interdependence between the media and terrorism. Nacos, Bloch-Elkon, and Shapiro (2011) find that that the major TV networks (ABC, CBS, and NBC) played a significant role in supporting the government following 9/11 by highlighting the threat posed by terrorism. These news organizations featured announcements of the rise in the terrorist threat level but paid significantly less attention to announcements of the decrease in threat levels. They find that all 23 announcements of an increase in the threat level were reported as "lead stories" by the traditional television networks; in contrast, 87% of stories about the reductions in threat levels were treated as secondary stories. Stories on the increase in threat levels received significantly more airtime than stories on the decrease in threat level. There was also little interest in covering complicated stories about the preparedness of the public health system or urban areas for response to a terrorist attack (Nacos, 2016).

Presidents and government officials often dominate the news with announcements, speeches, news briefings, press conferences, and visits to military bases and foreign countries. Their spokespeople appear on television to reinforce their message. Very few individuals who argue that the threat of terrorism is exaggerated or that Islamic terrorism is reasonable response to American foreign policy find themselves invited to appear on a major news network.

Presidents who employ military force historically have found that using this force enhances their popularity and poll numbers. After Ronald Reagan had Libya bombed in 1986 in retaliation for the bombing of a Berlin disco, which resulted in the death of two U.S. servicemen, his popularity rose from an impressive 62% to 67%, and more than 70% of Americans approved of the attack. Following the raid on Osama bin Laden's compound, popular approval of Barack Obama rose from 47% to 57%. The appetite of the news media for dramatic coverage may at times be exploited by presidents with declining poll numbers, who undoubtedly are aware that the announcement of military action will receive significant coverage and enhance their poll numbers. The most controversial example is Bill Clinton's ordering missile attacks on Afghanistan, along with an attack on an alleged chemical factory in Sudan in retaliation for al Qaeda's attacks on U.S. embassies in Kenya and in Tanzania. Skeptics suggested that the Sudan attack was a "Wag the Dog" scenario intended to draw attention away from the sex scandal (Nacos, Bloch-Elkon, & Shapiro, 2011). It should be noted that as the American public has grown increasingly tired of foreign military involvement, lengthy foreign interventions may not necessarily lead to a meaningful increase in a president's poll numbers—particularly when this policy is subject to criticism by politicians both within and outside of the president's own political party.

What is the impact on viewers who watch coverage of terrorism? A preliminary answer is provided by studies that found that individuals who paid a great deal of attention to the news following the 9/11 attacks were more likely to believe that another terrorist attack would occur within the next 12 months than those who paid little or moderate attention to the news. Psychological experiments found that individuals who perceived a high likelihood of attack are more likely to display intolerance and to support a restriction on civil liberties and other government actions (Nacos, 2016).

Any discussion of media coverage of terrorism would be incomplete without noting that American attitudes towards terrorism are shaped to a significant extent by television entertainment programs like *24* and *Homeland*. Studies find that knowledge about terrorism is based on a combination of news, entertainment, and political advertisements. These fictional accounts are given credibility by the fact that they are referenced by politicians in their public statements. This pattern is most pronounced among those age 18 to 34. The entertainment industry's portrayal of terrorism as a fight against "good" and "bad," and that the use of torture yields almost-instantaneous results without severe suffering likely had some role persuading roughly half of Americans by 2011 to view the use of torture against suspected terrorists to gain important information (Nacos, 2016).

THE NEW MEDIA AND TERRORISM

The struggle against terrorism exists both in physical conflict on the battlefield and in ideological conflict in cyberspace. Terrorists have taken advantage of the open and accessible nature of the Internet to promote their cause. In 2005 Ayman al-Zawahiri proclaimed that half the battle is in media in a struggle for the hearts and minds of the Muslim community. Al Qaeda accordingly began relying on the Internet both to promote itself and to attract support in the Muslim world.

Osama bin Laden hoped to provide Muslim a point of view that was different from the content available from CNN, the BBC, and from mainstream Arabic stations such as Al Jazeera and Al Arabiya. Sahab (meaning *the Clouds*) was the arm of al Qaeda. It was in charge of designing and producing videos. Once a video was shot and edited, it was uploaded to various al Qaeda–affiliated websites throughout the world. Al Qaeda adherents then copied and distributed the video. Osama bin Laden was featured in more than two dozen videos and audiotapes following the 9/11 attacks. By 2007, Sahab was producing nearly 100 videos a year—including posts on how to plan an assassination, fire a shoulder-fired missile, and use an automobile to deliver a car bomb. Al Qaeda also had a public relations arm, the Global Islamic Media Front, charged with translating and distributing the statements of Bin Laden and other al Qaeda leaders. Another media branch, Al Fajr (meaning *the dawn*) al Qaeda, produced an online magazine and a publication that offered instructions on how to use the Internet. Most importantly, al Qaeda began posting videos on websites it was hosting (Seib & Janbeck, 2011).

The Internet has been referred to as the "al Qaeda University of Jihad Studies" because the organization employed the Internet as a "virtual training camp," which provides detailed instructions on topics such as how to construct and deploy explosives. Hundreds of English-language terrorist sites, many of which are affiliated with al Qaeda, are aimed at recruiting people to organizations or inspiring lone wolves. Abu Musab al-Zarqawi posted a series of well-known videos called *Heroes of Fallujah*, one of which showed terrorists planting a roadside bomb and watching as the mine blew up an American armored personnel carrier. One of his most widely viewed videos showed al-Zarqawi beheading American businessman Nicholas Berg. The video was downloaded more than 500,000 times. Al-Zarqawi made his videos available in multiple formats that were compatible with various devices.

Al Qaeda also pioneered the use of the Internet to communicate with supporters by posting messages or documents to a secure website where the material can be viewed by members of the group.

ISIS, perhaps more than any other terrorist organization, appreciates the importance of the Internet in the ideological struggle against Western nations and their allies. ISIS regards its computer corps as of equal importance to its armed combatants. ISIS sponsored tens of thousands of Twitter accounts, posted high-production videos reminiscent of Hollywood films, spread reports on Facebook, sponsored chat rooms, and used every available app to distribute reports and photos.

Nacos (2016) notes certain characteristics of the Internet make it an attractive vehicle for terrorists. These include the fact that material can be disseminated anonymously all over the world in an inexpensive, unregulated fashion. The Internet is used by terrorists for various tasks—such as searching for information like the architectural structure of targeted buildings, coordinating and planning attacks, recruiting, raising money, and spreading propaganda.

The Somali terrorist group al-Shabaab tweeted throughout the attack that was launched against the Westgate Mall in Nairobi, Kenya, which resulted in 67 deaths. Another example of terrorists using the Internet to gather information is the use of Google Earth by the terrorists who carried out the attacks in Mumbai, India, in 2008 to locate targets in the city. During the attack, terrorists used a New Jersey–based Voice Over Internet Protocol (VoIP) service to converse between terrorists in Pakistan and terrorists in Mumbai.

ISIS spread propaganda by filming their attacks and then posting the videos online and distributing DVDs of the attacks. The pictures of alleged Western atrocities against Muslim women and children proved to be a powerful force in radicalizing new recruits. ISIS also used social media to spread psychological fear—posting the names, photographs, and addresses of 100 members of the U.S. military with the warning that the soldiers would be "dealt with" by ISIS supporters in the United States.

Various analysts argue that the struggle against terrorism is a conflict between the ideology of Western democracy and the ideology of radical Islamic ideology for the hearts and minds of young people, which ultimately will be decided in cyberspace rather than on the battlefield. Seib and Janbeck (2011), however, caution that the importance of Internet posting can sometimes be exaggerated, because these postings only reach about 1% of the global population. Nonetheless, in 2016, Facebook, Microsoft, Twitter, and YouTube all have agreed to collaborate in identifying and removing terrorist propaganda from their platforms. The program creates a database of digital "fingerprints" to automatically identify videos or images that the companies agree should be deleted.

Personalities and Events

On October 31, 2017, **Sayfullo Saipov**, age 29, drove a rented pickup truck down a crowded bike path adjacent to the Hudson River in New York City, killing eight people and injuring 11. The truck came to a halt after crashing into a school bus. Saipov jumped out of the truck and ran onto the highway waving a pellet gun and a paintball gun and, in the heat of the moment, left three knifes and a stun gun in the trunk of his vehicle. Saipov, while shouting "Allahu akbar" (*God is great*), was shot in the abdomen by a police officer. Handwritten notes in Arabic indicating allegiance to ISIS were found near the truck. ISIS later would claim Saipov as a soldier of the caliphate. Five of those killed in the attack were a group of friends from Argentina celebrating a high school reunion; another foreign victim was a Belgian mother of two children.

Saipov was born in Uzbekistan. In 2010 he had been selected in a lottery to emigrate to the United States and at the time of the attack, he was a permanent U.S. resident and had a green card. After moving around the United States, Saipov settled in Patterson, New Jersey, where he worked as an Uber driver.

The October 2017 attack was reminiscent of a 2016 attack in Nice, France, in which a cargo truck was driven into a crowd of individuals celebrating Bastille Day. Another similar attack was committed by an ISIS terrorist who drove a tractor into a crowded Christmas market in Berlin in December 2016. These attacks were followed by three vehicle attacks in London. Each of these events were seemingly a response to an in the ISIS magazine *Rumiyah*, calling adherents to attack pedestrians with motor vehicles and to continue the attack after exiting the vehicle with a knife or a gun. Several days prior to Saipov's attack, a French website affiliated with ISIS had called for attacks on Halloween. The site stressed the potential for motor vehicles to cause significant carnage if employed in a premeditated fashion against crowds of pedestrians.

(continues on next page)

(continued from previous page)

There were several photos of Abu Bakr al-Baghdadi, the leader of ISIS, on Saipov's phone—along with 3,800 other images, 90 videos, and propaganda material. One of the videos recorded the execution by ISIS of captives forced to wear orange jumpsuits similar to those worn by detainees at Guantanamo. Although Saipov did not appear to have pledged loyalty to al-Baghdadi prior to the attack, information on his cell phone indicated that he might have had access to secret ISIS chat rooms on the app Telegram. These chatrooms, called *channels*, provide instruction on carrying out terrorist attacks—for example, the steps to manufacturing an explosive—and also is used by ISIS organizers to locate potential attackers.

The United States and other Western countries are involved in hacking terrorist sites as well as websites meant to counter the message of terrorist groups. These counterterrorist sites feature videos recording terrorist defeats, the personal stories of individuals who left terrorist organizations, and the messages of Muslim imams who point out that Islam is a religion of peace, and that Muslim-inspired terrorists have distorted the Muslim religion. ☐

MEDIA CENSORSHIP

The First Amendment protects people's freedom of expression—including that of journalists. A free press is viewed as vital to ensure an informed citizenry and to hold government leaders accountable. Prior government restraint or the prohibition on the media from reporting a story before it is published or broadcast is only permissible when publishing that story would pose an immediate threat. The media attempts to act responsibly and refrains from publishing material that would cause harm.

Most important, the First Amendment is based on a belief in the so-called marketplace of ideas, in which various points of view compete with one another. The theory is that from this competition of ideas, the public is presented with the opportunity to make informed and intelligent decisions.

Keep in mind that although censoring the media usually violates the First Amendment, reporters and newspapers may be held criminally and/or civilly liable following publication.

There are instances when the American and foreign media have jeopardized counterterrorism efforts. Following the 2017 suicide bombing of a concert hall in Manchester, England, that killed 22 people, American newspapers ran a leaked story that the British security services were closing in on arresting individuals involved in the bombing. British prime minister Theresa May protested to U.S.

president Donald Trump that the story jeopardized these planned arrests in Great Britain. During the 1972 Munich Olympics, the Palestinian militia took Israeli athletes hostage. In East Germany, television broadcasts showed the preparation of West German security services to invade the compound. The West Germans decided against storming the compound as a consequence because the Palestinians had likely been alerted to the armed intervention by the broadcast, and a number of West German commandos could have been killed or gravely wounded had they stormed the compound.

During the conflict in Northern Ireland, British radio and television was prohibited from broadcasting interviews with members of 11 alleged terrorist organizations— although the media could report on the content of the interview. Media organizations skirted the ban by using actors to repeat the words of the terrorist leaders. One fear was that the statements might contain hidden messages to adherents.

There are various arguments for and against the censorship of the media (Schmid & de Graaf, 1982).

The arguments for media censorship include the following.

Assist terrorists. Media coverage provides terrorists with propaganda and aids their recruiting efforts.

Inspiration. Media coverage inspires others to commit acts of terrorism.

Assistance. Media reporting can provide helpful information to terrorists during an attack.

Retribution. Publicizing terrorist events can result in revenge attacks against innocent members of a community who share a heritage with the attackers.

Morale. Reporting on terrorism can demoralize the public.

Self-interest. The media cannot be counted on to perform responsibly because of the need and desire to attract a significant audience.

The arguments against media censorship include the following.

Information. Failing to report terrorism deprives the public of information required to make intelligent decisions about the causes and consequences of terrorism.

Credibility. The media may lose credibility and believability if reporting is dictated by the government.

Integrity. The imposition of censorship would allow terrorists to succeed in eroding democratic principles and values.

False reporting. Censorship encourages the spread of rumors and false news.

Abuse of power. The government may label journalists and media organizations that are critical of public policies as terrorists and demand they promote ideas that support the government.

Past performance. The media has proven responsible and reliable, and it has helped maintain an informed, intelligent public and can be counted on to avoid jeopardizing national security.

The ability of a democratic government to censor information in the world of the Internet would appear limited without a commitment to shut down websites and closely monitor online activity. A recent development is the increased commitment of Twitter, Facebook, YouTube, and other sites to remove and to prohibit postings by individuals or groups promoting terrorism. This is complicated by the large number of posts made by terrorists and by the ability of a group to continue to post material after it is taken down. It should be noted that a number of authoritarian regimes have severely restricted their citizens' access to the media.

Personalities and Events

FIGURE 9.3 Anwar Al-Awlaki

Anwar al-Alwaki, the deceased Yemeni cleric inspired numerous acts of terrorism—including the Fort Hood killings, the Boston Marathon bombers, the 2009 underwear bomber, and mass murders in Orlando, Florida, and San Bernardino County, California. Yet YouTube looked the other way and allowed al-Alwaki's lectures to be downloaded by potential jihadists across the globe. In November 2017, 6 years following al-Awlaki's killing by an American drone, YouTube decided to block most of the 70,000 videos referencing his lectures. YouTube located the videos with fingerprinting technology, and technicians blocked access to the material. As of November 2017, there were roughly 18,000 remaining videos—most of which discussed al-Awlaki's life and the legality of his killing by an American drone.

Al-Awlaki had been calling for jihad for years against the United States and the West. The first calls for al-Awlaki's removal from the Internet followed his November 2009 post calling Nidal Hassan, who killed 13 soldiers at Fort Hood, a hero. Al-Awlaki was particularly popular and effective because he was born in New Mexico to Yemeni parents, spent roughly half his life in the United States, and spoke flawless English. He was elevated to a revered status when President Obama ordered a drone attack in 2011 that killed al-Awlaki and three other members of al Qaeda (Simon, 2016).

The number of videos including al-Awlaki's lectures doubled between 2014 and 2017. Perhaps his most infamous lecture was a 12-minute call to jihad that urged Muslims to wage jihad at home. The video remained accessible until 2016.

Although YouTube, Facebook, Google, and Twitter claim to be neutral platforms that allow virtually all views to be articulated, the question is whether these companies should allow postings by people and groups who want to harm the United States. YouTube changed course after internal debate, explaining its decision based on the site's prohibition on content intended to "recruit for terrorist organizations, incite violence, celebrate terrorist attacks or otherwise promote acts of terrorism" (Shane, 2017). Although not all of al-Awlaki's recordings call for violence or terrorism, YouTube decided to remove all of the videos. Critics lambasted YouTube for taking down the recordings—especially given that most of them are freely available on other sites. There also is no persuasive evidence, according to these critics, that his videos contributed to acts of violence. Others warned against Internet sites losing their independence and being intimidated by governments into censoring or removing content that officials find objectionable. YouTube responded that at the very least, removing al-Awlaki's videos made them less accessible.

CHAPTER SUMMARY

Terrorist groups depend on the media to publicize their attacks and to enhance the impact of their attacks. Terrorism in the United States, Europe, and allied countries receive the most amount of media coverage; terrorism by Muslims receive more attention than terrorism committed by non-Muslims. There is evidence that newspaper coverage of terrorism inspires other acts of terrorism. Media, however, supports the practice of reporting government counterterrorism polices. Nonetheless there is the argument that the media does not perform a positive, patriotic role in combating terrorism and that a form of government censorship over the media is needed.

CHAPTER REVIEW QUESTIONS

1. Compare and contrast the new media and the old media.

2. Discuss whether the media should use the terms *terrorist* and *terrorism*.

3. Explain the concept of mass-mediated terrorism.

4. What types of terrorism receive the most media coverage? What areas of the world receive the most media attention? What accounts for these differences in coverage?

5. How does media coverage of terrorism compare to media coverage of other public policy issues? What accounts for the difference in coverage?

6. In your opinion, does media coverage promote terrorism? Why or why not?

7. How does the media cover counterterrorist policies?

8. Based on the discussion in this chapter, would you advocate for or against the censorship of media reporting on terrorism?

9. Is there interdependence between terrorists and the media?

10. Do you believe that the media performs responsibly in reporting on terrorism?

TERMINOLOGY

mass-mediated terrorism   new media   Saipov, Sayfullo
media contagion   old media

CHAPTER 10

The Legal and Historical Basis of Homeland Security

INTRODUCTION

In the aftermath of the 9/11 attacks, a number of measures were taken to protect the U.S. homeland. This chapter provides a brief introduction to the government departments and agencies charged with protecting the homeland, along with a historical overview of steps taken in the past to protect the United States. The next chapter looks at some of the public policy questions involved in counterterrorism programs.

Following 9/11, numerous commentators expressed alarm at the vulnerability of the United States to a terrorist attack and to the inadequate domestic protection of bridges, water-treatment and power plants, and seaports, as well as the lack of food security. Intelligence experts warned that al Qaeda "sleeper cells" had penetrated the United States and were waiting to attack (Mueller & Stewart, 2011).

A significant amount of money, resources, and attention is devoted to airline security, which following 9/11 became a particular area of concern. An attack made on an airliner can lead to the tragic loss of life and devastate countless families, relatives, and friends. Most people in the United States rely at least to some extent on air travel and threats of this type of attack can spread panic and fear. The data indicates that attacks on airplanes reverberate through the economy, discouraging travel and tourism and harming tourism-related services.

Skeptics, however, point out that there have been relatively few successful attacks on aircraft, and the screening of checked bags has effectively eliminated the threat of a bomb being smuggled onto an aircraft. In the 12 years from 1999 to 2010, 9,605 individuals were killed in airline accidents. During this period, 363 passengers were killed by terrorist attacks on airliners, including 265 individuals on the four planes attacked on 9/11 and 98 individuals in two 2004 attacks on Russian aircraft. In other words, airline passengers were significantly more likely to be killed in an airline accident than from a terrorist attack during this 12-year period. There was one chance in 11 million that a flight would be hijacked or attacked by terrorists (Mueller & Stewart, 2011).

Mueller and Stewart (2011) note that airliners are remarkably vulnerable to an attack by explosives and that the most effective method for bringing down an airliner is with a shoulder-fired missile. Between 1987 and 2007, there only were two successful shoulder-fired missile attacks on airliners—only two of which resulted in the catastrophic loss of aircraft.

The logical conclusion is that steps taken to protect aircraft have proven remarkably effective. Mueller and Stewart (2011), however, identify 21 separate layers of security surrounding air travel, the vast majority of which are of limited effectiveness. The researchers refer to these layers as **national security theater** that is designed to reassure and calm the public rather than effective protections against a terrorist attack.

Most individuals' contact with homeland security is the **Transportation Security Administration (TSA)** screening before boarding an airplane. In tests conducted in 2017, TSA screening failed to detect a weapon between 70% and 80% of the time. This was an improvement over tests in 2015, in which the failure rate was over 90%.

TSA agents are immune from being sued for a violation of an individual's civil liberties, although they may be held criminally responsible for misconduct.

The TSA preboarding screening is supplemented by the TSA's **Screening Passengers by Observation Techniques (SPOT) program**. The SPOT program involves trained observers evaluating whether the behavior of individuals in security lines and in the airport is suspicious. Various behaviors are listed as constituting suspicious behavior and are assigned points. An individual whose score is 6 or more is pulled out of the boarding line for closer inspection. SPOT officers also observe individuals after they have gone through the screening line. The General Accounting Office, which reviews the effectiveness of government programs and the wasteful expenditure of money, reviewed hundreds of studies and concluded that there is little evidence that terrorist activity can be detected by briefly observing an individual's physical behavior or facial expressions. Analysis of individual behavior is complicated by the fact that individuals often are nervous or apprehensive about flying and their behavior may appear suspicious. Only about 1% of the hundreds of thousands of individuals seized by SPOT officers are arrested, and these are arrests are most often for narcotics possession. There has yet to be an arrest for terrorist-related activity. The SPOT program also has been marred by allegations of racial profiling. Because of these difficulties, the SPOT program is being significantly revised.

A third airport security program is the **no-fly list**. The no-fly list is a list of people who are prohibited from boarding commercial aircraft within, into, or from the United States that is maintained by the **Federal Bureau of Investigation's (FBI)** Terrorist Screening Center. The number of names on the no-fly list and the identity of these individuals are a matter of national security and are not available to the public. Estimates are that the no-fly list contains as many as 81,000 names, although fewer than 1,000 are American citizens or nationals. Another list, termed the *TSA selectee list*, precipitates enhanced scrutiny of a passenger but does not prevent them from boarding an aircraft. This list contains roughly 28,000 names; fewer than 1,700 are Americans. There is a larger list of as many as 1 million mostly non-Americans on the terrorist watchlist who are individuals suspected of terrorist activity.

It is not clear why individuals are placed on the *no-fly list*, other than the finding that they are involved in terrorist activity or suspicion that they are involved in terrorist activity. Individuals have complained that they have been placed on the list because of travel to particular countries, social media posts, or that they were mistakenly placed on the list because their name is similar to that of a suspected terrorist. Individuals on the list also have alleged that they have experienced difficulty in being removed from the list. In 2015 officials boarded an aircraft and informed the family that their infant was on the no-fly list and had to be removed from the plane. There also are isolated instances of people on the no-fly list being able to board an aircraft. A successful application of the no-fly list was the case of Faisal Shahzad.

Shahzad attempted to ignite a car bomb in Times Square and the next day boarded a plane for Dubai before being removed from the plane at the gate and arrested.

A new program developed by TSA known as the "95 List" identifies difficult and unruly passengers who are thought to pose a threat to TSA screeners. Yet another recent program titled "Quiet Skies" involves the development of a watch-list based on undisclosed factors, which results in individuals being placed under surveillance during their flight.

Once on board the aircraft, passengers are protected by air marshals, which involves placing armed undercover law enforcement agents on aircraft to prevent disruptions or hijacking. Although there are thousands of marshals, only roughly 5% of flights have air marshals on board. The program is expensive and accounts for 10% of the TSA budget. The TSA argues that the marshals provide protection on high-risk flights, although there has not been a concerted effort to take over an American aircraft since 9/11. In addition, there is a program to train and equip pilots with firearms and to secure cockpit doors. There is anecdotal information that because of their hectic schedule, the air marshals often are sleep deprived and less than attentive. Mueller and Stewart (2011) estimate that the air marshal program only reduces the risk of a successful hijacking by 1.7%.

Morale in the TSA, which has an annual budget of more than $7.5 billion a year, is ranked nearly at the bottom of government agencies. Critics of the TSA assert that the TSA is wasting resources by screening every passenger rather than focusing on individuals who pose a threat. The no-fly list, although a more focused program, lacks clear standards for inclusion and includes various ordinary Americans who pose no terrorist threat. Some experts advocate additional pro-cedures such as securing entrances to airports, inspecting arriving automobiles, and increasing the use of bomb-sniffing dogs and surveillance cameras. Although each of the TSA programs has shortcomings, the thinking is that so-called layered security ensures that a would-be attacker who evades one layer of security will be detected by another layer of security. What is your view of whether airline security is effective in protecting against a terrorist attack?

The next sections of this chapter outline the agencies, institutions, and laws that protect the United States.

DEPARTMENT OF HOMELAND SECURITY

On October 8, 2001, President George W. Bush signed Executive Order (EO) 13228 titled "Establishing the Office of Homeland Security and the Homeland Security Council." The EO stipulated that the "functions of the Office [of Homeland Security] shall be to coordinate the executive branch's efforts to detect, prepare for, prevent, protect against, respond to, and recover from terrorist attacks within the United States" (Bush, 2001). In other words, the **Department of Homeland Security (DHS)** is charged with protecting the nation from terrorist attacks. Although the focus of this chapter is its role in preventing terrorism, keep in mind that DHS also is responsible for responding to natural and technological disasters and other threats to the nation.

Terrorist threats are constantly changing as terrorists develop new tactics. A country as large and complex as the United States has a number of vulnerabilities, ranging from airlines and airports to rail, truck, and sea transport. The northern and southern borders and coastline need to be secured against infiltration by terrorists. The vulnerable infrastructure also requires protection, including nuclear power and water-treatment plants, high-rise buildings, iconic landmarks, bridges and roads, and sports venues. Hospitals need to be equipped with sufficient resources to respond to a terrorist attack, and urban areas require evacuation plans and secure communication systems. First responders need to be equipped and trained to respond to a range of emergency situations. There also must be coordination between local, state, and federal agencies in protecting homeland security. A much-overlooked aspect of security is assisting private industry to address vulnerabilities in areas ranging from cybersecurity and power grids to high-rises.

A number of federal agencies were integrated into the DHS to ensure a coordinated and comprehensive response to terrorist threats and to other threats and emergencies (see Table 10.1). As a result of the reorganization of federal agencies, the DHS has a workforce of 225,000 employees and is the third largest federal agency, behind the Department of Veterans Affairs and the Department of Defense. The director of the DHS is part of the president's official Cabinet.

TABLE 10.1 Federal agencies incorporated into the Department of Homeland Security

Coast Guard. The Coast Guard is charged with securing the national seaports of entry and American coastline.

Customs and Border Protection (CPB). Customs and Border Protection is charged with enforcing immigration laws at the nation's borders and with inspecting items and containers brought and shipped into the United States.

Federal Emergency Management Agency (FEMA). FEMA is charged with coordinating the response to all varieties of national disasters, including floods, storms, and physical attacks.

Immigration and Customs Enforcement (ICE). ICE is responsible for enforcing immigration laws against individuals unlawfully in the United States and against businesses that employ unauthorized workers. ICE also is responsible for preventing illegal foreign trade involving the unlawful transportation of money, narcotics, the trafficking of people, and the export of prohibited technology.

Secret Service. An agency charged with the protection of the president and high-level executive personnel.

Transportation Security Administration (TSA). The TSA is responsible for ensuring that dangerous individuals do not gain access to the nation's transportation system.

CRITICAL INFRASTRUCTURE

Various agencies are concerned with specific sectors of the economy that include *critical infrastructure* that needs to be protected against a terrorist attack. The damage or destruction of these sectors would have a debilitating impact on the economy, public health, transportation, food, and agriculture. The agencies listed below are concerned with vital areas of the economy which may not come to mind when discussing terrorism, but they work with DHS in protecting the homeland.

U.S. Department of Agriculture (USDA). The USDA has primary responsibility for the food security of the U.S. food supply and for ensuring that the infrastructure supports the continued development and growth of the nation's food supply.

Department of Energy (DOE). The DOE is responsible for the development and protection of nation's energy resources, which includes responsibility for power plants, nuclear weapons production facilities, and research sites. The DOE and the Nuclear Regulatory Commission, which is an independent agency concerned with public health and safety, work with state agencies and with private industry to protect the nation's nuclear stockpile and nuclear power plants.

Department of Health and Human Services (DHS). The DHS is concerned with the health of Americans including the ability of the health care system to respond to an emergency.

Department of the Interior. The Department of the Interior is responsible for securing national monuments and federal lands for parks.

Environmental Protection Agency (EPA). The EPA has the responsibility to secure drinking water and water treatment plants and facilities and other environmental health concerns.

FEDERAL LAW ENFORCEMENT

In terms of law enforcement, the DHS coordinates with the Department of Justice (DOJ), which includes the FBI, the Drug Enforcement Agency (DEA), and the Bureau of Alcohol, Tobacco, Firearms and Explosives (ATF) to detect, investigate, and arrest terrorists. DOJ lawyers are charged with prosecuting terrorists.

The FBI is the lead agency in detecting and investigating domestic terrorism. The FBI is assisted in their investigations by the ATF, which enforces laws regarding gun crimes and by the DEA. The Diplomatic Security Service (DSS) is involved with protecting U.S. embassies and personnel abroad and with protecting foreign dignitaries visiting the United States. The DSS is concerned with terrorist threats to State Department facilities abroad and administers the Rewards for Justice program, which provides cash payments for information leading to the arrest of terrorists on the most wanted list. Each branch of the U.S. military has an investigative arm (for example, the Naval Investigative Service) which, among other concerns, investigates threats of terrorism against and within their specific branch of the military.

Joint Terrorism Task Forces (JTTFs) are cooperative arrangements between federal, state, and local law enforcement. The FBI coordinates JTTFs through the National Joint Terrorism Task Force.

DOMESTIC AND FOREIGN INTELLIGENCE

The collection, analysis, and distribution of intelligence are crucial to protecting the United States and American facilities around the world from a terrorist attack.

FIGURE 10.1 The Bombing of the Murrah Federal Building

Source: https://commons.wikimedia.org/wiki/File%3AFEMA_-_1573_-_Photograph_by_FEMA_News_Photo_taken_on_04-26-1995_in_Oklahoma.jpg.

The U.S. **intelligence community** includes 16 intelligence-gathering operations. Following 9/11, federal agencies realized that these various intelligence branches failed to share information on potential terrorist threats. The Intelligence Reform and Terrorism Prevention Act of 2004 created the **Office of the Director of National Intelligence (ODNI)** to centralize the collection of intelligence from each of these agencies and to identify areas of concern. The central components of the U.S. intelligence community include the following:

Central Intelligence Agency (CIA). The **Central Intelligence Agency (CIA)** collects and analyzes intelligence using human intelligence and also specializes in the analysis of open-source material (such as newspapers). The CIA is yet another partner agency of the DHS. In protecting the border, the DHS works with the CIA to identify individuals entering the country who may pose a terrorist threat.

Defense Intelligence Agency (DIA). The **Defense Intelligence Agency (DIA)** is located within the Department of Defense and is the central source of intelligence for the American military. The DIA gathers information from the intelligence bureaus of each of the branches of the military.

Federal Bureau of Investigation (FBI). The FBI is located within the Department of Justice and is the primary federal law enforcement agency. The FBI engages in domestic surveillance of suspected terrorists and is involved in the investigation of attacks on American facilities abroad.

Department of Homeland Security (DHS). The DHS, in conjunction with other agencies, is involved in collecting information on domestic terrorism, issues of immigration, and the import of contraband into the United States.

A number of agencies have their own intelligence arms, including the ATF, the DEA, and Department of State. In addition, the U.S. Postal Service monitors the country's mail for threats to national security.

National Security Agency (NSA). The National Security Agency collects foreign intelligence using electronic (for example, wiretapping, computer monitoring, and hacking) and satellite technology. The NSA devotes considerable resources to developing new methods of surveillance. The Five Eyes (FVEY) is an alliance comprised of Australia, Canada, New Zealand, the United Kingdom, and the United States that shares information and conducts joint surveillance. There are a number other information-sharing arrangements, including the arrangement between members of the North Atlantic Treaty Organization (NATO).

Keep in mind that the vast amount of information collected by intelligence agencies must be analyzed to determine its importance. Analysis requires individuals that have the language skills and familiarity with the culture and politics of various countries. In the past, the United States has experienced a shortage of individuals with the required skills in Southeast Asia and in the Middle East. There also are areas of the world—such as North Korea—in which it has been proven difficult to gather accurate information.

FEDERAL COUNTERTERRORISM LAWS

Two congressional laws discussed below are of particular importance in counterterrorism: the **PATRIOT Act** and the **Antiterrorism and Effective Death Penalty Act.**

The PATRIOT Act. In October 2001 the U.S. Congress passed and President George W. Bush signed a new law to provide the legal tools to combat terrorism titled the Uniting and Strengthening America by Providing Appropriate Tools Required to Intercept and Obstruct Terrorism Act of 2001. Commonly referred to as the PATRIOT Act, the law includes 10 titles and more than 50 sections and modifies more than nine existing laws. Congress periodically has renewed various sections of the PATRIOT Act with some modification of the text. The law primarily is concerned with defining new federal criminal offenses relating to terrorism, and with introducing reforms to criminal procedure that makes it easier to investigate, detect, and prosecute terrorism.

An example of a tool provided to law enforcement under the **PATRIOT Act** is national security letters (NSL). The FBI is authorized to issue an NSL under Section 505 of the PATRIOT Act to obtain information without a court order that is "relevant to an ... investigation to protect against international terrorism or [secret] intelligence activities" (U.S. Congress, 2001b). Another important provision in the PATRIOT Act is Section 203, which breaks down the so-called wall between national intelligence and domestic law enforcement and allows information obtained in electronic surveillance by NSA for purposes of national security to be shared with domestic law enforcement. Roving wiretaps allow a federal court to issue a warrant that authorizes the electronic surveillance of all telephones, computers, or other devices utilized by an individual without requiring that law enforcement obtain a separate warrant to monitor each device. Sneak-and-peek searches allow law enforcement to enter and examine material in a dwelling and then obtain a warrant and execute a formal search (U.S. Congress, 2001b).

To ensure that the provisions of the PATRIOT Act did not lead to governmental abuse and were at the same time sufficiently strong, civil libertarians and conservative lawmakers demanded that various provisions would automatically expire unless extended by Congress. For example, the USA PATRIOT Improvement and Reauthorization Act of 2005 provided additional protections for libraries and enhanced criminal penalties for financial support for terrorism, among other provisions.

The 1996 Anti-Terrorism and Effective Death Penalty Act. In 1996, following the explosion of a bomb at Centennial Park during the Atlanta Olympics and the unsolved explosion that brought down TWA Flight 800 over Long Island, New York, the U.S. Congress passed and President Bill Clinton signed the Anti-Terrorism and Effective Death Penalty Act. The legislation allows the death penalty for acts of terrorism and broadens the authority of the secretary of state to designate groups as terrorist organizations, which are prohibited from raising funds in the United States. An important provision requires the inclusion of taggants in plastic explosives in order to assist law enforcement to locate the individuals who purchased the explosives used in a terrorist attack.

Also keep in mind that most states have their own terrorism laws. These laws are typically used to prosecute acts of terrorism that are not prosecuted by federal authorities. In some instances, individuals may be prosecuted in both state and federal courts.

IDENTIFING STATE SPONSORS AND FOREIGN TERRORIST ORGANIZATIONS

Each year, the Department of State publishes the *Country Reports on Terrorism*, which lists state sponsors of terrorism and foreign terrorist organizations (FTOs). As previously noted, state sponsors of terrorism are governmental regimes that support terrorism; FTOs are terrorist groups.

In accordance with congressional legislation, the secretary of state may designate a government as a state sponsor of terrorism if the country has consistently provided support for acts of international terrorism. A government remains on the list of state sponsors until removed by the secretary of state. A state sponsor of terrorism is subject to various penalties, including a prohibition on arms exports and sales, a prohibition on economic assistance, and restrictions on American exports of dual-use technology (goods that may be used for both civilian and military purposes). The Trump administration has listed North Korea, Iran, and Syria as state sponsors of terrorism but removed Sudan from the list.

An FTO is a foreign organization that engages in terrorist activity or possesses the capability and intent to engage in terrorist activity. In order to be designated an FTO, the organization must threaten the security of American nationals or national security (for example, national defense, foreign relations, or economic interests) of the United States (Luna & McCormack, 2015).

CHECKS AND BALANCES

The authority and ability of the federal government to combat terrorism is limited by the system of checks and balances provided in the U.S. Constitution. The DHS and other administrative agencies are subject to oversight from Congress. Administrative regulations and Congressional laws may, in turn, be ruled unconstitutional by the courts. Elected officials must also stand for election and are accountable to the American electorate.

10.1 You Decide

Muhammad Youssef Abdulazeez, a Kuwaiti-born American citizen, attacked two military facilities in Chattanooga, Tennessee, killing five people and wounding another two. Despite a history of mental illness, Abdulazeez was able to legally purchase the firearm used in the assault (Cassidy, 2016).

In December 2015, Syed Rizwan Farook and Tashfeen Malik, described as homegrown violent extremists, killed 14 people and wounded 22 in San Bernardino, California. Farook was a U.S. citizen of Pakistani descent, and Malik was a lawful permanent resident born in Pakistan. They had legally purchased handguns and had persuaded a neighbor to purchase two rifles for them.

Omar Mateen, a 29-year-old American citizen of Afghan descent who in June 2016 killed 50 individuals and wounded 53 at the Pulse nightclub in Orlando, Florida. Investigators determined that he had legally purchased a pistol and an assault rifle a few days prior to the attack. Mateen had spent 10 months on the terrorist watchlist until removed by the FBI on the grounds that he did not pose a threat (Cassidy, 2016).

President Barack Obama, in an address from the Oval Office 4 days following the San Bernardino attack, said that Farook and Malik "had gone down the dark path of radicalization, embracing a perverted interpretation of Islam that calls for war against America and the West." President Obama called on Congress to "make sure no one on a no-fly list is able to buy a gun," and asked, "What could possibly be the argument for allowing a terrorist suspect to buy a semi-automatic weapon? This is a matter of national security" (Tau, 2015).

Individuals purchasing firearms from federally licensed dealers are required to undergo background checks. There are at least 10 categories of individuals who are prohibited from obtaining a firearm, including convicted felons, undocumented individuals unlawfully in the country, and individuals institutionalized for mental illness. A sale can be approved in less than an hour if the background check using the National Instant Criminal Background Check System does not indicate that the purchaser is prohibited from owning a firearm. A sale can be delayed for as long as 72 hours if FBI examiners find reason to believe that the purchaser of the weapon is prohibited from owning a weapon. Background checks are not required to buy a gun from an unlicensed seller at a gun show or online.

(continues on next page)

(continued from previous page)

The U.S. Congress, dominated by a Republican majority, disregarded President Obama's proposal to prohibit individuals on the no-fly list from purchasing a firearm. It was pointed out that prohibiting individuals on the no-fly list from purchasing firearms would not have prevented any of the recent terrorist attacks in the United States. The no-fly list is based on loose standards and contains inaccuracies which might unjustly prevent a law-abiding American from purchasing and possessing a firearm. A determined terrorist will find a way to obtain a firearm despite any restrictions that are imposed, and like the Boston Marathon bombers, a dedicated terrorist will employ methods of attack that do not involve firearms. Foreign nationals are ineligible to purchase a firearm in the United States in any event. A more effective approach, according to opponents of President Obama's proposal, would be to improve intelligence on extremists in the United States. A middle ground would delay sale to an individual whose name appears on a terrorist database to determine whether there is any concern that the firearm will be used for acts of terrorism.

Between 2004 and 2015, 2,477 people on the terrorist watchlist attempted to buy a firearm or explosive through a licensed dealer. The General Accounting Office of the federal government reports that 2,265 were allowed to make the purchase and 212 were denied. The denials presumably were based on a reason other than the fact that the individual was on the terrorist watchlist.

What is your view on whether individuals on the no-fly list should be allowed to purchase firearms? ▯

INTERNATIONAL COUNTERTERRORISM AGREEMENTS

Terrorism inevitably involves more than a single government. Terrorists may use a country as a safe haven, raise money or obtain weapons abroad, assassinate foreign leaders, or launch attacks on a target in another country. The international community has responded by entering into a number of agreements or treaties in which they agree to cooperate in combating terrorism. Keep in mind that an international agreement does not have a binding impact in a country unless it is incorporated into a country's internal domestic law. A treaty that is accepted by a country, although not made part of a country's domestic law, may take on the status of customary law that has the force of binding law based on general acceptance by the international community. Examples include international agreements that prohibit genocide and torture.

The most significant international agreements regulate areas that require international cooperation to be effective and are of concern to most countries in the world. Air transport is vital to the movement of people and cargo, the protection of diplomats and hostages abducted abroad, and restricting the movement of money across borders.

The major international treaties on terrorism are listed below.

Tokyo Convention on Offenses and Certain Other Acts Committed Aboard Aircraft (1963). Countries agree to restore the control of aircraft to the pilot and to send the passengers and containers on their intended route.

Hague Convention (1970). Signatories agree to extradite air hijackers to their country of origin or to prosecute hijackers.

Montreal Convention (1971). Sabotage and attacks on airports and grounded aircraft are to be prosecuted or sent to a country that seeks their extradition. Offenders are subject to severe penalties.

Protection and Punishment of Crimes Against Internationally Protected Persons Including Diplomatic Agents (1973). Violent acts against diplomats, the kidnapping of diplomats, and attacks on diplomatic premises and means of transport are to be subject to criminal penalties. Offenders are either to be prosecuted or extradited to a county asserting jurisdiction.

International Convention Against the Taking of Hostages (1979). An international agreement to punish hostage takers or to extradite hostage takers for trial abroad.

International Convention for the Suppression of the Financing of Terrorism. This treaty obligates signatories to prevent and punish the financing of terrorism.

The international community has been unable to agree on a general treaty to prevent and to punish terrorism. There has been intense disagreement, for example, on whether to punish state terrorism and whether individuals fighting for freedom should be considered terrorists or freedom fighters.

In addition to these international agreements, the 1949 Geneva Conventions and the related protocols of 1977 regulate the law of war and prohibit attacks on civilians and civilian objects. The treaties significantly regulate the treatment of prisoners of war during both international and noninternational conflicts. There also are international treaties regulating landmines, chemical and biological weapons, poison gas, torture, genocide, extrajudicial killings, and a newly drafted treaty on nuclear weapons.

There are several international courts with jurisdiction over international terrorism.

International Court of Justice (ICJ). The ICJ is a body established by the United Nations to consider disputes between nations and to issue advisory opinions on various issues. The ICJ, for example, issued an advisory opinion on the legality of the wall constructed by Israel to separate the country from the West Bank and an advisory opinion on the legality of nuclear weapons.

International Criminal Court (ICC). The court is based on a 1988 treaty and at present 128 states have joined the court which has jurisdiction to prosecute nationals of these states for international crimes, including torture, genocide, extrajudicial executions, and war crimes.

Regional human rights courts in Europe, Latin America, and Africa have jurisdiction to hear challenges to the treatment of terrorist detainees by courts. The European court has condemned the state torture of detainees accused of terrorism.

Personalities and Events

FIGURE 10.2 Chelsea Manning

Copyright © Tim Travers Hawkins (CC BY-SA 4.0) at https://commons.wikimedia.org/wiki/File%3AChelsea_Manning%2C_18_May_2017_(cropped).jpeg.

Chelsea Manning (born Bradley Manning, December 17, 1987) was a member of the U.S. military. In July 2013, she was convicted of violating the Espionage Act after transferring roughly 750,000 classified and sensitive (unclassified) military and diplomatic documents to the website Wikileaks. Manning was sentenced to 35 years in military prison and was released by President Obama in 2017.

Manning was born in Oklahoma City, Oklahoma, in 1987. Her father was a member of the Navy who married Manning's mother after meeting her in Wales in the United Kingdom. Both parents reportedly abused alcohol and Chelsea's health suffered. As an adult she only reached 5ft 2in and weighed around 105 pounds. Despite her unstable home life, Chelsea excelled at science and exhibited an aptitude for computers.

Manning moved with her mother to Wales before returning to the United States at age 17. After being fired from a position as a software developer, Chelsea held a series of low-paying jobs but found the confidence to live as an openly gay person.

In 2007 Chelsea's father persuaded her at age 20 to join the military with the understanding that she could take advantage of college benefits to eventually pursue a doctorate in physics. After surviving a difficult and challenging experience during basic training, Chelsea was assigned to serve as an intelligence analyst, which gave her access to a massive amount of classified information. Manning was then posted to Fort Drum in upstate New York and became romantically involved with a Brandeis University student who introduced Chelsea to the Boston-area hacker community. Although Manning finally seemed happy, she continued to exhibit emotional unevenness, instability, and insecurity. She was nonetheless assigned to Iraq in October 2009 and was promoted from private first class to specialist.

Manning reportedly found herself lonely, in crisis over her gender identity, and with grave misgivings about the war in Iraq. The military's "don't ask don't tell" policy prevented her from living openly as a transgender women. On January 5, 2010, Manning downloaded documents that were later labeled the Iraq War logs. Three days later she downloaded more documents, later known as the Afghan War logs. She saved the material on a CD-RW which she smuggled through security and copied onto her computer. The files then were copied from her laptop to an SD card for her camera. On January 23, 2010, Manning flew to the United States for 2 weeks' leave (Shaer, 2017). On February 3, 2010, after corresponding with Julian Assange, the founder of WikiLeaks, Manning began sending files to the website. Material shortly thereafter also began appearing in the *New York Times, Washington Post,* the *Guardian*, and *Der Spiegel*.

Manning was arrested shortly after the documents began to appear. The documents included:

Afghanistan war logs. Excerpts from 91,731 reports of U.S. military actions in Afghanistan known as the Afghan War logs. These files included information on a 2007 attack by American forces in the city of Jalalabad that killed 19 and wounded 50 civilians.

Iraq war logs. In October 2010, documents were released that included revelations of reports of abuse, torture, rape, and killing by Iraq police and soldiers. Some documents recorded that prisoners were shackled, hung by their wrists or ankles, and were whipped, kicked, and were subject to electric shock. Details of 100,000 deaths following the invasion of the country were compiled, which was contrary to representations that there was no official list of deaths.

(continues on next page)

(continued from previous page)

State department cables. On November 10, 2010, 251,287 Department of State cables written by 217 American embassies and consulates in 180 countries were released (WikiLeaks, 2010). This included cables on Saudi Arabia, the Soviet Union, and an intelligence operation directed against United Nations officials.

Baghdad airstrike. A video showing two American helicopters in 2007 firing at a group of roughly a dozen men. Two of the men who were killed were Reuters journalists; the pilot mistook their cameras for weapons. A van is attacked in the video, killing an innocent father who is attempting to assist the wounded—as well as his two young children.

Granai airstrike. A video of an air strike in 2009 on the village of Granai, Afghanistan, killing between 86 and 147 Afghan civilians. The video appears to have been destroyed by a member of Wikileaks and was never posted online.

Guantánamo. In April 2011, 758 "detainee assessment" dossiers were released on individuals held at Guantánamo Bay prison drafted between 2002 and 2009. The files detailed the detainees' connections with al Qaeda or the Taliban. The files revealed that some prisoners had long been cleared of involvement with terrorist organizations.

Manning was held in the Marine Corps Brig in Quantico, Virginia, from July 2010 to April 2011 under Prevention of Injury status—which required solitary confinement and constant surveillance. She was incarcerated in a 6-by-12-foot cell with no window. Manning was temporarily placed on suicide watch, her clothing and eyeglasses were removed, and she was required to remain in her cell 24 hours a day (Nakashima, 2011). Her conditions led to international criticism; the United Nations Special Rapporteur on torture, Juan E. Mendez, described her treatment as cruel and degrading.

On April 20, 2010, Manning was transferred to medium-level custody at Fort Leavenworth, Kansas, and pled guilty to 10 of 22 charges. She stood trial beginning in June 2013 on the remaining charges and on July 30, 2013, was convicted of 17 of the original charges and amended versions of four others—although she was acquitted of aiding the enemy (Pilkington, 2013).

A military psychologist who treated Manning testified at her trial that she was isolated in the Army and had difficulty dealing with her gender-identity issues in a hypermasculine environment. Another psychiatrist testified that Manning had narcissistic personality traits and demonstrated signs of fetal alcohol syndrome and Asperger's syndrome. According to the testimony, in leaking the material Manning was acting out a sense of her own grandiosity and believed that the leaked information was going to change the world and persuade people that the Afghan and Iraq wars were not worth pursuing (Shaer, 2017).

On August 14, Manning apologized to the court: "I am sorry that my actions hurt people. I'm sorry that they hurt the United States. I am sorry for the unintended consequences of my actions. When I made these decisions I believed I was going to help people, not hurt people." Manning was sentenced to 35 years in a maximum-security disciplinary barracks at Fort Leavenworth. The day after sentencing, Manning's attorney issued a press release announcing that his client was female and asked that she be referred to by the name Chelsea and that feminine pronouns be used. Manning requested and eventually received hormone replacement therapy (Hartmann, 2013; Tate, 2013).

On January 17, 2017, President Obama commuted all but 4 months of Manning's remaining sentence. President Obama stated in a press conference in January 2017 that Manning's original 35-year prison sentence was "very disproportionate relative to what other leakers have received" and that "it makes sense to commute—and not pardon—her sentence." She was released on May 17, 2017. In response, President Trump tweeted that Manning was an "ungrateful traitor" and should "never have been released" (Savage, 2017b; Nelson, 2017).

Manning's behavior may have been a product of her emotional instability and confusion. On the other hand, she may have been a well-meaning—if not naïve—idealist. Following the leaking of the documents to Wikileaks, Manning contacted Adrian Lamo, a well-known hacker, to discuss the leaks. Manning shared that the incident that had affected her most was when 15 detainees had been arrested by the Iraq Federal Police for printing material that was critical of the government. Manning reportedly told authorities that the arrests were unjustified because the arrestees had uncovered and were attempting to share information on corruption in the Iraqi government. Manning's commanding officer dismissed her concerns and ordered her to help the Iraqi police locate more subversives. Manning shared that it made her aware that she was "actively involved in something that I was completely against." On several occasions, Manning stated that she hoped the material that she leaked would hopefully lead to "worldwide discussion, debates, and reforms. if not ... than [sic] we're doomed as a species" (Shaer, 2017).

Some individuals view Manning as a traitor to her country. Admiral Michael Mullen, then chair of the Joint Chief of Staffs, and other high-ranking officials and analysts continue to insist that Manning's disclosures jeopardized the lives of Americans and of Afghan informants.

(continues on next page)

(continued from previous page)

Others contended that Manning was a whistleblower who had rallied opposition to the Iraq and Afghan war. A Department of Defense study released to the public in July 2017 found that Manning's release of documents had no significant strategic impact on American national security.

Manning has received numerous prizes from organizations in the United States, Germany, Scandinavia, and various magazines for inspiring public debate over war and peace, and encouraging government openness and transgender rights. On September 13, 2017, Manning was named a visiting fellow at Harvard University to participate in a limited number of events on campus and to discuss LGBTQ issues with students. The acting director of the Harvard Institute of Politics welcomed her contribution to a series of thought-provoking events on race, gender, politics, and the media (Stack, 2017) Mike Morell, former deputy director and twice acting director of the CIA, resigned as a nonresident senior fellow at Harvard's Belfer Center for Science and International Affairs in protest over Harvard honoring Manning, whom he stated was a convicted felon and leaker of classified information. CIA director Mike Pompeo—now Secretary of State—withdrew from a scheduled speaking engagement at Harvard, calling Manning a traitor. Douglas Elmendorf, dean of the Kennedy School at Harvard, subsequently withdrew Chelsea Manning's designation as a visiting fellow (Haag & Bromwich, 2017).

A lingering question is how a young, unstable enlisted soldier could be permitted access to sensitive national security documents. What is your view of Chelsea Manning? ☐

HISTORICAL FOUNDATION OF HOMELAND SECURITY

Throughout the country's history, the United States has confronted domestic challenges that the government has viewed as a serious challenge to the security and stability of the government.

Alien and Sedition Acts

President John Adams (1797–1801) and the Federalist Party strongly supported England against Napoleon Bonaparte's French regime, which was supported by Thomas Jefferson's Democratic Republican Party. The Federalists feared that the Democratic Republicans would foment revolutionary fervor in the United States and overthrow the government. The initial **Alien and Sedition Act** was intended to restrict the liberty and freedom of the Jeffersonians and their immigrant supporters. The Alien and Sedition Acts were made of the following four acts:

Alien Enemies Act. The president may deport or imprison citizens of "enemy" countries.

Alien Friendly Act. The president may deport citizens of friendly countries who are considered dangerous.

Naturalization Act. Immigrants are required to live in the United States for 14 years before being considered for citizenship.

Sedition Act. Individuals may be imprisoned for criticizing the government.

President Thomas Jefferson (1801–1809) and Democratic Republican Party repealed three of the Acts, although the Sedition Act remained in place and would form the basis for the Espionage Act which was employed to restrict dissent during World War I.

THE CIVIL WAR

The writ of habeas corpus is a fundamental right established in English common law, which was made part of English statutory law by parliament in 1671. The so-called Great Writ was later incorporated into the U.S. Constitution. An incarcerated individual may file a writ of habeas corpus and compel authorities to appear in court and justify the basis of his or her detention. Habeas corpus is thus a check on the ability of the government to imprison individuals without reason and/or without following required legal procedures. In 1861 President Abraham Lincoln imposed martial law and suspended habeas corpus in Maryland and in the Midwest. The U.S. Supreme Court rejected President Lincoln's suspension of habeas corpus as unconstitutional. Lincoln disregarded the Court's decision and extended the suspension of habeas corpus to all the states in the Union in cases involving prisoners of war, spies, traitors, or Union soldiers. Under Lincoln's order, detainees were to be prosecuted before military tribunals. Lincoln detained between 13,000 and 38,000 individuals under this order, many of whom were outside the immediate war zone and were guilty of nothing more than publishing articles and commentators critical of Lincoln's conduct of the war. In *Milligan*, the U.S. Supreme Court subsequently affirmed their earlier decision rejecting President Lincoln's suspension of habeas corpus and held that the use of military tribunals to prosecute civilians when civilian courts are still open and functioning is unconstitutional (*In re Milligan*, 1866). Keep in mind the issues of military tribunals and suspension of habeas corpus reemerged in prosecuting the War on Terror following the 9/11 attacks.

THE PALMER RAIDS

In 1915 President Woodrow Wilson warned that various American immigrants were sources of disloyalty and unrest and must be eliminated from the nation. His fears were fueled by the Russian Revolution of 1917 and a series of domestic bombings and labor strikes. In August 1919, attorney general Mitchell Palmer named 24-year-old J. Edgar Hoover to head an intelligence division in the Department of Justice. The newly established Bureau of Investigation amassed thousands of names of suspected anarchists and subversives. On November 7, 1919, the second anniversary of the Russian Revolution, agents of Hoover's Bureau of Investigation aided local police in carrying out **Palmer raids** in 12 cities against the Union of Russian Workers, arresting 250 so-called dangerous radicals. Only 43 of these detainees were ultimately deported. A second series of raids were initiated in January 1920 and extended over 6 weeks, leading to the arrest of roughly 3,000 suspects in 30 cities and 23 states—a large percentage of whom simply were at the "wrong place at the wrong time."

In the end, 10,000 were arrested, 3,500 were detained, and 556 immigrants were deported.

Palmer responded to criticism by emphasizing that drastic measures were required to meet the threat of an epidemic of subversion and violence that posed a threat to the government and to society. In June 1920, Massachusetts district court judge Georg Anderson ordered the discharge of 17 immigrants, denouncing the Palmer raids and proclaiming that "a mob is a mob, whether made up of Government officials acting under instructions from the Department of Justice, or of criminals and loafers and the vicious classes" (*Coyler v. Skeffington*, 1920). Judge Anderson's decision marked the end of support for Palmer's campaign against internal subversion.

THE POST-DEPRESSION RED SCARE

In 1938 the House of Representatives formed the House Un-American Activities Committee (HUAC) which investigated radical groups active in the United States during the Great Depression (1933–1938) and during the initial portion of the Cold War with the Soviet Union (1945–1951). The committee issued subpoenas (court-like orders) to individuals to appear and to testify before the committee. Critics claimed that HUAC was formed to link President Franklin Delano Roosevelt's New Deal with domestic left-wing groups. As Russia emerged as America's Cold War rival, HUAC increasingly turned its attention to identifying members of the Communist Party.

Individuals called before HUAC were asked to identify other suspected Communists disloyal to the United States. The committee believed that Communists had infiltrated every aspect of American life and called academics, actors, artists, and civil servants to testify. A refusal to provide names resulted in being held in contempt of Congress. Individuals claiming that they would not testify on the grounds that the testimony would incriminate them were denounced as "Fifth Amendment Communists" and found themselves terminated by their employer and blacklisted from employment.

In 1948 Whittaker Chambers accused Alger Hiss, a former important State Department official of spying on behalf of the Soviet Union. Chambers's testimony led to Hiss being convicted of perjury. Hiss served 44 months in prison. The case lent credibility to the claim that Communists had infiltrated the U.S. government.

The encouragement of public fear and panic about the spread of communism in American institutions and society has been termed by historians as the **Red Scare** (Communists were known as "Reds" based on the red Bolshevik Russian flag).

THE COLD WAR AND THE RED SCARE

Senator Joseph McCarthy of Wisconsin conducted hearings on the alleged infiltration of the U.S. government by individuals who were accused of being loyal to China or Russia rather than to the United States. His often false or exaggerated allegations and attacks became known as **McCarthyism**. Hundreds of individuals had their careers destroyed as a result of being singled out as Communists or as Communist sympathizers.

In 1940 Congress passed the Alien Registration Act (also called the Smith Act) making it a crime to "knowingly or willfully advocate the overthrow of the U.S. government or to organize any association which teaches the overthrow of the U.S. government or to become a member of such an association" (*Dennis v. United States*, 1951). The Smith Act provided the legal basis for the criminal prosecutions in 1949 and subsequent imprisonment of 11 leaders of the Communist Party and of more than 100 other members of the Communist Party. More than 130 other members of the Communist Party were prosecuted after the 1949 prosecutions, many of whom were imprisoned.

In 1947 President Harry S. Truman issued Executive Order 9835 (the Loyalty Order) which required that federal employees be examined to determine whether they were loyal to the U.S. government.

The Red Scare reached its height in 1951 when Julius and Ethel Rosenberg were brought to trial and convicted for conspiracy to commit espionage by allegedly turning information regarding the design of nuclear weapons over to the Soviet Union. The Rosenbergs were both executed in 1953.

McCarthy's assault on the government ended in December 1954 when Joseph Welch, General Counsel of the U.S. Army, confronted him during a Senate hearing and exposed him as an irresponsible bully. McCarthy was officially condemned by the Senate for contempt against his colleagues. During the next 2½ years,

McCarthy deteriorated and spiraled downhill into alcoholism. He died while in office in 1957.

WORLD WAR II INTERNMENT

The attack on Pearl Harbor on December 7, 1941, by Japan led to a fear among many Americans that Japanese Americans posed a threat of subversion and sabotage. There also was a fear that Japanese Americans were communicating with enemy submarines and ships and assisting in targeting missiles towards vulnerable targets within the United States.

President Franklin Delano Roosevelt established the War Relocation Authority which, with the assistance of the U.S. Army, transferred as many as 112,000 Japanese Americans to internment camps on the West Coast and in the Western states. Internees often lost their businesses, careers, and most of their valuable possessions. President Ronald Reagan, decades later in the 1980s, apologized for the actions of the United States in the internment of Japanese Americans and Congress authorized reparation payments of $20,000 to surviving internees.

VIETNAM PROTESTS

The U.S. government conducted a selective service draft of men 18 years of age and older to serve in the Vietnam War. The war became increasingly unpopular—particularly on college campuses. The government reacted strongly against any efforts to impede the draft. In 1968 famed pediatrician Benjamin Spock and Yale chaplain William Sloane Coffin, along with others were prosecuted for conspiring to aid, abet, and counsel draft registrants to violate the Selective Service Act. Their conviction was overturned by an appellate federal court in 1969. A number of the thousands of young men who committed a criminal offense by burning their draft cards were prosecuted and sentenced to prison.

Protests at the 1968 Democratic Convention turned violent in what a report termed a *police riot*. The federal government charged eight antiwar and civil rights activists with conspiracy to cross state lines to incite a riot. The convictions of six of the defendants were reversed on appeal.

The disclosure that American forces had expanded the Vietnam War by sending troops into Cambodia sparked nationwide protests. On May 4, 1970, 28 members of the Ohio National Guard fired 67 rounds over a period of 13 seconds and killed four students and wounded nine others. Criminal charges against the guardsmen were dismissed.

The COINTELPRO program (COINTELPRO stands for Counter Intelligence Program) was an FBI surveillance program that targeted antiwar and other activists. Undercover agents were used to disrupt demonstrations, infiltrate the movement, and harass antiwar leaders.

HOMELAND SECURITY AND CIVIL LIBERTIES

The historical record suggests that American government, in part, has responded strongly against what were viewed as internal domestic threats. This at times has involved a severe and seemingly unnecessary limitation on civil rights and liberties. How do we know when the response to an internal threat is unnecessary and a product of mass hysteria rather than a reasoned and prudent reaction? At what point is there a danger that the restriction on rights and liberties are compromising the very values that Western societies are fighting to uphold? How can we be confident that the threat is as severe as politicians indicate? Despite possible misgivings, is it better to take extreme measures—even if in retrospect they were too restrictive to secure national security and safety?

CHAPTER SUMMARY

Following the 9/11 attacks President George W. Bush issued an Executive Order establishing the Department of Homeland Security (DHS). The purpose of the DHS is to coordinate the detection, preparation, prevention, response to, and recovery from terrorist attacks within the United States. A number of agencies are under the umbrella of the DHS and the DHS coordinates with other agencies in protecting the nation's critical infrastructure. The FBI and a number of federal agencies are primarily responsible for the domestic investigation of terrorism and prosecutions are carried out by the Department of Justice. Other agencies are responsible for the collection and analysis of foreign intelligence. The international community has entered into a number of agreements to coordinate efforts on airline safety, the protection of international diplomats, combating the taking of hostages, and the financing of terrorism.

The United States has a history of taking strong action against internal threats that impinge on the rights and liberties of Americans. A number of these presidential and congressional programs remain of debatable effectiveness.

CHAPTER REVIEW QUESTIONS

1. Discuss the purpose of the Department of Homeland Security and the various agencies that constitute the Department of Homeland Security. Does it make sense to have created such a large bureaucratic organization to combat terrorism and other threats?

2. List some elements of the critical infrastructure of the United States.

3. What are the major agencies involved in federal law enforcement and in collecting and analyzing domestic and foreign intelligence?

4. Summarize the major federal counterterrorism laws.

5. What areas are addressed by the primary international counterterrorism agreements? Why is there no comprehensive agreement addressing terrorism?

6. Sketch the historical response in the United States to what are viewed as internal domestic threats.

7. Are there lessons from the past in terms of how to respond to domestic threats?

TERMINOLOGY

Alien and Sedition Act
Antiterrorism and Effective
    Death Penalty Act
Central Intelligence Agency
    (CIA)
Country Reports on Terrorism
Defense Intelligence Agency
    (DIA)
Department of Homeland
    Security (DHS)

Federal Bureau of Investiga-
    tion (FBI)
intelligence community
Joint Terrorism Task Forces
    (JTTFs)
Manning, Chelsea
McCarthyism
national security theater
no-fly list

Office of the Director of
    National Intelligence
    (ODNI)
Palmer raids
PATRIOT Act
Red Scare
Screening Passengers by
    Observation Techniques
    (SPOT) program
Transportation Security
    Administration (TSA)

CHAPTER 11

Counterterrorism

TEST YOUR KNOWLEDGE

1. List two of the major approaches to counterterrorism that have been followed by recent U.S. presidents.
2. Understand the advantage of relying on predator drones in conducting the War on Terror.
3. Comprehend the reasons for establishing the Guantánamo detention camp.
4. Understand the reasons the Bush administration introduced enhanced interrogation.
5. Understand the advantages of prosecuting detainees before military commissions.
6. Comprehend the requirements of the Foreign Intelligence Surveillance Act.
7. List the arguments against relying on racial profiling in detecting terrorism.
8. Understand the relationship between immigration and terrorism.
9. Know why terrorism presents a challenge to social media.

INTRODUCTION

The Joint Chiefs of Staff of the U.S. military define **counterterrorism** as "activities and operations taken to neutralize terrorists, their organizations, and networks in order to render them incapable of using violence to instill fear and coerce governments or societies to achieve their goals" (Crenshaw & LaFree, 2017, p. 169). The range of activities included in counterterrorism according to the Joint Chiefs include domestic law enforcement, acts undertaken by first responders and military, and foreign assistance efforts.

Ganor (2005) lists three broad goals of a counterterrorism strategy:

Eliminating terrorism. The eradication of terrorism by defeating terrorists, deterring terrorists through the use of violence or intimidation, or meeting terrorist demands.

Minimizing damage. Reducing the number, severity or types of attacks, or limiting the human and/or physical consequences of attacks.

Preventing the escalation of terrorism. Limiting the growth of domestic and international support for terrorists and impeding the spread of the terrorist attacks and development of new types of terrorist attacks.

Various counterterrorism programs can be grouped under each of these strategic goals. Infrastructure protection, for example, is intended to minimize damage and deradicalization programs are intended to eliminate the threat of terrorism.

A major pillar of American counterterrorism policy is that the United States is at "war" with terrorists and with terrorism. This means that terrorists can be attacked and killed wherever they are found, even they are not on the battlefield or do not pose an immediate threat. Terrorists and their supporters receive minimal protections under the Geneva Convention and may be prosecuted before military tribunals rather than civilian courts.

An alternative to the **war-fighting approach to counterterrorism**, at the other extreme, is to view terrorists as "common criminals" who are subject to arrest and are to be accorded with constitutional protections when captured. They are to be prosecuted before conventional criminal courts and afforded a jury trial. The focus of this **crime-control approach to counterterrorism** is on combating the radicalization of individuals and in combating the conditions that lead to terrorism by promoting economic development and democracy. Military force, whenever possible, should be undertaken in a multilateral fashion in conjunction with other countries.

In practice, counterterrorism policy in the United States combines the war-fighting approach and the crime-control approach, although the primary focus of American efforts has been on the reliance on military force.

In 1984 the Reagan administration invoked the phrase *war against terrorism* in asking Congress to pass legislation to bolster the military following the 1983 bombing of an American military barracks in Beirut, Lebanon, which resulted in the death of 241 Americans. In a 2017 speech, Vice President Mike Pence noted that the Beirut attack marked the beginning of the war on terrorism.

In 2001, following the 9/11 attacks, President George W. Bush in an address to Congress observed that the war on terror would not be complete until every global terrorist organization has been defeated. Three years later, he stated that the effort against terrorism was not a "law enforcement and intelligence-gathering operation." Counterterrorism required the "full use of American power." The goal is to 'defeat terror' by ... destroying terrorists" (Crenshaw & LaFree, 2017, p. 172).

The early Bush policy had a decidedly military emphasis and was based on what was termed *four Ds*; Defeat, Deny (state support), Diminish (by addressing root causes), and Defend (the homeland and Americans abroad). This policy stressed that the United States would take the initiative in self-defense against terrorists and would seek international allies but would not hesitate to act alone (Crenshaw & LaFree, 2017).

The legal basis for this War on Terror was soon thereafter established following the 9/11 attacks by the **Authorization for the Use of Military Force (AUMF)** passed by Congress in the aftermath of the 9/11 attacks and signed by President Bush on September 18, 2001. The law authorized the president to employ all necessary and appropriate force against those nations, organizations, or persons determined to have planned, authorized, committed, or aided the terrorist attacks on September 11, 2001, or who harbored such organizations or persons in order to prevent future acts of terrorism against the United States (U.S. Congress, 2001a).

By 2006, the Bush counterterrorism policy became less focused on unilateral military force in defense of America and more focused on countering jihadist ideology through so-called soft power. The spread of democracy, bolstering the economy of other countries, and strengthening moderate Muslims at home and abroad were considered essential in combating the root cause of terrorism, which was described as *violent extremism*. The United States at this point was hesitant to act alone or use military force without consultation and support from allied nations (Crenshaw & LaFree, 2017)

In April 2007, the British government publicly abandoned the use of the term *War on Terror* explaining that the terrorists were criminals rather than soldiers. President Barack Obama generally avoided use of the term *Global War on Terror* and following his election, in a speech at Cairo University in Egypt he outlined a counterterrorism policy based on human rights, religious freedom, economic development, multilateral cooperation, and rejecting violent extremism (Crenshaw & LaFree, 2017).

President Obama aspired to dismantle al Qaeda and to diminish and degrade imminent terrorist threats, rather than defeat terrorism militarily across the globe. Terrorism was to be controlled rather than entirely eliminated. An important focus was on continuing to counter the spread of terrorism by challenging the growth of violent extremist ideology. President Obama stated that, in his opinion, "our efforts to work with other countries to counter the ideology and root causes of extremism will be more important than our capacity to remove terrorists from the battlefield" (Crenshaw & LaFree, 2017, p. 176).

President Obama, however, did not abandon the view that the United States was engaged in a so-called war against terrorists that transcended geographic boundaries. In May 2013 President Obama stressed that the United States was at war with al Qaeda and the Taliban and that this was a so-called just war that was being waged against terrorist groups across the globe that threatened the United States. President Obama stressed that military action should be a collective effort between America and its allies, and that the United States should not act alone. The Obama administration's counterterrorism policy also stressed the need to deny terrorists access to nuclear material and weapons (Crenshaw & LaFree, 2015).

The direction of American counterterrorism policy under Presidents Bush and Obama moved in the direction of defeating terrorism through challenging violent extremist ideology and by spreading democracy and economic development. Muslim communities came to be viewed as partners in the fight against terrorism. Military force increasingly was to be undertaken in conjunction with allied nations.

President Donald Trump shifted the focus of American counterterrorism policy back to a reliance on unilateral military force. President Trump, in honoring the anniversary of the 9/11 attacks, proclaimed that "we are making plain to these savage killers that there is no dark corner beyond our reach, no sanctuary beyond our grasp and nowhere to hide anywhere on this very large earth ... we will never, ever yield ... we pledge ... to fight together and to overcome together every enemy and obstacle that's ever in our path" (Trump, 2017). President Trump authorized military commanders in the field to act without consultation to attack terrorists, expanded military operations across the globe, and supported an increase in military bombing strikes. He also has threatened to limit the United States' commitment to countries that do not support America's war on terrorism. In August 2017, President Donald Trump announced the creation of a memorial to American soldiers killed in the War on Terrorism.

American counterterrorism policy, although differing under Presidents Bush, Obama, and Trump, has several broad components.

Military. A willingness to rely on the unilateral use of force against terrorists when it is not possible to rely on a coalition force of American, European, and Middle Eastern countries. The United States is involved in training and equipping local counterterrorism troops in Afghanistan, Iraq, Syria, Southeast Asia, and Africa. Foreign assistance is provided to countries participating in the effort against terrorism.

Intelligence. A vigorous intelligence program intended to detect and disable terrorist plots. This also involves the sharing of information among security agencies in various countries and cooperation in apprehending and interrogating suspected terrorists.

Diplomacy. Cooperation with other member-states of the UN Security Council and other nations to sanction countries that sponsor terrorism and the withdrawal of foreign assistance from countries that do not cooperate in combating terrorism. A crucial component of diplomacy is working with foreign countries to prevent state sponsors of terrorism and terrorist groups from obtaining weapons of mass destruction.

Homeland security. Combating terrorist threats within the United States; control over immigration and borders; the creation of a legal structure that facilitates the investigation, detection, and prosecution of terrorists; and the protection of critical infrastructure.

Ideology. Challenging terrorist propaganda in cyberspace.
As you read the about the various issues discussed in this chapter, consider whether they are primarily based on a war-fighting or crime-control approach to terrorism. The next sections of the chapter outline several issues involved in American counterterrorism.

DRONE WARFARE

Drones, or remote targeted aerial vehicles, are a central component of the war on terrorism. These unmanned, armed vehicles are equipped with cameras and are used to track terrorists. Images are sent back to operators stationed outside the battlefield who control the guidance and targeting of the armed drones.

Signature strikes target training camps and groups of fighters and are carried out in active war zones. Profile strikes target specific individuals and may be employed wherever the target is located. For the most part in the past, profile strikes were carried out by the Central Intelligence Agency (CIA). International humanitarian law requires that attacks be directed at military targets. An attack on a military object which could cause collateral damage to civilians is permissible only when the military advantage of the attack outweighs the harm to civilians.

President Bush authorized drone strikes, although during his administration only about 50 attacks were launched in Pakistan, most of which took place in his last year in office. Within 2 years of taking office, President Obama escalated the number of strikes, most of which took place in Afghanistan. Strikes also targeted terrorists linked to al Qaeda in Yemen, in the tribal areas of Pakistan, in Libya, and against al Shabaab in Somalia.

Profile strikes were carried out based on broad standards, such as a gathering of males who appeared to be terrorist fighters and as a consequence, these strikes resulted in civilian casualties. In March 2011, a CIA attack in Pakistan mistakenly killed a gathering of tribal elders. Another attack killed 83 people, including 45 civilians, who were attending the funeral of Khwaz Wali Mehsud, a middle-ranking Taliban commander. The British Bureau of Investigative Journalists identified 18 other occasions in which funerals were targeted by CIA drone attacks (Jaffer, 2016),

Under the Obama administration, so-called kill lists of individuals to be targeted in signature strikes were developed by government officials who convened periodically to develop a roster of individuals to be targeted. The final decision on the individuals to be tracked and killed was made by President Obama.

Perhaps the most controversial and widely reported drone strike was the October 11, 2012, attack that killed American-born Yemini cleric Anwar al-Awlaki, a leading operative in al Qaeda in the Arabian Peninsula. Al-Awlaki's online lectures reportedly inspired the attacks by Major Nidal Hassan at Fort Hood, a 2009 attack on the New York City subway system, and an attempted bombing of Times Square in New York City by Faisal Shahzad in 2010. Al-Awlaki also played a role in the attempt by "underwear bomber," Umar Farouk Abdulmutallab, to attack an airliner over Detroit on Christmas Day 2009.

The drone strike against al-Awlaki also killed Samir Khan, a 25-year-old American who was editor of the al Qaeda online magazine, *Inspire*. At the time they were killed, neither al-Awlaki nor Khan posed an immediate threat to American combatants or to the United States. Two weeks later, Awlaki's 16-year-old American-born son, Abdulrahman, was killed in a drone strike on a gathering of men congregating at an outdoor restaurant in Yemen.

In 2013, in response to criticism of the drone program, President Obama signed a presidential policy guidance popularly known as the drone playbook that attempted to restrict drone attacks (Presidential Policy Guidance, 2013). The guidance stipulated that attacks would be focused on individuals who presented an imminent threat to U.S. citizens, in which there was a near certainty that the individual being targeted is present at the site of the attack, and that there was a near certainty that noncombatants would not be injured or killed. The guidance also required that capture was not feasible, the country on whose territory the strike would take place was unable or unwilling to address the threat, and that there were no other reasonable available alternatives. The Obama administration also announced that responsibility for drone strikes would be shifted from the CIA to the military in order to provide a greater degree of information to the public regarding the occurrence of drone strikes. These reforms, according to various analysts, limited but did not eliminate civilian causalities (Jaffer, 2016).

The Obama administration continued to rely on drone attacks, contending that the United States was at war with al Qaeda and that the drone strikes were justified on the battlefield and in other areas of the world as a matter of self-defense. Members of the administration denied that drone attacks resulted in a significant number of civilian deaths. In 2016 the Obama administration announced that over a 7-year period ending on December 31, 2015, drone strikes outside of the battlefield had killed between 64 and 116 noncombatants.

Nongovernmental organizations list the number of civilian casualties between 2009 and 2015 as numbering between 200 and 900. As of the end of 2017, according to the Bureau of Investigative Journalism, the United States had conducted 4,705 drone strikes, which had killed between 7,207 and 10,511 people, approximately 70% of whom have been noncombatant civilians. As many as 330 of these casualties were children.

Drone strikes were undoubtedly responsible for crippling, if not eliminating, the leadership of al Qaeda. However, the resulting civilian casualties in Pakistan and Afghanistan have led to a backlash against the United States and to a reluctance by the domestic population to cooperate with American forces. Drone strikes inevitably result in the killing of civilians because without accurate intelligence on the ground at the site of attack, it is difficult to determine whether civilians are present within the strike zone.

Critics of President Obama's drone policy asserted that rather than focusing on killing high-level terrorists, the United States should attempt to capture them and gather intelligence on terrorist activity. On the other hand, this would inevitably place American forces at risk and could result in an even greater number of civilian casualties.

President Donald Trump announced that his administration has delegated the decision to employ drone attacks to the military and CIA and authorized profile attacks in an increased number of countries. Military commanders and the CIA are also authorized to attack terrorist leaders as well as ordinary foot soldiers who do not pose an immediate threat. In July 2017, the Columbia Law School's Human Rights Clinic and the Sana'a Center for Strategic Studies reported that in the first months that President Donald Trump was in office, the monthly rate of American drone strikes has increased by roughly 4 times over the monthly rate of drone attacks under President Barack Obama. The U.S. government, according to the report, only acknowledged 20% of drone strikes that had taken place but admitted to killing between 2,867 and 3,138 individuals in strikes in countries like Pakistan, Somalia, and Yemen. During his two terms in office, President Obama approved one drone strike every 5.4 days. Under President Trump, a drone strike during his first months in office was carried out roughly every 1.25 days.

Defenders of drone attacks note that war is violent enterprise and that it is unrealistic to criticize tactics to defeat terrorists, who pose a serious threat. Attempting to introduce restrictions on the use of drones impedes the campaign against terrorism. The terrorists do not respect human life or restraints on the use of military force, and the defeat of terrorism requires authorizing the military and CIA to employ the necessary force to eliminate terrorist networks. On the other hand, the use of violence that threatens civilians may increase support for terrorists and make waging the War on Terror more difficult to win. What is your view?

11.1 You Decide

In October 2017, the bodies of four members of the U.S. Special Forces were found near a remote village in Niger. Three of the deceased, Staff Sergeants Bryan Black, Jeremiah Johnson, and David Wright had apparently died in a gunfight. A fourth American fighter, Sergeant La David Johnson, had reportedly been captured by ISIS fighters. After leaving a village, the American soldiers were attacked by terrorists. The area of the attack had been the site of more than 40 terrorist attacks in the previous 18 months, but the Americans seemed unprepared for the armed assault. They were in unarmored pickups and lightly armed when confronted with an attack by over 30 terrorists armed with rocket-propelled grenades and automatic weapons mounted on troops. The 2-hour attack only halted when French Mirage jets were flown into the area. The jets were unable to drop bombs because they were not in radio contact with the Americans and feared hitting Nigerien or U.S. forces.

The involvement of the Americans in the mission appeared to be contrary to the rules of engagement, which specify that American troops are to train and to assist Nigerien fighters and only may accompany Nigerien fighters when enemy contact is unlikely.

Niger is twice the size of Texas and has been a center of terrorist activity, drawing fighters from North Africa and the Middle East. American involvement has gradually expanded in the country and has grown from 100 under President Barack Obama in 2013 to the present commitment. In reaction to the killing of the four American fighters, Niger has asked the United States to arm the two surveillance drones provided to the country.

Another 300 U.S. forces are in Cameroon. There are an additional 400 troops in Uganda, the Central African Republic, and South Sudan pursuing the Lord's Resistance Army. This is all part of what is termed *shadow wars* against terrorism.

Members of the U.S. Congress claimed that they were unaware that there were 800 American counterterrorism troops in Niger who were training counterterrorism troops and carrying out joint patrols on the Mali–Niger border. In 2006 roughly 1% of U.S. forces deployed abroad were in Africa, by 2010 this had increased to 3% and by 2016, 17% of

American counterterrorism troops were in Africa. There are more U.S. Special Operations personnel in Africa (1,700 in 20 countries) than in any geographic location other than the Middle East. At any given time, American troops are involved in close to 100 missions in Africa. Critics warn that the growing American presence may anger local residents and result in them aligning with terrorists. There also is the concern that the United States may find itself in a position of spending money to prop up fragile and unpopular governments because of their support for the fight against ISIS.

Do you agree that American should be stationed abroad to train and advise foreign troops in Africa as part of the War on Terror? ▯

Personalities and Events

Beaudry Robert "Bowe" Bergdhal, at age 23, was serving in Afghanistan with the U.S. Army when he was captured and held captive by the Taliban-affiliated Haqquini network. He was held as a prisoner from June 2009 to May 2014. He was captured after deserting his post and only was released in exchange for five Taliban detainees detained at Guantánamo Bay.

Bergdhal was to be tried by a general court-martial for desertion and misbehavior before the enemy. On October 16, 2017, he entered a guilty plea in a court-martial proceeding and was sentenced to dishonorable discharge, reduced in rank from sergeant to private, and fined $1,000 per month from his pay for 10 months—but was not sentenced to prison (Oppel, 2017).

Bergdahl was born in Sun Valley, Idaho, and was homeschooled and was called a free spirit by many, spending time in a Buddhist monastery. He was discharged after 26 days from the Coast Guard for psychological reasons. Two years later, in 2008, Bergdahl enlisted in the army and was deployed in Afghanistan the next year and assigned to a counterinsurgency unit stationed at an outpost in eastern Afghanistan on the Pakistani border. Throughout his military career Bergdahl was described as a loner and he was reportedly shaken when a fellow soldier with whom he was close was killed by a roadside bomb. Several days later, Bergdahl allegedly wandered away from his unit and was captured. He had previously sent his parents an e-mail that was highly critical of the U.S. military:

(continues on next page)

(continued from previous page)

> The US army is the biggest joke the world has to laugh at. It is
> the army of liars, backstabbers, fools, and bullies. The few good
> SGTs are getting out as soon as they can, [...] I am sorry for
> everything here. These people need help, yet what they get is
> the most conceited country in the world telling them that they
> are nothing and that they are stupid, that they have no idea how
> to live. ... We don't even care when we hear each other talk
> about running their children down in the dirt streets with our
> armored trucks. ... We make fun of them in front of their faces,
> and laugh at them for not understanding we are insulting them
> [...] I am sorry for everything. The horror that is America is dis-
> gusting. There are a few more boxes coming to you guys. Feel
> free to open them, and use them (Hastings, 2012).

The circumstances surrounding Bergdahl's disappearance are highly
contested and uncertain. For example, soldiers in his unit contend he
left an explanatory and bitter note, although the Pentagon claims there
was no such note. Various soldiers who served with Bergdahl called him
a deserter and attacked him for placing thousands of soldiers at risk
when searching for him and for diverting soldiers from counterinsurgency
missions. Although it was alleged that six soldiers died searching for Bergdahl, the Pentagon concluded that the soldiers' deaths were unrelated to
the search.

In July 2009 the Taliban released the first in a series of videos showing
Bergdahl's capture. His capturers initially demanded $1 million and the
release of 21 Afghan prisoners along with a Pakistani scientist convicted
in the United States (Stein, 2014). This demand eventually was reduced
to five prisoners held at Guantánamo.

Bergdahl alleged that while imprisoned, he attempted to escape and
that after being captured he was tortured and detained in a cage in the
dark for weeks at a time.

On May 31, 2014, Bergdahl was released and exchanged for five Taliban members, including the Taliban army chief of staff, a Taliban deputy
minister of intelligence, a former Taliban interior minister, and two other
senior Taliban figures (Schmitt & Savage, 2014).

The same day that Bergdahl was released, President Obama appeared
with Bergdahl's parents in the White House Rose Garden where he
announced the prisoner exchange (Schmitt & Savage, 2014). The decision was criticized for rewarding the Taliban for taking U.S. soldiers as
prisoners and encouraging future efforts to capture American soldiers.
Negotiating with the Taliban also was attacked as contrary to the practice
of not negotiating with terrorists and, in effect, providing them recognition
as a military force rather than as terrorists.

A psychiatric exam following Bergdahl's capture concluded that "[al] though Sgt. Bergdahl did have a severe mental disease or defect at the time of the alleged criminal conduct, he was able to appreciate the nature and quality and wrongfulness of this conduct" (Wong, 2016). A 59-day investigation concluded that there was no evidence that Bergdahl was sympathetic to the Taliban or intended to desert. He was described as having "idealistic and unrealistic expectations of people" and as being an extreme individualist, and that there was no evidence that any soldiers had been killed attempting to rescue Bergdahl. The report concluded that imprisonment would be an "inappropriate penalty" for Bergdahl (Lamothe, 2015).

President Donald Trump during the presidential campaign attacked the Bergdahl controversy, saying he was a traitor.

Should the United States have negotiated Bergdahl's release? What is your view? What was the appropriate sentence? []

GUANTÁNAMO

Following the 9/11 attacks, the Bush administration reportedly wanted to house detainees outside the geographical boundaries of the United States at a prison constructed at Guantánamo Bay, thinking that American courts lacked the jurisdiction to review the legality of the detentions and of the treatment of detainees held at the offshore facility. Al Qaeda and Taliban detainees were considered unlawful combatants who should not receive the legal protections accorded to prisoners of war under the law of war, which is adhered to by virtually every country in the world. President Bush reasoned that the detainees had no regard for the rule of law and did not merit recognition as prisoners of war because they did not satisfy the requirements for lawful combatants set forth in the Geneva Conventions—they did not carry their weapons openly, wear identifiable symbols, adhere to the law of war, or operate under the command of a responsible military officer.

Guantánamo Bay detention camp was opened in January 2002 and since opening, it has housed 780 detainees. The island is leased by the United States from Cuba for a fee of $2,000 a year. The fee is based on a 1903 agreement between the two countries following the Spanish-American War. It has been termed the "most expensive prison on earth" and costs roughly $445 million per year to run—roughly $10 million for each detainee.

The U.S. Supreme Court rejected the notion that the detainees at Guantánamo existed in a no-law zone and held that courts had jurisdiction over the detainees housed at Guantánamo because the naval base was under American control. The detainees accordingly possessed the right to petition federal courts for habeas corpus review to determine whether they were being lawfully interned. Habeas corpus originated in England and provides prisoners the ability to ask courts to determine whether they are being legally interned. A number of detainees petitioned courts under habeas review, although the appellate courts in virtually every instance deferred to the judgment of military officials and held that based on the facts that the detainees were lawfully detained (*Rasul v. Bush*, 542 U.S. 466 (2004); *Boumediene v. Bush*, 553 U.S. 723 (2008). The Supreme Court also held that detainees were entitled to various fundamental protections under the law of war.

President Obama was intent on closing Guantánamo. He argued that Guantánamo was a symbol of American disregard for Muslims and inspired terrorist activity. American allies refused to extradite individuals to the United States to stand trial without a promise that the individual, if criminally convicted, would not be held at Guantánamo. Guantánamo was a blemish on the United States' commitment to the rule of law and made it difficult for the United States to criticize the human rights records of other countries. The U.S. Congress, however, passed legislation prohibiting the use of federal funds to transfer detainees to a prison in the United States. Various communities also expressed concern that the incarceration of convicted terrorist in a nearby prison would make the community a target for a terrorist attack. Keep in mind that hundreds of individuals convicted of terrorism are incarcerated in American prisons.

Congress authorized the transfer of detainees to other countries if the secretary of defense certified that the country had a security plan in place and that the detainee did not pose a risk of engaging in terrorist activity.

Detainees have been transferred to roughly 58 countries across the globe. The Bush administration transferred roughly 548 detainees from Guantánamo who were determined to no longer pose a threat or to have been incarcerated by mistake. These detainees either were sent back to their country of origin or to other countries that agreed take them. President Obama transferred 197 detainees, and roughly 40 presently remain at Guantánamo, four of whom are scheduled to be sent to other countries. Twenty-three of these detainees are scheduled to be detained indefinitely, and 10 are to be charged or are in pretrial hearing before the military commission (see below). Three detainees are serving prison sentences or are awaiting sentencing.

The Director of National Intelligence has certified that 21.2% of detainees transferred by the Bush administration have been confirmed to have engaged in terrorism and 13.9% are suspected of engaging in terrorism. Roughly 4.4% of detainees transferred by the Obama administration are confirmed to have engaged in terrorism and 7.1% are suspected of engaging in terrorism.

President Trump has criticized the release of Guantánamo detainees and has expressed an intent to use the institution to house domestic terrorists. Nonetheless, the United States in 2018 released Ahmed al-Darbi, a 42-year-old Saudi citizen who in 2014 pled guilty to planning a 2002 terrorist attack on a French oil tanker off the coast of Yemen that killed one crew member (Savage, 2018). Al-Darbi had agreed to cooperate with the prosecution in the trial of the terrorists that attacked the USS *Cole* in exchange for being sent to Saudi Arabia after 4 years of imprisonment to serve the remainder of his 13-year prison sentence.

In 2018 President Trump announced a revised policy for Guantánamo which provides that individuals captured abroad who pose a significant threat to the security of the United States will be interned at the prison camp rather than in a civilian facility (Pilkington, 2018).

11.2 You Decide

The John Jay College of Criminal Justice in New York City in October 2017 sponsored an exhibit of art created by current and former Guantánamo detainees titled "Ode to the Sea." The exhibition online provided the e-mail addresses of artists so that anyone interested in the art could arrange to purchase the pieces. The Department of Defense (DOD) had a policy of releasing art after it was subjected to a "censorship and security" review.

The DOD responded to the exhibit by stating that the art belonged to the U.S. government and that in the future, it would halt the release of art created by detainees and that the art would be destroyed after a prisoner was released. The DOD also threatened to confiscate any money paid for the art.

Detainees at Guantánamo would continue to be permitted to create artwork, but they only would be allowed to keep a limited number of pieces in their cells—the other pieces would be destroyed. The Federal Bureau of Prisons allows inmates to mail "art and hobby craft" to their family, give items to visitors, and display the art in public space that meets the warden's standard of taste. The warden under the Federal Code of Regulations "may restrict for reasons of security and housekeeping, the size and quantity of all products made in the art and hobby craft program. Paintings mailed out of the institution must conform to both institution guidelines and postal regulation" (Code of Federal Regulations, n.d.).

Art classes were introduced at Guantánamo to break the monotony of imprisonment and were the most popular activity in the prison. The paintings were prohibited from depicting the prison and were typically based on recollections of their home or of seascapes. Other internees created three-dimensional models of ships and other objects.

Should inmates at Guantánamo be offered art classes? Should they be allowed to keep or sell their art? □

ENHANCED INTERROGATION

The Bush administration determined that the United States was not obtaining the intelligence required to effectively combat al Qaeda. It was decided that it was necessary to employ **enhanced interrogation** techniques against high-level detainees. The Office of Legal Counsel (OLC) of the Department of Justice was asked to clarify the definition of the terms *torture* and *cruel, inhumane, and degrading treatment*, which are considered crimes under international and American domestic law and to offer an opinion on authorized interrogation techniques (US Senate, Select Committee on Intelligence, 2014).

A 2001 OLC memo advised that interrogation methods had to meet a high standard to constitute unlawful torture. Physical pain to constitute torture "must be equivalent in intensity to the pain accompanying serious physical injury, such as organ failure, impairment of bodily function, or even death." Mental pain or suffering to constitute torture must "result in significant psychological harm of significant duration ... lasting for months or even years." The memo also argued that the president as commander in chief possessed unrestricted authority to take whatever steps which were required to defend the United States. In response to public and media criticism, the OLC rescinded the memo in 2004.

In a separate August 2002 memo, the OLC approved 15 interrogation methods, including sleep deprivation, nudity, cramped confinement in a box filled with insects, stress positions, sleep deprivation, denial of food and water, ice water baths, and shackling of individuals to the floor. At least five detainees were subjected to "rectal feeding."

The most controversial enhanced interrogation technique was **waterboarding**. The detainee is strapped to the bed and a cloth is placed over the nose and mouth and water is poured onto the cloth causing the individual to feel as if he or she is being suffocated by water. Abu Zubaydah, director of terrorist operations for al Qaeda, reportedly was waterboarded 83 times. Khalid Sheikh Mohammed, a central figure in planning the 9/11 attacks, was waterboarded an estimated 183 times.

The Bush administration argued that enhanced interrogation resulted in valuable intelligence, although a number of analysts as well as the report on torture of the Senate Intelligence Committee (2014) dispute whether these methods yielded important information. Critics of enhanced interrogation contend that individuals who are abused by interrogators will provide whatever information the interrogators "want to hear" in order to end their abuse. Although the best approach to obtain information is to establish a relationship with a detainee, the imminent threat of terrorism does not always allow interrogators the time and opportunity to establish a trusting relationship with detainees.

Torture was carried out in many instances in conjunction with **extraordinary rendition**, which involved turning foreign nationals detained in American custody over to another country for enhanced interrogation without going through legal procedures. In other instances, extraordinary rendition was carried out by transferring individuals to so-called secret black sites for interrogation by the CIA and allied countries. In some instances, individuals were literally kidnapped off the street and sent for interrogation abroad.

U.S. allies also were involved in the rendition program. In 2018, a British Parliament report documented the involvement of intelligence officials in extraordinary rendition and the abuse of suspected terrorists. British officers were involved in the direct abuse of individuals in only three instances, although they assisted in the financing, rendition, and questioning and received intelligence in several hundred cases in which they were aware that individuals were subject to abuse (Perez-Pena, 2018).

In one infamous episode, Maher Arar, a Canadian citizen of Syrian descent, was mistakenly identified as a "terrorist" during a stopover in New York City and was sent to Syria where he was detained and tortured for a nearly a year before being released at the request of Canadian authorities.

The 2005 **Detainee Treatment Act** prohibited the use of cruel, inhumane, or degrading treatment. The primary sponsor and advocate for the legislation was the late Senator John McCain of Arizona, who himself had been tortured while a prisoner of war during Vietnam. When he took office, President Barack Obama stated that terrorist detainees would be accorded the rights of prisoners of war,

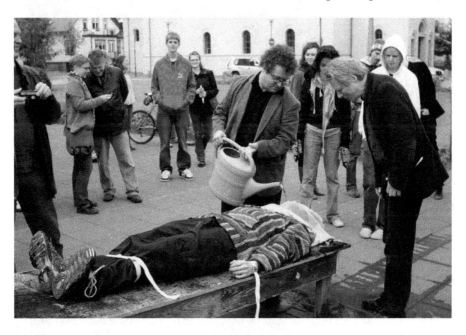

FIGURE 11.1 Waterboarding

Copyright © Karl Gunnarsson (CC BY-SA 2.0) at https://commons.wikimedia.org/wiki/File%3AWaterboarding.jpg.

and he prohibited the use of enhanced interrogation and directed that both military and CIA interrogators follow the requirements of the law of war as set forth in the U.S. Army Field Manual.

There is continuing debate over whether terrorist suspects brought to the United States should be read their *Miranda* rights and informed of their rights to silence and to a lawyer, and that anything they may say can be used against them. Umar Farouk Abdulmutallab, who in 2009 attempted to ignite a bomb on board an airliner landing in Detroit, was read the *Miranda* rights and invoked his right to silence. Although Abdulmutallab subsequently talked to authorities, federal officials were criticized for treating Abdulmutallab as a "common criminal" rather than as a terrorist and for reading him the *Miranda* rights. Detainees now are subjected to a two-track interrogation. The first involves national security concerns without the *Miranda* rights based on the public safety exception to *Miranda*, and during the second interrogation terrorist suspects are read *Miranda*. FBI agents most recently relied on the national security exception in their interrogation of Boston marathon bomber Dzhokhar Tsarnaev (Lippman, 2016).

What is your view on whether enhanced interrogation is justified?

11.3 You Decide

In September 1999, the Israeli Supreme Court issued a judgment holding that several interrogation methods relied on by the Security Services, when questioning Palestinian detainees who were considered terrorists, violates suspects' dignity and the right to not be subject to degrading and inhumane conditions. In the *Shabach* position, a "detainee's hands are tied behind his back, he is seated on a small and low chair whose seat is tilted toward the ground. One hand is tied behind the suspect and placed inside the gap behind the chair against the back support. His [or her] second hand is tied behind the chair against the back support"(Israel Supreme Court, 1999). A heavy bag is placed over the detainee's head and loud music is continuously piped into the room. Suspects are secured in this position for lengthy periods of time and are periodically interrogated.

The Israeli Supreme Court held that an interrogator prosecuted for the criminal abuse of a detainee during interrogation may rely on the necessity defense. The interrogator may be exonerated in instances in which the harm caused by the interrogator's criminal act is outweighed by the harm the interrogator intended to prevent.

An interrogator, for example, would be able to rely on the necessity defense in the so-called ticking time bomb scenario in which torture was relied on to obtain information to prevent an imminent terrorist bombing. Critics assert that torture is rarely effective in obtaining information from detainees and that society should never accept that torture is justified. Recognition of torture is considered a slippery slope because courts will be reluctant to find that an interrogator's actions were unjustified.

Harvard law professor Alan Dershowitz has advocated "torture warrants" that allow government authorities to go before a federal judge and to obtain a warrant authorizing the use of torture in interrogating a detainee.

Should an interrogator who tortures a terrorist detainee be criminally prosecuted? If criminally prosecuted, should an interrogator be allowed to rely on the necessity defense? What of the proposal for torture warrants?

MILITARY COMMISSIONS

On November 13, 2001, President George W. Bush, as commander in chief of the U.S. armed forces, issued a military order providing that enemy combatants were to be prosecuted before **military commissions**. A military commission is a court composed of members of the military that has jurisdiction to prosecute enemy soldiers. Military commissions provide the basic rights that are essential to a fair trial while providing the flexibility to limit these rights in the interests of national security. The trial of terrorists, for example, necessarily involves the testimony of unnamed confidential informants and reliance on confidential information.

In *Hamdan v. Rumsfeld*, the U.S. Supreme Court held that the military commissions had several fatal flaws such as the admission of evidence obtain through torture, the limited right for defendants to have access to the evidence against them, and a limited right to appeal. President Bush responded by consulting with Congress which, passed the **Military Commissions Act of 2006**. The act provides military commissions with jurisdiction over any foreign unlawful combatant who has been involved in hostilities against the United States or who has supported hostilities against the United States. The commission under the Act is to consist of a military judge and at least five commissioned military officers (Lippman, 2016).

In 2008 Salim Hamdan, who served as a bodyguard for Osama bin Laden and had driven him to various meetings became the first individual convicted before a military commission. This conviction was later overturned on appeal along with two other subsequent convictions. A total of eight individuals have been convicted before military commissions. In a conviction in early 2014 Ahmed al-Darbi pled guilty to aiding and abetting a suicide bombing of a French flagged oil tanker off the coast of Yemen.

In February 2018, Judge Colonel Vance Spath suspended pretrial hearings in the death penalty case against Abd al-Rahim al-Nashiri, accused of directing the 2000 bombing of the American destroyer USS *Cole* that killed 17 sailors. The entire defense team had withdrawn from the case after discovering that their communications with their client were being monitored. The al-Nashiri prosecution, along with the effort to prosecute five coconspirators, was initiated in 2012 and had made little progress.

The Obama administration favored prosecuting individuals before civilian courts rather than military commissions. In 2009 Attorney General Eric Holder announced that the Department of Justice would bring criminal charges in New York City against five 9/11 defendants. The holding of civilian trials in New York City were meant to communicate that the United States would not be intimidated by terrorists and as a democracy, society would provide full due process protections to accused terrorists. In November 2010 a New York jury convicted Ahmed Khalfan Ghailani of conspiracy to damage or destroy two U.S. embassies in 1998 in Africa by bombings that killed 224 people, including 12 Americans. Ghailani was acquitted of 284 counts, including murder and attempted murder, and was the first and only Guantánamo detainee prosecuted in civilian court. He was sentenced to life imprisonment. Critics of the Obama administration alleged the verdict indicated that civilian courts cannot be trusted to prosecute terrorists. Others responded that the trial proved that terrorists can be successfully prosecuted before civilian courts and that if convicted, they will be severely punished (Lippman, 2016).

The plan to conduct trial of the 9/11 defendants in New York City collapsed when city officials protested that the trial posed a threat to the city. Charges against the 9/11 defendants were subsequently filed before military commissions, and the defendants continue to await the start of their trials.

The Obama administration nonetheless continued to bring charges against foreign terrorists captured abroad in domestic courts. In 2013 the guilty plea of Ahmed Abdulkadir Warsame to a nine-count indictment was unsealed in federal court. Warsame, a Somali national, had pled guilty to providing material support to al Shabaab and al Qaeda in the Arabian Peninsula. In 2015 Russian national and Taliban terrorist Irek Hamidullin was convicted of conspiracy to attack Afghan and American forces in Afghanistan. A second prosecution in September 2017 resulted in the conviction of Muhanad Mahmoud Al-Farekh for participation in an attack on an American military outpost in Afghanistan. A third prosecution for foreign terrorist activity in civilian court was the conviction in 2017 of Libyan militia leader Ahmed Abu Khattala, who was found guilty of various offenses relating to the Benghazi attacks in which four Americans were killed. In another 2017 prosecution, a jury convicted Ibrahim Suleiman Adnan Harun for a conspiracy to murder American military personnel in Afghanistan and a conspiracy to bomb the U.S. embassy in Nigeria. Harun was subsequently sentenced to life in prison (Ellis & Kupperman, 2018).

Other recent convictions include Sulaiman Abu Gheith, Osama bin Laden's son-in-law; Abid Naseer, convicted of conspiring with al Qaeda to bomb shopping malls; Abu Hamza who was sentenced to life imprisonment for involvement of the abduction of tourists in Yemen and organizing a terrorist training camp in Oregon; and Khalid al-Fawwaz, who was convicted of conspiracy to bomb two American embassies in East Africa and was sentenced to life imprisonment.

A number of terrorist trials have been prosecuted in the United States against individuals apprehended within the country. The more than 600 convictions before American courts include Faisal Shahzad, who attempted to explode a car bomb in Times Square in New York City; David Coleman Headley, convicted of involvement in the 2008 attack on Mumbai, India, that resulted in the deaths of 164 persons, including six Americans; and a number of individuals involved in a conspiracy to bomb the New York City subway system. In 2017 Abdirahman Sheik Mohamud was the first American convicted of training with ISIS in Syria and returning to the United States with the intent to commit acts of terror. In 2017 Ahmad Khan Rahami, the so-called Chelsea bomber, was convicted of planting two bombs in New York City, one of which was detonated and injured 30 individuals. In another case, David Daoud Wright was convicted in a federal trial in Boston of plotting to kill Americans on behalf of the Islamic State. In 2018 Nicholas Young, a former patrol officer in the Washington D.C. regional Metrorail system, became the first law-enforcement officer to be convicted of terrorism. Young was sentenced to 15 years in federal prison for attempting to provide gift cards to the Islamic State. He was friends with another Islamic convert, Zachary Chasser, who was sentenced to 25 years in prison for attempting to join al Shabab in Somalia and for making threats against the creators of the *South Park* for segments he considered insulting to Islam.

The question whether to prosecute foreign terrorists before military commission or civilian courts remains a point of contention. The Trump administration has announced that it will keep Guantánamo open and that there are plans to prosecute detainees before military commissions (Pilkington, 2018). Following Sayfullo Saipov's driving of a truck onto a bicycle path in New York City killing eight people and injuring 12, President Trump called the American criminal justice system laughable and argued that military commissions were much more effective that civilian courts in bringing detainees to justice.

In June 2018, federal prosecutors persuaded a judge to sentence a former Columbia University student to supervised release. The defendant faced a possible prison sentence of 25 years in prison, based on his having traveled to Syria to fight with ISIS. Prosecutors recounted that after the defendant fled an ISIS encampment, he had assisted the American government for roughly 4 years (Feur, 2018).

SURVEILLANCE

Most experts argue that intelligence that detects terrorist plots is the most effective method of defeating terrorism. Since the attack on the World Trade center, New York City has prevented more than 26 terrorist attacks through intelligence, investigation, and intervention.

In 1976 a Senate Select Committee documented widespread warrantless spying on Americans by U.S. intelligence activities. This surveillance was based on the claim of various Democratic and Republican presidents that the president, as commander in chief, possessed the inherent power to protect national security and that the president was not required to obtain a search warrant to engage in the wiretapping of individuals. The Congress, in 1978, enacted the **Foreign Intelligence Surveillance Act (FISA)** to establish procedures for the electronic surveillance of threats to national security. In 1994 FISA was extended to cover physical searches. Keep in mind that FISA regulates surveillance within the United States of international threats to national security and of international terrorist activities.

FISA established the **Foreign Intelligence Surveillance Court**, composed of 11 district court judges selected by the chief justice of the United States. Requests for a warrant to conduct surveillance of a potential threat to national security, or for a warrant to conduct surveillance involving international terrorism, are filed before a single judge and a request that is turned down may be appealed to the entire court. The standard for approval of FISA surveillance is whether there is probable cause to believe that the target is an agent of a foreign power, is affiliated with a terrorist group, or is engaged in terrorism.

In 2005 it was disclosed that 3 years prior, President George W. Bush signed a secret order authorizing the National Security Agency (NSA) to intercept communications within the United States without a warrant (Risen & Lichtblau 2005). President Bush explained that the **Terrorist Surveillance Program** was part of his responsibility as commander in chief to protect the United States, and that the FISA procedures were overly complicated and interfered with his responsibility to protect the United States. Congress, although affirming that warrants were required to monitor the communications of Americans, authorized the attorney general and director of national intelligence to continue to engage in the electronic surveillance of foreign nationals located abroad and to specify how the surveillance would avoid the warrantless surveillance of Americans who may be involved in the conversation.

In 2014 **Edward Snowden**, a 33-year-old former Central Intelligence Agency (CIA) and NSA contractor, leaked confidential information. Since 2006, the NSA had engaged in the bulk collection of the domestic and foreign telephone numbers dialed by Americans, along with digital data. This secret "metadata" program, referred to as **PRISM**, was based on bulk search warrants issued every 3 months by the surveillance court that directed nine Internet providers to turn phone call and other records over to the government. The collection involved "chaining" of the collection of the numbers dialed by the target, all numbers dialed by individuals called by the target, and all numbers dialed by these individuals.

Studies concluded that the collection of the numbers dialed by an individual could reveal virtually every aspect of an individual's life. In those instances where there was reasonable suspicion based on the numbers dialed that an individual was involved with terrorism, the government was authorized to obtain a search warrant to monitor the content of phone calls.

Snowden was concerned that this warrantless secret surveillance violated the provision in the Fourth Amendment to the U.S. Constitution that prohibited unreasonable searches and seizures that are conducted without probable cause. The government responded that the American public did not possess an expectation of privacy in the numbers they dialed, and that the program was essential to combat terrorism.

A review commission appointed by President Obama concluded that the program had not been significant in protecting national security, and that information obtained through the program could have been obtained by relying on the established FISA warrant procedure. After extensive debate, Congress adopted the USA Freedom Act, which mandates that phone providers retain metadata rather than turning the information over to the government. The NSA only may obtain access to these records by obtaining a warrant from the surveillance court where there is a reasonable suspicion that the target is involved in terrorism. Once a warrant for metadata is secured, the NSA may obtain the record of the phone numbers dialed and text messages sent by the target as well the numbers dialed by the individuals who have been in contact with the target. In 2017 the NSA obtained the phone records of 40 individuals and the individuals linked to these targets. This amounted to over 500 million communications (Savage, 2018).

Are there too many restraints being placed on surveillance to combat terrorism? What of the threat of a surveillance state like that being constructed in China with 200 million surveillance cameras, facial recognition technology and the tracking of internet use and communications and an integrated system that collects data on nearly every aspect of an individual's life (Mozur, 2018).

Personalities and Events

FIGURE 11.2 Edward Snowden

On June 9, 2014, the British newspaper the *Guardian* released a video interview with Edward Snowden (Poitras & Greenwald, 2014), a 33-year-old former CIA and NSA contractor who had released top-secret information regarding NSA programs to several newspapers. Initially denied asylum in Hong Kong and several other countries, Snowden es received temporary asylum in Russia.

Snowden reportedly never received a high school diploma, briefly attended community college, and joined military with the goal of joining the Special Forces. He was discharged after breaking both his legs and in 2007, based on his aptitude for computers, obtained employment in Geneva, Switzerland, as a contractor for the CIA maintaining network security. He was next hired by Dell as a contractor engaged in computer analysis for the NSA in Japan and was then transferred to Hawaii.

Snowden took a job with CIA contractor Booz Allen Hamilton (BAH) and worked as an ethical hacker charged with detecting vulnerabilities in American technology which might be exploited by foreign countries. This provided Snowden with access to top-secret Internet programs. He inadvertently discovered a report that detailed the Bush administration's warrantless surveillance of both Americans and foreigners following 9/11. His sense of shock was heightened in March 2013 when James Clapper, the director of national intelligence, denied before a congressional committee that the NSA had been collecting data on American citizens, a statement that Snowden was aware was false. Snowden unlawfully transferred information about the warrantless surveillance program to journalists at the *Guardian* and the *Washington Post*.

The American government charged Snowden with espionage, and government officials characterized him as a coward for fleeing rather than taking responsibility for his actions. Officials claimed that Snowden's actions jeopardized national security and had made American less safe. In addition, his claim that he was a defender of liberty and freedom seemingly was in conflict with his seeking asylum in an authoritarian regime like Russia.

Polls indicated that the majority of Americans considered Snowden a whistleblower rather than a traitor. Without Snowden's leaking of information, the "metadata" program likely never would have been revealed (Lippman, 2016).

Should Snowden be prosecuted for espionage if he returns to the United States or granted a pardon and allowed to return to the United States? ☐

RACIAL PROFILING

The Fifth and Fourteenth Amendments to the U.S. Constitution provide individuals equal protection of the law, which means that individuals may not be discriminated against based on race, religion, or gender. In terms of law enforcement, individuals may not be targeted for **racial profiling**: investigative stops, arrests, prosecution, and sentences based on race, religion, or gender. In other words, the law is concerned with what you did—not with who you are.

In the aftermath of the 9/11 attacks, various analysts advocated the use of racial profiling to combat terrorism. This was based on the fact that al Qaeda was a Muslim group and the 9/11 hijackers were Muslims from the Middle East. The Bush administration almost immediately initiated a detention program of Muslims. The only precedent for this this type of mass roundup of individuals was the detention of 112,000 Japanese Americans during World War II, an event for which President Ronald Reagan and Congress later apologized and paid compensation to the individuals who had been harmed. The Bush initiative involved three programs.

In the 2 months following the 9/11 attacks, the U.S. government detained well over 1,000 individuals based on immigration violations. Attorney general John Ashcroft explained that this was motivated by a desire to deter future acts of terrorism by identifying individuals who participate in or support terrorist activities. Citizens of more than 20 predominantly Muslim countries who had violated immigration law were detained—roughly one third of whom came from Pakistan. In April 2003, the Office of the Inspector General of the Department of Justice released a report analyzing the detention of 762 individuals, all of whom were nationals of various Middle Eastern countries or Pakistan. The average length of detention was 80 days, and although a small number of individuals were suspected of terrorist activities, the vast majority were detained because of minor immigration violations such as overstaying their visa or working without authorization. In all likelihood most of the detainees ordinarily would not have been jailed and would have been released and directed to report for a deportation hearing. None of the men who were detained were subsequently charged with terrorism or with terrorism-related activities. They were incarcerated on a hold-until-clear policy while they were investigated for terrorist activity. Individuals guilty of immigration violations were ordered to be deported. The inspector general, Glenn A. Fine, determined that several detainees at the Brooklyn detention facility had been subjected to unduly harsh conditions and 12 individuals reportedly had been subjected to physical abuse. "High interest' detainees were held in restrictive conditions and were confined in their cells for 23 hours a day and handcuffed with leg irons when moved out of their cells. The Bureau of Prisons imposed a communications blackout that restricted the efforts of detainees to contact their family and lawyers" (Office of the Inspector General, 2003, Ch. 7).

On November 9, 2001, Ashcroft directed the FBI and immigration authorities to interview upward of 5,000 men between the ages of 18 and 35 who had lawfully entered the United States in the previous 2 years and originated from countries thought to be linked to terrorism. The list of individuals subject to interview was based on national origin and there was no basis for suspecting that any of these individuals were involved with terrorism. In March 2002, an additional 3,000 Arab, Muslim, and South Asian men in the United States who had entered the United as visitors or students were interviewed.

In June 2002, Ashcroft announced the initiation of the National Security Entry Exit Registration System (NSEERS), required Arab and Muslim noncitizen immigrants to register and to be fingerprinted, photographed, and questioned. In 1 year, the now-abandoned NSEERS program registered 83,310 individuals and deported more than 13,000. The program was subsequently abolished (American Civil Liberties Union, 2004).

In 2003 the Department of Justice issued now-abandoned guidelines prohibiting racial profiling although exempted relying on race or ethnicity in national security investigations. The 2014 guidelines, promulgated by the Attorney General Eric Holder, eliminated the authorization to rely on racial profiling in national security cases. Critics argue that the notion that terrorism can be effectively combated based on racial profiling is misguided. It is thought to be a waste of resources to track individuals because they are Muslim rather than to focus on individual behavior. Muslims are a diverse community with various beliefs and backgrounds, and Islamic terrorists within the United States have very little in common with one another. Richard Reid, the so-called "shoe bomber," is of Canadian and Jamaican background. The 9/11 hijackers all were lawfully within the United States and were from Saudi Arabia and Egypt, both of which are allies of the United States. Law enforcement depends on cooperation from the Muslim community, and singling the entire group out as terrorists breeds distrust of law enforcement, discourages cooperation, and damages American prestige throughout the world. Programs that target individuals because of their race and religion run the danger of a "slippery slope" that may lead to an acceptance of severe restrictions on the civil liberties of members of the group and on the civil liberties of members of other groups.

On the other hand, proponents of racial profiling note that individuals should be willing to sacrifice a small degree of liberty and freedom in the interests of protecting society. Terrorism is difficult to detect, and it makes sense to focus law enforcement efforts on individuals who fit the broad pattern of individuals involved in terrorist activity. Following 9/11, it was reasonable to believe that individuals unlawfully in the United States may be associated with al Qaeda. The view that Muslims are more sympathetic to terrorist violence than other Americans is shared by roughly one third of Americans and a higher percentage among individuals who hold conservative political and religious views.

IMMIGRATION

Individuals involved in terrorist activities are prohibited from entering the United States. Terrorist activities are broadly defined in the Immigration and Nationality Act. This includes planning or engaging in a terrorist activity, soliciting individuals to engage in terrorism, providing material support to a terrorist organization or membership in a terrorist organization, and soliciting or recruiting members for a terrorist organization.

After he took office, President Donald Trump banned immigration from seven predominantly Muslim countries. Several federal courts held the ban unconstitutional on various grounds including a finding that the so-called Muslim ban was at least partially based on discriminatory intent. The ban was subsequently modified to include additional non-predominantly Muslim nations. The Trump administration has consistently contended that immigration, unless accompanied by enhanced vetting of individuals applying to emigrate to the United States, poses a threat to national security because of the threat that terrorists will enter the United States and engage in acts of violence.

It is a crime to unlawfully enter the United States. An estimated 11 million individuals are unlawfully in the United States and are subject to deportation back to their country of origin. There are various categories of individuals who are authorized to enter and to remain in the United States.

Visitors/Tourists. Individuals visiting the United States are required to obtain a visa, although nationals of various European and other nations are not required to obtain a visa under the Foreign Visa Waiver program.

Refugees. Individuals are eligible to enter the United States if they experience a well-founded fear of persecution or violence in their country of origin.

Asylum. Individuals who enter the United States and immediately apply for asylum based on a well-founded fear of persecution or violence in their country of origin.

Students. Individuals may enter to pursue higher or graduate education.

Immigrants. Individuals lawfully in the United States under various employment programs or family reunion programs. Green Card holders are authorized to work in the United States.

Marriage. Individuals entering the United States based on marriage to an American citizen.

Temporary Protected Status (TPS). Nationals of 10 countries have been granted temporary residency in the United States because of war, natural disasters, and severe and threatening conditions which makes it unsafe for individuals to return home. These countries are: El Salvador, Haiti, Honduras, Nepal, Nicaragua, Somalia, Sudan, South Sudan, Syria, and Yemen. The TPS program is administered by the Secretary of the Department of Homeland Security and TPS status typically is granted in 6- to 18-month intervals that can be renewed so long as the secretary considers the designation necessary. Under the Trump administration, the DHS has revoked TPS for 100,000 individuals from Haiti, 25,000 from Nicaragua, roughly 1,000 from Sudan, 800 from Nepal, as many as 200,000 from El Salvador, and 57,000 from Honduras, many of whom have established businesses and have children born in the United States and are thus American citizens (Miroff, 2018).

The most comprehensive study of the relationship between immigration and terrorism was undertaken in 2016 by Alex Nowrasteh of the Cato Institute (Nowrasteh, 2016).

Nowrasteh cautions against concluding that deporting immigrants or closing American borders will eliminate terrorism on U.S. soil and concludes that the risk of an American being killed by a foreign-born terrorist over the 41-year period between 1975 and 2015 is one in 3.6 million per year. The possibility of an American dying in a terrorist attack by a refugee is one in 3.64 billion; and by an individual granted asylum based on political persecution is one in 2.7 billion. The odds of being murdered in an attack by an illegal immigrant is one in 10.9 billion per year, and the odds of being murdered by a foreign tourist on the widely issued B visa is 1 in 3.9 million per year. No murder was committed by a visitor who entered on the Foreign Visa Waiver program. Student visa holders pose a threat to one in 3.8 million individuals.

The U.S issued 1.14 billion visas between 1975 and 2015; 154 of these visas were issued to terrorists. In other words, only 0.0000136% of visas were issued to terrorists. One foreign-born terrorist entered the United States for every 7.38 million nonterrorists. Excluding the 9/11 terrorists, 134 foreign-born terrorists entered the United States out of the 1.14 billion visas issued between 1975 and 2015 (0.00001%). Excluding the 9/11 terrorists, for each visa granted to a terrorist, 8.48 million visas were issued to nonterrorist foreigners.

Of the 19 9/11 terrorists, 18 were on tourist visas and one entered on a student visa. Zacarias Moussaoui—who was not a hijacker, but was involved in the conspiracy, entered without a visa based on his French citizenship.

Excluding the 9/11 attackers, 21 foreign-born terrorists succeeded in murdering 41 individuals between 1975 and 2015. Sixteen of those terrorists committed their attacks prior to 9/11, and these terrorists killed a total of 17 people. There were five successful attacks following 9/11 that killed 24 people. Egyptian-born Hesham Mohamed Hadayet killed two people in July 2012 at Los Angeles International Airport; the Tsarnaev brothers killed three people in the Boston Marathon bombing on April 15, 2013; Muhammad Abdulazeez killed five people at two military installations in Chattanooga, Tennessee, on July 16, 2015; and Tashfeen Malik, along with her American-born husband, killed 14 individuals in December 2015 attack in San Bernardino, California.

Nowrasteh argues that a halt to all immigration is unrealistic because of the contribution of immigrants to the United States. At any rate, this would prevent a relatively small number of terrorist attacks. An alternative would be to eliminate tourist visas. The vast majority—93.7%—of all murders by foreign-born terrorists were committed by the 34 terrorists who entered the United States on tourist visas. He concludes that this would not be realistic given that tourists add $94.1 billion directly and indirectly to the American economy. Consider also that 99.7% of murders committed by foreign-born tourists occurred on 9/11.

David Bier, who is Nowrasteh's colleague at the conservative Cato Institute, created a database of all terrorist suspects between 2015 and the initial portion of October 2017. He found very few instances of foreign terrorists entering the United States as a result of a failure in the vetting (screening) process. He found that at most that there were 17 vetting failures. These individuals came from 12 different countries and only eight attempted to carry out an attack; the other nine were guilty of aiding a foreign terrorist organization. Only one of the 17 individuals succeeded in killing an individual on American soil (Bier, 2017).

In yet another study issued in April 2018, Bier concluded that the United States was effectively vetting refugees. He found that only 13 of the 531 persons convicted of a terrorism-related offense or killed while participating in a terrorist attack since 9/11 had managed to pass through immigration screening and enter the United States. Only one of these 13 individuals participated in a deadly assault in the United States, a rate of one for every 379 million individuals entering the country with a visa or individuals who obtained a change in status allowing them to remain lawfully in the United States between 2002 and 2016 (Nixon, 2018).

In other words, the data suggests that very few terrorists are able to avoid detection and enter the United States. A relatively small number of lethal terrorist offenses are committed by individuals born abroad who enter the United States on a visa, and the odds are very small that an individual in the United States will be killed by a foreign-born terrorist. This suggests that the overwhelming number of terrorists are homegrown rather than foreign born. On the other hand, there is no way of knowing about the number of terrorist attacks that were planned and then abandoned by the perpetrators. It also might be argued that it is better to be safe than sorry, and that all available steps should be taken to prevent terrorism by limiting the number and background of individuals entering the United States.

Keep in mind that studies indicate that when individuals are polled, they vastly overestimate the number of immigrants in their country, as well as the share of immigrants who are Muslim, and they overestimate immigrants' poverty rate and social benefits. These misperceptions are concentrated in individuals with the least amount of education who possess low skills and who have right-wing political views (Porter & Russell, 2018).

Personalities and Events

Sayfullo Saipov, age 29 (discussed in Chapter 10), arrived in the United States from Uzbekistan in 2010. He married and worked as a truck driver, drifting from Ohio to Florida with his wife and children without success before settling in Patterson, New Jersey. In November 2017, Saipov drove a rental truck onto a New York City bicycle path, killing eight people and injuring more than a dozen. Witnesses said he exited the truck yelling "Allahu Akbar" and carrying a pellet gun and paintball gun. Saipov was fortunately subdued by an alert law enforcement officer. He left behind a note in the truck endorsing ISIS and investigators found 90 ISIS propaganda videos and about 3,800 pro-ISIS images on his phone. According to law enforcement, Saipov had followed instructions for a vehicle attack that appeared in the ISIS online magazine *Rumiyah*.

The evidence is that Saipov held moderate political views when he entered the United States and had become increasingly extremist after experiencing personal and economic frustrations.

In 2010 Saipov received a visa, along with nearly 3,300 people from Uzbekistan who were granted diversity visas. The Diversity Visa program was established by Democrats and Republicans in 1990 and signed by President George H. W. Bush. The purpose of the program is to increase immigration from countries and regions that are underrepresented in the ordinary immigration program. Individuals place their name in a lottery and roughly 50,000 individuals are selected out of more than 1 million applicants. No country may receive more than 7% of available slots. To be eligible, an individual must have a high school diploma and go through a vetting process. Between 2007 and 2016, roughly 473,000 people were granted a diversity visa. The largest number were from Africa, which accounted for 43% of those awarded in 2016. This compares with the 32% that went to Europeans, 19% to Asians, 3% to Latin Americans, and 1% to people from Oceania. President Trump has called for an end to diversity visas even though Saipov is only the second person on a diversity visa to commit an act of terrorism.

The same pattern of radicalization following arrival in the United States was followed by Akayed Ullah. Ullah, aged 27, was born in Bangladesh. In November 2017, he strapped a pipe bomb to his chest which he ignited in a Times Square subway station. Ullah arrived in the United States in 2011 on visa for family members (chain migration) after an uncle had received a visa in the lottery program. Ullah was radicalized online after entering the country. He ignited his bomb in response to an online call from ISIS to launch Christmas attacks. President Trump has advocated an end to the family reunion program that allowed Ullah to enter the United States. Commentators supporting family reunion visas argue that the program promotes stability and a sense of community among immigrants to the United States.

A third individual, Akhror Saidakhmetov, an immigrant from Kazakhstan, was arrested in 2015 for attempting to travel abroad to join ISIS, and he was sentenced to 15 years in prison. Saidakhmetov, 19 at the time of his arrest, was simply unprepared to attend an American high school or adjust to life in America when he arrived in the United States at age 16. He was radicalized online by an Uzbek cleric and was abandoned by his mother because of his increased criticism of her Western dress and of her failure to adhere to Islam. He moved in with an older male whom he met at the mosque and began posting pro-ISIS messages on various sites and expressing admiration for the ISIS massacre of Iraqi soldiers.

These three individuals all were radicalized primarily on social media after entering the United States. In each instance, they were unable to adjust to American society, lived in insulated communities, and found meaning by becoming part of the ISIS electronic community. The important point is that enhanced vetting of individuals entering the United States may not fully protect America from attacks by foreign-born terrorists, because many of these individuals are radicalized after entering the country. A focus on foreign-born terrorists clearly does very little to combat homegrown terrorism. ⬜

SOCIAL MEDIA

David Patrikarakos argues in his 2017 book, *War In 140 Characters*, that the nation-state in the 20th century exercised power in two crucial areas: the government monopolization of armed force and the domination of the flow of information. He notes that the development of Web 2.0 in the 21st century has allowed individual citizens to challenge governmental dominance of the flow of information. Governments, although able to militarily dominate terrorist groups, find themselves struggling to slow the radicalization of young people and dissemination of political criticism on social media (Patrikarakos, 2017).

Al Shabaab in Somalia was one of the first groups to establish Twitter accounts which they organized under their media wing, called HMS Press. In September 2013, al Shabaab attracted worldwide attention by live-tweeting a terror attack on the Westgate shopping mall in Nairobi, Kenya. An al Shabaab tweet read: "What Kenyans are witnessing at #Westgate is retributive justice for crimes committed by their military, albeit minuscule in nature." Shortly thereafter al Shabaab posted the following message: "Since our last contact, the Mujahideen inside the mall confirmed to @HMS_Press that they killed over 100 Kenyan kuffar & battle is ongoing" (Higham & Nakashima, 2015). More than 60 people were killed in the attack on the mall, and an additional 175 were wounded. Twitter almost immediately took down the accounts, reportedly one of the first times the company removed material posted by a terrorist organization. Al Shabaab responded by creating new Twitter accounts under different names (Howden, 2013). The attack and the use of Twitter in real time was noted and copied by terrorists across the globe. Adam Gadahn, the late American-born al Qaeda media specialist observed in 2013 that the organization must make an effort to "reach out to Muslims through the new media like Facebook and Twitter" (Higham & Nakashima, 2015).

In 2017 Twitter, Facebook, Microsoft, and YouTube initiated the Global Internet Forum to Counter Terrorism with the mission of developing technology for detecting terrorist posts online and providing online counternarratives to challenge terrorist appeals. There are at least four challenges identified by commentators in controlling social media. First, the content typically is in the form of videos. Photos are easily scanned, but videos contain thousands of frames and pose a greater challenge to scan for terrorist material. Second, the quantity of the videos poses a challenge. Facebook reports that around 100 million hours of video are watched on a daily basis and often are copied and shared; many of these videos are reposted after having been removed. Third, social media companies must undertake the difficult task of balancing freedom of expression against safety and profits. Lastly, governments must depend on the cooperation of private business entities organized to make a profit to regulate terrorist content.

In response to governmental pressure to take action against terrorist material, Twitter suspended roughly 300,000 accounts linked to terrorism in the first half of 2017 and 935,897 accounts between August 2015 and June 2017. Twitter has roughly 328 million users, approximately 68 million of whom are in the United States.

Restricting hate speech can be a difficult task for social media companies. Facebook has hired 1,200 moderators to monitor hate speech on its platform in Germany. The company received criticism from Muslim groups in Myanmar for failing to curb hate speech, incitements to violence, and fake news on its platform. It is estimated that Facebook would have to employ roughly 800 Burmese-speaking monitors to restrict hate speech in Myanmar. Human rights activists in other countries have articulated similar concerns. In March 2018, Sri Lanka ordered Facebook blocked in an effort to end mob violence against Muslims (Roose & Mozur, 2018).

The focus on social media in combating terrorism only addresses a portion of the problem. In their personal communications and recruitment, terrorists rely on encryption. American governmental authorities unsuccessfully pressured Apple to assist them in breaking into the phone of one of the San Bernardino terrorist attackers. The British Conservative Party government reported that moments before Khalid Masood drove a car into pedestrians on the Westminster Bridge in London and stabbed a policeman to death outside Parliament, he had communicated through the use of an encrypted messaging service. Technology companies argue that their customers expect that their communications will remain private but governments insist that technology companies should not provide terrorists with a safe haven from governmental surveillance.

In the past, Telegram has been the app of choice for ISIS, and ISIS has used the encrypted app to recruit and direct attacks in France, Germany, Russia, and Turkey. The app was developed in Russia, has more 100 million users, and primarily appeals to individuals who want end-to-end encryption (which prevents anyone except the sender and receiver from accessing a message), secret chatrooms, and self-destructing messages. Telegram also has a reputation for being less aggressive in closing terrorist channels of communication than other apps (Tan, 2017).

11.4 You Decide

In December 2017, the police in Cologne, Germany, posted a Christmas message reading "Celebrate—With Respect," which appeared in German, English, French, Persian, and Arabic. Beatrix von Storch, a far-right parliamentarian, tweeted, "What the hell is wrong with this country? Why is the official page of police ... tweeting in Arabic ... Are they seeking to appease the barbaric Muslim, rapist hordes of men?" (Eddy, 2018).

(continues on next page)

(continued from previous page)

Von Storch, who is a member of the anti-Islamic party Alternative for Germany, was referring to the fact that in Cologne on New Year's Eve 2015, a number of women had been harassed and assaulted. She told her supporters that the "overwhelming majority of the perpetrators were young Muslim men for whom women and followers of other faiths are second-class citizens" (Eddy, 2018).

The day after von Storch's message, a new law went into effect requiring social media companies to remove hateful comments within 24 hours or confront fines of as much as $57 million. A fine may be imposed after a company systematically refuses to remove objectionable material or fails to establish an effective complaint management system (Eddy, 2018).

Twitter responded by withdrawing von Storch's account for 12 hours. Von Storch next posted a picture of the Twitter message suspending her account on her Facebook page. She wished her 83,000 followers a "Happy New Year in a free country in which everyone can call barbarians, barbarians, even if they are Muslims" (Eddy, 2018). Facebook reacted by removing her post (Eddy, 2018). The Twitter feed of Alternatives for Germany showed two lawmakers with red tape over their mouth with the caption, "Call for freedom of speech in Iran and preventing it in Germany" (Eddy, 2018).

Germany, unlike the United States, prohibits hate speech directed at individuals and groups. However, individuals of every political persuasion opposed the imposition of criminal penalties on social media companies that failed to remove objectionable material as a violation of freedom of expression, because companies could begin to remove lawful posts to avoid possible fines.

There also was the possibility that an Internet provider would make a mistake and remove nonoffensive material or material that served an important public purpose. A member of Berlin's Jewish community, for example, posted a video of an anti-Semitic speech by a prominent German politician on Facebook to highlight the prevalence of anti-Semitism in the country. Facebook following protests restored the post (Eddy, 2018).

Would you favor the imposition of criminal penalties on social media companies that fail to delete hateful comments, terrorist appeals, or propaganda? □

How Terrorism Ends

Audrey Kurth Cronin (2011) finds that the ends of terrorist campaigns follow several patterns. In other words, why do terrorist groups disappear, evolve into peaceful political parties, or succeed? What are the lessons of Cronin's analysis for strategies of counterterrorism? Six "primary patterns" emerge.

Decapitation. The killing or arrest of a terrorist leader is intended to eliminate those who unite a group and articulate the group's goals. The elimination of leadership also demonstrates the group's vulnerability and demoralizes adherents. A leader's arrest also may yield valuable intelligence. An example of a successful decapitation is the arrest of Abimael Guzmán, the founding figure of Sendero Luminoso ("Shining Path") in 1992 in Peru. The group rapidly declined and largely disappeared. The death of Osama bin Laden appears to have seriously weakened al Qaeda. This strategy may backfire—such as by eliminating a leader who is able to control the desire of various factions within the organization to engage in an increased level of violence. Killing a leader also may create a martyr and heroic figure whose apprehension or death inspires increased violence. Eliminating a leader also may splinter an organization and make negotiated settlement more difficult. A government that engages in the killing of a terrorist leader also may be placed on the defensive in explaining why violence by terrorists is criminal when violence by the state is legitimate.

Negotiations. There are isolated instances of governments engaging in unannounced negotiations with terrorist groups. The goal is to determine what concessions may lead to an end to violence and to reach a peace accord. Negotiations can demonstrate to a terrorist group that there are alternatives to violence to achieve the group's aims and goals. Negotiations also may enable the government to weaken the group by creating tension between individuals who favor negotiation and those who reject negotiations. On the other hand, negotiations provide terrorists recognition and legitimacy, reward a group for engaging in unlawful violence, and may give the impression that the government is weak and vulnerable and can encourage additional terrorist violence. The historical record indicates that negotiations only have taken place in isolated instances in which a group has successfully carried out a terrorist campaign that the government has been unable to defeat. Terrorist groups are most likely to negotiate when the group possesses a strong centralized leadership that commands loyalty; when there are other insurgent groups that are competing for popular support; when preconditions are not demanded to negotiations; when the international community intervenes to ensure fair negotiations; and when the group believes that it cannot sustain the terrorist campaign in the long term. In these instances negotiations generally have resulted in a settlement, such as in Northern Ireland.

(continues on next page)

(continued from previous page)

Success. Terrorist groups possess various aims and goals. Examples of successful terrorist campaigns are the Jewish terrorist groups Irgun and Lehi, which contributed to the British decision to exit Palestine, the African National Congress (ANC) transition to power in South Africa, and the success of the FLN in Algeria. Groups have been most successful when they attract a measure of popular and international support for their goals. A foreign power like the French in Algeria is most likely to exit when its continued presence is increasingly unpopular at home and abroad.

Failure. Terrorist groups on average have a lifespan of roughly 8 years. Terrorists are killed and captured, and financial support and resources become increasingly difficult to attract. Fighters grow disillusioned or tired with the struggle or with the lack of clear success. Terrorists may be offered amnesty if they give up the struggle and decide to leave the battlefield. A terrorist group also may find that their goals are no longer relevant because of government concessions or reforms. The end of the Vietnam War left New Left groups in the United States without a cause that could attract popular support. An escalation of violence by a terrorist group may result in a group losing credibility and support. There also is a tendency for terrorist groups to splinter into various factions that differ on whether to continue to rely on violence or to shift to an electoral strategy or to open negotiations.

Repression. A government may take aggressive actions to weaken or to eliminate a terrorist group. The use of force may be used to affirm the strength of the government, deter additional attacks, maintain domestic and foreign support, and gain revenge and retribution. There is an obvious danger that the government reaction is viewed as too severe or as needlessly harming civilians and will weaken the government's support in the country. Excessive violence, although it may lead to short-term success, can create resentment that impedes unification of the country and inspires future acts of rebellion. Examples of the successful repression of terrorist groups include Peru and Uruguay.

Reorientation. A terrorist group may be transformed into a political organization or wage a guerilla or conventional war campaign. Kashmir is an example of a conflict in which terrorism evolved into a series of conventional armed conflicts. The ANC in South Africa made the transition from a terrorist organization to a political party that elected Nelson Mandela as president of the country in 1994. A terrorist group also may react to a lack of success by employing its political networks and skills to engage in criminal activity. FARC in Colombia, although it was a self-identified Marxist terrorist group, evolved into an organization that devoted a disproportionate amount of its resources to furthering the cocaine trade. ▯

CHAPTER SUMMARY

A number of public policy issues in counterterrorism, some of which have yet to be fully resolved, have been discussed in this chapter.

Drone warfare has proven effective in killing terrorists and in dismantling terrorist networks, although it risks endangering and alienating civilians. Current American policy is to maintain the Guantánamo Bay prison camp to detain and to isolate terrorists, although critics assert that the facility is expensive, is unnecessary, and inspires terrorism. The use of enhanced interrogation is considered torture, which is prohibited under American and international law. Some commentators question whether enhanced interrogation constitutes torture and assert that these methods prove effective in detecting terrorist plots and are justified for protecting national security. Military commissions have proven to be an inefficient method of prosecuting accused terrorists, although they are viewed by some as preferable to providing terrorists with the full due process of protections granted in civilian jury trials. Civilian trials also present a target for terrorist attacks. The issues of surveillance and racial profiling starkly raise the question of how to balance civil liberties and the right to privacy with national security. Among the primary reasons why a significant number of people favor limiting immigration is to prevent terrorists from entering the United States. Studies suggest that immigrants are responsible only for a small number of terrorist attacks. Social media companies are expected as responsible citizens to balance the desire for free and open access and debate and the desire to attract as many users as possible with the responsibility to limit terrorist incitement and recruitment and hate speech.

CHAPTER REVIEW QUESTIONS

1. Compare and contrast the counterterrorism policies of Presidents Bush, Obama, and Trump. As president, what aspects of the counterterrorism policies of these three presidents would you continue?

2. Discuss the decision to incarcerate detainees at Guantánamo? As president, would you favor incarcerating detainees in prisons within the continental United States?

3. What are the arguments for and against enhanced interrogation of terrorists? What is your view as to whether enhanced interrogation should be used to question terrorists?

4. Why are military commissions used to prosecute suspected terrorists? Should suspected terrorists be prosecuted before military commissions or before civilian courts?

5. Outline the development of the use of electronic surveillance against suspected terrorists.

6. Define racial profiling. Should racial profiling be relied on to detect and to investigate terrorism?

7. What is the relationship between immigration and terrorism? Would you support restricting immigration to combat terrorism?

8. Should social media companies be held responsible for racist material or material advocating terrorism that is posted on their platforms?

9. Discuss the various ways that Cronin argues terrorism ends.

TERMINOLOGY

Authorization for the Use of
   Military Force (AUMF)
counterterrorism
crime-control approach to
   counterterrorism
Detainee Treatment Act
drones
enhanced interrogation
extraordinary rendition

Foreign Intelligence Surveillance Act (FISA)
Foreign Intelligence Surveillance Court
Guantánamo Bay detention
   camp
Military Commission Act of
   2006
military commissions

PRISM
racial profiling
Snowden, Edward
Terrorist Surveillance
   Program
war-fighting approach to
   counterterrorism
waterboarding

CHAPTER 12

Donald Trump and Contemporary Terrorism*

INTRODUCTION

This brief concluding chapter offers a perspective on the current state of American terrorism policy under the administration of President Donald J. Trump. Events, of course, are nearly impossible to predict, although some broad trends can be identified.

As with each and every president who has sat in the Oval Office, President Trump has proclaimed the protection of the American people and the United States as a priority. His counterterrorism policy demonstrates both a continuity and a profound change from the counterterrorism policies of Presidents Bush and Obama. The primary pillars of President Trump's terrorism policy sketched in this chapter include the following:

Nuclear weapons. A reinvigorated nuclear program and less restrictive use of nuclear weapons.

International counterterrorism. A more aggressive use of military force and pressure.

---

* AUTHOR'S NOTE: This chapter is meant to serve as an addendum to the book. It is a brief overview rather than an in-depth discussion, and for that reason, it does not include all the features that have been presented in the previous chapters. The topics are in flux, and the relevance of the subject matter is difficult to anticipate.

Domestic terrorism. A reluctance to criticize or to act against right-wing violence within the United States.

National security. A pursuit of "leakers" and espionage, along with a reluctance to act against Russian meddling in the American political process.

Immigration. A restriction on legal immigration, the prevention of illegal immigration, and the deportation of undocumented immigrants.

NUCLEAR WEAPONS

The United States' 2018 National Defense Strategy states that after nearly 2 decades of focusing on terrorism, the United States is turning its attention to the challenges presented by Russia and China, and by rogue regimes like North Korea and Iran. Although President Trump has been skeptical of whether the United States benefits from foreign alliances, the new defense strategy stresses the importance of multilateral cooperation. In this new strategy, terrorism continues to be a concern although no longer is the primary focus of American defense policy. Of course, even the best conceived plans may be derailed by unanticipated events.

The Trump administration plans to devote $1.2 trillion to upgrading America's nuclear arsenal and has expressed unhappiness with agreements limiting nuclear weapons, stating that it is difficult to envision the renewal of an existing agreement with Russia that expires in 2021. Under the 2010 New START treaty, both sides are limited to 1,500 nuclear warheads.

The Trump administration has announced plans to develop mobile medium-range nuclear weapons—a violation of a treaty agreement with Russia. Russia has allegedly already begun to deploy this type of missile system. In the past, both sides pledged not to develop mobile medium-range missile systems, because they can be deployed in countries reasonably proximate to Russia and to the United States—which would provide limited reaction time to verify that an attack is underway or to respond to an attack. Russian premier Vladimir Putin further escalated tensions in March 2018 when he threatened the West with a new generation of nuclear weapons—including what he called an invincible intercontinental cruise missile, and a nuclear torpedo that is able to evade all American defenses.

A controversial U.S. government document titled the *Nuclear Posture Review* indicates that in the future, nuclear weapons may be deployed for surgical strikes in response to various nonnuclear attacks—including cyberattacks and attacks on the nation's infrastructure. In the past, the United States has limited the first-strike use of nuclear weapons to extreme circumstances—such as threat of nuclear attack or a biological weapons attack on the United States or its allies. These "surgical" attacks are to be carried out by a new generation of small low-yield nuclear weapons that are currently under development as part of the United States' trillion-dollar investment in nuclear weapons. The Trump administration believes that other countries are planning to develop these low-yield nuclear weapons, and that the United States needs to have the same capacity in order to deter the use of these types of weapons against the United States.

In July 2018, President Trump and Russian Premier Vladimir Putin met in Helsinki, Finland, and surprisingly appeared to agree to open negotiations on renewing the treaty on Measures for the Further Reduction and Limitation of Strategic Offensive Arms (known as the New START Treaty). This treaty is central to limiting both sides' strategic nuclear arms and nuclear delivery systems (Wintour, 2018b).

There is the larger threat of nuclear exchange between the United States and North Korea, which now has sufficient missile technology to reach Hawaii and the U.S. mainland with a nuclear weapon. President Trump, like his predecessors, came into office vowing that he would not permit North Korea to develop a nuclear weapon capable of threatening the United States. He initially proclaimed that the era of "strategic patience" has drawn to an close and that his goal was the complete denuclearization of North Korea.

The United States has imposed increasingly harsh economic sanctions on North Korea and enlisted the United Nations and countries across the globe to place pressure on the nation. In November 2017, the Trump administration added North Korea to the list of State Sponsors of Terrorism, which includes countries which repeatedly provide support for acts of international terrorism. The country had been off the list for 20 years.

There was a major breakthrough in April 2018 when the leaders of North and South Korea met and pledged to pursue a peace agreement that would officially end the Korean War. The joint statement also put forth the goal of denuclearizing the Korean Peninsula. President Trump and North Korean leader Kim Jong Un also met in Singapore to discuss ending North Korea's nuclear program in exchange for lifting sanctions and providing economic assistance and military-related concessions (Sanger, 2018a; Sang-Hun, 2018).

President Trump was an outspoken critic of the nuclear agreement between the United States and five other countries with Iran. The United States, along with major European powers, agreed to lift economic sanctions on Iran in return for a commitment by Iran to end their nuclear weapons program and to delay enriching uranium to the level required for a nuclear bomb for 15 years. The International Atomic Energy Agency inspectors have certified that Iran has abided by the agreement. Despite support for the agreement from America's European allies, in May 2018, President Trump withdrew from the nuclear agreement with Iran and reimposed sanctions. He insisted that Iran must permanently renounce the possession of nuclear weapons and stop exporting terrorism throughout the Middle East (Baker & Davis, 2018; Gearan & De Young, 2018).

The United States has taken a strong stand against the use of chemical weapons and has joined a new organization to identify and punish countries and groups that use chemical weapons. In April 2017, the United States fired 57 Tomahawk missiles at a Syrian airfield, which the United States claimed had been used to launch the planes carrying out a gas attack that killed 100 people. Although the United States claimed that this would deter Russia from allowing Syria to carry out additional gas attacks, the Syria launched an additional attack in January 2018, and has reportedly carried out a number of chemical attacks since 2013 (Almukhtar, 2018). In April 2018, the United States, France, and Great Britain launched a missile attack in response to a Syrian chemical weapons attack which killed 40 civilians (Cooper, Gibbons-Neff, & Hubbard 2018).

The *Bulletin of the Atomic Scientists* maintains an influential "doomsday" clock that provides a measure of the likelihood of nuclear war. Based on the global instability in the world at the end of 2017, the group set the clock to 2 minutes to midnight (Bulletin of the Atomic Scientists, 2018).

INTERNATIONAL COUNTERTERRORISM

President Trump has adopted an "America First" foreign policy, which is based on the promotion of the self-interest of the United States—rather than on what President Trump views as tailoring policies and expending resources on behalf of other countries. He has threatened to end funding for international organizations like the United Nations, which at times he believes does not support America's point of view.

The United States nonetheless does not seem ready to withdraw from a global role in fighting terrorism. The war in Afghanistan against insurgent terrorism has lasted more than 16 years and has resulted in the death of more than 2,000 American troops. The Trump administration has agreed to negotiations with the Taliban in Afghanistan, and President Trump has sent 4,000 additional troops into the country (a total of 15,000 troops) and has predicted victory. The United States under President Trump has adopted what is described as a more aggressive policy of taking the fight to the Taliban. A BBC study finds that as of February 2018, the Taliban controlled or were active in 70% of Afghanistan, in areas that also house roughly half the country's population. In 2018 Taliban fighters demonstrated their continued strength by carrying out serious terrorist attacks in urban areas in retaliation for the 4,000 bombs dropped by the United States on rural areas. As a result of the American and Taliban attacks, civilian casualties in 2017 remained at near-record levels. The situation in Afghanistan is complicated by the recent involvement of ISIS, which is competing with the Taliban for rural dominance (Sharif & Amadou, 2018).

The United Nations reported in 2017 that deliberate terrorist attacks on civilians accounted for 27% of all civilian casualties. This includes suicide bombings and targeted killings but excludes airstrikes and attacks on military targets. Civilian casualties from American airstrikes only rose 7% (despite the increased number of aerial attacks) because of more precise targeting. The number of civilians killed in "complex attacks" (which involves two or more commandos with suicide vests seizing a building or taking hostages and detonating their explosives) and other suicide bombings increased from 398 in 2016 to 605 in 2017. A United Nations report found that the first 6 months of 2018 were the most lethal 6 months of any year during the Afghan conflict for civilians. ISIS was responsible for 52% of civilian deaths, and the Taliban were responsible for 40% of civilian deaths. Only 3% were attributed to the international coalition forces (Nordland & Sukhanyar, 2018).

A Pentagon report found that in 2017 American military attacks killed 499 civilians and injured 169 civilians in Iraq, Syria, Afghanistan, and Yemen. Data were not broken down by country, and data were not reported on Somalia. The nonprofit organization Airwars has reported a figure of 6,259 civilian casualties (Cooper, 2018).

President Trump has proclaimed that countries which do not support the United States will have their foreign aid restricted. Pakistan lost billions of dollars in security assistance because of the country's "lies and deceit"—continuing to provide safe haven to the Taliban. The Trump administration threatened that foreign assistance would only be reinstated when the country's intelligence services stopped working with Taliban-affiliated groups and prevented Pakistan's northern frontier territory from being used as a base for Taliban-affiliated terrorist groups like the Haqqani network. Haqqani militants enter and fight in Afghanistan, and then quickly cross back over the border to a safe haven in Pakistan. Defense experts warned that the ruling Pakistani regime would risk being voted out of office if it cooperates too closely with the United States, which is viewed with suspicion by the majority of the population. There also the belief that the United States runs a risk in withholding assistance from Pakistan. Pakistan is vital for supplying U.S. and U.S.-allied troops in Afghanistan, although supplies may be routed through Russia and Central Asian countries. Most importantly, Pakistan is a nuclear-armed state and the United States has a direct interest in ensuring the security of the country's weapons.

In another example of Trump restricting American assistance to advance foreign policy goals, $65 million was cut from the UN Relief and Works Agency for Palestine Refugees in the Near East, which helps to support nearly 5 million Palestinians living in refugee camps. The United States objected to the alleged mismanagement of the fund and expressed the view that countries in the Middle East should contribute a greater share of the agency's budget. The termination of assistance also was a reaction to Palestine's objection to the United States moving the embassy in Israel to Jerusalem, which was intended to push the Palestinians into negotiating a peace agreement by removing a historic impediment to an agreement from the negotiating table. The movement of the embassy was condemned across the Middle East and has encouraged skepticism among Palestinians about whether the United States can be trusted to fairly negotiate peace between Israel and Palestine (De Young & Morello, 2018).

The Trump administration has extended the definition of a "war zone" (areas of active hostilities) to Yemen and Somalia. This policy authorizes drone and other military and CIA attacks without Congressional approval against terrorists in these two countries as well as in Iraq, Syria, Libya, and Afghanistan. The logic is that the Obama administration purportedly impeded the War on Terror by requiring approval for most drone attacks. The requirements for launching attacks against enemy fighters outside war zones also have been made less restrictive. Attacks outside war zones, for example, no longer require that the target pose an immediate threat to Americans and no longer require the guarantee that civilians will not be killed.

The Trump administration also engaged in increased bombing of terrorist targets in Afghanistan and in Syria. Critics of the Trump strategy objected that the Trump policy placed civilians at risk, and that the military has devoted limited resources to investigating civilian casualties (Qui, 2017).

ISIS has been driven out of urban areas in Iran and Syria and no longer can claim a caliphate. The territory ISIS controls has shrunk from a land mass equivalent to the size of Portugal to merely a few isolated outposts. However, ISIS continues to command 6,000–10,000 fighters, which is roughly 14 times more fighters that it possessed in 2011, and continues to have a strong social media presence. A number of ISIS fighters remain in Syria awaiting instructions on encrypted communication platforms. Others have joined al Qaeda or terrorist groups in Libya, North Africa, the Philippines, and Afghanistan.

An estimated 5,000 ISIS fighters in Syria were originally from Europe, and roughly 1,500 have returned to Europe. ISIS-directed attacks continue to take place in spite of the defeat of ISIS in Syria and Iraq. In 2017 ISIS claimed responsibility for three attacks in Great Britain that killed an estimated 38 people. An attack on a Sufi Muslim mosque in Egypt in November 2017 killed 235 people and wounded 109 others. ISIS considers the Sufi, a minority Muslim sect, to be an impure form of Islam. In January 2018, ISIS carried out two suicide bombings in Baghdad, indicating a renewed focus on soft and small-scale targets.

President Trump has expressed a desire to withdraw the remaining U.S. troops from Syria even though the United States continues to support the Kurdish militia in the Syrian civil war against the Assad regime. American advisors and Kurdish forces occupy territory on the Turkish border, despite objection from Turkey that the Kurds pose a terrorist threat to the country.

An issue that has yet to be resolved is the accountability of ISIS fighters for atrocities. The UN Security Council appointed a special advisor to assist Iraq in investigating the mass killings committed by ISIS. There are well over 60 mass graves that have been uncovered in Iraq that contain the victims of mass murders committed by ISIS. Sweden has brought charges against members of ISIS who are responsible for crimes against Swedish nationals in Iraq and Syria, and Germany has relied on universal jurisdiction to begin the process of prosecuting nearly 20 ISIS fighters for war crimes. In February 2018, Kurdish forces apprehended two British ISIS members thought to be responsible for beheading 27 individuals, including American journalists James Foley and Steven Sotloff as well as Abdul-Rahman Kassig, a U.S. aid worker. Russia has blocked efforts to bring Syrian officials to trial before the International Military Court for torture, murder, and the use of chemical weapons. In May 2018, Iraqi forces arrested five important leaders of ISIS, including the senior aide to ISIS leader Abu Bakr al-Baghdadi (El-Ghosbashy & Salim, 2018).

The Trump administration has continued to support Saudi Arabia. Arms sales to Saudis valued at billions of dollars began in the late 1960s and continued under the Bush and Obama administrations—and now under the Trump administration. Each of these administrations viewed the Saudis as a bulwark against terrorism and Iranian expansionism in the Middle East.

The Trump administration has strongly backed significant reforms adopted by Saudi Arabia and has supported and encouraged the country's modernization and commitment to a more moderate brand of Islamic theology at home and abroad (Ignatius, 2018).

The Trump administration has been particularly supportive of Saudi Arabia (Sunni Islam) in combating the influence of Iranian (Shia Islam) dominance in the Middle East. An ugly example is the conflict in Yemen, in which Saudi Arabia (with the assistance of U.S. air strikes and weaponry) is waging a campaign against the Iran-supported insurgent Houthis. The Pentagon has admitted that American troops carried out roughly 130 ground operations in Yemen, and in 2017 Americans carried out roughly 130 aerial bombing attacks. The United States also is providing intelligence to the Saudi military and assisting in securing the Saudi border. There are no accurate figures on the casualties, although the conventional wisdom is that at least 10,000 civilians—roughly one fifth of whom are children—have been killed, 3 million have been displaced, and hundreds of thousands have fled the country. A blockade lasting several years has caused 1 million people to suffer from cholera, and thousands have died from disease.

The Saudi Arabia–Iran conflict also has led to an air and sea boycott by Saudi Arabia and the United Arab Emirates of the fellow Sunni gulf state of Qatar. The boycott—which is in response to Qatar's close relationship with Iran, alleged financing of terrorism, provision of a safe haven for Arab dissidents, and hosting the news network al Jazeera—which has been critical of Arab rulers. President Trump endorsed and encouraged the Saudi boycott, despite the fact that Qatar is home to two American military command posts and a center from which the United States and allied nations conduct the air war on ISIS in Iraq and in Syria. Although tensions remain, the conflict between the Qatar and its neighbors appears on the way to being resolved (Wintour, 2018a).

The United States did join Europe in condemning Russia's attempted assassination of double agent Sergei Skripal and his daughter using a nerve agent. Sixty Soviet diplomats were expelled from the United States in retaliation for the attack—the second carried out by Russia in Great Britain (Hjelmgaard, 2018).

A major change in American policy is the decision for the American Cybercommand to engage in offensive attacks to disable foreign computer networks, weapon and radar systems, and infrastructure. In the past, the Cybercommand was generally viewed as a defensive organization charged with intercepting attacks against the U.S. defense establishment and infrastructure (Sanger, 2018b). Iran is viewed as posing a particular threat. In 2016, Iranian hackers were indicted for penetrating the computers of a New York dam in an effort to affect water levels and flow. Iranian hackers are alleged to be responsible for roughly a dozen attacks on critical infrastructure in the United States (Perlroth, 2018).

The Trump administration, according to critics, seems to have abandoned human rights as a significant factor in American foreign policy and has praised nationalist leaders with little regard for the rights of its citizenry. Critics note that the Department of State omitted Afghanistan, Iraq, and Myanmar from the list of countries using child soldiers—presumably because U.S. law prohibits countries relying on child soldiers from receiving financial and military assistance. The United States lifted sanctions of Sudan, whose president faces charges of crimes against humanity, war crimes, and genocide stemming from his regime's sponsorship of attacks on the region of Darfur in Sudan. The Trump administration points out that, however important human rights are, the American national interest requires support for regimes like Rodrigo Duterte's in the Philippines, responsible for killing thousands in a war against drugs. The Trump administration also joined various repressive regimes and Russia by calling for the abolition of the International Criminal Court.

At the same time, relations with American allies like Australia and Mexico at times have been strained. In June 2017, President Trump expressed solidarity with Great Britain in the wake of a terrorist attack in which a car sped across the London Bridge, killing seven people and seriously injuring 21. Two knife-wielding assailants emerged from the car and were shot dead by eight armed officers. This was the third major terrorist attack in England in 3 months. President Trump seemingly distorted the meaning of the comments of Muslim mayor of London, Sadiq Khan, and attacked Khan in a tweet, leading to a "war of words" between the two of them. Before this exchange, the British government had protested President Trump's false allegation that the British security services had been involved in assisting the FBI in engaging in electronic surveillance of the president-elect following the November election. Britain also complained that the United States had leaked details of the May 2017 Manchester bombing at a time when they were pursuing possible coconspirators. President Trump further alienated Great Britain by retweeting an anti-Muslim video from a White supremacist website in Great Britain.

South American countries were surprised when President Trump tweeted that he is prepared to unilaterally send troops to restore order in Venezuela, which suffers from a collapsing economy, food shortages, crime, violence, corruption, and political conflict. The announcement came as a shock to Latin American leaders who are negotiating a settlement between the contending factions in Venezuela.

President Trump has also stated that he will keep Guantánamo open and has suggested that members of ISIS captured during the Syrian conflict should be housed at the prison. At various times he has expressed some support for harsh interrogation practices as well as prosecuting domestic terrorists before military tribunals.

A number of Democratic and Republican members of Congress have expressed the need to pass new legislation restricting the president's use of armed force without Congressional approval. Both Presidents Obama and Trump have relied on the Authorization for Use of Military Force (AUMF), passed by Congress following the 9/11 attacks, to provide legal justification for their use of military force.

DOMESTIC TERRORISM

A significant development is the rise of domestic terrorism. Conservative observers point to the left-wing Antifa, a loosely organized group whose roots can be traced to the 1920s and 1930s when the organization fought in the street against fascists in Nazi Germany, Italy, and Spain. Antifa has recently been reconstituted to fight against racist movements. There are as many as 15,000 members of Antifa, a number of whom have appeared at various rallies to confront White supremacists and Nazis and to protect antiracist protestors.

On the right, there is the growth of what is termed the *alt-right*. This is a political movement that has embraced the racist, anti-immigrant, and gun rights positions that have characterized right-wing terrorist groups. The alt-right views the greatest threat as coming from the "deep state," the federal employees and law enforcement agencies that the alt-right believes work in a conspiratorial fashion to prevent policies that they oppose from being formulated and enforced. The "deep state" is a conspiracy of unelected individuals who exercise more power than elected representatives. The investigation into Russian meddling in the 2016 presidential election is viewed as an effort by the "deep state" to prevent an improved relationship between the United States and Russia.

There has been a substantial increase in right-wing violence. The Anti-Defamation League (2017), a Jewish civil rights organization, reported that in 2017, 34 people were the victims of right-wing extremists, the militia movement, and racist groups. Eighteen were killed by White supremacists, a 157% increase over the 7 killed by White supremacists in 2016. The number of Americans killed by White suprem-acists was double the number killed by domestic Islamic extremists. Right-wing extremists have been responsible for 274 of the 374 murders committed by extrem-ists over the past 10 years.

Overall, there were 307 incidents of anti-Muslim hate crimes in 2016, marking a 19% increase from the previous year. There was even a sharper increase the year before, when the total number of anti-Muslim incidents rose 67%, from 154 in 2014 to 257 in 2015. The largest number of hate crimes in 2016 were against Jews, increasing from 666 in 2015 to 684 in 2016.

In 2017 a Pew Research Center survey found 75% of Muslim Americans believe there is a great deal of discrimination against Muslims—a sentiment shared by nearly 70% of non-Muslim Americans. One half of Muslims believe that discrim-ination is getting worse.

The Southern Poverty Law Center (SPLC), a nonprofit organization that works to combat hate groups in the United States, reports that in 2017 the number of hate groups increased from 917 from 954. Neo-Nazi groups grew 22% and anti-Muslim groups increased 13%. The SPLC also reports an increase in Black nationalist groups, anti-immigrant groups, and armed militias (Beirich & Buchanan, 2018).

In one widely reported incident in May 2017, Jeremy Christian stabbed three men—two of whom died—who were attempting to protect two young women, one an African American and the other wearing a hijab, on a Portland, Oregon, light-rail train. In another incident, James Fields, Jr., a 20-year-old White nationalist from Toledo, Ohio, drove his car into a crowd in Charlottesville, Virginia, killing Heather Heyer, who along with other demonstrators was protesting a White nationalist gathering in the city. The night before the rally, right-wing partici-pants marched through the campus of the University of Virginia while carrying torches and chanting Nazi slogans. President Trump, in a controversial statement, seemingly apportioned equal blame for the violence in Charlottesville to the right-wing demonstrators who rallied in Charlottesville and to the residents and other individuals who had gathered to protest the march. He later retweeted an anti-Muslim video originally posted by a British neo-Nazi organization and made unsubstantiated comments about violence perpetrated by migrants in Sweden, which were condemned by the Swedish government.

In April 2018, three members of a militia group in Kansas were convicted of a conspiracy to violate civil rights and a conspiracy to use a weapon of mass destruction to destroy apartments housing Somali immigrants who worked at a meat-packing plant (Smith, 2018).

Following the incident in Charlottesville, the Trump administration withdrew funding from groups involved in combating the radicalization of young people by extremist right-wing groups. Although members of the Trump administration have denounced violence by right-wing groups, President Trump has been relatively silent when confronted with this type of violent extremism.

NATIONAL SECURITY

There is a renewed espionage competition between the United States, Russia, and China that undoubtedly will continue in cyberspace as well as in the use of human intelligence. Hackers suspected of being linked to Russia managed to steal hacking tools developed by the National Security Agency. These hackers used this malicious software to launch ransomware attacks in 74 countries, demanding payment in digital currency to restore data to hospitals, banks, and industry. The stolen hacking tools allowed hackers to break into smartphones, computers, and even computer-based television stations. Chinese hackers penetrated U.S. government computers and obtained the names of individuals working in diplomacy and intelligence, whom they may potentially target. The United States has identified and criminally charged individuals in Russia, China, and Iran for cybercrimes.

There have been at least four major security breaches that have been disclosed since President Trump took office. The United States arrested former CIA intelligence officer Jerry Chun Shing Lee and charged him with one count of illegally possessing classified information—although the underlying suspicion is that he helped China kill or imprison as many as 10 American spies working in China. Harold T. Martin was arrested for possession of a literal library of stolen security documents that he had unlawfully removed from his work at the National Security Agency. Reality Winner, a young NSA contractor, pled guilty to leaking a report on Russian interference in the 2016 election to an online publication. In June 2018, a grand jury indicted former CIA employee Joshua Schulte for leaking information to Wikileaks that described the CIA's attempts to break into various computer operating systems and devices.

There have been a number of leaks from sources inside the federal government during the tenure of the Trump administration, which administration officials have expressed a determination to investigate and to prosecute. At the same time, there is an obvious obligation for news organizations to protect their sources, so they view the pursuit of their confidential sources with alarm.

There have been continued calls for President Trump to investigate and to take action to counter Russian interference in the U.S. electoral process. However, he has remained reluctant to pursue Russian meddling—meddling that has been corroborated by all 16 American intelligence agencies and by the heads of the FBI, CIA, and by the director of national intelligence. In February 2018, the Justice

Department charged 13 Russians and three Russian companies in an intricate network designed to undermine the 2016 presidential election by promoting discord and undermining confidence in American democracy. Russian operatives waged a campaign of so-called information warfare meant to disparage Hillary Clinton. After failing to fully implement sanctions on Russia that were adopted by Congress, the Trump administration responded by imposing sanctions against those indicted, along with others involved in cyberattacks (Baker, 2018). In July 2018, indictments were brought against 12 Russian intelligence operatives for hacking into the e-mails of Hillary Clinton and the Democratic National Committee. This was followed by the arrest of Maria Butina, a Russian national resident in the United States who is alleged to have been working to influence the outcome of the 2016 presidential election (Mazetti & Benner, 2018).

President Trump's criticisms of American intelligence agencies and the FBI, however demoralizing to these agencies, are unlikely to affect the determination of these agencies to protect U.S. national security. In July 2018, the FBI arrested Demetrius N. Pitts, 48, who told an undercover informant that he wanted to ignite bombs and launch attacks against cities across the United States. Pitts planned to launch his first attack at an Independence Day parade in Cleveland, Ohio (Haag, 2018).

IMMIGRATION

Restricting legal and illegal immigration continues to be the central component to President Trump's counterterrorism strategy. He argues that people entering the United States constitute the greatest terrorist threat to the United States. Keep in mind that there are three prongs to President Trump's immigration policy: restricting legal immigration, preventing illegal immigration, and deporting undocumented individuals.

The details of immigration policy likely will continue to evolve over the next several years. The important point is that immigration is viewed by President Trump and by the Department of Homeland Security as a vital component of counterterrorism. On several occasions, President Trump has attributed violence and terrorism in Europe to immigration. In January 2018, the Trump administration released a report attempting to connect immigration to terrorism in the United States. The report purported to demonstrate that the overwhelming majority of individuals convicted of international terrorism or terrorism-related charges in the United States in the past 15 years were born abroad. Kirsten Nielson, the head of Homeland Security, stated that the report is utterly chilling. Individuals who have analyzed the findings of the report say it is misleading, noting that among other points, the report included individuals extradited to the United States to stand trial.

President Trump's initial immigration order issued on January 27, 2017, was in effect until March 2017—when it was held unconstitutional by various federal courts as a violation of equal protection. The order effectively blocked travel to the United States from the majority-Muslim countries of Iran, Iraq, Libya, Nepal, Somalia, and Sudan until a country satisfied various requirements. The so-called Muslim ban on travel—which was rejected by federal judges, whether appointed by Republicans or by Democrats—was superseded by Executive Order 13780, which somewhat modified the ban by limiting the prohibition on the issuance of visas to six countries. This prohibition also was blocked by federal courts and a third order focuses on eight countries—six of which are predominantly Muslim—and also includes North Korea and Venezuela, limits the number of refugees, and contains various other restrictions. The restrictions imposed for entry vary somewhat from country to country, although in general it will be extremely difficult for individuals from the countries designated in the order to enter the United States to live, work, study, or visit. The process for vetting refugees—which already takes 2 years—has been significantly tightened. President Trump also drastically reduced the number of refugees admitted into the United States. The end result of all these provisions is a drastic reduction in the number of Muslims and other individuals from abroad admitted to the United States. The Supreme Court lifted a temporary injunction preventing the president's immigration order from being implemented (Gerstein, 2017) and subsequently uphold the legality of the President Trump's immigration order. The Court reasoned that President Trump has the authority to control immigration to protect national security. An interesting aspect of the case was the pronouncement that the 1944 decision in *Korematsu v. United States*, upholding the forcible relocation of Japanese Americans to concentration camps, was wrongly decided (Siddiqui, 2018).

President Trump has argued that immigration should be based on merit, and that the diversity visa lottery and chain migration (wherein people who have family members already living in the United States are allowed to immigrate) should be restricted, if not eliminated. He expressed the view during negotiation with members of the Senate that these programs result in the admission of individuals from "s__hole countries."

The second component of President Trump's immigrations policy is the deportation of undocumented immigrants. Immigration and Customs Enforcement (ICE) arrests of undocumented immigrants have increased by nearly 40%—including those accused but not convicted of minor offenses, some of whom have lived in the United States for a number of years. President Trump's immigration policy has led to a stand-off, so to speak, with so-called sanctuary cities—local jurisdictions that have a policy of not notifying ICE when undocumented immigrants are arrested for minor offenses or when they come into contact with law enforcement. Keep in mind that these jurisdictions do notify ICE when an individual is arrested for certain serious crimes or when there is a federal arrest warrant for the individual. The thinking of sanctuary cities is that victims will be reluctant to contact or cooperate with the police for any reason if they believe that the local police will turn them over to ICE. An example of this phenomenon is a noticeable decline in reports of domestic violence in Hispanic areas of major urban areas.

A related policy is the decision to end Protected Visitor status for individuals from El Salvador, Haiti, Honduras, Nepal, and Sudan who were lawfully admitted to the United States on a temporary basis because of natural disasters or massive violence in their country of origin. In spite of the fact that some of these disasters occurred several years ago, these countries remain in a state of emergency and crisis. The Trump administration reasons that these programs were intended to be temporary and thus should be terminated. Most controversially, President Trump announced his intent to end the Deferred Action for Childhood Arrivals (DACA) program implemented by President Obama, unless Congress endorsed the program by March 2018. Congress has failed to act, and the future of the program remains uncertain.

The most important symbol of President Trump's anti-immigration policy is the proposed border wall with Mexico. The wall, which would cost an estimated $18 billion according to President Trump, is essential to limiting illegal immigration and the transport of drugs across the border. President Trump insisted throughout the presidential campaign that Mexico would pay for the wall—although following the election he has continued to seek Congressional funding and there is some indication that he no longer believes that this wall must be a physical barrier. Despite the Trump administration's continued advocacy for the wall, in 2017 there was a 40% decline in incidents along the border as compared to 2018 and incidents, according to the DHS, were the lowest they had been in 45 years. Experts argue that the greatest cause of illegal entry and importation of narcotics is through people entering legally as visitors rather than crossing the border with Mexico.

The Trump administration, in an effort to deter unlawful entry into the United States by individuals from Central America, a number of whom were fleeing violence, implemented a "zero-tolerance policy" in which individuals illegally entering or present in the United States were charged with a misdemeanor and criminally prosecuted. First-time offenders typically were sentenced to time-served and turned over to ICE for deportation. Individuals awaiting trial in most instances were separated from their minor children, who were detained in facilities across the United States. In various instances, parents were deported before being reunited with their children. The Trump administration claimed that a significant percentage of individuals entering the United States unlawfully were affiliated with criminal gangs and that a "get-tough policy" was required to put a halt to unlawful entries into the country. Popular opposition led the Trump administration to return to a policy of keeping families together and processing individuals in civil deportation hearings. Individuals awaiting deportation hearings will be detained along with their children in detention centers or released and monitored by an ankle bracelet until a hearing is conducted. Individuals also may "waive" a hearing and accept immediate deportation. Keep in mind that "expedited removal" permits immigration authorities to deport an individual who is not claiming asylum without a hearing if detained within 100 miles from the border and within 14 days of the individual's entering the United States (Shear, Nixon, & Benner, 2018). The Trump administration also has articulated opposition to allowing individuals who unlawfully cross the border to file claims for political asylum and has eliminated asylum in cases in which a government has demonstrated an inability or disinterest in protecting individuals from domestic violence and gang-related violence (Dickerson, 2018).

As the debate over immigration became increasingly heated, the Trump administration issued a report in February 2018 listing 15 individuals accused or convicted of terrorism-related charges who either were admitted into the United States through the diversity visa lottery or family reunion program. The release highlighted Akayed Ullah, a Bangladeshi-born immigrant who ignited a pipe bomb in the New York City subway in December 2017 and Sayufullo Saipov, a Uzbekistan-born immigrant who killed eight people when he drove a truck onto a bike lane in New York City (discussed in Chapter 11). Studies indicate that immigrants are less likely than those born in the United States to commit crimes and much less likely to be imprisoned than those born in the United States.

FUTURE CHALLENGES

The ever-changing nature of events and the difficulty of anticipating events make the future virtually impossible to predict. However, it can confidently be predicted that over the next few years, the United States will confront a new map of terrorism. Terrorism is increasingly spreading to African countries like Nigeria, Chad, Kenya, and Somalia. The competition between Saudi Arabia and Iran, between Israel and Palestine, and between competing factions in Syria will continue to be a source of instability and proxy wars in the Middle East.

A free and open Internet will continue to provide a mechanism to radicalize and to recruit terrorists. Experts note that ISIS, despite losing a territorial base, will continue to represent an ideology that will inspire adherents. The splintering of ISIS will likely lead to asymmetrical low-level attacks by ISIS and ISIS-inspired lone wolves on so-called soft targets that are difficult to defend or to anticipate.

The great danger is that nuclear weapons technology will continue to proliferate, and the risk increases that these weapons fall into the hands of terrorists. There also is the very real threat posed to the United States by North Korea and Iran.

Global instability, regional wars, a weak global economy, the gap between the poor and the wealthy, and environmental crises will continue to fuel immigration and place pressure on Western societies to admit refugees. The backlash against immigration, when combined with a growing gap between rich and poor, may mean a continued drift towards nationalistic and intolerant policies in the United States and in Europe. In addition to domestic terrorism, American democracy remains under threat from Russian and other foreign efforts to promote political and racial divisions and to undermine confidence in American institutions.

There is the constant danger that in an effort to control and to curtail terrorism, individual freedom will be restricted. The ability of governments to monitor individuals though technology and the Internet gives regimes an unprecedented ability to track individuals' activities and communications. Striking the balance between freedom, liberty, and security will continue to pose a challenge.

Appendix

MAP OF AFGHANISTAN

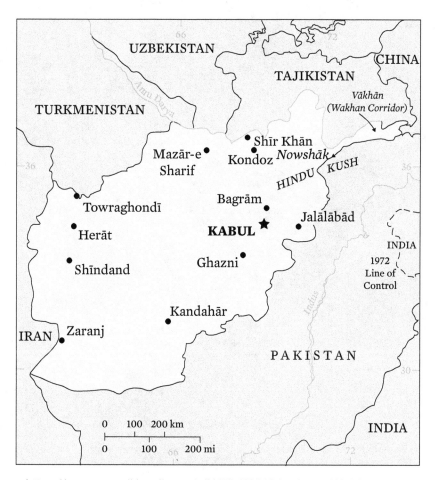

Source: https://commons.wikimedia.org/wiki/File%3AAfghanistan-CIA_WFB_Map.png.

MAP OF AFRICA

Source: https://commons.wikimedia.org/wiki/File%3A%22Political_Africa%22_CIA_World_Factbook.jpg.

MAP OF ASIA

MAP OF CENTRAL AMERICA

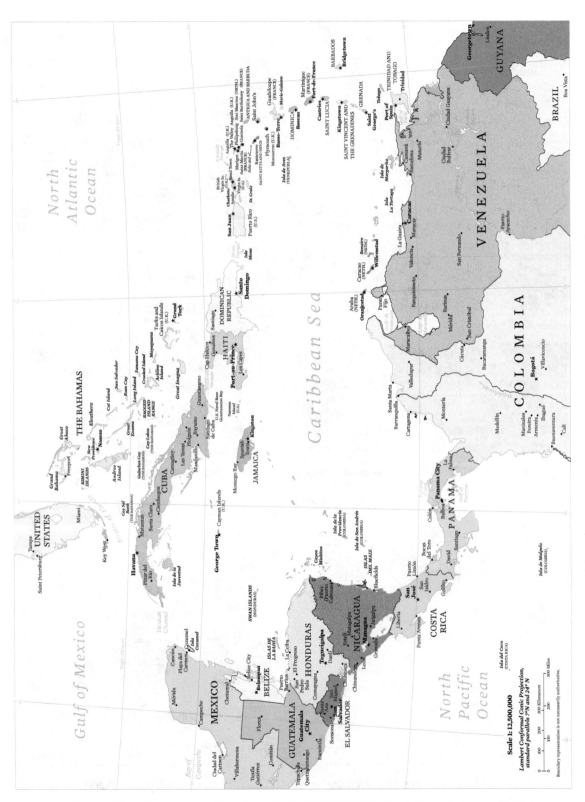

MAP OF EUROPE

Source: https://commons.wikimedia.org/wiki/File%3A%22Political_Europe%22_CIA_World_Factbook.jpg.

MAP OF ISRAEL

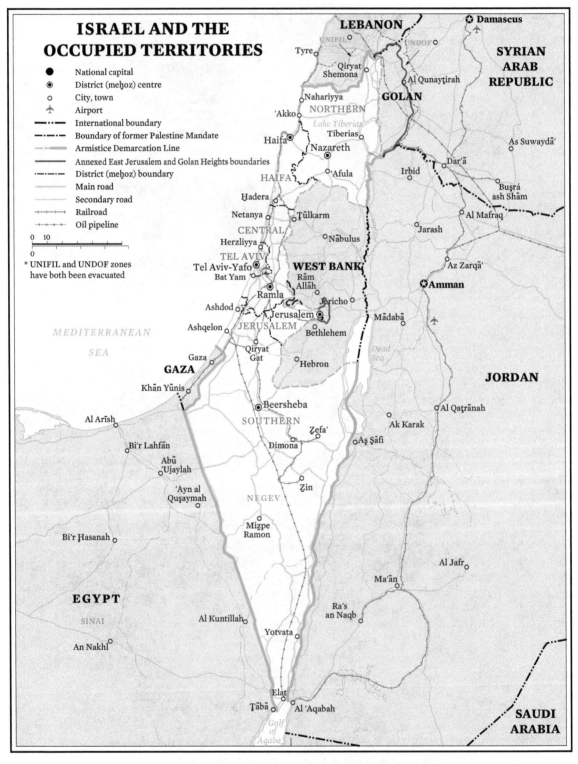

MAP OF OCEANIA

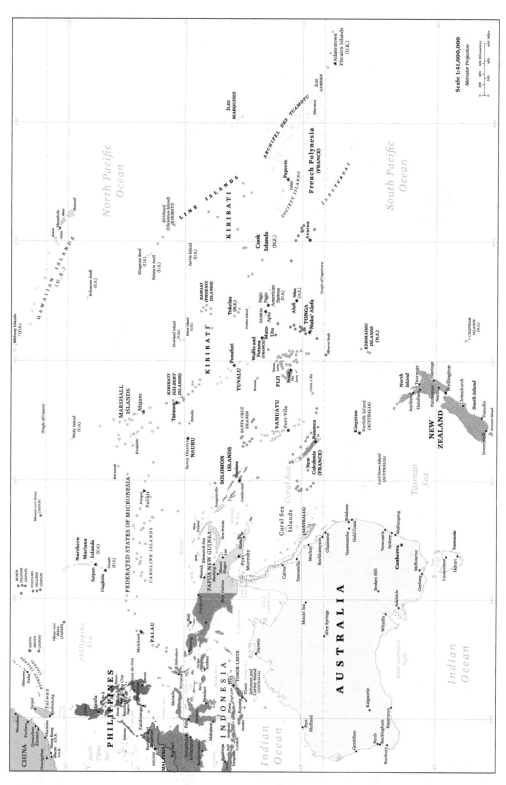

MAP OF SOUTH AMERICA

MAP OF THE MIDDLE EAST

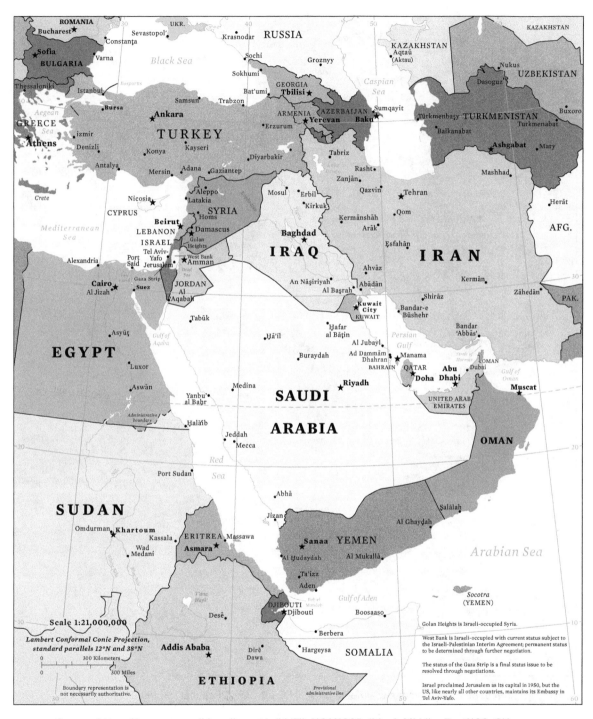

Source: https://commons.wikimedia.org/wiki/File%3A%22Political_Middle_East%22_CIA_World_Factbook.jpg.

MAP OF SOUTHEAST ASIA

Source: https://commons.wikimedia.org/wiki/File%3A%22Political_Southeast_Asia%22.
jpg.

MAP OF LIBYA

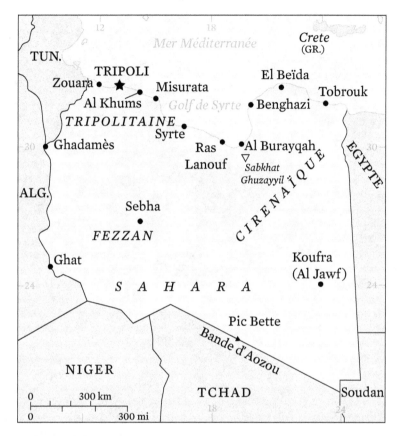

MAP OF T

CAL WORLD

Antarctica

MAP OF SYRIA

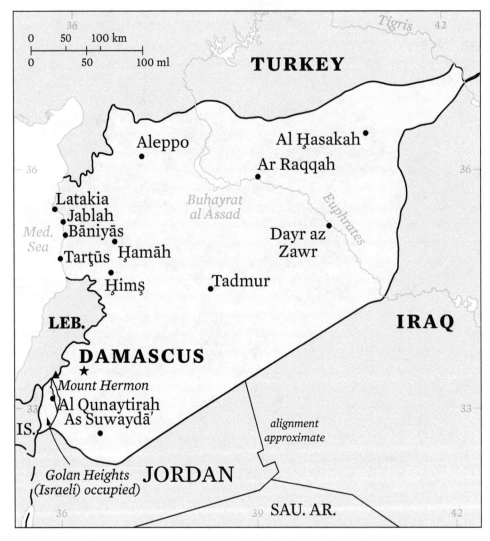

Source: https://commons.wikimedia.org/wiki/File%3ASyria-CIA_WFB_Map.png.

MAP OF THE UNITED STATES

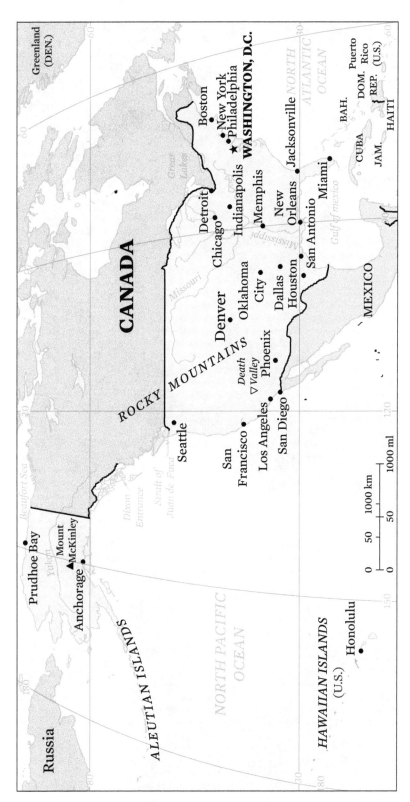

Source: https://commons.wikimedia.org/wiki/File%3AUs-map.png.

References

Abrams, M. (2014). Suicide terrorism is a political failure. In S. Gottlieb (Ed.), *Debating terrorism and counterterrorism: Conflicting perspectives on causes, contexts, and responses* (pp. 152–171). Thousand Oaks, CA: Sage.

Adams, J. (1986). *Financing of terrorism*. New York, NY: Simon & Schuster.

Agnew, R. (2010). A general strain theory of terrorism. *Theoretical Criminology, 14*(2), 131–153.

Aderman, L. (2018, June 29). France indicts cement giant on charge of aiding terror groups in Syria. *New York Times*.

Allison, G. (2004). *Nuclear terrorism: The ultimate preventable catastrophe*. New York, NY: Holt.

Almukhtar, S. (2018, April 14). Aid group says Syria has often used gas on civilians. *New York Times*.

American Civil Liberties Union. (2004). Sanctioning bias: Racial profiling since 9/11. Retrieved from https://www.aclu.org/files/FilesPDFs/racial%20profiling%20report.pdf

American Declaration of Independence. (1776). USHistory.org. Retrieved from http://www.ushistory.org/declaration/document

Anti-Defamation League. (2017). *Murder and extremism in the United States*. New York, NY: Anti-Defamation League. Retrieved from https://www.adl.org/resources/reports/murder-and-extremism-in-the-united-states-in-2017

Argentine National Commission on the Disappeared. (1986). *Nunca mas: The Report of the Argentine National Commission on the Disappeared*. New York, NY: Farrar, Straus and Giroux.

Armstrong, T., & Matusitz, J. (2013). Hezbolah as a group phenomenon: Differential association theory. *Journal of Human Behavior in the Social Environment, 23*(4), 475–484.

Atkins, K., & Winfree, I. T., Jr. (2017). Social learning theory and becoming a terrorist: New challenges for a general theory. In J. Horgan & K. Braddock (Eds.), *Terrorism studies: A reader* (pp. 133–149). New York, NY: Routledge.

Baker, P. (2018, March 16). White House puts new sanctions on Moscow over election meddling and cyberattacks. *New York Times*.

Baker, P., & Davis, J. H. (2018, April 24). Trump signals openness to a "new deal" to constrain Iran. *New York Times*.

Balfour Declaration. (1917). Avalon Project. Retrieved from http://avalon.law.yale.edu/20th_century/balfour.asp

Beckman, M. (2016). Which countries' terrorist attacks are ignored by the U.S. media? FiveThirtyEight. Retrieved from https://fivethirtyeight.com/features/which-countries-terrorist-attacks-are-ignored-by-the-u-s-media

Beirich, H., & Buchanan, S. (2018). The year in hate & extremism. *Intelligence Report, 164*, 33–42.

Bellew, K. (2018). *Bring the war home: The white power movement and paramilitary America*. Cambridge, MA: Harvard University Press.

Bennett, D. H. (1988). *The party of fear: From nativist movements to the New Right in American history.* New York, NY: Random House.

Bergin, P. (2016). *United States of jihad: Who are America's homegrown terrorists, and how do we stop them?* New York, NY: Crown.

Bergman, R. (2018). *Rise and kill first: The secret history of Israel's targeted assassinations.* New York, NY: Random House.

Beydoun, K. (2017, October 2). Stephen Paddock a "lone wolf": Our stunning double standard when it comes to race and religion. *Washington Post.*

Bier, D. (2017). Very few vetting failures of terrorists since 9/11. Cato Institute. Retrieved from https://www.cato.org/blog/very-few-immigration-vetting-failures-terrorists-911

Blakeley, R., & Raphael, S. (2016). Targeted killing and drone warfare. In R. Jackson (Ed.), *The Routledge handbook of critical terrorism studies* (pp. 159–160). New York, NY: Routledge.

Bloom, M. (2007). *Dying to kill: The allure of suicide terror.* New York, NY: Columbia University Press.

Boot, M. (2013). *Invisible armies: An epic history of guerilla warfare from ancient times to the present.* New York, NY: Liveright.

Boumediene v. Bush, 553 U.S. 723 (2008).

Bulletin of the Atomic Scientists. (2018). 2018 doomsday clock statement. Retrieved from https://thebulletin.org/2018-doomsday-clock-statement

Bunn, M. (2014). Is nuclear terrorism a real threat? In S. Gottlieb (Ed.), *Debating terrorism and counterterrorism: Conflicting perspectives on causes, contexts, and responses* (pp. 174–187). Thousand Oaks, CA: Sage.

Bureau of Counterterrorism. (2015). *Country reports on terrorism 2015.* Washington, DC: U.S. Department of State.

Bureau of Counterterrorism. (2016). *Country reports on terrorism 2016.* Washington, DC: U.S. Department of State.

Burrough, B. (2015). *Days of rage: America's radical underground, the FBI, and the forgotten age of revolutionary violence.* New York, NY: Penguin.

Bush, G. W. (2001). *Executive Order 13228, Establishing the Office of Homeland Security and the Homeland Security Council.*

Byman, D. (1998). The logic of ethnic terrorism. *Studies in Conflict & Terrorism, 21*(2), 149–169.

Canetti-Nisim, D., Halperin, E., Sharvit, K., & Hobfoll, S. E. (2009). A new stress-based model of political extremism: Personal exposure to terrorism, psychological distress, and exclusionist political attitudes. *Journal of Conflict Resolution, 53*(2), 363–389.

Capron, T. A., & Mizrahi, S. B. (2016). *Terrorism and homeland security: A text/reader.* Thousand Oaks, CA: Sage.

Carr, M. (2007). *The infernal machine: A history of terrorism.* New York, NY: New Press.

Carson, J. V. (2017). Left-wing terrorism: From anarchists to the radical environmental movement and back. In G. LaFree & J. D. Freilich (Eds.), *The handbook of the criminology of terrorism* (pp. 323–338). New York, NY: Wiley.

Cassidy, J. (2016, July 17). Gun laws and terrorism: An American nightmare. *New Yorker.* Retrieved from https://www.newyorker.com/news/john-cassidy/lax-gun-laws-are-becoming-a-national-security-issue

Chaliand, G., & Blin, A. (2016). Zealots and assassins. In G. Chaliand & A. Blin (Eds.), *The history of terrorism: From antiquity to ISIS* (pp. 55–78). Oakland: University of California Press.

Claridge, D. (1996). State terrorism? Applying a definitional model. *Terrorism and Political Violence, 8*(3), 47–63.

Clark, R. V., & Newman, G. R. (2006). *Outsmarting the terrorists*. Westport, CT: Praeger Security International.

Cochrane, J. (2018, May 15). Suicide attacks by families, with children in two. *New York Times*.

Code of Federal Regulations. (n.d.). 28 CFR §544.35.

Cohen, L., & Felson, M. (1979). Social change and crime rate trends: A routine activity approach. *American Sociological Review, 44*(4), 588–608.

Columbia Law School Human Rights Clinic & San'a Center for Strategic Studies. (2017). *Out of the shadows: Recommendations to advance transparency in the use of lethal force*. Retrieved from https://www.outoftheshadowsreport.com/#new-page

Combs, C. C. (2013). *Terrorism in the twenty-first century* (7th ed.). New York, NY: Pearson.

Commission on the Prevention of WMD Proliferation and Terrorism. (2008). *World at risk: The report of the Commission on the Prevention of WMD Proliferation and Terrorism*. Washington, DC: Author.

Cooper, H. H. A. (2001). Terrorism: The problem of definition revisited. *American Behavioral Scientist, 44*(6), 881–893.

Cooper, H. (2018, June 2). American strikes killed nearly 500 civilians in '17. *New York Times*.

Cooper, H., Gibbons-Neff, T., & Hubbard, B. (2018, April 13). U.S., Britain and France strike Syria over suspected chemical weapons attack. *New York Times*.

Coyler v. Skeffington, 265 F. 17 (D. Mass. 1920).

Crenshaw, M. (1972). The logic of ethnic terrorism. *Journal of Conflict Resolution, 16*(3), 383–396.

Crenshaw, M. (2012). The causes of terrorism. In J. Horgan & K. Braddock (Eds.), *Terrorism studies: A reader* (pp. 99–114). New York, NY: Routledge.

Crenshaw, M., & LaFree, G. (2017). *Countering terrorism*. Washington, DC: Brookings Institution Press.

Cronin, A. K. (2011). *How terrorism ends: Understanding the decline and demise of terrorist campaigns*. Princeton, NJ: Princeton University Press.

Crotty, W. J. (1971). Assassinations and their interpretation within the American context. In W. J. Crotty (Ed.), *Assassinations and the political order* (pp. 3–51). New York, NY: Harper & Row.

DeFronzo, J. (2015). *Revolutions and revolutionary movements*. Boulder, CO: Westview.

Dennis v. United States, 341 U.S. 494 (1951).

Detter, I. (2000). *The law of war* (2nd ed.). New York, NY: Cambridge University Press.

De Young, K., & Morello, C. (2018, February 23). U.S. embassy in Israel will move to Jerusalem in mid-May, State Department says. *Washington Post*.

Diamant, J. (2017). American Muslims are concerned but also satisfied with their lives. Pew Research Center. Retrieved from http://www.pewresearch.org/fact-tank/2017/07/26/american-muslims-are-concerned-but-also-satisfied-with-their-lives

Dickerson, C. (2018, July 19). Trump administration seeks to further curb U.S. asylum system. *New York Times*.

Duvall, R. D., & Stohl, M. S. (1988). Government by terrorism. In M. Stohl (Ed.), *The politics of terrorism* (pp. 231–271). New York, NY: Dekker.

Duyvesteyn, I. (2017). How new is the new terrorism? In J. Horgan & K Braddock (Eds.), *Terrorism studies: A reader* (pp. 27–40). New York, NY: Routledge.

Dwyer, J. (2017, May 3). "I want to live it out," says Brink's driver after denied parole. *New York Times.*

Eddy, M. (2018, January 2). German lawmaker who called Muslims "rapist hordes" faces sanctions. *New York Times.*

El-Ghosbashy, T., & Salim, M. (2018, May 10). A deputy to ISIS leader Baghdadi is among 5 key members captured by Iraqi forces. *Washington Post.*

Ellis, R., & Kupperman, T. (2018). Al Qaeda operative sentenced to life in prison. CNN.

Ezekiel, R. S. (2016). An ethnographer looks at neo-Nazi and Klan groups: The racist mind revisited. *American Behavioral Scientist, 46*(1), 51–71.

Fahey, S. (2017). Assessing aerial hijacking as a terrorist tactic. In G. LaFree & J. D. Freilich (Eds.), *The handbook of the criminology of terrorism* (pp. 323–352). New York, NY: Routledge.

Federal Bureau of Investigation (FBI). (2006). *Terrorism 2002–2005.* Retrieved from http://www.fbi.gov/stats-services/publications/terrorism-2002-2005

Feur, A. (2018, June 29). ISIS recruit gets a second chance after years of cooperation with U.S. *New York Times.*

Gaetan, V. (2016, February 9). "Industry of death": Pope Francis on arms dealers and causes of World War III. *National Catholic Register.*

Ganor, B. (2005). *The counter-terrorism puzzle: A guide for decision makers.* Piscataway, NJ: Rutgers University Press.

Gearan, A., & De Young, K. (2018, May 8). Trump pulls United States out of Iran nuclear deal, calling the pact "an embarrassment." *Washington Post.*

Gentry, C., & Sjoberg, L. (2016). Female terrorism and militancy. In R. Jackson (Ed.), *The Routledge handbook of critical terrorism studies* (pp. 145–156). New York, NY: Routledge.

Gerstein, J. (2017, December 4). Supreme Court lets Trump fully impose latest travel ban. *Politico.*

Goodman, M. (2015). *Future crimes: Everything is connected, everyone is vulnerable and what we can do about it.* New York, NY: Doubleday.

Grabosky, P., & Stohl, M. (2010). *Crime and terrorism.* Thousand Oaks, CA: Sage.

Gunaratna, R. (2002). *Inside al Qaeda: Global network of terror.* New York, NY: Berkley Books.

Guiora, A. N. (2011). *Global perspectives on counterterrorism* (2nd ed.). New York, NY: Kluwer.

Gurr, T. R. (1970). *Why men rebel.* Princeton, NJ: Princeton University Press.

Gurr, T. R. (1989). Protest and rebellion in the 1960s: The United States in world perspective. In T. R. Gurr (Ed.), *Violence in America* (Vol. 2, pp. 101–130). Newbury Park, CA: Sage.

Haag, M. (2018, July 3). Man arrested in terror plot after a sting. *New York Times.*

Haag, M., & Bromwich, E. (2017, September 14.) Harvard disinvites Chelsea Manning and the feeling is mutual. *New York Times.*

Hacker, F. J. (1976). *Criminals, crazies, terror and terrorism in our time.* New York, NY: Norton.

Halbfinger, D. M., & Patel, J. K. (2018, April 14). 300 meters in Gaza: snipers, burning tires and a contested fence. *New York Times.*

Halbfinger, D. M., & Abuheweila, I. (2018, April 14). One Killed, hundreds injured at Gaza-Israel fence in 3rd protest week. *New York Times.*

Hamdan v. Rumsfeld, 54 U.S. 557 (2006).

Hamm, M. S. (2013). *The spectacular few: Prisoner radicalization and the evolving terrorist threat.* New York, NY: New York University Press.

Hamm, M. S., & Spaaij, R. (2017). *The age of lone wolf terrorism*. New York, NY: Columbia University Press.

Hartmann, M. (2013, August 15). Ahead of his sentencing, Bradley Manning says "I'm sorry I hurt the United States." *New York Times Magazine*.

Hastings, M. (2012, June 7). Bowe Bergdahl: America's last prisoner of war. *Rolling Stone*.

Hjelmgaard, K. (2018, March 26). U.S. expels 60 Russian diplomats after Sergei Skripal poisoning: What we know. *USA Today*.

Higham, S., & Nakashima, E. (2015, July 16). Why the Islamic State leaves tech companies torn between free speech and security. *Washington Post*.

Hoffman, B. (2006). *Inside terrorism* (Rev. ed.). New York, NY: Columbia University Press.

Honderich, T. (2002). *After the terror*. Edinburgh, Scotland: Edinburgh University Press.

Horgan, J. (2014). *The psychology of terrorism*. New York, NY: Routledge.

Howden, D. (2013, October 4). Terror in Nairobi: The full story behind al-Shabaab's mall attack. *Guardian*.

Hubac-Occhipinti, O. (2016). Anarchist terrorists of the nineteenth century. In G. Chaliand & A. Blin (Eds.), *The history of terrorism: From antiquity to ISIS* (pp. 113–151). Oakland: University of California Press.

Hubbard, D. G. (1971). *The skyjacker: His flights of fantasy*. New York, NY: Macmillan.

Hudson, R. A. (1999). *Who becomes a terrorist and why: The 1999 government report on profiling terrorism*. Guilford, CT: Lyon Press.

Human Rights First. (2013). President Obama's record-breaking arms sales are enabling human rights abuses. Retrieved from https://www.humanrightsfirst.org/blog/president-obamas-record-breaking-arms-sales-are-enabling-human-rights-abuses

Ignatius, D. (2018, March 1). Are Saudi Arabia's reforms for real? A recent visitor says yes. *Washington Post*.

In re Milligan, 71 U.S. (4 Wall) 2 (1866).

Israel Supreme Court. (1999). Judgment concerning the legality of the GSS's interrogation methods.

Jackson, R., Jarvis, L., Gunning, J., & Breen-Smyth, M. (2011). *Terrorism: A critical introduction*. New York, NY: Palgrave Macmillan.

Jaffer, J. (Ed.). (2016). *The drone memos: Targeted killing, secrecy and the law*. New York, NY: New Press.

Jenkins, B. (1981). *The psychological implications of media-covered terrorism*. Santa Monica, CA: Rand Corporation.

Jetter, M. (2017). The effect of media attention on terrorism. *Journal of Public Economics, 153*, 32–48.

Jiang, B. (2017). An empirical analysis of maritime terrorism using the global terrorism database In J. Horgan & K. Braddock (Eds.), *Terrorism studies: A reader* (pp. 433–449). New York, NY: Routledge.

Jones, A. (2017). *Genocide: A comprehensive introduction* (3rd ed.). New York, NY: Routledge.

Juergensmeyer, M. (2003). *Terror in the mind of God: The global rise of religious violence* (3rd ed.). Berkeley: University of California Press.

Kerns, E., Betus, A., & Lemieux, A. (2017). Why do some terrorist attacks receive more media attention than others? *Justice Quarterly*. Retrieved from https://papers.ssrn.com/sol3/papers.cfm?abstract_id=2928138

Kershner, I. (2018, July 4). Israelis vote to penalize payments for "martyrs." *New York Times*.

LaFree, G., & Bersani, B. E. (2014). Country-level correlates of terrorist attacks in the United States. *Criminology & Public Policy, 13*(3), 455–481.

Lamothe, D. (2015, September 18). General: "Unrealistically idealistic" Bowe Bergdahl does not deserve jail. *Washington Post.*

Landler, M. (2018, February 16). In pursuit of peace, friction with Israel. *New York Times.*

Laqueur, W. (1999). *The new terrorism: Fanaticism and the arms of mass destruction.* New York, NY: Oxford University Press.

Laqueur, W. (2001). *A history of terrorism.* Piscataway, NJ: Transaction.

Law, R. (2016). *Terrorism: A history* (2nd ed.). New York, NY: Polity.

Lesser, I. O., Hoffman, B., Arquilla, J., Ronfeldt, D., & Zanini, M. (1999). *Countering the new terrorism.* Santa Monica, CA: Rand Corporation.

Levitas, D. (2002). *The terrorist next door: The militia movement and the radical right.* New York, NY: Dunne.

Lewis, J. W. (2012). *The business of martyrdom: A history of suicide bombing.* Annapolis, MD: Naval Institute Press.

Lifton, R. J. (1999). *Destroying the world to save it: Aum Shinrikyo, apocalyptic violence and the new terrorism.* New York, NY: Picador.

Lippman, M. (1993). Vietnam: A Twenty Year Retrospective. *Dickinson Journal of International Law, 11,* 325–421.

Lippman, M. (2007). Darfur: The politics of genocide denial syndrome. *Journal of Genocide Research, 9*(2), 193–213.

Lippman, M. (2016). *Criminal procedure* (3rd ed.). Thousand Oaks, CA: Sage.

Luna, E., & McCormack, W. (2015). *Understanding the law of terrorism* (2nd ed.). Durham, NC: Carolina Academic Press.

Mandala, M. (2017). Terrorist assassinations: A criminological perspective. In J. Horgan & K. Braddock (Eds.), *Terrorism studies: A reader* (pp. 353–369). New York, NY: Routledge.

Martin, G. (2016). *Understanding terrorism: Challenges, perspectives, and issues* (5th ed.). Thousand Oaks, CA: Sage.

Masco, J. (2014). *The theater of operations: National security affect from the Cold War to the War on Terror.* Durham, NC: Duke University Press.

Masters, D. (2008). The origin of terrorist threats: Religious, separatist, or something else? *Terrorism and Political Violence, 20*(3), 396–414.

Matusitz, J. (2013). *Terrorism & communication: A critical introduction.* Thousand Oaks, CA: Sage.

Mazetti, M., & Benner, K. (2018, July 13). 12 Russian agents indicted in Mueller investigation. *New York Times.*

Matusitz, J. (2015). *Symbolism in terrorism: Motivation, communication and behavior.* Lanham, MD: Rowman & Littlefield.

McAllister, B., & Schmid, A. P. (2011). Theories of terrorism. In A. P. Schmid (Ed.), *The Routledge handbook of terrorism research* (pp. 201–271). New York, NY: Routledge.

McCants, W. (2015). *The ISIS apocalypse: The history, strategy, and doomsday vision of the Islamic State.* New York, NY: St. Martin's Press.

McConville, S. (2003). *Irish political prisoners 1848–1922.* New York, NY: Routledge.

McConville, S. (2014). *Irish political prisoners 1920–1962.* New York, NY: Routledge.

McKinley, J., Jr. (2018, April 27). Getaway driver in Brink's heist merits new parole hearing, judge rules. *New York Times.*

Meisels, T. (2014). Terrorist violence is never justified. In S. Gottlieb (Ed.), *Debating terrorism and counterterrorism: Conflicting perspectives on causes, contexts, and responses* (pp. 71–82). Thousand Oaks, CA: Sage.

Merari, A. (1993). Terrorism as a strategy of insurgency. *Terrorism and Political Violence, 5*(4), 213–251.

Merari, A. (1998). The readiness to kill and die: Suicidal terrorism in the Middle East. In W. Reich (Ed.), *The origins of terrorism: Psychologies, ideologies, theologies, states of mind* (pp. 192–210). Washington, DC: Wilson Center.

Miller, M. A. (2013). *The foundations of modern terrorism: State, society and the dynamics of political violence.* New York, NY: Cambridge University Press.

Miroff, N. (2018, January 9). What's TPS and what will happen to the 200,000 Salvadorans whose status is revoked? *Washington Post.*

Mozur, P. (2018, July 9). With cameras and A.I., China closes its grip. *New York Times.*

Mueller, J. (2006). *Overblown: How politicians and the terrorism industry inflate national security threats, and why we believe them.* New York, NY: Free Press.

Mueller, J., & Stewart, M. G. (2011). *Terror, security, and money: Balancing the risks, benefits, and costs of homeland security.* New York, NY: Oxford University Press.

Mueller, J., & Stewart, M. G. (2016). *Chasing ghosts: The policing of terrorism.* New York, NY: Oxford University Press.

Nacos, B. L. (2013). The portrayal of female terrorists in the media. In S. Mahan & P. L. Griset (Eds.), *Terrorism in perspective* (3rd ed., pp. 249–272). Thousand Oaks, CA: Sage.

Nacos, B. L. (2016). *Mass-mediated terrorism: Mainstream and digital media in terrorism and counterterrorism.* Lanham, MD: Rowman & Littlefield.

Nacos, B. L., Bloch-Elkon, Y., & Shapiro, R. Y. (2011). *Selling fear: Counterterrorism, the media, and public opinion.* Chicago, IL: University of Chicago Press.

Nakashima, E. (2011, March 5). In brig, WikiLeaks suspect Bradley Manning ordered to sleep without clothing. *Washington Post.*

National Advisory Commission on Civil Disorders. (1968). *Report of the National Advisory Commission on Civil Disorders* (Kerner Report). Washington, DC: U.S. Government Printing Office.

National Commission on Terrorist Attacks Upon the United States. (2002). *The 9/11 Commission Report: Final report of the National Commission on Terrorist Attacks Upon the United States.* New York, NY: Norton.

Nelson, L. (2017, January 26). Trump calls Chelsea Manning an "ungrateful traitor." *Politico.*

Nixon, R. (2018, April 18). Want "extreme vetting"? U.S. has had it for years. *New York Times.*

Norris J. J., & Grol-Prokopczyk, H. (2015). Estimating the prevalence of entrapment in post-911 terrorism cases. *Journal of Criminal Law and Criminology, 105*(3), 609–677.

Nordland, R., & Sukhanyar, J. (2018, July 18). Taliban leaders declare a halt to bombings in civilian areas. *New York Times.*

Nowrasteh, A. (2016). Terrorism and immigration: A risk analysis. Policy Analysis No. 798, Cato Institute. Retrieved from https://www.cato.org/publications/policy-analysis/terrorism-immigration-risk-analysis

Office of the Inspector General. (2003). *A review of the treatment of aliens held on immigration charges in connection with the investigation of the September 11 attacks.* Washington, DC: U.S. Department of Justice.

O'Malley, P. (1990). *Biting at the grave: The Irish hunger strikers and the politics of despair.* Boston, MA: Beacon Press.

Oppel, R., Jr. (2017, October 16). Bergdahl, called a "traitor" by President Trump, pleads guilty. *New York Times.*

Pape, R. (2005). *Dying to win: The strategic logic of suicide terrorism.* New York, NY: Random House.

Pape, R., & Feldman, J. (2010). *Cutting the fuse: The explosion of global suicide terrorism & how to stop it.* Chicago, IL: University of Chicago Press.

Parkin, W. (2017). Victimization theories and terrorism. In J. Horgan & K. Braddock (Eds.), *Terrorism studies: A reader* (pp. 162–174). New York, NY: Routledge.

Patrikarakos, D. (2017). *War in 140 characters: How social media is reshaping conflict in the twenty-first century.* New York, NY: Basic Books.

People v. Morales, 982 N.E.2d 580 (N.Y. 2012).

Perez-Pena, R. (2018, June 29). Britain abetted torture of terrorism suspects by the U.S., Parliament finds. *New York Times.*

Perlroth, N. (2018, May 11). Without constraints on Tehran, experts warn of Iranian cyberattacks. *New York Times.*

Piazza, J. (2014). Poverty is a weak causal link. In S. Gottlieb (Ed.), *Debating terrorism and counterterrorism* (2nd ed., pp. 35–51). Thousand Oaks, CA: Sage.

Pilkington, E. (2013, July 31). Bradley Manning verdict cleared of "aiding the enemy" but guilty of other charges. *Guardian.*

Pilkington, E. (2018, May 2). Guantánamo prisoner released in surprise move by Trump administration. *Guardian.*

Poitras, L., & Greenwald, G. (2013, June 9). Whistleblower Edward Snowden: "I don't want to live in a society that does these sorts of things"—video. *Guardian.*

Pomper, P. (2001). Russian revolutionary terrorism. In M. Crenshaw (Ed.), *Terrorism in context* (pp. 63–104). University Park, PA: Penn State University Press.

Porter, E., & Russell, K. (2018, June 23). Migrants are on the rise around the world, and myths about them are shaping attitudes. *New York Times.*

Post, J. M. (2007). *The mind of the terrorist: The psychology of terrorism from the IRA to al-Qaeda.* New York, NY: St. Martin's Griffin.

Power, S. (2002). *"A problem from hell": America and the age of genocide.* New York, NY: Basic Books.

Presidential Policy Guidance. (2013). Procedures for approving direct action against terrorist targets located outside the United States and areas of active hostilities.

Qui, L. (2017, October 18). Can Trump claim credit for gaining on ISIS? *New York Times*

Quinney, R. (1970). *The social reality of crime.* Boston, MA: Little, Brown.

Rapoport, D. C. (1990). Sacred terror: A contemporary example from Islam. In W. Reich (Ed.), *The origins of terrorism: Psychologies, ideologies, theologies, states of mind* (pp. 103–130). Washington, DC: Wilson Center.

Rapoport, D. C. (2012). Fear and trembling: Terror in three religious traditions. In J. Horgan & K. Braddack (Eds.), *Terrorism studies: A reader* (pp. 41–62). New York, NY: Routledge.

Rasul v. Bush, 542 U.S. 466 (2004).

Reilly, S. (2015, March 24). Bracing for a big power grid attack: "One is too many." *USA Today.*

Richardson, L. (2006). *What terrorists want: Understanding the enemy, containing the threat.* New York, NY: Random House.

Risen, J., & Lichtblau, E. (2005, December 16). Bush lets U.S. spy on callers without courts. *New York Times.*

Roose, K., & Mozur, P. (2018, April 10). Hate messages in Myanmar get long-awaited response. *New York Times.*

Ryan, J. (2007). The four p-words of militant Islamist radicalization and recruitment: Persecution, precedent, piety, and perseverance. *Studies in Conflict and Terrorism, 30,* 985–1011.

Sageman, M. (2004). *Understanding terror networks.* Philadelphia: University of Pennsylvania Press.

Sageman, M. (2008). *Leaderless jihad terror networks in the twenty-first century.* Philadelphia: University of Pennsylvania Press.

Sanger, E. D. (2018a, April 28). Two Koreas unite in goal to banish nuclear weapons: Parameters are set for Trump meeting. *New York Times.*·

Sanger, E. D. (2018b, June 18). U.S. easing reins on cyberattacks. *New York Times.*

Sang-Hun, C. (2018, April 28). Two Koreas unite in goal to banish nuclear weapons: Kim and Moon vow to forge official end to the war. *New York Times.*

Savage, C. (2017a). *Misunderstanding terrorism.* Philadelphia: University of Pennsylvania Press.

Savage, C. (2017b, January 17). Obama commutes bulk of Chelsea Manning's sentence. *New York Times.*

Savage, C. (2018, February 20). U.S. misses deadline to repatriate detainees who pleaded guilty. *New York Times.*

Schmid, A. P. (2011). The definition of terrorism. In A. P. Schmid (Ed.), *The Routledge handbook of terrorism research* (pp. 39–98). New York, NY: Routledge.

Schmid, A. P. (2017). The response problem as a definition problem. In J. Horgan & K. Braddock (Eds.), *Terrorism studies: A reader* (pp. 91–96). New York, NY: Routledge.

Schmid, A. P., & de Graaf, J. (1982). *Violence as communication: Insurgent terrorism and the Western news media.* Beverly Hills, CA: Sage.

Schmid, A. P., & Jongman, A. J. (2005). *Political violence: A new guide to actors, authors, concepts, data bases, theory, and literature.* Piscataway, NJ: Transaction.

Schmitt, E., & Savage, C. (2014, May 31). American soldier freed by Taliban in prisoner trade. *New York Times.*

Seib, P., & Janbeck, D. M. (2011). *Global terrorism and new media: The post–al Qaeda generation (media, war and security).* New York, NY: Routledge.

Selerstad, A. (2016). *One of us: The story of a massacre in Norway—and its aftermath* (reprint edition; S. Death, Trans.). New York, NY: Farrar, Straus and Giroux.

Shaer, T. (2017, June 13). The long lonely road of Chelsea Manning. *New York Times Magazine.*

Sharif, S., & Adamou, L. (2018). Taliban threaten 70% of Afghanistan, BBC finds. BBC.

Shane, S. (2017, November 12). In "watershed moment" YouTube blocks extremist cleric's message. *New York Times.*

Shear, D. M., Nixon, R., & Benner, K. (2018, June 23). Migrants order tosses a wrench into the system. *New York Times.*

Siddiqui, S. (2018, April 15). Supreme Court appears to lean in favor of Trump's right to impose travel ban. *Guardian.*

Simi, P., & Bubolz, B. F. (2017). Far right terrorism in the United States. In G. LaFree & J. D. Freilich (Eds.), *The handbook of the criminology of terrorism* (pp. 297–309). New York, NY: Wiley.

Simon, J. D. (2016). *Lone wolf terrorism: Understanding the growing threat.* New York, NY: Prometheus Books.

Singer, P. W., & Friedman, A. (2014). *Cybersecurity and cyberwar: What everyone needs to know*. New York, NY: Oxford University Press.

Slutka, J. (Ed.). (2000). *Death squads: An anthropology of state terrorism*. Philadelphia: University of Pennsylvania Press.

Smith, B. L. (1994). *Terrorism in America: Pipe bombs and pipe dreams*. Albany: State University of New York Press.

Smith, M. (2018, April 19). Verdict is guilty for men in plot to bomb migrants. *New York Times*.

Soufan, A. (2017). *Anatomy of terror: From the death of Bin Laden to the rise of the Islamic State*. New York, NY: Norton.

Springzak, E. (2012). "Right-wing terrorism in a comparative perspective:" The case of split delegitimization,. In J. Horgan & K. Braddock (Eds.), *Terrorism studies: A reader* (pp. 187–205). New York, NY: Routledge. (Original work published 2005)

Stack, L. (2017, September 13). Sean Spicer and Chelsea Manning join Harvard as visiting fellows. *New York Times*.

Stampnitsky, L. (2013). *Disciplining terrorism: How experts invented "terrorism."* New York, NY: Cambridge University Press.

Stein, S. (2014, June 3). The Bowe Bergdahl controversy could be politics at its very worst. *Huffington Post*.

Stern, J., & Berger, J. M. (2015). *ISIS: The state of terror*. New York, NY: HarperCollins.

Stohl, M. S. (2006). The state as terrorist: Purposes and types. *Democracy and Society, 1*, 1–25.

Sutherland, E. H. (1939). *Principles of criminology* (3rd ed.). Philadelphia, PA: Lippincott.

Swaine, J. (2013, August 4). Fort Hood shooter Nidal Hasan "left free" to kill. *Telegraph*.

Tan, R. (2017). Terrorists' love for Telegram explained. *Vox*.

Tate, J. (2013, August 21). Judge sentences Bradley Manning to 35 years. *Washington Post*.

Tau, B. (2015, December 8). No-fly list is only one of many U.S. watchlists. *Wall Street Journal*.

Taylor, L. (2017, May 9). Nearly 10,000 Yazidis killed, kidnapped by Islamic State in 2014, study finds. *Reuters*.

Terrorist Research and Analytical Center. (1996). *Terrorism in the United States 1995*. Washington, DC: U.S. Department of Justice.

Townshend, C. (2011). *Terrorism: A very short introduction*. New York, NY: Oxford University Press.

Toy, E. V., Jr. (1989). Right-wing extremism: From the Ku Klux Klan to the Order, 1915–1988. In T. R. Gurr (Ed.), *Violence in America* (Vol. 2, pp. 131–152). Newbury Park, CA: Sage.

Trump, D. (2017). Remarks by President Donald Trump at the 9/11 Memorial observance. WhiteHouse.gov. Retrieved from https://www.whitehouse.gov/briefings-statements/remarks-president-trump-9-11-memorial-observance

United Nations. (1945). UN charter. Retrieved from http://www.un.org/en/sections/un-charter/un-charter-full-text

United Nations. (1960). Declaration on the granting of independence to colonial countries and people. Resolution 1514 (XV).

United Nations. (2002). *Report of the Ad Hoc Committee established by General Assembly Resolution 51/210 of 17 December 1996*. Sixth Session (January28–February 1). General Assembly, Official Records, 57th Session, Supplement no. 37 (A/57/37).

United Nations Office of the High Commissioner for Human Rights. (2014). Myanmar: UN expert raises alarm on Rakhine State. News release. Retrieved from http://www.ohchr.org/EN/NewsEvents/Pages/DisplayNews.aspx?NewsID=14476&

U.S. Code, Title 18, Section 3077 (n.d.).

U.S. Congress. (1978). *Foreign Intelligence Surveillance Act.* Retrieved from https://www.law.cornell.edu/uscode/text/50/chapter-36

U.S. Congress. (2001a). *Authorization for the use of military force.* Retrieved from https://www.congress.gov/107/plaws/publ40/PLAW-107publ40.pdf

U.S. Congress. (2001b). *Uniting and Strengthening America by Providing Appropriate Tools Required to Intercept and Obstruct Terrorism Act of 2001* (PATRIOT Act). Retrieved from https://www.uscis.gov/ilink/docView/PUBLAW/HTML/PUBLAW/0-0-0-24178.html

U.S. Congress. (2005). *Detainee Treatment Act.* Retrieved from https://www.dni.gov/index.php/ic-legal-reference-book/detainee-treatment-act-of-2005

U.S. Congress. (2006). *Military Commissions Act.* Retrieved from https://www.loc.gov/rr/frd/Military_Law/pdf/PL-109–366.pdf

U.S. Department of Defense. (2010). *Dictionary of military and associated terms.* Washington, DC: Author.

U.S. Department of Justice. (2002). *Memorandum for Alberto Gonzalez: Counsel to the president.* Office of Legal Counsel. Retrieved from https://nsarchive2.gwu.edu/NSAEBB/NSAEBB127/020801.pdf

U.S. Holocaust Museum. (2015). *"They want us all to go away:" Early warning signs of genocide in Burma.* Washington, DC: Author. Retrieved from https://www.ushmm.org/m/pdfs/20150505-Burma-Report.pdf

U.S. Senate, Select Committee on Intelligence. (2014). *The Senate Intelligence Committee report on torture: Committee study of the Central Intelligence Agency's detention and interrogation program.* Brooklyn, NY: Melville House.

Walzer, M. (2015). *Just and unjust wars: A moral argument with historical illustrations.* New York, NY: Basic Books.

Warrick, J. (2015). *Black flags: The rise of ISIS.* New York, NY: Anchor Books.

Webber, D., & Kruglanski, A. W. (2017). Psychological factors in radicalization: A "3N" approach. In J. Horgan & K. Braddock (Eds.), *Terrorism Studies: A Reader* (pp. 33–46). New York, NY: Routledge.

Weimann, G., & Winn, C. (1994). *The theater of terror: Mass media and international terrorism.* New York, NY: Longman.

Weinberg, L., Pedahzur, A., & Hirsch-Hoefler, S. (2012). The challenges of conceptualizing terrorism. In J. Horgan & K. Braddock (Eds.), *Terrorism studies: A reader* (pp. 76–90). New York, NY: Routledge.

White, J. R. (2017). *Terrorism and homeland security* (9th ed.). Boston, MA: Cengage Learning.

Whittaker, D. J. (2012). *The terrorism reader* (4th ed.). New York, NY: Routledge.

Wikileaks. (2010). Secret U.S. Embassy cables. Retrieved from https://wikileaks.org/Press-Release-Secret-US-Embassy.html

Wilkinson, P. (2011). *Terrorism versus democracy the liberal state response* (3rd ed.). New York, NY: Routledge.

Wintour, P. (2018a, March 6). Gulf states considering plans to bring end to Saudi-led Qatar. *Guardian.*

Wintour, P. (2018b, July 17). Helsinki summit: What did Trump and Putin agree? *Guardian.*

Wood, G. (2017). *The way of the strangers: Encounters with the Islamic State.* New York, NY: Random House.

Wong., K. (2016, March 17). Army: Bergdahl had mental illness when he walked off post. *The Hill.*

Wright, L. (2006). *The looming tower: Al-Qaeda and the road to 9/11.* New York, NY: Knopf.

Wright, L. (2016). *The terror years: From Al-Qaeda to the Islamic State.* New York, NY: Knopf.

Index

A

Abdulazeez, Muhammad Youssef, 257–258
Abedi, Salman, 64, 83
Abrams, Max, 88
absolute deprivation, 40
Adams, James, 71
African American Liberation Movements, 208
African National Congress (ANC), 39
air hijackings, 66
aji, Abu Bakr, 143
al-Adnani, Mohammed, 159
al-Awlaki, Anwar, 3, 92, 244–245
al-Baghdadi, Abu Bakr, 60, 156
Alcohol, Tobacco, Firearms and Explosives (ATF), 252
Alexandrovich, Sergei, 84
Alfred P. Murrah Federal Building, 35
Algeria, 124–125
Alien and Sedition Acts, 264–265
alienation, 30
Alien Enemies Act, 265
Alien Friendly Act, 265
al-Jihad, 48, 50
Allison, Graham, 77
al Qaeda, 14, 16, 19, 70, 147–150
  Egyptian Islamic Jihad, 148
  guerilla warfare branch, 73
  honey trade, 149
  sleeper cells, 248
  training camp, 28

Al Qaeda in the Arabian Peninsula (AQAP), 151
Al Qaeda in the Islamic Maghreb (AQIM), 151
al Qaeda University of Jihad Studies, 240
al Shabaab, 92, 152
Al-Turabi, 19
al-Zarqawi, Abu Musab, 154–155
al-Z awahiri, Ayman, 48–51, 49
American Airlines Flight, 219
American Cultural Center, 28
American Federation of Scientists, 80
American Flight, 220
American humanitarian organizations, 170
anarchism, 102–104, 204–205
Anarchist bombing of Paris Café, 228
Animal Liberation Front (ALF), 215–217
Ansar al-Sharia (Libya), 152
Ansar al-Sharia (Tunisia), 152–153
Ansar Bait al Maqdis, 152
anticolonial terrorism, 120
anti-Klan law, 196
1996 Anti-Terrorism and Effective Death Penalty Act, 255–256
apocalyptic narratives, 144–145
Arafat, Yasser, 89, 111
Árbenz, Jacobo, 131
Ariana Grande concert, 64

Armed Forces of National Liberation (FALN), 210–211
Armstrong, Taylor, 41
Aryan Nations, 200
assassinations, 65
assassins, 83, 97, 98
asymmetrical warfare, 65
Atta, Mohamed, 31
Authorization for the Use of Military Force (AUMF), 273
Azimov, Khmzat, 62

B

Baader-Meinhof gang, 69
Balfour, Arthur James, 110
Basque Nation and Identity (ETA), 121
  symbol, 121
Basque separatists (ETA), 21–22
Bataclan and Nice attacks, 63
Bataclan theatre, 62
Ben Gurion International Airport, 46
Bergman, Ronen, 115
biological agents, 75–77
biological terrorism, 216–217
Black Panther Party, 208–209
Black Widow suicide bombers, 51
blistering agents, 74, 75
blood and choking agents, 74
Bloom, Mia, 85
Boko Haram, 153
Bonaparte, Napoleon, 101
Bosnian Muslims, 28, 29

351

Bosnian Serbs, 28
Bosnian War, 13
botulism, 82
Bouhlel, Mohamed
    Lahoauiej, 62
Bush, George W., 155

C

Caesar, Julius, 116
caliphate, 141
capital punishment, 173
Carbonari, 101
Carrero, Luis, 121
Carter, Jimmy, 112
Central Intelligence Agency
    (CIA), 183
Cesare Lombroso, 104
Charlie Hebdo, 60–61
Charlie Hebdo attack, 62
Chechen Republic of
    Ichkeria, 123
Chechnya, 123
chemical agents, 74
Chemical And Biological
    Weapons, and
    Radiological and Nuclear
    Weapons (CBRN), 72
chemical weapons, 74–76
    blistering agents, 75
    blood and choking
        agents, 74
    chemical agents, 74
    nerve agents, 74
Chinese communists, 14
Christian Identity (CI)
    movement, 199
civil liberties, 4
    and homeland security,
        269
Civil Rights Workers, 197
civil war, 265
Claridge, David, 172
Clark, Ron, 44
Clinton, Bill, 51
collective strains, 42
Collins, Michael, 109
Colombia, 129–130
Colombian Communist
    Party, 46
Columbia Law School, 55
conflict diamonds, 71

conspiracy theories, 195
counterinsurgency, 109
counterinsurgency
    campaign, 130
counterterrorism, 271
    crime-control approach,
        272
    media coverage of,
        237–239
    war-fighting, 272
coup d'état, 183
Covenant, Sword and Arm
    (CSA), 200
Crenshaw, Martha, 39, 40,
    127
criminal ownership, 102
criminological theories,
    40–47
crisis of confidence stage, 31
crisis of legitimacy phase, 31
critical infrastructure, 252
critical terrorism, 168
Cromitie, James, 56
Crotty, William J., 192
crowded venues, 66
cyberterrorism, 16, 90–92
Cynthia Combs, 51

D

Daesh, 158
Davidians, Branch, 193
Day of Judgment, 138
delegitimization, 22
Democratic People's
    Republic of North Korea,
    186–187
Denial of Service (DoS), 90
Department of Defense, 2
Department of Energy
    (DOE), 252
Department of Health and
    Human Services (DHS),
    252
Department of Homeland
    Security (DHS), 11,
    250–251
    Federal agencies
        incorporated, 251
Department of State, 11
differential association
    theory, 40–41

Diplomatic Security Service
    (DSS), 252
dirty bomb, 79
Disaster. *See* Nakba
domestic and foreign
    intelligence, 253–254
domestic state-sponsored
    terrorism, 173, 179
domestic state terrorism,
    173, 174–175
domestic terrorism, 11,
    315–317
drone warfare, 275–281
Dutch Afrikaners, 39
Duterte, Rodrigo, 169

E

early religious terrorism,
    98–99
Earth Liberation Front
    (ELF), 215–216
Easter Uprising, 108
ecoterrorism, 17
educational rights, 122
Egyptian Islamic Jihad,
    148
electronic media, 227
English Civil War, 99
enhanced interrogation,
    284–286
Ensslin, Gudrun, 51
entrapment, 55
Environmental Protection
    Agency (EPA), 252
ethnonationalist
    communal terrorism,
    125–126
Ethnonationalist separatist
    terrorism, 119–125
Euroarabia, 38
Europe
    religious conflict, 99
    revolutionary terrorism,
        132–133
explosives, 64
external state-sponsored
    terrorism, 182–184,
    185–186
external state terrorism,
    173, 181–182
extrajudicial execution, 173

F

Federal Bureau of
    Investigation's (FBI), 249
federal counterterrorism
    laws, 254–256
Financial Action Task
    Force, 70
financial gain, 36
Finsbury Park Mosque, 67
firearms, 66
Foreign Terrorist
    Organizations (FTO)
    and state sponsors, 256
Fort Hood, 3
Fortier, Michael, 193
Fourteen Words, 200
fourth estate, 237
Freedom Birds, 51
French Calvinist
    Huguenots, 99
French colonial forces, 14
French company Lafarge
    SA, 71
French Revolution, 98, 100–
    102, 134, 139
frustration-aggression
    theory, 33
Furrow, Buford, 41

G

Gandhi, Indira, 126
Gandhi, Rajiv, 52
Ganor, Boaz, 9
Gaza Strip, 113
General Strain Theory of
    Terrorism (GSTT), 41
Geneva Conventions and
    Protocols, 13
genocide, 174
    in Kampuchea, 171
Gentry, Caron, 54
Gheith, Suleiman Abu, 77
globalism, 195
global jihadist movement,
    30
gold standard, 192
Goldstein, Baruch, 89
Greenpeace, 5
Grol-Prokopczyk, Hanna, 55
group identification, 42–43
guantánamo, 281–283

Guantánamo prison camp,
    33
Guerilla Army of Poor, 131
guerilla warfare, 73
    defined, 13–14
    war and terrorism, 12–15
Guiora, Amos, 9
Gunpowder Plot, 99
Gurr, Ted, 172

H

Hacker, Frederick, 15
Hague Convention, 1898, 13
Hague Convention, 1970,
    259
Hakim, Boubaker, 60
Hamas, 89, 113, 232
Hamm, Mark S., 33
Hansen, Fjotolf, 37–38
Haqqani network (HQ), 153
hard targets, 65
Hasan, Nidal, 1–3
hawala system, 72
Heinzen, Karl, 102
Hezbollah suicide attack on
    U.S, 87
Highly Enriched Uranium
    (HEU), 78
Hinckley, John, 14
Hiroshima and Nagasaki,
    atomic bomb, 23
Hitler, Adolf, 175–176
Hoffman, Bruce, 9, 12, 14
homeland security
    and civil liberties, 269
    historical foundation of,
    264–265
honey trade, 149
Horgan, John, 29
Hostage taking, 67
House Un-American
    Activities Committee
    (HUAC), 266
Hubbard, David, 28
human rights abuses, 169
Human Rights Watch, 55
Hunger Strike Mural, 93
Hussein, Saddam, 75

I

Idris, Wafa, 53

immigration, 318–321
implosion-type bomb, 78
imposition of life-
    threatening conditions,
    173
Improvised Explosive
    Device (IED), 64
indoctrination, 86
innocent victims, 10
International Convention
    Against Taking of
    Hostages (1979), 259
International
    counterterrorism, 307,
    310–316
International
    Counterterrorism
    Agreements, 258–260
International Court of
    Justice (ICJ), 260
International Criminal
    Court (ICC), 260
internationalism, 206
Internationally Protected
    Persons
    protection and
    punishment, 259
international terrorism, 11
    United States,
    216–220
international violence, 16
International Workingmen's
    Association (IWA), 103
internment, 173
Intifada, 89, 113
Ireland ethnonationalist
    violence, 107–109
Irish Republican Army, 16
Irish Republican Army
    (IRA), 39, 53, 69, 93, 108,
    120
    provisional, 120
Irish Revolutionary
    Brotherhood (IRB), 108
Islamic Group (IG), 153
Islamic radicalization, 30
Islamic Resistance
    Movement, 114
Islamic State in Syria (ISIS),
    33
Islamic state of Iraq,
    155–160

Islamic State of Iraq and al-Sham (ISIS), 138, 157
Islamic State of Iraq and the Levant (ISIL), 157
Islamic State of Iraq (ISI), 156
Israel Defense Force, 9–10
Israeli Knesset, 90
Israeli-Palestinian conflict, 109–111
Italian Red Brigades, 67

J

Jabhat al Nusra, 153
Jackson, Richard, 74
Jahiliyyah, 147
Jamaah Islamiyah, 91
Jamaat Isamiyya/Lashkar Jihad (Indonesia), 161
Japanese Red Army, 51
Japanese Red Army (JRA), 72
Jemaah Islamiyah (JI), 153
Jihad, 20, 142, 143
Jihadi Salafism, 142
jihadist, 3
Joint Terrorism Task Forces (JTTFs), 253
Juergensmeyer, Mark, 139

K

Kamikaze. *See* Tokubetsu Kougekitai
Khalid, Leila, 52
Khan, Mohammad Sidique, 83
Khomeini, Ayatollah Ruhollah, 50, 163
Khomeini, Ruholllah, 162
knives, 65
knowledge, 4–5
Koran-memorization, 138
Kouachi, Chérif, 59, 60
Kouachi, Said, 59, 60
Kropokin, Pyotr, 103
Ku Klux Klan (KKK), 195–197
Kurdistan Workers' Party (PKK), 124

L

labor violence, 203–204
Laden, Osama bin, 18–21, 29, 49, 77, 148–150
Laqueur, Walter, 9, 52
Lashkar-e-Taiba (LeT), 92, 160
leaderless resistance, 201
learning organizations, 68
Lebanese Shi'a group, 41
Left-Wing Revolutionary Violence, 212–213
  May 19 Communist Organization (M19CO), 213
  United Freedom Front (UFF), 213
left-wing terrorism, 16, 203–205
Lewis, Jeffrey William, 86
LGBT rights, 8
Liberation Tigers of Tamil Eelam (LTTE), 14
Liberty City Seven, 56
local control, 194
London School of Economics, 27, 29
lone-wolf terrorists, 34–38
  financial gain, 36
  five types, 35–37
  idiosyncratic, 36–37
  religious, 35–36
  secular, 35
  structural theory, 38–40
  terrorist-coordinated lone-wolf attack, 37
  terrorist-directed lone-wolf attack, 37
  terrorist-inspired lone-wolf attack, 37
lone wolves, 203, 216–217
Lopez, Ivan A., 3
Los Angeles International Airport, 20
Louis XVI, 100
Luddites, 101

M

Madrid bombing, 150, 233
magnitude, 42
Mahdi, 144

Manning, Chelsea, 260–264
Marie Antoinette, 100
Marighella, Carlos, 128
maritime attacks, 65–66
Marxism, 45–47
Marxist theory, 46
Marx, Karl, 45, 106–107
Masood, Khalid, 67
mass-mediated terrorism, 231–233
  legitimacy, 231–233
  public attention and intimidation, 231
Mateen, Omar, 221
Matusitz, Jonathan, 41, 67
Maximilien Robespierre, 100
May 19 Communist Organization (M19CO), 213
McVeigh, Timothy, 16, 35, 192
media
  and terrorism, 239–241
  censorship, 242–244
  contagion, 235–237
Meinhof, Ulrike, 51
messianism, 140
MH-60 Black Hawk, 148
military commissions, 287–290
militia groups, 201–202
minutemen
  and posse comitatus, 198–199
missile strikes, 51
modern left-wing terrorism, 205–214
  internationalism, 206
modern state-sponsored political terrorism, 98
Mohammed, Khalid Sheikh, 66, 219
money laundering, 72
Montreal Convention (1971), 259
moral equivalence, 23
moralist movements, 202–203
Moro Islamic Liberation Front (MILF), 161

Moro National Liberation Front (MNLF), 161
Most, Johann, 103
Motassadeq, Mounir, 31
Mueller, John, 4
Munich Olympics, 243
Murrah Federal Building, 193
Muslim cleric, 3
Mzoudi, Abdelgham, 31

N

Nakba, 111
nanking massacre, 182
narcissistic–rage approach, 33
Narodnaia Volia. *See* People's Will
narodniki. *See* populists
nationalist terrorism, 17
Nationalist violence, 210
National Liberation Front (NLF), 124, 170
national security, 317–318
national security theater, 248
Naturalization Act, 265
Navy Seal Team Six, 21
Nechaev, Sergei, 104
negative-identity approach, 33
Neo-nazi extremists, 198
nerve agents, 74
Newman, Graeme, 45
new media, 228
new terrorism, 17–18
    leaderless resistance, 18
    personnel, 18
    technology, 18
    weaponry, 18
New World Order, 201
nihilism, 104
Nobel, Alfred, 102
no-fly list, 249
Norris, Jesse J., 55
Northern Ireland, 120–121
nuclear bomb, 77
Nuclear emergency support teams (NESTs), 77–79
nuclear terrorism, 77–79

Nuclear weapons, 307, 308–310

O

Obama, Barack, 3
October Revolution, 108
old media, 228–229
Operational Forces Action, 63
Operation Infinite Reach, 20
Order, 200
overreaction, 22

P

Padilla, José, 80
Palestine
    and Sri Lanka, 66–70
Palestine Liberation Organization (PLO), 21, 84, 111–112
Palestinian response, 111–114
Paris Attacks, 2015, 61
Paris Café
    Anarchist bombing of, 228
Paris Opera House, 62
Paris Stock Exchange, 103
Parkin, William S., 48
Party of Socialist Revolutionaries (PSR), 84
PATRIOT Act, 254
Pearl, Daniel, 28
Pentagon, 3, 48
People's Republic of China, 124
People's Will, 105
persecution, 32
perseverance, 32
personal security, 4
Peru, 130
piety, 32
Plutonium, 78
Popular Front for the Liberation of Palestine (PFLP), 66
populists, 105
portable rockets, 64
posse comitatus
    and minutemen, 198–199

post-9/11 international Jihadist attacks, 220–221
post-depression red scare, 266–267
Prabhakaran, Velupillai, 87
precedent, 32
Precision-guided Munitions (PGMs), 64
predatory terrorism, 133–134
predisposition, 55
print media, 227
prisoner-of-war, 13
progressive intensification, 30
property theft. *See* sabotage
Protestant police, 74
Protestant Reformation, 99
psychological disorientation, 22
psychological liberation, 127
public attention, 22
public spaces, 66–67
pure evil, 233

Q

Qutb, Sayyid, 49, 145

R

racial profiling, 293–295, 295–300
racism, 194
radicalization, 29–30
    Islamic, 30
    persecution, 32
    perseverance, 32
    piety, 32
    precedent, 32
    process of, 30–34
    progressive intensification, 30
    recruitment, 30–34
    social affiliation, 30
    theory of, 54
Radical Marxist criminological theory, 45
radiological bomb, 79–82
Ramamoorthy, K. R., 92
Ramzi bin al-Shibh, 31
Rapoport, David, 137
rational choice theory, 40

Red Army Brigade, 46
Red Army Faction (RAF), 69, 132
Red Brigades, 133
red scare, 267
regional Islamic movements, 160–161
relative deprivation, 39
religion, 194
    and new terrorism, 139–141
religious terrorism, 17
Republic of New Afrika (RNA), 209–210
Reserve Officer Training Corps (ROTC), 207
resources, 4
Ressam, Ahmed, 20
Revolutionary Armed Forces of Colombia (FARC), 14, 46, 129
revolutionary terrorism, 127–133
    Colombia, 129–130
    Uruguay, 129
Richardson, Louise, 9, 29, 46, 168
right-wing philosophy, 38
right-wing terrorism, 16–17, 194–203
Rockwell, George Lincoln, 198
Roman sicae, 98
Roosevelt, Franklin Delano, 266
Rousseau, Jean-Jacques, 117
Ruby Ridge, 202
Rudolph, Eric, 36
Russian regime, 106
Russian Revolution, 134
Russian revolutionary violence, 104–107
Russo-Turkish War, 1877–1878, 105
Rwandan Genocide, 178
Ryan, Johnny, 32

S

sabotage, 67, 90
sacred sacrifice, 140
Sadat, Anwar, 112

safe houses, 51
Saipov, Sayfullo, 241–242
salafism, 31, 141–144
Screening Passengers by Observation Techniques (SPOT) program, 249
second amendment, 194
Sedition Act, 265
self-determination, 135
separatist terrorism, 119
September 11, 2001 Attacks, 219
sexual-social approach, 34
sexual violence, 173
shaheed batal, 89
sharia, 141
Shehade, Salah, 116
Sheikh, Ahmed Omar Saeed, 27
Shia Muslim sect, 83
Shia terrorism, 162–163
Shia tradition, 162
Shining Path, 130
Shinrikyo, Aum, 80, 81–82
signature method, 67
Simon, Jeffrey D., 35, 54
single-issue terrorism, 215–217
situational approach, 44–45
Sjoberg, Laura, 54
sleeper cells, 248
social activities theory, 43–44
social affiliation, 30
social change, 39
social conservatism, 194
social disorganization theory, 43
social disruption and delegitimization, 22
social distance, 42
social divisions, 22
Socialist Revolutionary (SR) Party, 105
social learning theory, 40, 41
social media, 159, 300–304
soft targets, 65
Southern Thai Insurgent Groups, 160
sovereign citizens movement, 199

Spain
    Basque Region of, 121–122
Springzak, Ehud, 31
Sri Lanka
    and Palestine, 87–90
    Tamil region of, 122–123
Stalin, Josef, 175
Stampnitzky, Lisa, 5, 8
state-sponsored terrorism, 173
state sponsors
    and Foreign Terrorist Organizations (FTO), 256
state sponsors of external terrorism, 179–181
state terrorism, 167
    defining, 171–174
    domestic, 174–175
    domestic state-sponsored terrorism, 179
    types of, 174–188
Stern Gang, 110
strategic logic terrorism, 85
structural theory, 38–40
Students For A Democratic Society (SDS), 207
suicide attacks, 88
suicide bombing, 16, 82–88
    women, 87
suicide terrorism, 16, 85, 86
Sunni Muslim, 83
Sunni tradition, 162
superbomb, 78
surveillance, 290–293
surveys typologies, 1
survivalists, 202
Sutherland, Edwin, 40
symbiosis, 238

T

Takfir, 143–144
Taliban, 14, 20, 70–71, 147, 160
Tamil Tigers. See Liberation Tigers of Tamil Eelam (LTTE)
Tamil United Liberation Front (TULF), 87

Tanweer, Shehzad, 83
targeted killings, 115
Taymiyyah, Taqi al Din ibn, 142
terrorism
    act, 7
    and Effective Death
        Penalty Act, 254
    and media, 239–241
    and women, 51–54
    anticolonial, 120
    anticolonial separatist, 119, 124
    biological, 216–217
    checks and balances, 256
    civil liberties, 4
    critical, 168
    Department of
        Homeland Security, 11
    Department of State, 11
    diverse phenomenon, 7
    domestic, 11, 315–317
    domestic state, 173
    domestic state-
        sponsored, 173, 179
    early religious, 98–99
    ethnonationalist
        communal, 125–126
    Ethnonationalist
        separatist, 119–125
    extent of media
        coverage of, 234–235
    external state, 173
    external state-
        sponsored, 173,
        182–184, 185–186
    Federal law in the
        United States Code, 18
        U.S.C. Section 3077, 12
    financing of, 259
    focus of media coverage, 234
    four waves, 137
    harm, 10
    history, 7
    initial thoughts on
        defining, 7–9
    intent, 7, 10
    international, 11
    knowledge, 4–5
    left-wing, 16, 203–205

    legitimacy, 24
    logic of, 21–22
    mass-mediated, 231–233
    modern left-wing, 205–214
    modern state-sponsored
        political, 98
    morality of, 23–24
    motivation, 7
    motive, 7, 11
    nationalist, 17
    need of definition, 6
    new, 17–18
    nuclear, 77–79
    organization of, 73
    overreaction, 22
    personal security, 4
    perspective, 6–7
    power, 7
    predatory, 133–134
    problems with defining, 6–7
    psychological
        disorientation, 22
    psychological impact, 10
    psychological theories, 28–29
    public attention, 22
    religion and new, 139–141
    resources, 4
    revolutionary, 127–133
    right-wing, 16–17, 194–203
    separatist, 119
    Shia, 162
    single-issue, 215–217
    social disruption and
        delegitimization, 22
    social divisions, 22
    sociological and
        criminological
        theories, 37
    some definitons of, 9–12
    State, 171–174
    state-sponsored, 173
    state sponsors of
        external, 179
    strategic logic, 85
    suicide, 16
    surveys typologies, 1
    tactic, 8

    target, 8
    transnational, 17
    typologies of, 15–20
    U.S. Department of
        Defense, 11
    violence, 4
    war and guerilla
        warfare, 12–15
terrorist. See terrorist
    organization
Terrorist Brigade, 84
terrorist-coordinated lone-
    wolf attack, 37
terrorist-directed lone-wolf
    attack, 37
terrorist financing, 70–72
terrorist-inspired lone-wolf
    attack, 37
terrorist organization, 6
    types, 68–69
    unlikely, 27
    violence, 68–69
    weapons and targets, 63–67
Thatcher, Margaret, 68
Thugs, 97
Tokubetsu Kougekitai, 84
Torture, 173
Townshend, Charles, 140
trains, 65
transformational
    delegitimization, 32
transnational terrorism, 17
Transportation Security
    Administration (TSA), 248
Trans World Airlines, 53
Tupamaros, 129
Turkey, 124
turner diaries, 200

U

United Flight 93, 220
United Flight 173, 219
United Freedom Front
    (UFF), 213
United States
    international terrorism, 217
    Jihad, 218
unlikely terrorist, 27

Uruguay, 129
U.S. Department of
    Agriculture (USDA), 252
U.S. Department of Defense,
    11
Uyghur, 124

V

victimology, 48–52
Vietnam
    protests, 268
violence, 4, 10, 23
    international, 16
    Ireland
        ethnonationalist,
        107–109
    labor, 203
    terrorist organization,
        68
    threat of, 9
Viral Hemorrhagic Fevers
    (VHF), 76
Virginia Tech, 3

W

Wahhab, Abdul, 142
Wahib, Abu, 35
war
    defined, 13
    terrorism and guerilla
        warfare, 12–15
war crimes, 174
Washington Post, 228
Weapons Of Mass
    Destruction (WMD), 16,
    72
weather underground, 207
Weimann, Gabriel, 91
White, Jonathan, 76
White supremacist, 44
women
    and terorism, 51–54
    suicide bombing, 87
    Yazidi, 138
World Trade Center, 48
    firefighters, 2
World War II Internment,
    268

Y

Yazidi women, 138
Yousef, Ramzi, 66

Z

Zealots, 97
Zedong, Mao, 128
Ziad Amir Jarrah, 31
Zionism, 109

CPSIA information can be obtained
at www.ICGtesting.com
Printed in the USA
LVHW052244140423
744410LV00011B/56

9 781516 523702